The Waldemar Story

Camping in the Texas Hill Country

Dining Hall

The Waldemar Story

Camping in the Texas Hill Country

Compiled by Marsha English Elmore

1928–1978
Written by Sue Van Noy Willett
Edited by Mary Brooke Oliphint Casad

1979–1996
Written by Carolyn Carmichael Wheat
Edited by Julie Menges

With gratitude to these who shared:

Sarah Jayne Johnson Manning
Ellen Easley
Margaret Gladney Savage
Mary Ellen Kirven Marchman

Margaret Manor Richards
Downs Lander Fordyce
Pat Glen Cunningham
Maybelle Smith Harris

Karen Turner Harlan

EAKIN PRESS   ★   Austin, Texas

FIRST EDITION

Published in the United States of America
By Eakin Press
An Imprint of Sunbelt Media, Inc.
P.O. Drawer 90159   ★   Austin, TX 78709-0159

ISBN 1-57168-190-6

Library of Congress Cataloging-in-Publication Data

Van Noy Willett, Sue.
   The Waldemar Story : camping in the Texas Hill Country / by Sue Van Noy Willett and Carolyn Carmichael Wheat, edited by Mary Brooke Oliphint Casad and Julie Menges. Compiled by Marsha English Elmore.
      p.   cm.
   ISBN 1-57168-190-6
   1. Camp Waldemar (Tex.)–History. 2. Camping–Texas–Texas Hill Country–History. 3. Outdoor recreation for women–Texas–Texas Hill Country–History. I. Casad, Mary Brooke. II. Title.
GV194.T42W358   1998
796.54'09764'272–dc21
                                                                                97-18750
                                                                                CIP

Contents

Prologue and Dedication

Joshua Foster Johnson—young, ambitious, adventurous—left Tennessee for Texas in 1845, settling in Mount Vernon in East Texas. He became a force in local politics, representing his county in the state legislature and later serving as a member of the Constitutional Convention which drafted the present Texas state constitution.

His recognition of the importance of education in his adopted state caused him to sponsor the Mount Vernon male and female academy bill, which led to the establishment of the public school system in that community. A Texas historical marker was unveiled at his graveside in Mount Vernon in 1975.

One of Joshua Foster Johnson's nine children by Amanda Wright Johnson was William Thomas Johnson. He married Laura Bolin, whose family had moved to Texas from North Carolina, and among their seven children were W. T., Ora and J. F. Johnson, all of whom played leading roles in the story of Camp Waldemar—W. T. as advisor to his sister Ora (the founder), and J. F. as advisor to his daughter, Doris (niece of the founder), who succeeded her aunt and dedicated her life to Waldemar.

In 1937 at the first vesper of the second term, "old-timers," both campers and counselors, were asked to share their impressions of Waldemar with the new campers. Doris Johnson, by this time the director, rose and said, "I eat, breathe, sleep and live Waldemar—it's my very life."

And so it was—for forty-seven years until her retirement in 1979. She died in November of 1985.

It is to her memory that this story of Waldemar is dedicated.

Acknowledgments

Sue Willett, lovingly known as Squish (from her wet tennis shoe sound to her hometown of Tishomingo, OK), came to Waldemar in 1941. She stayed off and on until 1988, when her health forced her to retire. Squish wore many "hats," from tribal sponsor, administrator, Hilltopper kampong counselor, to prolific writer of and director of Waldemar's Final Programs, and now the Waldemar history. She was the perfect person to take on the enormous task of writing Waldemar's history. Doris, Ellen, and many of the Waldemar old-timers were her best friends. Squish was at Waldemar during the transition from the original family to the new family and assured that traditions were preserved and continued.

May you enjoy reading this as much as I enjoyed writing it.

—Squish

Carolyn Carmichael Wheat was the only person who could have written the next twenty years of history, having been a part of it since the beginning. She came to Waldemar as Marsha's best friend and advisor. She had watched the Elmores—Dale, Marsha, Teak, Meg, Josh—and Dr. English come from their hometown of Beaumont, Texas, to take on the enormous and wonderful opportunity of being the next owners and caretakers of Waldemar.

Carolyn has written from a background rich in Waldemar experience. She has been a parent and grandparent of Waldemar girls, counselor of Outdoor Skills, assistant director for twelve years directing IWG and Final Program ceremonies, writing programs, and countless other jobs. In 1980 she started Waldemar's Women's Week with Marsha and directed it for twelve years. She has taken time from her successful business career to write an inspired version of Waldemar's history from 1979 to 1996.

It was my great privilege to come to work at Waldemar with the "changing of the guard" in 1979. From my fond memories, I have written a brief account of Waldemar, 1979–1996, and of the Elmore family and their life there.

—Carolyn Wheat

This history could not have been completed as effectively without the contribution of Mary Brooke Oliphint Casad, who worked with Squish editing the final draft and putting it on computer. Karen Turner Harlan spent many hours compiling the names of all the Waldemar campers from the card file, yearbooks, and Waldemar "bibles." Julie Menges, Waldemar's secretary and office manager, has edited names and records, put final drafts on disc, and been the contact person for all involved.

I am so grateful to these two extraordinary ladies for their dedication to this task, their love of Waldemar, and all the special people it has taken to "carry on."

—Marsha English Elmore

Chapter 1

1920s

MISS ORA JOHNSON

"Providence!"

That's what Miss Ora Johnson said it was. Her friends in educational and religious circles in San Antonio and across the state, as well as her admirers in the San Antonio business community, all labeled it politics and jealousy.

In 1928, Miss Ora Johnson, the first woman principal of a major co-educational high school in Texas, had been summarily dismissed as principal of San Antonio's Brackenridge Senior School. Her unprecedented successes and her universal popularity had rankled the members of a men's organization of teachers who were opposed to women holding executive positions in the San Antonio school system, and they had been able to get the backing of the superintendent of schools and enough members of the board to dismiss her.

It was no doubt difficult for men not to be jealous of the successes of the dynamic Ora Johnson. On October 18, 1925, shortly after she was named principal, the *San Antonio Express,* a leading newspaper in the city, devoted two pages of pictures and text to the story of Miss Johnson's transformation of the physical aspects of Brackenridge Senior School:

Holding that the environment and surroundings of senior school students have a great bearing upon the sort of education they acquire and that an attractive and home-like atmosphere make for good manners and good morals, Miss Ora Johnson, principal of Brackenridge Senior School, San Antonio, has expended a vast amount of time and energy in this, her initial year as principal, in turning the school buildings into a veritable center of harmony and good taste. . . . So thoroughly is she imbued with the desire to make

Brackenridge a model school in every respect and so well has her spirit been transferred to the student body that many of the students labored through the entire summer vacation assisting her in the work of redecorating and refurnishing many of the principal rooms in the building.

Businessmen had been impressed by Miss Johnson's theory of beautiful surroundings for growing boys and girls as an aid to mental and moral development, and their firms had joined school patrons in contributing liberally to the renovation project. Thus fine furniture, art, wall hangings, art objects and rugs enhanced the school, and other firms had provided labor for floor refinishing, painting and landscaping.

After her dismissal some three years later, the editor, in chastising the Board of Education, wrote:

Until Miss Ora Johnson became principal of Brackenridge Senior School, it was known chiefly as the largest building in the city equipped with more than the usual facilities for special studies as the result of the generosity of the late George W. Brackenridge for whom it was named. Under Miss Ora's energy and leadership it became known as the institution in which pupils suddenly developed an amazing ability to bring recognition to San Antonio. In one year no less than seven national honors open to high school students of the United States found their way to pupils of Brackenridge.

Ora Johnson had come to San Antonio in 1910 as a grade schoolteacher, had soon been named to teach history at Main Avenue Senior School, and in 1918 went to Brackenridge as history teacher and vice-principal. When she was elected principal of Brackenridge in 1925, the forty-eight-year-old Miss Johnson was exuberant. She was quoted in a San Antonio newspaper as having said, "I would rather be

1

principal of Brackenridge than president of the United States."

Ora Johnson had prepared herself well for advancement in her profession. At an early age she was graduated with a bachelor of science degree from Baylor College, Belton, Texas (now Mary Hardin Baylor). Then she received a bachelor of arts degree from Baylor University, Waco, and pursued her studies further at Columbia University, where she took a master of arts degree and earned a dean's diploma. Her thorough preparation for teaching was later enhanced by special work at the Universities of Chicago, Texas, and Tennessee.

Much of her college work was done in summer sessions because Miss Johnson taught school in the winter, beginning when she was about sixteen years old. She had "finished" the school she was attending and had studied at "summer normal" when she began her teaching career in a small East Texas community near Omaha before the turn of the twentieth century.

From that time on Ora Johnson believed that teaching was the world's most important profession because "school teachers shape lives." Her respect for young people and theirs for her, her ability to inspire her students to reach for excellence, her insight into human nature, her exceptional executive ability, her energy and her personal charm had lifted her to what was then the pinnacle of women public school educators—the principalship of a large co-educational high school.

Her dismissal from that position in the summer of 1928 became a cause célèbre in San Antonio with parents, teachers, students, former students, editors and businessmen—indeed all who knew her—fighting to reverse the board's decision. They deplored what had happened to their "Miss Ora" and thus to their school system, while she calmly called it "providence." The *San Antonio Express* labeled a series of editorials condemning the Board of Education: "Because She Is a Woman."

She considered her dismissal providential because now the decision had been made for her. It meant that the Lord intended that she should turn her tremendous energy, which by this time was legendary, to the girls' camp she had started in 1926 near the headwaters of the Guadalupe River in the Texas Hill Country. She had originally intended that the camp should occupy only her summers, but she was discovering that perhaps operating a successful summer camp could be a full-time occupation.

Thus Miss Ora Johnson didn't look back with regrets and recriminations—she looked forward with enthusiasm and confidence to a new and exciting challenge.

THE DREAM BEGINS

Because of her interest in all matters educational, Ora Johnson was aware of the proliferation of summer camps in the East, and early in her career at Brackenridge she began musing about the possibility of establishing a camp for girls in Texas. She read of the enthusiasm of Dr. Charles Eliot of Harvard, a much-publicized educator, for the organized summer camp, and she decided that her experience, her ability, and her money would be well invested if she used them to establish a summer institution which would offer unusual advantages for physical, mental, cultural, and moral growth for girls in the Southwest.

The vice-principal of Brackenridge Senior School under Miss Ora was a young man from North Carolina, a minister's son named Alex Waite. He had watched the camping movement grow in the East and take root in his home state, and he realized that he would like to work with boys in the summer as well as during the school year. Waite had recognized the beauty of the Hill Country near Kerrville, with its sparkling Guadalupe River guarded by tall cypress trees and gentle hills, as being ideal for a summer camp, and he had acquired property three miles downstream from the eventual Waldemar site (near the River Bend Lodge location) for his Lone Star Camp for Boys. His camp was in operation before 1926.

Waite's enthusiasm for his project was infectious, and before long he had inspired his principal, Ora Johnson, to walk the banks of the Guadalupe River searching for a spot for her camp for girls. Perhaps it was the beauty of the riverfront which offered a superb "swimming hole"—or perhaps it was the rough, overgrown scruffy hill upon which she envisioned cabins nestling but which those less visionary saw as unaccommodating to a camp situation. Whatever the lure this particular spot held for her, in February of 1926 Miss Ora Johnson and Alex Waite signed a twenty-five-year lease with the option for a ten-year extension with T. V. Lawson for twelve acres of land along the Guadalupe River with the intent of starting a camp for girls the following summer. The Brackenridge faculty applauded.

THE LAND

Miss Ora Johnson did not "acquire 320 acres of splendid camp property in February, 1926" as Florence Wolkewitz was to write in her history for the camp newspaper in 1932. She acquired only a twelve-acre tract, leasing it instead of buying it, and she had a partner. Terms of the partnership agreement between the two schoolteachers, signed on February 23, 1926, follow:

1. The parties agreed to associate themselves as co-partners for the purpose of operating a Girls' Summer Camp in Kerr County, Texas.
2. Ora Johnson agreed to advance the partnership the sum of $4,000 to be used for equipping and conducting the camp for the 1926 season.
3. Alex Waite agreed to contribute and pay into the partnership <u>within a period of two years</u> from this date the sum of $4,000.
4. It was agreed that until Waite's $4,000 was paid, the partnership property would be a lien to Ora Johnson in the amount of $4,000 and that she would receive from the partnership business 8% per annum of the sum of $4,000. After Waite paid the $4,000 no more interest would be paid to her.
5. It was further agreed that Ora Johnson would be the managing partner, doing the hiring, firing, and making all decisions regarding operation of the camp. However, she did not have the power to borrow money on the credit of the firm or to sell or purchase property without the written consent of Alex Waite.
6. It was agreed that Ora Johnson would receive a salary of $1,000 per year as Waldemar's business manager and director.

Waldemar has two copies of a small green booklet announcing the opening of Camp Waldemar for Girls in the summer of 1926 and listing prestigious advisors and counselors who would serve on the Waldemar staff. Three were on the staff of Alex Waite's Lone Star Camp for Boys. An announcement at the end of the booklet reads:

> The Lone Star Camp for Boys, of which Waldemar is an associate camp, is located three miles from Waldemar and is under the direction of Mr. Alex Waite, an owner in the Waldemar Camp.

The agreement of February 1926 could be dissolved by mutual consent of the partners at any time. That may indeed have been the case, or Mr. Waite, whose Lone Star Camp soon fell on hard times, may have been unable to meet the $4,000 financial obligation to Waldemar in February 1928. In any event, a new lease was executed in March of 1928 between only Miss Ora Johnson and T. V. Lawson for the original twelve acres, and Alex Waite was no longer associated with Waldemar.

This 1928 lease set the fee at $80 per year for the twelve acres for a period of twenty-five years, at which time the lessee had the option of extending the lease for ten more years.

Evidently, in 1928 Miss Ora's creativity was being stifled by the limitation of only twelve acres, and so at the same time a separate lease was executed with Mr. Lawson for two additional tracts of land of 160 acres each. The annual lease fee was $400.

On September 22, 1930, a few days after her fifty-third birthday and little more than a year before her death, Ora Johnson and Mr. and Mrs. Lawson signed a new lease agreement and contract. The need for a more comprehensive document was no doubt brought about by two events—the Great Depression, which was crippling the economy of the nation, and the disastrous fire in August of the 1930 season, which destroyed the elaborate dining hall and hotel which Miss Ora had built in 1928. The fire no doubt called attention to the value of the buildings she was erecting on Mr. Lawson's land, thus provoking tax discussions.

Conditions of this 1930 document paid tribute to the depression by lowering the annual rental fee from $400 to $200 with the lease to run until May 31, 1951. But Miss Ora agreed to pay all taxes, including state, county, "and any and all of the political subdivisions thereof, as the same now exist, and which may be hereafter created."

At the termination of the lease, the owner could "acquire any improvements on the payment of a fair and reasonable valuation therefore, to be agreed upon by the parties at that time." Should the owner not care to buy the improvements, the lessee had the right to remove such from said premises within ninety days. Mental pictures of moving the dining hall dance in the head!

Thus during Ora Johnson's few years at Camp Waldemar she was erecting expensive architecturally designed buildings on leased land. It wasn't until several years after the camp had passed into the hands of Miss Ora's niece, Doris Johnson, Doris' father J. F. Johnson, and her brother Billie that the land upon which Camp Waldemar is built belonged to a Johnson family member. Doris bought it in 1938.

1926

A teacher of English at Brackenridge Senior School is credited with suggesting the name "Waldemar" for the girls' camp venture. Although the name appears in books now and then as belonging to a twelfth-century Danish king, the best guess is that the English teacher knew it meant "sea of woods" in the Germanic family of languages, that it had a certain euphony, and that the campsite chosen by her friend was truly a "sea of woods" of Spanish oak, pecan, cedar, elm, and cypress.

And someone on the excited Brackenridge staff must have visited the Malay peninsula, or at least read extensively about it. The word "kampong" literally means "a small village or community of houses in Malay-speaking lands." The houses in those villages were built on stilts, and so Miss Ora decided to use the word "kampong" for the distinctive cabins on stilts which she would erect, a building device which allowed her hillside to accommodate them.

There would be no record of the erection of Waldemar's first buildings or of its first camping season, 1926, had not Mrs. J. R. Wolkewitz of Tyler written a short, informal history in 1932 which was serialized in the camp newspaper, the *Waldemar War Whoop.* Her history, in four parts, takes up only about a dozen columns in the tabloid-sized paper, but in those twelve columns Mrs. Wolkewitz preserved for later generations of Waldemar girls historical facts as well as the flavor of those early years.

Florence Wolkewitz and Ora Johnson had met when they were in their mid-twenties, and the two East Texans found their interests and backgrounds such that they became close friends. Mrs. Wolkewitz, a teacher in Tyler, held a master of arts degree from the University of Chicago, and she was much involved in church work as was Miss Ora. She probably did not join the Waldemar staff until the summer of 1930, but there is no doubt that she and her husband Jack were frequent visitors before that time. She wrote:

> Mine was the opportunity of knowing Ora Johnson thoroughly, of working with her, sharing her confidence, her ambition, her sorrows, and her joys.

A patron of that first summer wrote that her family had learned about Miss Johnson's plan to open a camp for girls in 1926 "from Mrs. Wolkewitz who was making a trip to Trinity [Texas] in the interest of church affairs and staying in our home." They en-rolled their two daughters for that first summer, and so Mrs. Wolkewitz may well hold the title of "Waldemar's first representative." Her contributions to the success of Camp Waldemar were tremendous, and both Miss Ora and later Doris drew heavily upon her judgment and wisdom for advice and inspiration.

Florence Wolkewitz wrote about the activities of that exciting February of 1926 as she had heard the story from her friend Ora Johnson:

> Intensive work began at once. Small green booklets, a prospectus of the camp, found their way into the homes of many girls. Workmen began the clearing of grounds. Vines and undergrowth were cut away. The sound of the hammer and the saw sent the wild folk scurrying further into the hills. Houses began to take shape.

The first practical imperative for the camp was a lodge—a meeting place—a lounge with dining hall and kitchen adjoining. Waldemar Lodge, a substantial rustic building, was built at the west end of the property. It faced the river, and flagstone steps led down to several plateaus and eventually to the Guadalupe. The area between Waldemar Lodge and the river, known as Tejas Chapel since 1957, became the heart of camp where all sorts of campfires, dramatic performances, Indian dances, and all-camp meetings took place. In a brochure Miss Ora described the lodge:

> A large stone fireplace, a wagon wheel chandelier, bear skin rugs, Mexican pottery, books, magazines and musical instruments created an atmosphere for relaxation and genial companionship.
>
> Here may be found a piano, an Edison [an early-day record player], many current magazines of art, travel and fiction, and a library well equipped for the literary explorations of the wide-awake girl. Under the same roof is a well-appointed dining room and a kitchen, both screened.

Miss Ora built twelve kampongs for that first summer, eleven for the girls she planned to enroll and one to house the office, telephone, and director. In an early catalog, a kampong was described as being

> built well above the ground with side walls high enough to prevent drafts on the sleeper, but open above on all sides, so that it gives the effect of sleeping out of doors. Each kampong is furnished with four Simmons hospital beds, built in on one side, and two spring cots on the other, supplied with good mattresses, making accommodations for five girls and a counselor.

Mrs. Wolkewitz adds:

The kampongs had only canvas flaps and no screens. The first campers crawled into bed from the outside as often as from within. Oil lamps furnished lights, and a stone reservoir held water for showers.

The kampongs, built at the west end of the camp near Waldemar Lodge, were named rather than numbered: "Hi-Hi," "Rodeo," "Seventh Heaven," "Bug House," and "Check Inn" were among the first.

The natural Athletic Field, a large somewhat level space between the hill and the river just east of Waldemar Lodge, was covered with rocks, and there was no grass. When workmen cleared and leveled the area before the camp session started, they found an Indian mound and many arrowheads, perhaps presaging the Waldemar "tribes" which were soon to glory in the place.

A tennis court was built on the east end of the Athletic Field (it later became the Playhouse), and Miss Ora invested in two canoes and borrowed ten horses. The stable was just northeast of the present dining hall near where the cowboy dining hall is now. Mrs. Wolkewitz wrote:

Ambrose was the first stable man, and not a single paint was among the first group of horses—nor was there a cowboy. But it wasn't long before Waldemar was famous for its "paint ponies."

Camp opened in July of 1926 for an eight-week term. Somehow this dynamic educator was able to enroll fifty-four girls for that first summer, a few more than half from San Antonio and none from outside the boundaries of Texas. Among those fifty-four campers was Miss Ora's niece, Laura Jean Johnson, whose association with Waldemar has continued through the years.

The names of Waldemar's first counselors for 1926 have been lost, but Mrs. Wolkewitz was quick to point out that

Miss Johnson chose as counselors only those persons with superior qualities in the field of education. All counselors on the senior level were required to hold college degrees or their equivalent in the various fields.

The following paragraphs, taken from Mrs. Wolkewitz's history, are revealing not only about Miss Ora's thorough planning but about the dress of the day. Miss Johnson had recruited a talented young girl cornetist from San Antonio to play bugle calls for reveille, classes, assemblies, and taps.

As the sun rose on Waldemar's first day of activity, the bugle's clear notes sounded reveille. Happy girls tumbled from their bunks, pulled on shirts and knee trousers, or knickers, and three-quarter hose and shoes. Down the hillside from the eleven kampongs they came to form a double line before the flagpole and pledge allegiance to the flag.

(The flagpole was fashioned from an East Texas specimen pine tree grown by an enthusiastic patron and presented to Miss Ora for her camp. It was set to the southeast of Waldemar Lodge, where the oval road curves to follow the river downstream.)

Breakfast, lunch and dinner were interspersed with singing—good things to eat. Will Hicks was the first cook. "Come out of the kitchen, Oh Will, Oh Will" sang the enthusiastic campers when some particularly good thing was served, and the applause brought his smiling face and white cap to the door.

(Finding a talented chef for her girls' camp was high on Miss Ora's list of priorities, and she turned to one of the most prestigious sources of excellently prepared food of that era—the railway dining car. Will Hicks had been head chef on a diner.)

A study of Waldemar's history brings with it a realization of the strength of its first planning. A patron bringing her two daughters to camp on the first day described it as "a perfectly equipped camp," and so it was for its day and its purpose. In the beginning Miss Johnson formulated an activity program for Camp Waldemar which, although enlarged each succeeding summer to meet the growing demands, satisfied the need of every type of child. The elasticity of her program by plan allowed for all individual differences in physical ability and tastes. The physical, mental and spiritual phases of life were incorporated for an all-round development of the girls.

With special stress on horseback riding and swimming, she offered a varied athletic program including canoeing, camp-craft, archery, tennis, volleyball, soccer, baseball, hiking, and tumbling. Not overlooking the cultural side of life, she provided many advantages for her campers in the highly developed Fine Arts department which featured all phases of music, dancing, drama and art. For the girl who must attend summer school, she built a strong academic department affiliating with Baylor College for Women, Belton. Thus she felt that she was affording a wonderful opportunity to obtain school credits under the most advantageous circumstances.

(When Baylor College discontinued its academy in 1936, the camp's academic department became accredited with Schreiner Institute at Kerrville. The department was discontinued in the late 1940s.)

From the first a wonderful camp spirit was shown. Through her marvelous ability to inspire to achievement both her co-workers and campers and her belief with Thomas Edison that "no amount of genius can take the place of hard work," Ora Johnson achieved great results. With megaphone in hand she was everywhere directing all activities—her contagious enthusiasm spreading to every group. Her conception of the camp and its future was magnificent. A veritable seer, with a breadth of vision prophet-like in scope, she saw the girls of '26 as the first of many who through the generations should come to this beautiful spot which should grow with the years into a place of usefulness and of service—making finer, better and truer girls with strong bodies and clean hearts: "the women of tomorrow, guardians of the world's ideals."

As her associates in the work of the camp, Miss Johnson chose helpers, or counselors, who were well qualified by preparation and experience for the work which they were to direct. Her own words describe them thus: "The most important part of every camp is the personnel of its staff. The director prides herself that her staff is made up of Christian men and women whose sympathetic guidance and helpful interest will prove of inestimable value to a girl in shaping her ideas of a happy useful life. They are educational leaders peculiarly qualified to carry out the program of Camp Waldemar and above all preeminently fitted to guide girls in their daily contacts and activities."

Mrs. Wolkewitz wrote that service points and picture day had their places from the first. A kampong "yard contest" was staged, paths were cleared, grass was planted—and work at each of these was rewarded with "service points."

What more expedient and time-honored way was there to get the athletic field cleared of rocks or rock-bordered paths laid on the hill than by the campers, who enjoyed it because fun-loving "Aunt Ora," as they called her, was working right along beside them? The tribes were yet to come, and so the service points they earned went toward the campers' individual scores which determined who would be named "Best All-Round Camper" in her division—the camp's highest honor.

Miss Ora believed that "a picture is worth a thousand words" and from the first she scheduled "picture days" on which a photographer would come to Waldemar to record photographically the summer's activities. His expertise was respected by Miss Johnson, but she knew camping and he didn't, and she knew what she wanted in the upcoming catalog, which would be published before the 1927 season rolled around. Megaphone in hand, she "ran" picture day. In addition to being director of the camp, she was its consummate public relations director. Mrs. Wolkewitz wrote:

Not only were group and individual pictures made of the first swimmers, but motion pictures as well. These were shown in many theaters in Texas . . .

(The first term of 1928 ended on July 19, and the second term began on July 17. The catalog explained that "the three overlapping days are arranged in order that the girls of both terms may become acquainted and be present for the motion pictures to be made on those dates." Those familiar with Miss Ora's brand of promotional activity knew also that this maneuver would swell the number of campers in the pictures.)

Because their mother had died, this busy woman Ora Johnson was helping one of her younger brothers, J. F., "look after" his daughter Doris and her younger brother Billie. Doris was at the University of Texas in summer school in 1926 working toward a degree in history, and Miss Ora had planned that Billie, who was a teenager, would attend Lone Star Camp owned by her friend, Alex Waite. It was just down the road.

Wrote Mrs. Wolkewitz:

Billie at that time, hardly old enough for "longs," ran away from Lone Star to Waldemar.

"A girls' camp is no place for boys," said Aunt Ora as she took him back to Lone Star.

History records that three times Billie appeared, pleading with tears to be allowed to stay. Perseverance won, and with many promises to "stay away from the girls and work hard," Billie became a vital part of Waldemar.

At first young Billie was Miss Ora's "errand boy" and handyman, but he promptly made himself indispensable to her, to the counselor staff, and to the campers. Later he became the camp's purchasing agent, a position which quickly grew in importance and volume of work as Waldemar grew.

A 1926 camper who visited Waldemar in 1932 while Mrs. Wolkewitz was preparing her history gave her some sidelights on her memories of that first summer:

Fishing, the laying of trot lines at night and running them early in the morning, moonlight canoe rides (when chaperoned), kampong inspection when in addition to sweeping, dusting and mopping, lamp chimneys had to be cleaned . . .

The girls sang the following song to Miss Johnson:

> Oh, Miss Johnson you're a wonder
> And when you are old and gray
> We will tell them, "Yes, by thunder,
> You were some girl in your day."

The girls rode horseback to Hunt that first year for the mail. The laundry wagon came from Kerrville once a week. For disobedience to camp rules girls were sentenced by campers to haul rocks and place them on paths on the mountainside or around the athletic field. Girls had to pump water from the well. Miss Johnson's call up the hill "Goodnight, girls," was full of meaning when voices were not stilled at 10 p.m.

Mrs. Wolkewitz concludes her story of Waldemar's first year:

Not only did Ora Johnson work with the girls of Waldemar but she played with them. Many were the picnics, the barbecues, the excursions to places of interest, with an overnight trip for seniors to Junction and the Seven Hundred Springs going across the Division through some of the most picturesque country of Texas.

Not forgetting her juniors, Miss Ora took them on an overnight trip to the home of a camp friend in the Bandera Hills.

The final excursion of the 1926 season was a trip to San Antonio where the San Antonio girls were hostesses to the campers for two festive days. Visits to Missions, the old cathedral, the Mexican Market place and the beautiful park ended with Waldemar's final banquet in the patio of the Menger Hotel.

This was no doubt a stroke of genius by the creative PR director. She was giving awards that night, some in the form of impressive silver cups, others in the form of pins typifying the sport they represented, and San Antonio patrons would be on hand to see how mature, how attractive, how healthy and how happy were Waldemar's fifty-four campers.

The first summer was over, but there was little time for Ora Johnson to savor the memory of the pleasures of the summer. She was wise enough to know that her project was not yet crowned with success even though the first season had been better than she had dreamed it could be. True, she was a long way from making her camp financially profitable or even self-supporting, but that really wasn't the point. She had founded Waldemar to enhance the physical, mental, and moral growth of girls and she was satisfied that the first summer had achieved that

goal along with fostering a lot of good wholesome fun and genuine happiness. She had savings which she had accumulated and invested wisely through the years. She had an excellent credit rating at more than one San Antonio bank—and she had her brother, W. T. Johnson.

Of the seven children in the Johnson family, W. T. was the eldest. But his sister Ora was only two years younger, and very early these two developed a closeness of mind and spirit which was to last throughout her life. They loved each other, trusted each other, admired each other, and each took pride in the accomplishments of the other.

W. T. Johnson had left his East Texas home at an early age "to seek his fortune" and eventually made his way to Denton, Texas, where he married, had children, and became president of a bank. But the banking business was not satisfying to him and soon he moved his family to San Antonio, where he engaged successfully and happily in ranching and the cattle business.

When in the mid-1920s his sister confided to him her ambition to enter the camping business, which was new to Texas, W. T. encouraged her, pledged his support, and promised to lend her ten fine saddle horses from his own ranches for her first Waldemar stables.

Horseback riding was the most popular activity that first summer, and W. T. Johnson was a frequent visitor. He watched—and he began dreaming about the horses that would inhabit the future stables at his sister's camp for girls!

1927

Because age eligibility to attend Camp Waldemar was "from six to twenty" (and that was sometimes negotiable), Miss Ora became very much aware during the first summer of camp that she needed two separate recreation halls, one for junior girls and one for senior girls. Although there were many programs and exercises that the campers attended together, and even though the older girls were loving and kind to the younger ones, their natural interests called for separation upon occasion.

Thus when campers arrived for the 1927 season they found a handsome new building located on the north side of the road which circled the oval Athletic Field, almost marking its center.

The two-story structure combined stone and cedar. On the lower level were an art room and a bedroom for Miss Ora and the camp secretary. An uncovered stone verandah, about fifteen feet above the road and running all across the front of the building, was a feature of the lower level. Art students moved their projects to this pleasant working space during class periods. Fifteen-foot wide stone steps led from the verandah to the road which encircled the Athletic Field.

Wide, inviting wooden steps at the east and the west ends of the structure led to the upper level, which was fronted by a long cedar railed porch. According to Mrs. Wolkewitz, it served as "a lounging place with an unexcelled view of the river and surrounding country and an observation point for events on the Athletic Field."

The huge upstairs room was furnished with rustic tables, chairs and bookshelves "made from natural cedars from Waldemar's hills." It was a cozy lounge which could be transformed quickly into a large room for games, plays, or dances.

This building was named "Cedar Lodge" and its second floor became known as "Senior Rec," for Senior Recreation Hall. Waldemar Lodge became "Junior Rec," the home of junior activities.

Although not as visually pleasing or exciting as fine new Cedar Lodge, certain basic advancements had been made before the 1927 season which were equally, if not more, important. After spending the first season with oil lamps—inconvenient, inefficient, and perilous—Miss Ora installed her own "Delco" system, and Waldemar had electricity. Sometimes it worked better than it did others, but any lights at all were wonderful after the dangerous lamps whose smoky chimneys had to be cleaned daily.

(Later when the Rural Electrification Association brought electricity to Waldemar, the small honeycomb rock building just northwest of Cedar Lodge which had first housed the Delco system became a shower house, then the camp store and in the 1980s it was enlarged to accommodate both the store and the post office.)

Perhaps more satisfying to campers and counselors than electric lights was the addition of running water and septic toilets.

A rock dam was built across the river before the 1927 season, deepening water for swimming and adding to the beauty of Waldemar. Again quoting Mrs. Wolkewitz:

Below the dam the sparkling rapids were known from the first as "Riverside Laundry," later shortened to "Riverside." It was here that the washing of socks and underwear was not a task but fun. Many were the merry chases down the river to rescue garments carried away by the swift current.

Later day ecologists recommended the discontinuance of the river-polluting soapsuds of "Riverside."

Two counselors came to Waldemar in 1927 who made such basic and necessary contributions to its success and continued to be a part of Waldemar for so many years that a history of this period would not be complete without mentioning them.

Ann Miller (later Crockett), of Austin, taught violin in 1927, and was multi-talented. Clever skits for campers and counselors flowed from her pen, and she was the irrepressible master of ceremonies at many programs. Early on she directed the orchestra, and later she qualified as a water safety instructor and taught on the waterfront. Ann was an accomplished golfer and helped in that department when needed. Two of the three tribes, Aztec and Comanche, benefited from her originality and enthusiasm, and many early Comanche traditions were begun by Ann when she served as their tribal sponsor. She was a second-term Waldemar counselor for a quarter century, and Ann Miller Crockett continued to be Waldemar's Austin representative until the late 1980s, having served in that capacity since Waldemar's beginnings.

Miss Johnson decided she needed a dietitian for her camp for its second summer, and she engaged the services of a young woman who was trained in dietetics at the College of Industrial Arts, now Texas Woman's University, Denton. When circumstances prevented her coming, she sent in her stead her equally qualified friend, Ripple Frazer of Dallas, and Ripple was the first of the three capable, talented, flamboyant Frazer sisters to enliven Waldemar. Through the years Ripple or her sister, Katherine "Kat" Gannon, also of Dallas, alternated the dietitian's duty to fit their own busy lives, making certain that the high standard of Waldemar food which Ripple had set continued to receive praise from camp personnel, patrons, and guests. Ripple Frazer's salutary influence was felt at Waldemar during five decades.

Music, drama and dancing played important roles in early-day camp life. Violin, piano, and voice lessons were offered without additional charge. For her first two summers, Miss Ora was able to secure Otto Zoeller, director of music in the San Antonio schools and a staff member of Lone Star Camp, to head the music department. A picture of the 1926 orchestra shows a group of twenty-three musicians including seven violinists. (This was two years before

Interlochen Music Camp was founded in Michigan in 1928.)

Porter Sargent, early-day authority on schools and camps, wrote in his *Handbook of Camps* for 1934:

> There are few girls' camps that do not present photographs of barefoot girls in cheese cloth on the lawn.

Waldemar's first catalog pictures at least six. Only "aesthetic" dancing was taught in 1926 and 1927, and the 1928 catalog states:

> Dancing is without doubt the most comprehensive form of physical education, cultivating not mere strength and bodily controls, but wonderful poise, good posture, and harmony and grace of movement. . . . Its appeal is universal because its essential quality is joy. Classical and folk dancing are taught at Waldemar by competent instructors.

Soon ballet, tap, acrobatic, ballroom, interpretative, and modern dance showed up on the Waldemar class schedule.

And something else showed up at the Waldemar stables in 1927—PAINT PONIES. Not many, but a few.

Mrs. Wolkewitz wrote of the horses and of W. T. Johnson's enthusiasm for them:

> Becoming more keenly interested in his sister's new undertaking, W. T. Johnson determined to secure for the camp a group of saddle horses unequaled in any camp in the country.
>
> Arabian horses are noted for their gentleness and their amiable disposition. Paint horses are picturesque and attractive, so Arabian paints were selected to add to the beauty and superior equipment of Waldemar.
>
> The distinguishing mark of an Arabian paint is the border fringe between the colors, and these horses are all imports. Regardless of price or location, when Mr. Johnson found one he wanted, he bought it. The cost of some ran into four figures and many were brought from great distances. They were carefully tested from large numbers to insure safety.

Knowledgeable horse fanciers, including Marsha English Elmore, Waldemar's owner and director since 1979, object to the use of the term "Arabian Paints." By 1929 the horses had become famous as "the paint ponies of Camp Waldemar" and the controversial term gradually disappeared.

In 1926 Maj. B. J. Reilly of the United States Cavalry—erect, disciplined, and horsewise—had come to Waldemar from Lone Star Camp to teach horseback. (In the winter he was the officer in charge of ROTC at Brackenridge High School.) Major Reilly introduced "target practice" the second year, and Mrs. Wolkewitz wrote:

> Under Major Reilly's expert instruction, interest in riflery soared and horseback riding became an art.

Miss Ora believed that trips to interesting places away from Waldemar were not only appealing to the girls but educational as well. In 1926 the trip had been the two-day outing to San Antonio for the final banquet, but in 1927, Miss Ora branched out a little. The trip was to the Rio Grande Valley, and W. T., a popular travel companion, is pictured with the group. There is no record of the fee for the trip, but the catalog lists the camp fee as $190 for six weeks and $350 for twelve.

1928

The turmoil within the San Antonio school system over Ora Johnson's principalship of Brackenridge Senior School was reaching its climax when camp opened in 1928, and the beleaguered but resilient Ora Johnson countered by directing all her energies and talents toward perfecting her girls' camp. The school board took formal action dismissing her on August 8.

Five days later, August 13, she established the *Waldemar War Whoop* and announced on its first page that Waldemar would be open as an adult camp for a time in the fall.

On August 21, the *San Antonio Express,* always her strong supporter, included a story she wrote about Kerr County and camping and devoted an entire pictorial page to Camp Waldemar, its director and its sports program—perhaps a ladylike "thumb of the nose" to the school board.

Doris Johnson once said that if her aunt had stayed in the school system, the demands on her time might have made it impossible for her to continue the Waldemar project, certainly not on the grand scale on which she embarked in 1928. She was building a large dining hall-hotel and sparing no expense.

Ora Johnson was always open to suggestions from her talented counselor staff, and when San Antonian Olive McCormick, who had been a counselor at a well-established Eastern camp, suggested dividing the girls into two "tribes" to promote healthy competition, the director acted immediately. The catalog promoting the 1928 season announced:

For competitive sports . . . the campers are divided into two tribes, the Tejas and the Comanches, representing tribes that inhabited in early days the very grounds of Waldemar.

It is possible that Miss Ora and Olive McCormick chose the names Tejas and Comanche as well as the colors purple and orange. Miss McCormick, who was chairman of the Bexar County Chapter (San Antonio) of Red Cross Life Saving, also suggested that Miss Ora buy each tribe a War Canoe, and according to the catalog for 1928:

Waldemar has eight Old Town canoes, and two War Canoes have been recently added to the Waldemar Fleet.

Miss Ora was proud of her War Canoes and showed them off to "visitors from neighboring camps" on July 27 of the 1928 season when, in an exhibition race, the Comanches beat the Tejas by "half a length of the canoe." Of special interest in the story published in the *Waldemar War Whoop* is the revelation that both canoes had coxswains sitting in the bows in the manner of racing shell crews.

The catalog states that in the year 1928 the juniors were aged eight to twelve inclusive, low seniors were thirteen to fifteen, and high seniors were sixteen and above. The most prestigious awards given were cups for the Best All-Round Senior, Best All-Round Low Senior, and the Best All-Round Junior. These honors were decided by a vote of both campers and counselors. Being "high point" senior, low senior, or junior was also a goal.

The third catalog, announcing the 1929 season but imparting 1928 rules, has this to say about camp awards and shows Miss Ora's continuing influence upon Waldemar:

Girls keeping the health rules and making an excellent rating on the required number of teams are classed as All-Star-Campers. The first season that a camper makes the high score the award is a felt star for sweater, the second season the silver star pin, third, the gold star pin, and the fourth season is the gold star set with a diamond.

A great number of cups and pins are given for progress in the various camp activities, but no girl will receive honors at Waldemar who has not kept the health rules. All awards are made at the final banquet given at the close of camp. On this occasion the winning tribe will be announced. In addition to these, a number of pins and cups are awarded for individual skill and progress. In no case do juniors and seniors compete with each other.

(No doubt the girls of 1928 knew the all-important health rules, but they were not recorded until 1930.)

Thus in its third summer Waldemar was becoming "well established," and the *Waldemar War Whoop* made its official debut on August 13, 1928. Although the issue of that date is the only one preserved for the year 1928 and probably the only one published that year, it makes a few interesting disclosures.

The tribes met together rather than separately at a campfire by the river on Saturday nights, and after some yells,

different groups have very unusual and interesting performances. . . . Twice the Comanches have sung out on the river in canoes.

One night Indian legends were told and

the most imaginative and fascinating one was of a Comanche maiden and a Tejas brave who ended their lives many years ago on this very spot.

At the next campfire:

The Tejas acted out the Indian story beautifully.

This was, no doubt, the first presentation of "The Legend of the Guadalupe," but it was not until 1932 that this version was selected as the traditional Waldemar legend. Many others were written, published, and presented in the meantime.

From the catalog it is known that 1928 is the first summer Waldemar was divided into two six-week terms, but campers were encouraged to come for twelve weeks. The fee for six weeks was $190 and for twelve, $350. One hundred and forty-two girls attended Waldemar that summer in 1928, but there is no information on how many were in camp each term. Nor is there information on how many kampongs had been built by this time, but Miss Ora was far-sighted and it can be assumed that she built several each year.

Neither is there mention of the arrival of several people who spent their summers at camp for many years and put their indelible stamps on Waldemar, helping to develop wise and lasting policies, most of which are still valid. Laura Wallace, of Mineral Wells, and Frances McCluskey and Mary Strange, of Waco, came to Waldemar in 1928 and returned for many summers. Laura told of seeing an advertisement— "Counselors needed at Camp Waldemar"—on the movie screen at Mineral Wells. She wrote and was accepted so promptly, without being seen or interviewed, that she thought, "Camp Waldemar can't be much!"

Upon arrival, she learned that she had quite recently been highly recommended to Ora Johnson and was on her list to contact at the time her application arrived.

The two became close friends, and after Miss Ora's death, Laura often joined Mrs. Wolkewitz in telling about their friend at the first vesper service of the term. Laura, a Latin scholar, was the head of the academic department for many years. When that department was discontinued, she became the camp librarian and the kampong inspector.

Frances McCluskey was for many years the song leader and the camp hostess. At that time, with space in the dining room, guests were often invited to eat with the girls and "Mac" was able to introduce to the campers, without notes, any number of newcomers whom she herself had just met. With the small group of campers, there was room for a grand piano in the dining room, and a wide center aisle was left for dancing between courses. "Mac" played piano for this activity when the orchestra was not on the stage. At other times she played camp songs and promoted spirited singing. She continued to enliven Waldemar for many years.

Mary Strange was the only "arts and crafts counselor" in 1928, but she stayed long enough to head an art department of a half-dozen counselors. Waldemar had many "banquets" in the dining room in those days—all with a theme—and Mary was automatically head of the decorating committee. The tables were centered with an elaborate product of Mary's ingenuity, and oftentimes each place had a nut cup of her design. Streamers festooned the dining hall making the most casual "banquet" a gala. She, and later her department, was in charge of designing sets for the final banquet and awards program.

Doris Johnson, the founder's brown-eyed dark-haired niece, qualified as a counselor in 1928 by virtue of receiving her college degree from the University of Texas. She had been in and out of camp the first two summers, and she gloried in her aunt's progress and shared her confidence, gaining insight into the operation of such an establishment. In 1928 her responsibilities were limited to running the store and handing out the mail.

There were three others who came to Waldemar in 1928, two men and a woman, whose phenomenal expertise in their fields and their devotion to Camp Waldemar and Miss Ora—and later to Doris—make them the real stars of the 1928 Waldemar story: Ferdinand Rehbeger and U. S. and Lucille Smith.

The biggest news of the 1928 season was the building of the large dining hall-hotel which was under way when the first-term campers arrived. The limited space for kitchen and dining facilities in Waldemar Lodge was no longer adequate; and besides, Miss Ora planned to build one handsome building at Waldemar each year. She had engaged Henry Steinbomer of the architectural firm of Albaugh and Steinbomer in San Antonio to draw the plans for the building, and although the native stone and cedar building was not completed on opening day, it was ready within a month.

Above the dining hall with its huge cedar beams were several guest rooms for friends and patrons, and the infirmary was on that floor. On the ground level a large screened kitchen adjoined the dining room at the rear.

The principal workman on the building was a man who spoke Spanish with a thick guttural German accent. He was Ferdinand Rehbeger, who had just come to Camp Waldemar. More accurately, he had been brought to Waldemar by W. T. Johnson to help his sister build her dining hall. He remained until his death in 1963, and the man-made charm of Waldemar—the buildings of such beautiful stonework that strangers come just to admire them—is the handiwork of this unique man whom fate brought to Waldemar.

Ferdinand was a German with Russian citizenship, and he came to Waldemar from Mexico, where his path had crossed with that of W. T. Johnson. He was a shy man, not given to personal disclosures, but when Ellen Easley came to Waldemar, they became fast friends and he told her of his early life in Russia.

Soon after Ferdinand died, Ellen wrote a story about him for the first issue of the 1963 *Waldemar War Whoop* to try to help campers who loved him accept his death.

> The fateful trail, which spans from the banks of the Volga River in Russia to the banks of the Guadalupe River in Texas, is like an incredible chapter of predestination. It began on the Volga because the Rehbeger family and all their neighbors of German ancestry in the Ukraine were forced to exile inland during the early years of World War I. Being German, they were potential enemies in their adopted Russian land.
>
> Ferdinand was born near Kiev in the Ukraine, an area of rich agricultural land. His father was a prosperous farmer and a leader in the local Baptist Church, and Ferdinand grew up loving the soil, the things that grow on it, and the things that live on it.
>
> The Kaiser, the Czar, and the communists, interrupted a normal, peaceful existence for a young man who might have achieved an outstanding career as a student, an architect, or a scientist.

He witnessed the atrocities of the early Communists who were roaming and pillaging. . . . The long exile journey eastward to the Volga was made at gun point in railroad box cars, with people packed in like cattle. Ferdinand's mother became ill and, not caring to be bothered with a sick woman, the soldiers dropped her off at the first convenient station and refused to leave any of her family with her. They never knew what became of her.

Small wonder, then, that when the war was over and the Rehbegers were able to return to the Ukraine, Ferdinand had made up his mind to flee Russia. This would not be easy, for by this time his number had come up for the Russian draft, and he was scheduled to become a Communist soldier.

Using the "underground" route, he managed to reach Germany where he borrowed a cousin's passport and was able to escape from Europe. He traveled from Germany to Vera Cruz, Mexico, on a Holland-American liner, the *Edam*—and the borrowed passport he carried gained him admission to a land of new opportunity.

Ferdinand's first job in that strange land was as a dishwasher in a Monterrey cafe. Then he became a brick-layer's helper in Saltillo and he discovered that his employer was a German like himself who also liked farming. Together they leased a plot of irrigable land from a rancher near town and planted a farm. The rancher was W. T. Johnson, Miss Ora's brother, and there the paths of two vital men crossed.

W. T. Johnson recognized the steadfastness and the versatility of this talented transplanted man and, with Ferdinand's approval, he asked his ranch foreman to bring him across the border to help his sister build her building. No passport was produced and none was asked for, and Ferdinand Rehbeger never returned to Mexico. He was about twenty-eight years old when Waldemar became his home and the Johnsons became his family. Ellen continued,

For many years, he worked and lived at Waldemar, more or less oblivious of the rules of society which dictate where a man can legally live. Finally, during World War II, he did obtain U.S. citizenship as a result of serving in the army, but that didn't affect him very much one way or the other.

It didn't affect Ferdinand Rehbeger very much because long before this self-assured man had obtained the priceless papers attesting to his United States citizenship, he had privately declared himself a citizen of the world—and that world was Camp Waldemar, Hunt, Texas.

Miss Ora helped Ferdinand anglicize his name, but that didn't affect him very much either because

very few people remembered his last name anyway. He was "Ferdinand" and Ferdinand alone to all who knew him. Laura Wallace taught him to read and speak English, but he never lost his strong guttural accent. He became an avid reader and of the four magazines he read each week his favorite was *National Geographic.* As a result of this appetite for knowledge he was well informed on national and world affairs and was not reluctant to speak out when he thought somebody's freedom was likely to be compromised.

Ferdinand's construction work occupied his fall, winter and spring, but when summer rolled around he became responsible for the mechanical efficiency of the camp. In addition to the usual plumbing "emergencies" for which he was paged over the public address system with bedeviling regularity, Ferdinand replaced spent light bulbs, opened keyless trunks, built campfires, and checked on the camp's water supply, among other vital chores.

When drama counselors or tribal sponsors needed advice on and assistance with some intricate theatrical set they were planning, Ferdinand could be depended upon to design the plan and help execute it. Life had made his nature such that at first he assured the requester that it could not be done, but within a half day or so he was back to tell her, excitedly, just how he had worked it out and when he would be about it. One of his favorite expressions with which he exhorted counselors—as well as the camp director—was "Yoose your head." And Ferdinand Rehbeger did just that. He never set his extraordinary mind and skillful hand to learning to write English, though, perhaps because he felt he had no need for it.

The wonderful buildings, walls, steps, and walkways, every stone of which this patient man sculpted and caressed, are his legacy to Waldemar, his domain, the domain of the remarkable artist to whom Tejas Chapel was dedicated in 1963. It is so proclaimed on a bronze plaque near its entrance:

"Happy is the man who has found his work."
—Carlyle

Behind the plaque lie Ferdinand Rehbeger's ashes.

The first chef to enjoy Miss Ora's new kitchen and dining hall was Ulysses S. Smith of Fort Worth who, with his wife Lucille and their family, also came to Waldemar in 1928. Wrote Mrs. Wolkewitz:

Lucille, in the capacity of cateress in the house of the daughter of Mr. W. T. Johnson, met Miss Ora Johnson. Quick to recognize superior ability and eager to acquire the best for her beloved camp, Miss Johnson began to negotiate for the service of Lucille.

A faithful wife and a loving, conscientious mother could be interested only when the plan for three months' absence from home included her family. Investigations disclosed that U. S. was a chef of renown and a barbecuer par excellence who could be persuaded to transfer his activities for the summer—that Armistead and Gladys, high school and junior high school age, could help their mother, and Sonny, eight years old, could water the flowers. Thus the Smith children grew up at Waldemar as the camp grew up.

Except for two years in the early thirties, either U. S. or Lucille or both were responsible for Waldemar's food from 1928 until the summer of 1973. When U. S. died in 1956, Armistead returned to help his mother and stayed until about 1965. Then Lucille ran things herself until her health dictated her retirement at the end of the summer of 1973. She died in 1985.

Ulysses Samuel Smith and Lucille Bishop Smith were uncommon people. At a time when few of their race attended college, they had both been graduated from Sam Houston College in Austin, a school for blacks which no longer exists. Lucille continued her education by doing graduate work at Prairie View State College.

During her early days at Waldemar, Lucille chaired the African-American division of Vocational Education in Fort Worth during the winter. In the 1940s, because of her organizational and executive ability as well as her knowledge of home economics, she was employed as Teacher Trainer of Industrial Educational of Texas in Charge of House Service Training with headquarters in Prairie View. During the five years she served, her sister Florence took over her duties in the Waldemar bakery with Lucille visiting often in a supervisory capacity.

Her home city of Fort Worth, where she was active in educational and religious circles as well as in the business community, did not fail to honor Lucille Smith. April 28, 1966, was proclaimed by the mayor of Fort Worth "Lucille B. Smith Day, in honor of her fifty years of Christian service to all humanity." That evening a testimonial banquet was attended by more than 300 persons, both white and black civic leaders.

In 1969 she was named Texas Merit Mother of the Year in recognition of the fact that she was one of two runners-up for the title of Texas Mother of the Year. Lucille was the first black woman to receive this honor.

Her "touch" in the bakery was unequaled. She marketed "Lucille's Hot Roll Mix" in 1943 long before large baking companies marketed such a product. Because of this project, her picture has appeared in the entrepreneurial section of an exhibition of Texas women. "Lucille's Treasure Chest of Fine Foods," a card file of her recipes, required four printings to satisfy the demand. Many favorite recipes such as "blarney stones" and "blond top brownies" are in this file.

In 1931 Miss Ora sponsored a letter writing contest among the campers.

> Do we have swell food? Well, I say we do. U. S., the head cook, is my ideal cook. He wears a tall white hat and he weighs 200 pounds.

She no doubt underestimated his weight. He was tall and carried himself like the "king" he was. His tall white chef's hat and his high-collared chef's jacket—always impeccably clean and dazzling white—gave him a commanding presence. He was genial and affable, and the campers loved him.

> With a voluminous white chef's hat as a crown and a turning fork as a scepter, the central figure Monday noon when Waldemar's famous chicken barbecue is served to several hundred guests will be U. S. Smith, Barbecue King of the Southwest and head of the camp's efficient kitchen force for the past ten years. . . . U. S. earned his regal title when traveling with Col. W. T. Johnson's rodeos when he proved many times his favorite boast that he can serve 200 as easily as 20.

Fathers were drawn to U. S.'s outdoor barbecue pit on the Fourth of July to take notes from the master. U. S. was a showman who became even taller on guest days. When the Final Banquet was served on the lower tennis courts to all parents who made reservations (and all did), the Waldemar orchestra played stirring music as U. S. led in, single file, his starched and smiling staff, each member carrying a tray of preserved plates high in the air. The sight brought enthusiastic and appreciative cheers from patrons and campers.

U. S. did the hiring and firing and paying of his staff. Most of them were recruited from black colleges, and U. S. saw to it that they put their money in the bank for college costs the following year. They jumped when he breathed heavily. Practically every year the staff, headed by Lucille as director, presented an evening program which was eagerly awaited and heartily cheered.

U. S. and Lucille Smith, along with capable and faithful dietitians, set the high standard for food at Waldemar which has continued through the years.

What was the trip in 1928? Miss Ora chose to give the twelve-week campers a trip to Carlsbad Cavern, a wonderland 800 feet beneath the surface of the earth in the neighboring state of New Mexico.

And the catalog displaying wonderful pictures taken during the 1928 camping season featured STILL MORE PAINT PONIES! By this time they were housed in an up-to-date stable on the easternmost hill of the camp proper.

Word of the popular W. T. Johnson's quest for beautiful horses for his sister's girls' camp spread throughout Texas, and his rancher friends helped him "round up the cream of the crop." The elation he felt when he saw them at the camp or pictured so handsomely in the catalog caused him to look for a use for these magnificent animals after the camping season was over. According to the catalog, there were thirty-eight horses in the 1928 Waldemar string, many of them paints.

A "profile" of the colorful "Colonel," appearing in a 1940 San Antonio newspaper, states that he presented his first rodeo in the fall of 1928 in his hometown of San Antonio.

Obviously, W. T. Johnson had found an exciting off-season use for Waldemar's horses.

1929

It was June of 1929, and no hint of impending financial distress for the nation had yet blighted Wall Street, much less the banks of the Guadalupe River where Miss Ora's carefully tended flower was about to burst into full blossom.

The banner headline in the *War Whoop* read: "WALDEMAR CELEBRATES 4th ANNIVERSARY." The enthusiastic reporter wrote:

Four years ago 54 girls met at Waldemar, and with the help of the director, Miss Johnson, and a few counselors, began to make Waldemar history. Last week 165 girls from Texas, Oklahoma, Louisiana, Arkansas and California gathered at Waldemar to write Waldemar's fourth year of history.

The growth of Waldemar is due largely to the many improvements which are made as they are seen fit.

In 1926 there were girls only from the Lone Star State. Proud of their fine beginning, these campers realized that any gathering needed the broadening influence of contact with girls gathered from the different sections of the country. Today, as the fame of Waldemar spreads, the patrons of the camp are drawn from an even wider range.

The equipment of the camp has increased as the spirit has grown. A year ago the dining hall was built; the assembly hall has been recently remodeled and perfected; the stables have been enlarged; finer horses are added every year to Waldemar's collection; work has been started on the open air theater, which will give a beautiful background for the extensive dramatic ability found among camp girls, and this summer seven new kampongs have been erected, making a total of 29 bunk houses.

At the beginning of her fourth year, Waldemar starts with all her old traditions, and with the new improvements which symbolize the spirit of the camp.

Like the young reporter, Miss Ora had a good feeling about her enterprise. The fee for six weeks had been raised from $190 to $210, and for twelve weeks from $350 to $375. A reduction of $25 per term was made for girls who did not take horseback riding.

The year 1929 was the second of the rivalry between the Tejas and Comanche tribes. This innovation had worked as planned, inspiring girls to perfect their skills for the sake of their tribes, and all looked forward to the contests of 1929.

Still it was almost ten days after their arrival in 1929 before they elected their chieftains. It is noteworthy that the Tejas elected cheerleaders.

A regular pow-wow with a bonfire, war yells an' everything, was held Monday night by the Comanches and Tejas jointly.

After "heap much" celebration (not the Fourth of July variety) the tribes finally settled into their usual Indian stoicism and enough quiet was had to allow the tribes to elect their chiefs, etc.

The chief of the Comanches for this session will be Dunlop Glen of Oklahoma. Assisting her will be Jane Connellee of Eastland, Texas.

The Tejas chose as their leader the popular "Buster" Boyle of San Antonio, and Dot Milroy of Brenham will help her. Kathryn Heaney is to be Tejas yell leader, with Mary Pearle Garrett and Elizabeth Jacobs working with her.

The Comanches and Tejas both have many new yells and songs, and quite a few tribal members are working to compose more.

It will be a fair race to the finish this year, and there will be some close fight for supremacy. May the best team win.

Come on team, let's go!

Under the heading of "Sports" in the issue of July 7:

Despite the rain all Friday evening and early Saturday morning, the first big Tejas-Comanche meet of the season was held with great success on Saturday afternoon, June 29. There were two war canoe races, swimming events, and a soccer game. The Tejas came out on top with a final score of 43 to 26.

Both War Canoes still carried coxswains.

However, there was much more going on at Waldemar in 1929 than field meets and War Canoe races. Miss Ora's performing arts department was given frequent opportunity to realize heady successes.

Even though it would be fair to assume that Miss Ora Johnson did not let the Fourth of July go unheralded in the first three years of her camp's life, there is no record of these celebrations, but a patriotic pageant presented in 1929 was given generous coverage in the *War Whoop*. Because it is the first of many pageants to be reported in detail through the years, because the story includes a surprise for Miss Ora from the campers, and because the last line of the story predicts that the pageant "will go down in the history of Waldemar," the account of it follows.

WALDEMAR STAGES PATRIOTIC PAGEANT
Cedar Lodge Forms Background for Program

One hundred and sixty-five girls participated in the patriotic pageant which was given at Camp Waldemar on the evening of July 4th. The production of the pageant was the culmination of several days intensive practice for both dramatic and dancing parts.

The program was started by talks presenting to Miss Johnson the girls' plan of giving, as a token of their sincere appreciation of her gifts to them, a portrait of her to be painted by Arthur C. Morgan of New York and Shreveport, La. Dunlop Scott Glen spoke of the success Miss Johnson has made of the camp in the four years Waldemar has been run. Buster Boyle then told of the plan, which had already received the enthusiastic backing of the girls, and asked that they be allowed to complete the plans which they had started. After yells for Miss Johnson had been given, Mary Pearle Garrett gave a brief review of the life and fame of the artist chosen to paint the portrait.

The choir took its place on the porch of Cedar Lodge and sang "America the Beautiful."

The pageant was then begun with an Indian and Dutch group dance. Following this, a short patriotic play was given, showing the reception which the signers of the Declaration of Independence received as they left Liberty Hall. Then "Pioneer" and "War" came forward to the throne of "Peace" pledging themselves to banish "Poverty" and "Disease" and to guard the Liberty of the new democracy.

After the play, the girls of the lantern parade marched forward and took their places around Cedar Lodge. To further enhance the beautiful effect, they sang camp songs appropriate to the occasion. The program was ended with the singing of taps by the campers.

Spectators at the pageant, including approximately forty parents who came to Waldemar to celebrate the Fourth with their daughters, were enthusiastic in their praise of it. They adjudged it to be one of the most colorful and perfect programs they had ever witnessed. The costumes of the dancers, the picturesque lantern parade, and the graceful tableau revealed by torch light made an unforgettable picture—one which will go down in the history of Waldemar.

In an accompanying story, Miss Johnson announced that she would not have time to sit for a portrait, but she told of her appreciation of the spirit which moved the girls.

The success of the Fourth of July pageant inspired Miss Ora to schedule an even more challenging one for the end of the second term. This pageant marks the first time the Waldemar pier was lighted for theatrical use at night.

The pageant will be the biggest affair of the season. Tickets are to be sold for half a dollar by members of the Episcopal Church in Kerrville. Proceeds will go to a fund for an Episcopal church there. Patrons of the camp, however, will not be charged.

Miss Johnson is having extensive wiring done for the lighting effect, which will be magnificent. The pageant will be presented on the pier, thus making it possible to have water sports demonstrated, as well as to have the Guadalupe with its fringe of cypress trees, as a fitting background.

The pageant will be made up of a play, "The Pioneers," followed by the reading of a Waldemar poem by a girl who is to be selected as the most truly representative of Waldemar; demonstrations of the various sports will end the pageant.

The Waldemar poem was composed by Miss Ann Miller, of Austin, Texas. The representative girl who will read this has not yet been chosen.

Thus this pageant at the pier in 1929 hinted at the need for an award other than those given for achievement in sports. It was not until 1933 that the Ideal Girl Award was established, but the "representative girl of 1929" was certainly the forerunner. Neither her name nor a copy of the poem is available.

Recognizing that the quality of her staff determined the quality of her camp, Miss Ora gathered around her people of outstanding and unusual ability. In addition to their being eminently qualified in their fields, they were all entertainers: actors, dancers, violinists, pianists, and vocalists who could put together an impromptu program at the drop of their director's hat. And she worked at making the summers fun for them as well as for the girls. At bedtime, as a surprise, she would summon them to Waldemar Lodge for a bridge party. The old counselors would honor the new ones, which then demanded reciprocation, and the fun they had called them back to Waldemar each summer. They starred in camp pageants right along with the campers. They were talented and inventive, and Miss Ora's mind was always open to the suggestions of her superior staff, and their lives became caught up in the spirit which emanated from this dynamic woman.

Two of the new counselors who first came in 1929 and continued to come for many years were Carmen Crain (later Williams) of Fort Worth and Margaret Gladney (later Savage) of Beaumont.

In an early catalog, Miss Ora had written:

The most ancient of sports is Archery, perhaps forgotten for a few years, but such a fascinating sport can never die. The twenty lemon wood bows owned by the camp, the archery course trail, and the guidance of a live instructor has revived this "Perfect Posture" producing sport into one of the camp's most popular recreations.

The "live" archery instructor who was recruited by Waldemar in 1929 was Carmen Crain, a Fort Worth schoolteacher. In addition to heading the archery department for many summers and being loved by her kampong girls, Carmen became the Waldemar representative in Fort Worth serving the camp for many years. The esteem in which Carmen was held by Fort Worth patrons made her invaluable to Waldemar, and her contribution to the camp cannot be overstated.

Margaret Gladney came to Waldemar as a swimming teacher and as "Head of Sports," and she was quickly promoted to "Director of Activities." In this capacity she set up Waldemar's class schedule very much as it is today, planned evening programs, and was the one who answered all of the "Ask Maggie!" questions. When asked how she happened to come to Waldemar, "Maggie" said that before the 1929 season Miss Ora sent out "scouts" to schools having girls' physical education departments to recruit talent. The head of the Beaumont High School department was Beatrice Lytle, roommate of math teacher Margaret Gladney. Beatrice wasn't taken with the idea of recruiting campers, and Margaret stepped in and accepted the offer. Beatrice had second thoughts and came also in 1929.

When Margaret was called home temporarily because of the illness of her mother, a distraught reporter wrote the story as though she would never be back.

There was not a better liked counselor at Waldemar. Margaret was equally popular with girls and other counselors—she had the pep, the cooperation, even the voice of authority that go to make a model counselor.

The above news story was written in 1929, her arrival year. Maggie Gladney Savage continued to help shape Waldemar's policies until the summer of 1945.

But tribal competitions, pageants, and counselors' talents were not the real focus of Camp Waldemar in 1929.

W. T. Johnson, Miss Ora's brother, had earlier determined to secure for the camp a group of saddle horses "unequaled in any camp in the country," and by the summer of 1929 he had probably reached that goal. In her catalog for 1929 Miss Ora wrote:

While it has been the aim of the director to make Waldemar excel in every department, many people speak of it as the "Texas Horseback Camp" on account of its unusual horses, and instruction.

From the first issue of the paper in 1929:

Major Reilly reports that there are 52 girls taking English riding and 93 taking Western, which shows that the spirit of the west is still going strong, in Texas and Oklahoma girls at least. The total number of girls signed up for horseback riding is 145.

The Major is very proud of the 42 Waldemar horses. The majority of them, he says, are good, quiet saddle horses which were selected for the girls of the camp by W. T. Johnson, Miss Johnson's brother. In picking out these horses, Mr. Johnson went all over Texas, New Mexico, and Arizona, and money was no obstacle when he found one suitable for his purpose.

This next fall the horses will be taken to the State Fair at Dallas, and later to the New York Horse Show. In past years the Waldemar horses have carried off many prizes at the Fort Worth Fat Stock Show.

Two issues later a headline proclaimed:

WALDEMAR HORSES CHOSEN
FOR NEW YORK HORSE SHOW

Waldemar's horses have been chosen, as the finest group in this part of the country, to be taken to the New York Horse Show.

Representatives of those backing the show have offered Miss Johnson $5000 and free shipping, in order to present the horses in New York.

(When the Waldemar horses were shown in Madison Square Garden, Mrs. Wolkewitz remembered with pride that: "Mayor Jimmy Walker announced over the NBC network that they were the finest group of saddle horses ever shown in that noted place.")

The news story continued:

A recent addition to the stables is the beautifully marked and expensive white horse which Mr. W. T. Johnson bought near Bonham.

It is a most valuable addition to the Waldemar group and will be one of the outstanding horses at the New York and Dallas shows. Mr. W. T. Johnson, noted for his knowledge of horses, has chosen those now at Waldemar, and neither distance nor money has been any barrier when he found one which he thought the camp needed. Fine saddles, both English and Western have been bought, with a view to the comfort of both rider and mount. As a result of this careful selection, and of the expert care given the horses, those at Waldemar have taken many prizes at the Fort Worth Fat Stock Show. This fall the horses will be taken to the State Fair at Dallas.

The expensive white horse bought in Bonham was no doubt the subject of this paragraph:

One of the most interesting events that has recently happened at the stables is the arrival of a new horse which Mr. W. T. Johnson bought for Waldemar. No girl is allowed to ride the new mount until Mr. W. T. arrives at the camp.

Mr. W. T. came often. In Mrs. Wolkewitz's history she wrote:

Mr. Johnson has, because of his desire to bring every possible happiness to the girls of Waldemar, become their firm friend. "W. T.," as he is popularly known at camp, never fails to add his quota of excursions and entertainments to the regular camp program. He is unquestionably the camp's most popular visitor.

In the Christmas 1929 issue of the paper was this from Dallas:

October twelve was a day of fun and excitement for some of the Waldemar girls. Mr. W. T. had come to Dallas to put on the "World's Championship Rodeo" and had brought the Waldemar horses. Naturally he wanted the Waldemar girls to ride them in the BIG PARADE the opening day of the Texas State Fair. So Peggy Maxson, Christine Browning, Lida Mae Dudley, Dorothy Patterson, Gene Holland, Lucille Lipscomb, Martha Perkinson, Sara Frances White, Ripple Frazer, and Pat Patterson, all appeared upon the scene dressed "a la cowgirl" and rode in the parade and the Grand Entry of the rodeo.

This marks the first mention in the *Waldemar War Whoop* of Col. W. T. Johnson's "World Championship Rodeo," which he continued to sponsor in Madison Square Garden featuring Waldemar's horses until 1937.

On October 29, 1929 (an infamous Tuesday in financial annals), the *San Antonio Express* carried a feature story on Camp Waldemar. "Girls' Camp Brings South Texas Fame" was the heading above nine typical camp pictures and the complimentary story. The entire page was reproduced in the December 1929 Christmas issue of the *War Whoop*, which was mailed to campers, prospective campers, counselors, and friends.

A slick cream-colored "superior" grade of paper was used for this issue, and it has not stood the test of time as well as the ordinary newsprint used in other issues. It is rapidly disintegrating, and Waldemar has only one copy. Because of its rarity, and because the article compresses the history of the camp from its founding through the 1929 season into a few columns, it is reprinted here. There is no by-line, but it was no doubt written by R. F. Grant, editor, and a close friend and staunch supporter of Miss Ora's.

Although it would be hard to find in any writing of Emerson the celebrated quotation about the builder of the mouse-trap in the wilderness to whose door the world would make a beaten path, there is a South Texas institution which strikingly illustrates the idea. It is called Camp Waldemar, is located on the north fork of the Guadalupe in Kerr County, 17 miles upstream from Kerrville, and was founded by Miss Ora Johnson of San Antonio.

Getting national attention is not new for Miss Johnson. An experienced educator and an exceptional executive, her administration of Brackenridge Senior School as principal was marked by the greatest collection of national scholastic honors ever accumulated by pupils of that school. One first place after another in essay writing, journalism, annual publication, came to Brackenridge pupils while Miss Johnson was at the head and they were won in competition with pupils of the high schools in every city of the country.

Then Miss Johnson was removed as exceptional executives frequently are removed when they show outstanding ability in public service, and she turned her energies to a summer camp for girls in one of Kerr County's beautiful canyons. Her original plan was to have something to occupy vacation periods between school sessions as she expected to remain in the educational field.

But the summer camp for girls has grown into an institution that is bringing fame to South Texas, and this year it has received national recognition in a striking way.

Right now the "paint ponies of Camp Waldemar" are the feature attraction at a horse show being held in Madison Square Garden, New York, for the benefit of the Broad Street Hospital. From New York the ponies will travel to Boston to be featured at the horse show there. Already they have been shown this year in El Paso for ten days and at the State Fair in Dallas. Agents of the New York and Boston shows came to Texas, traveled the 89 miles from San Antonio to Waldemar by auto, marveled at what they declared is the best collection of "paint ponies" in America, and offered not only a handsome fee for the privilege of showing the horses, but guaranteed the cost of transporting them more miles with insurance for their safety.

A Texan accustomed to the phrase 'paint pony' will wonder what there is sensational about Miss Johnson's herd of ponies, but any lover of horse flesh would need only a glimpse of the sleek horses to open his eyes. The ponies really are beautifully marked in bay and white, and ranging in value from $250 to $1500 apiece. There are 51 in the herd and they were collected from all over the United States by Miss Johnson's brother, W. T. Johnson, a ranch man of wide experience. During camp periods the girls at Waldemar use these horses every day and despite the fact that every one of them is as spirited as an Arabian horse, they are so gentle that even novices ride them safely within a few weeks after their first lesson at the camp.

Riding, of course, is only one of Camp Waldemar's activities. It is a school where 150 girls may study under experienced teachers if they wish. For recreation they have riding, tennis, swimming, canoeing, hiking, soccer, football, archery, rifle practice, playing in the orchestra, or sketching. The camp's object is to promote the health and happiness of the girls who so eagerly look forward to the six or twelve weeks every summer they are permitted to spend there.

Dinner time is marked by stunts and impromptu entertainments. Every camp period brings its pageant, the one last summer being staged with all the brilliance which might have been expected of a professional production near a large city instead of many miles from any railroad. Electric lighting equipment, natural torches, water, moonlight, and cypress shadows give a pageant picture which several hundred citizens of Kerrville and San Antonio who went to see it say was never before equaled in this section. The camp occupies a site of more than 360 acres on both sides of the Guadalupe. Its dormitories are on the sides of the canyon and all through the summer the girls sleep under blankets every night. In appointments, according to national camp inspectors, Waldemar ranks among the most exclusive camps for girls in America. Buildings are of native stone and huge cedar logs. Fireplaces of boulders are in the large buildings. There are electric lights, running water, telephone, and conveniences unexpected so far from any city or town. The beamed-ceiling dining hall is unusually attractive, and the tables are hand-made with inlaid tops. Even the china is distinctive with pictures of Waldemar burned in the plates.

Still Miss Johnson is not satisfied. She had girls from seven states at Waldemar last summer and the largest attendance in the camp's history. Right now she is busy with Henry Steinbomer, camp architect, on plans for a new Fine Arts building of native rock, the most elaborate structure on the site. The administration building is being remodeled. Kamp McGinnis, landscape architect of Dallas, is at Waldemar working on plans for the further beautification of the grounds. Scores of San Antonions motor to Waldemar during the summer camp period just to see it.

The road along the Guadalupe from Hunt to the camp is one of the most attractive in South Texas. The climb to the camp from San Antonio is so gradual it is not easy to realize it is nearly 2000 feet above sea level.

No description of Waldemar would be complete without reference to the spirit which dominates its activities. Every employee of the camp has been selected by Miss Johnson to achieve a cooperative spirit, and while the camp's rules are of the strictest, they are enforced with such good nature that they are made pleasant even for the girls who sometimes don't want to get up in the morning or who want to smuggle in a two-pound box of candy for nibbling between meals. Nearly every camp employee is an entertainer and the impromptu shows which they give in the evenings are remembered with keen pleasure by the girls long after they have returned to their homes and their school work.

Chapter 2

1930s

1930

The summer of 1929—wonderfully successful and eventful—had nonetheless lacked a big building project, and Miss Ora Johnson was not completely fulfilled. In the fall of that year she directed that work begin on at least four building and remodeling projects.

The façade of Cedar Lodge, only three years old, had never been quite as attractive as she would have it, and so large rock columns, extending from the stones of the lower level up through the second floor porch to the roof, were added to lend charm to the building. The cedar railing around the upstairs porch displayed a rough cedar "W" in the center of its decorative vertical supports, and on the lower level stone retaining walls defining flower beds enhanced the exterior. Its austere face was gone and Cedar Lodge now smiled.

In the busy summer of 1929, tennis counselors had complained that tennis classes were much too crowded—that 115 campers had reported for tennis. And so two new cement tennis courts were under construction "in the space formerly occupied by the old garages," to be ready for the 1930 season. Miss Ora wrote in the Christmas issue of the *War Whoop* about the tennis courts just north and east of the dining hall (later referred to as "lower courts.")

Some of the old campers perhaps cannot visualize the location and, true, it has taken much time in excavation and building of rock walls.

When this work is finished, however, it will be an ideal location, for the huge trees will give shade to the players both morning and afternoon. As Mr. W. T. said, "Waldemar surely should have some good tennis players, moving a mountain to make the courts for them to practice on."

But by far the most dramatic improvement to the physical plant in 1930 was the new Fine Arts Building. Located near the entrance of the camp grounds proper, it welcomed campers and counselors of 1930 who marveled at the resourcefulness of their "Aunt Ora." The building was to be the home of Miss Ora in the winter and Waldemar's Fine Arts Building in the summer.

Henry Steinbomer, architect of the dining hall built in 1928, designed the building "which is being constructed by the same rock artist who built other camp buildings, known to camp girls as Ferdinand."

The following description of the building, which appeared in the 1929 Christmas issue of the *War Whoop*, was probably written by Miss Ora with the help of the architect while the building was under construction:

A beautiful Tower Hall will furnish entrance to the building through massive arched doors. The ceiling of adzed wood, the floor of tile lighted with antique electric lanterns, and the walls of highly colored rocks, produce a very distinctive entrance.

The living room is very spacious and the walls are being made of most unusual rock on the interior. The distinctive unit around which this room is decorated is the large fireplace, and this together with the built-in reproductions of Indian scenes, painted by the famous artist, Wiley Amick, make for a most unusual room. The Aztec design of the tile flooring carries out the Indian motif.

A real fountain in a Patio is to lend artistic beauty to the structure. The Patio is to be planted under the supervision of Kamp McGinnis, landscape architect of Dallas. There will be Flag Stone walks in the Patio and terrace. Tile topped wrought iron tables, each table in a different design and color scheme, will be seen in the Patio. So closely is nature followed that a most beautiful and natural effect will be presented.

Furnishings of the unique building are to be of the most modern. Lovely Venetian mirrors are to be put in the walls. Many special built-in features will be found most convenient, especially the bookcases. To adorn the top of the building will be an iron horse mounted as representative of the camp mounts.

In fact everything is being built for use and comfort as well as beauty, and with a four-foot cement foundation the building will stand to see many camp sessions come and go.

At the time Miss Ora wrote the article, she did not know that Ferdinand Rehbeger was going to make the walls of the entrance hall of that building, which has been known as Rippling Waters since 1937, a showplace for geodes and other geological wonders native to the area. The unfashionably high "built-in Indian scenes" were removed about 1950 and the resulting spaces expertly filled by Ferdinand's skillful hand and eye. Venetian mirrors were never installed.

As if all of this activity were not enough, a new wooden kampong for the younger girls was built to take the place of the "old improvised one used last summer." *War Whoop* articles suggest that the improvised "Doll House" of 1929 was the old kitchen in Waldemar Lodge which became "Kollege Kampong" for Junior Counselors in 1930, when the younger girls had their new house. A picture in a catalog shows the girls and their two counselors sitting on an inviting covered porch of a comfortable looking wooden ranch type house, located just across the road to the east of the Dining Hall and facing the Fine Arts Building and the river. The girls hold distinctive handmade dolls which decorated the building (and had decorated their quarters in Waldemar Lodge) and from which the house took its name rather than from the age of its occupants. It was not long, however, before the youngest campers became known as "Dolls."

The "studio for arts and crafts," located in the present position of the Craft House, was ready for the 1930 season. Other construction dates are difficult to establish. Either in 1929 or 1930 an attractive porch with stone columns was constructed on the east side of Junior Recreation Hall (the original Waldemar Lodge). Curving stone steps led from the porch south to the lower level or patio often used for church services. This addition gave the building a frontage on the road which encircled the Athletic Field.

At the "swimming hole," the wooden pier which had proved to be inadequate in 1929 was enlarged for the 1930 season, and a half-dozen stone steps for "theater seating" were built by Ferdinand. Audiences were sometimes seated across the river so that drama directors could use the stone steps for unusual staging effects.

The original gate to Waldemar's grounds was memorable only because it had "Camp Waldemar" neatly lettered on a wooden sign hanging between two small rock columns. In 1930 Ferdinand built two massive stone columns, and each bore, near its summit, a thick slab of pink granite upon which was carved "Waldemar." This gate was used until 1965.

Thus as she neared the end of Waldemar's fifth summer, a confident Ora Johnson surveyed her camp with pride and marveled at the beauty of its physical plant. Waldemar Lodge, Cedar Lodge, both with new facelifts, the Dining Hall, and then her sparkling new Fine Arts Building formed a crescent and outlined, along with the river, her spacious and inviting Athletic Field.

A few of Miss Ora's campers in the early days were either in college or planning to enter in the fall, and their maturity not only allowed them more freedom but improved their performance level, whether physical, theatrical, musical, or intellectual. In advertising her academic department in the early days, Miss Ora wrote:

> College courses may be given where enrollment is sufficient to justify offering the course.

In 1934 Waldemar was listed in the *Handbook of Summer Camps* as being "for girls from 6-20" and these were the prevailing age limits for girls' camps listed nationwide.

A very few girls, usually talented former campers or musicians, were invited by Miss Ora to become "Junior Counselors." They lived together rather than with campers, and they assisted counselors in teaching in the fields of the "JC's" expertise. Wrote Maggie Savage many years later:

> They were ineligible for awards and were on their own to behave, but they could participate in any classes if not clashing with their duties. They were great.

One of the national prizes which Brackenridge Senior School had won while Miss Ora was its principal was for "annual editing," and she decided that her older girls at Waldemar could do as well. Three or four brochures for promotional purposes had preceded it, but this "Waldemar Annual" was to be edited by the more mature campers with a counselor sponsor.

Among the distinctions this first annual in 1930 boasted were the first publication of the Waldemar crest on its title page and the first publication of "Waldemar Sea of Woods" on its last.

> The book will be in the nature of a catalog but will be truly representative of camp life and camp activities at Waldemar. A book with a beautiful paper back will be given to each camper who does not care to pay the small sum of one dollar for having her name put on a leather back in gold letters.

The idea of the annual lasted only four seasons, the difference in the two organs being that the annual carried no information about clothing lists, camp rules, fees, and the like. In the last two annuals the director, by then Doris, asked the girls' permission to include that information so that she could "send it to the new girls," and shortly it became a catalog again edited off season by the camp.

The *Waldemar War Whoop*, begun by Miss Ora near the close of the 1928 season, was traditionally edited by a selected group of older campers with a counselor sponsor. It was light-hearted, filled with "inside" jokes, feature stories, social notes, lists of camp visitors, original Indian legends, the goings and comings of both counselors and campers, and "What If—?" columns. There were editorials as appropriate and meaningful when Waldemar was fifty years old as when it was five. A sports column kept the readers abreast of progress in the various departments, and camp entertainment programs were reviewed, usually with puffery. Miss Ora introduced the familiar Indian chieftain's profile on the paper's nameplate for the Christmas issue of 1929.

Her words written for the 1929 winter issue of the *War Whoop* were exciting:

> A special feature of the horseback riding next summer [1930] will be the staging of two horse shows, one each term, and Waldemarites will have a chance to see the horses dance the old-fashioned quadrille, a most popular feature of the New York Horse Show. The audience of Madison Square Garden made repeated requests for the repetition of this act. . . .

"A Camper's Diary," a regular feature of early catalogs, carried this notation for August 28, 1930:

> Horse Show, a thrilling, colorful sight, and oh, those horses in that quadrille!

Thus it is safe to say that the quadrille was first performed at Waldemar on August 28, 1930, but it may have been ridden by cowboys instead of campers. Neither Miss Ora nor the 1930 diarist makes mention of camper riders. It is believed that Miss Ora intended to let the girls perform the fast-paced square dance on horseback during the 1931 season, but again the diary keeper simply says, "And oh, the horses in that quadrille!"

If the 1930 quadrille was performed by Waldemar's high flying cowboys, one of these was no doubt Jack Reeves, who came to Waldemar in 1930 and continued to be associated with the camp until his death in 1985. Jack was already working for "the Colonel" at one of his ranches, and the Colonel may have considered him "on loan" to his sister, but Jack liked it and became a Waldemar mainstay. The handsome, genial, witty Jack was popular with campers and counselors alike, and his marriage in 1943 to Constance Douglas, the much loved and admired matriarch of Waldemar's horseback department, gave unusual strength to that department which has continued into the decade of the 1990s.

Departments other than horseback had achieved outstanding successes in 1930, and the ebullient Miss Johnson was proud of them all. Emma Sealy, "the swimming instructor for beginners," had seen to it that sixty-seven girls who came to camp unable to swim had now passed the National Red Cross test, an accomplishment that brought both Mrs. Sealy and Waldemar recognition.

In 1930 the Tejas and Comanche tribes were largely pep organizations. Tribal members were kept busy writing new tribal songs and yells and trying to "out rah-rah" the opposition, and their tribal loyalty was strictly physical. The beauty and memory-making thrill of inspirational, character-building programs presented on their own tribal hills were not known to very early campers. However, an entry for July 11, 1930, in "A Camper's Diary" indicates that their meetings, even though pep rallies solely, were now conducted separately on hills. The entry read: "The Tribal Meetings on the mountain tops created pep!"

Sponsors had not yet been introduced into the tribal system in 1930, but if camp was to have Field Days, someone had to organize and supervise them. So Miss Ora appointed a few counselors as "supervisors," and the story they wrote for the next issue of the *War Whoop*, August 17, 1930, will delight later-day tribal sponsors:

> "What does she have this period?" "Oh, you can't

put her in canoeing, she has tennis." And so far, far into the night, or the morning, we should say. Did anybody hear any noise Friday night in Junior Recreation Hall? Well, if you did, you know it was some of the "Jolly Happy Crowd" fixing out programs for field day. We certainly hope everybody had a red-letter day, because we had a red-letter night before. Mrs. Baker said that we wanted this to be a day that everyone in camp would remember. I know that all of you had a good time and will never forget it, and I'm sure that none of us will. We apologize right now for any bad dispositions or inclinations to "gripiness" on the part of the so-called "Supervisors," but just consider the source and forgive, don't-cha know.

We tried to keep up the good camp spirit, folks, and make up a song to sing in the dining room, but we couldn't make the grade. All we could say was "Pooped, pooped, pooped." Hoping you had a hilarious time, we leave you. From Just the Sleepy Time Gals.

There is no clue as to who the supervisors were, but the story shows that the organized Field Day had come into being.

Most of the many guests who came from San Antonio and Kerrville to see Miss Johnson's camp saw only the buildings and the physical facilities, but during these five years, administrative decisions had kept her busy too—and kept her on her creative toes. Waldemar's counselor staff, its camper group, its program, its rules and its awards—indeed its success—were all under her aegis, and all decisions were made thoughtfully by her and her intelligent staff.

An early priority for Ora Johnson was setting up a fair and just point system to determine what the qualifications were for each all-star. As early as 1928 she brought in an "expert" (Agnes Murphy of Denton) for advice in this area. Margaret Gladney and Beatrice Lytle came to camp from Beaumont in 1929, and in 1930 they set up the point system in a ledger which soon became known as the Waldemar "bible." Frances McCluskey was charged with helping record in the large, ledger-like tome.

Each camper was listed along with such information as her tribal affiliation, her age and camp classification, her points earned by making "teams," the number of service points she received, and her "plus spirit" scores.

Keeping the "plus spirit" code was an important part of earning the all-star. "Plus spirit" was an all-inclusive term "which covered the willing execution of kampong duties, good sportsmanship, rest hour rules, punctuality, and morning exercises or morning dips." Each was listed in the "bible."

Infractions of rules were recorded in the "bible," and from the first it was stated that "no all-star will be awarded to any girl who breaks health rules." The information in the "bible" determined who received the all-star for which she was working and which tribe won the plaque.

On page three of the first "bible":

HEALTH RULES TO BE KEPT FOR 3 CONSECUTIVE WEEKS FOR ANY HONORS

1. At least 6 glasses of water every day besides water at meals
2. Eight hours of sleep every night
3. One hour of exercise daily
4. A bath or a swim every day
5. No eating between meals except fresh fruit or milk
6. No candy except within 15 min. after meals
7. No tea, coffee or soda water
8. A bowel movement every day
9. Three regular meals every day
10. One green vegetable daily
11. Each girl must use her own drinking cup

N.B. (1) No honors will be given to any girl who smokes or attempts to smoke while in attendance at camp

N.B. (2) All Health Rules are suspended if a girl is under the care of the nurse

[Editor's note: N.B. is Maggie's "scholarese" for NOTE WELL.]

EXTRA POINTS COUNTED AS OPTIONALS

	Points
1. Each extra team	25
2. No candy for six weeks	50
3. No gum for six weeks	25
4. No gum in public places for six weeks	15
5. Expense account	25
6. Service points	100
(do not carry over to 2nd term)	
7. Kampong honors for each girl in cabin 6 wks.	
For 6 consecutive 100 plusses	15
For 6 consecutive 100s	10
(a 100 plus makes a 98 equal 100)	
8. Original legend	10
9. Original song (must be "put over")	25
10. Captain of any team	10
11. Table Manners (every three weeks)	5
12. No "Homesick Blues"	5
13. Grade of A in academic subject	Team or 25
14. Weight points for over or underweight girls	10

Waldemar has continued to maintain its "bible" and in the 1990s is into its fifth ledger.

Certainly the highlight of the 1930 camping season was the presentation of the spectacular pageant "Hiawatha." The artfully designed printed program is dated August 27, 1930, but the "Camper's Diary" says that it was presented on the night of August 28, horse show day. A large audience made up of patrons and friends of Waldemar crowded the opposite bank of the river to watch Longfellow's story of "Hiawatha," specially arranged by Waldemar's talented counselors, unfold with bareback riders, swimmers, canoers, and archers taking part. The drama, dance, and music departments were much involved, and lighting for the production was done by Texas Power and Light Company, Kerrville. This was Miss Ora Johnson's kind of pageantry.

(The wonderful costumes, some handpainted, formed the nucleus for Waldemar's store of Indian costumes which were soon to be used annually for "The Legend of the Guadalupe.")

Thus in 1930 Camp Waldemar and Ora Johnson had reached a heady milestone. The camp was concluding its fifth year of operation, and its progress and successes were noteworthy to observers and exhilarating to camp personnel. Handsome native stone buildings—tourist stoppers—bordered the grass-covered Athletic Field, that magic oval where so many happy activities were centered. Strict rules, happily accepted, set boundaries as well as goals for the girls, and traditions had been born which were destined to live far into the future.

The summer of 1930 had been another happy and rewarding one for campers and counselors alike—to say nothing of the zestful and confident Ora Johnson. She was looking forward to the awards banquet at summer's end, which was to be held on her impressive new tennis courts just a stone's throw from the kitchen door, and she herself would try to be impressive as she bestowed cups, medals, and All-Stars on her campers who had earned them.

During these first five years, Miss Ora had amassed a variety of beautiful silver loving cups, appropriately engraved, which her department heads awarded to their winners at the banquet on the last night of camp. It was not necessary for her to buy them all because patrons and businessmen and friends of the camp were eager to furnish the cups which were taken home with pride, engraved with the name of the winner, and then returned for the following summer's contest. Three wins by the same camper retired the cup. Miss Ora also supplied pins

and medals of all kinds for her department heads to award, and she could hardly wait for the second-term 1930 event.

Everything was going so well. Certainly W. T. had made a name for himself and for Waldemar with those wonderful horses he had assembled. Horse fanciers in New York City and in Boston were now well familiar with the name of the Texas girls' camp on the Guadalupe River.

Ripple Frazer, dietitian, and U. S. and Lucille Smith were also looking forward to the grand night with confidence and enthusiasm. Much of their preparatory work was done the day before, and at eleven o'clock on the night before the big event they placed huge trays of hand-decorated angel food cake squares in the refrigerators and dozens of dressed chickens in the ice chest. They locked the store room, satisfied that they had done all they could for that night, and off they went to bed. Ripple had served on the costume committee for "Hiawatha" that night, and she was eager for a little rest.

Before dawn on the day of the final banquet, the kitchen was a mass of flames, and the entire building, only two years old, was destroyed.

Miss Ora, the Colonel, Ripple, U. S., Lucille and the kitchen staff—together with a team of volunteers which included campers, counselors, cowboys, and friends from other camps—"pulled it out of the fire," so to speak. The Colonel had pots, pans, dishes and cutlery, as well as food, brought from San Antonio before breakfast time. They had fruit, cereal, bacon, milk, and bread served at outdoor tables, the bacon having been cooked on the cowboys' stove. Breakfast was only one hour late, according to Mrs. Wolkewitz's chronicle.

Mrs. Wolkewitz credits Ripple Frazer's "unconquerable spirit" and the willingness and flexibility of U. S. and Lucille Smith with the complete success of the banquet that night. The former kitchen attached to Waldemar Lodge (which had become a haven for the youngest girls and then for the JCs) was hastily reactivated and the JCs put to work. Two years after the fire, Mrs. Wolkewitz wrote:

> Three hundred chickens were bought and dressed, 500 angel food squares were made and decorated, only the rolls were bought, and the menu consisted of fruit cocktail, barbecued chicken, potato surprises, asparagus salad, rolls, salted nuts, ice cream and cake. Only seeing was believing for truly it was a miracle brought about by Ripple Frazer and her competent staff.

The tables were placed out of doors at the west

end of the Athletic Field in order to be near the makeshift kitchen. The theme was a circus performance, and the tables ringed the "stage" upon which clowns made merry despite the unsettling events of the last twenty-four hours.

As she laughed with the clowns, applauded the ringmaster, and congratulated medal and cup winners, Miss Ora Johnson was marveling at the wonder of it all—and mentally planning her new dining hall.

1931

To design her new dining hall, Miss Johnson chose the talented Harvey P. Smith, a well-known San Antonio architect. She had seen his work in her home city, and she knew that he was able to blend the rustic, the Spanish and the Mexican into a distinctive Southwestern style that would personalize her camp to its region. He liked to use native materials, and he wanted the land and the trees and the hills to embrace his structures, which they inevitably did.

From the first Harvey Smith and Ferdinand Rehbeger genuinely liked each other, and each respected and admired the work of the other. They were both practical and resourceful men, and a wonderful chemistry grew between them which bred and nourished Waldemar's uniquely beautiful physical plant. The suited man from the city and the khaki-clad émigré from Russia became close friends, each understanding and respecting the ambitions and the needs of the other.

Their names are visibly and indelibly linked on Waldemar's Dining Hall, the first structure they built together. It bears a cornerstone of river rock placed to the right of the center doors leading into the senior dining room. The inscription reads:

1931
Harvey P. Smith
AIA
Architect
Ferdinand Rehbeger
Masonry

On a nearby stone is inscribed:

1926–1931
Dining Hall
Camp Waldemar
Ora V. Johnson
Founder

The catalog for 1931 carries wonderful architectural drawings of the new building, but no pictures. It is, however, described in detail by the delighted owner:

The biggest surprise for the 1931 campers will be the new dining hall, one of the finest rustic buildings in the United States. It is more than a hundred feet across the front and eighty feet deep, constructed of river rock from the vicinity, varying from great boulders at the base to the smaller cobble stones at the top. The strength and beauty of the building is greatly enhanced by the massive stone buttresses on all the corners. Across the front is a broad flagstone porch over which is a rustic balcony where one can get a panoramic sweep of not only the picturesque camp site, but the river and the range of hills beyond.

One enters from the porch directly into the Senior Dining Hall, a large hall with flagstone floor, timbered ceiling, and walls combining the gray honeycomb and red fossil rock. At either end are massive fireplaces in which are combined all varieties of stone found in the Kerrville hills, a veritable geologist's laboratory. Behind the many crystal rocks are concealed lights, which when turned on transport the visitor back to the Queen's Chamber of Carlsbad Cavern. In the center and at the rear is the grand staircase, and four steps give access to the large landing which serves as a stage. Flights to the right and left of the stage lead to the second floor.

To the left of the Senior dining hall is the Pioneer room, an octagonal room with cabinets for trophies and furnishings collected from the early pioneer days.

To the right of the Senior dining hall is the Junior dining hall. The cedar timbered gable, twenty-six-feet high, and the great fireplace and chimney breast lend this room the appearance of a baronial hall. At the second-story level around the chimney is a rustic balcony descending in short flights to the floor." [The Junior Dining Hall porch was not added until 1939.]

In the rear of the building is the large and modernly equipped kitchen and service portion.

On the second floor are guest rooms, bathrooms, and the hospital clinic. The appointments of these rooms and the colored tile baths are equivalent to any modern hotel accommodations.

There is a large recreation hall on the third floor with hardwood floors for dancing. The hall will be decorated as a hunting lodge, using a large collection of horns, blankets, and Indian relics.

The foundation for this massive building was placed on solid rock, and the fact that its masonry walls and asbestos shingled roof are of fireproof materials, make it not only beautiful, but also convenient, comfortable, and safe.

Miss Ora took pride in the fact that her building

was constructed entirely of materials found close to Waldemar, but Ferdinand Rehbeger, with a sly grin, would point out a particular rock in the east fireplace which a friend had brought him from Arkansas. He would assure the listener that it was the only import—except for the handsome Vermont slate which was used instead of flagstone for the floor!

The large third-floor ballroom, decorated as a hunting lodge, celebrated the American cowboy. Deer-antler light fixtures, fashioned with tiny light bulbs, colorful Indian blankets, Indian relics, a custom-designed firescreen and wrought-iron floor lamps—all of this personalized the large room with hardwood floors which became known as the "Colonel W. T. Johnson Ballroom" in honor of Miss Ora's brother and in recognition of his contributions to Waldemar.

So proud was Miss Ora Johnson of her new building that she abandoned for a time the Indian Chieftain nameplate of the *Waldemar War Whoop*, adopted only the year before, and chose instead to superimpose a photograph of the Dining Hall over attractive lettering for the 1931 season.

Sunday, August 17, was the day she chose for the dedication of her new building. A camp reporter wrote:

> The program is under the direction of the gold and diamond-star girls and a minister from the Westminster encampment will be the principal speaker. Arrangements are being made to take care of visitors from all over the state.

The *Kerrville Mountain Sun* pointed out that music by camp counselors, guests, and the Waldemar Glee Club would enhance the dedication:

> The dedication will be made to the Spirit of Waldemar which, it is declared, stands for character building for young womanhood of America.

Among the new counselors who joined the Waldemar staff in 1931 was Dolly Downes (later Kelton), whom Miss Ela Hockaday had brought from Boston to teach at Hockaday School for Girls in Dallas. Dolly was ready to go to a New Mexico camp in the summer of 1931, but Miss Hockaday "wouldn't hear of her going to any camp except Ora Johnson's." Dolly headed the Waldemar canoeing department during the decade of the 1930s, and the canoe pageants she designed are legendary. Dolly is important to the Waldemar story because she created the canoe drill which precedes the Ideal Waldemar Girl ceremony. Many talented canoeing counselors have made changes and additions, but the basic design of the drill is very much as Dolly created it.

The youngest of the three Frazer sisters, Hannah More Frazer, came to Waldemar in 1931 to teach lifesaving. She served as president of the Kerr County Life Saving Board, and later in the second term of 1934 she accepted a position with the Midwestern Division of the American Red Cross in St. Louis. She returned to Waldemar in 1937, but very soon she joined the National Red Cross Organization permanently. Hannah More is probably best remembered by "old-timers" of the 1930s as climaxing water pageants by diving through a wall of fire, sometimes accompanied by fireworks set off by the ubiquitous Miss Billie Johnson.

The campers of 1931 fell heir to many fun-filled Waldemar traditions. "Miss Newcomer Weds Mr. Oldcamper" was a hilarious evening program in which both campers and counselors took roles and which varied enough through the years to continue to entertain—and sometimes convulse—the audience.

The "Annual Movie Banquet," for which everyone costumed as a motion picture star of the day (including Miss Ora as sultry siren Gloria Swanson) called for costumes which had been carefully packed at home in anticipation of this one night.

Dolly's annual Canoe Carnival, in which kampong groups vied for honors in decorating canoes with swans, sails, rainbows and jack o'lanterns, was begun this year.

Sightseeing trips to San Antonio, Junction and Seven Hundred Springs, and later to Monterrey, Mexico, or to Carlsbad Caverns brought out dresses and hats. There was a trip to Austin in 1931 to acquaint campers with the lawmaking process and to meet Governor and Mrs. Sterling.

In the catalog for 1931 a smiling Miss Ora is pictured standing beside her new Federal Truck. It helped with the transportation for the all-camp excursions which were frequently on the Waldemar calendar. Some walked, some rode trucks, and some rode horseback, with transportation changing for the return trip. Vesper services were held at "Dripping Springs" (later known as the "second picnic ground"), and a dip at "Seagraves" (Mo Ranch) on the way made it a popular excursion. An eleven-mile trip to "The Great Divide," the spot where the two forks of the Guadalupe River rise, was successfully undertaken on Sunday after rest hour (over at 2:30 P.M.) for a vesper service. The glorious communion between God and nature was firmly established during these vesper services which were often conducted by minister friends of Miss Ora.

August 27, 1931, was the day of a horse show so important that special programs were printed for those who came from San Antonio and Kerrville to enjoy watching W. T. Johnson's fabulous horses and the riding skills of Waldemar campers. Six prestigious judges, three for English and three for Western, watched the thrilling Grand Parade made up of thirty-two riders. They named the winners of the coveted cups and judged a "musical chair contest" with contestants jumping from their mounts at a given signal to claim an empty chair. And then came the highlight of the afternoon:

MUSICAL QUADRILLE

Audrey Moody	Jean Blocker
Martha Gene Perkinson	Calada Waller
Martha Sanderson	Mary Ellen Kirven
Elizabeth Lou Everett	Maurice Finney
Mildred Goodrich	Charlotte Lane
Betty Briscoe	Charline Lane

If indeed Waldemar girls rode the flashy quadrille in 1930, the year before, it is a good bet that most of these girls were in it. Only three were newcomers to camp in 1931.

The chairman of the panel of judges was W. P. Knox, director of Arrow Head Ranch for Boys. Earlier that summer his boys, under the direction of Chief Blue Eagle from Shawnee, Oklahoma, who was on the Arrow Head staff, had secretly carved for Waldemar girls a large totem pole and presented it to the camp with much ceremony and ritual dancing. It was placed directly in front of Cedar Lodge. The totem pole, which had required much skill and originality, was a surprise for Miss Ora and the girls and she decided to honor Mr. Knox by making him the chairman of her horse show judges.

The proud Miss Johnson was sending about fifty girls the next day to Carlsbad Caverns, according to an article in the *Kerrville Mountain Sun*. This was to be a three-day trip, the first one to the caverns since 1928. The horse show had been a dazzling climax to a happy and successful season.

It was raining when second-term campers had arrived in 1931, and knowing that a rainy day can foster homesickness in new campers, the director used some psychology. A reporter wrote:

Sunday morning Aunt Ora shocked the camp by saying that everyone must write a letter home. Horrors!

She announced that this was to be a letter-writing contest on our first impression of the camp.

The winning letters were published, taking up much of the space in the one 1931 *War Whoop* issue in Waldemar's archives. These statements are excerpted:

"I am in camp now and I'm having the time of my life. I think it's because Miss Johnson is so jolly and sweet to us all."

"I like it so much I could live here the whole year round. I love the camp. I love Miss Johnson very much."

"The director of the camp, Miss Ora Johnson, or Aunt Ora, as all the campers call her, is the sweetest woman you ever met. She is just like a mother to you and the best sport of all."

"Dearest Aunt Ora: Your camp is so wonderful I don't just know what to say about my first impression of it. Maybe you had rather I'd say our camp, for you are so big-hearted you want everybody to feel like they are at home, and really and truly that's the way everybody feels."

"Miss Johnson is so sweet to us. Saturday when we arrived, Aunt Ora, as we call her, met us, and I wasn't a single bit homesick."

Thus Ora Johnson finished the second term of 1931 surrounded by campers and counselors who loved her as no other.

September 19, 1877 – December 1, 1931
MONDAY MORNING EPITAPH

Probably I should cry, but I don't feel like crying. Aunt Ora is dead. The neat orange column clipped from a San Antonio paper, telling of her death, with all the important data in the first paragraph, looks inconsequent among the letters on my desk, in the usual weekend mess, and covered with books and dust.

Ever since the first of my summers at her "character building camp for children," I've known that Aunt Ora was "a grand old girl." The orange clipping says she died at "5 a.m. in the morning, after two operations," and so on. Funny she should die at that hour, when she had awakened so many mornings at five o'clock, at the first note of the bugler's "Reveille," blown with an adolescent, if sleepy, enthusiasm. She used to hurry from her bedroom, fastening a georgette dress as she came into the dining room. She kept her white hair beautifully marcelled. She wore a navy blue georgette dress every day of the five summers I knew her; laughing rumors said she bought the dress the day before camp opened each summer, and at the end of the season, when the last camper had left for home, she solemnly walked down to the pier, wrapped the dress around a stone, and sank it in the river. During meals she used to wander from table to table, conferring with counselors, chatting with visiting parents, and absently taking a just-buttered muffin from someone's plate, asking a question and hurrying on in the midst of a careful answer.

"As a personal project," continued the clipping, "her camp has grown from a small affair to a large educational plant. . . ." The reporter erred there. The camp could never have grown from a personal project because it was developed as the realization of a dream. Aunt Ora told me so one night when she stayed with me in the infirmary because I had an ear-ache and was homesick. I was only fourteen; I snuggled up against her comfortable shoulder and sniffled while she rocked and talked me to sleep. "When you've grown up and remember these summers here, you'll understand," Aunt Ora told me, and she hushed my sobs when the bugler, silhouetted against the moonlighted river, played "Taps." I reached up to Aunt Ora's cheek and felt a wetness there. From then on, with childish loyalty, I hugged the secret to me that Aunt Ora cried when "Taps" was played. A few years later, when she called me into her office to reprimand me for neglecting my duties as a junior counselor, I remembered, and understood what she meant as she shouted that her camp was more important to her than any counselor's pleasures.

The clipping has writhed in the wind across my desk. "Members of the family were at the bedside when death came Tuesday morning." I wonder if she felt the strangeness of the final "Taps" at the hour when "Reveille" should have blown. Or was she amused at the sleeping stupidity of the bugler?

I should get rid of this litter on my desk. The scraps of the clipping are too vivid against the enameled blue waste basket. Outside on the limb of a maple tree in the backyard, a squirrel is idly waving his tail and watching me stuff the orange scraps to the bottom of my waste basket.

—Dunlop Scott Glen

Gone was the dreamer—but not the dream.

Miss Ora Johnson had brought together a group of uncommon women at her girls' camp. They were teachers known throughout their home states as innovative educators, inspirational role models, and jolly companions. Their love and admiration for Miss Ora had caused them to give their best to her girls' camp and to cherish it almost as much as she did, and her untimely death strengthened their determination to help it continue to blossom.

Margaret Gladney Savage remembers visiting the bedside of her stricken mentor at the Scott and White Clinic in Temple, and she recalls the poignant resolve with which she promised to "Carry On."

And so at Christmastime of that sad year, a group Mrs. Wolkewitz called "the old guard" met at Waldemar and rallied around Doris Johnson, the founder's young niece, and encouraged her to accept the responsibility of the Waldemar project.

The decision was made to "Carry On."

1932

Dunlop Scott Glen was a student at the University of Oklahoma when she wrote her poignant tribute to "a grand old girl." It was published on April 18, 1932, in a special issue of the camp newspaper under the nameplate *The Spirit of Waldemar*, which announced Miss Ora's family's decision to carry on the Waldemar project. The four-page newspaper was filled with letters, poems, and testimonials written by Texans prominent in religious, educational, and political circles as well as by camp friends, both counselors and campers. Above "Aunt Ora's" softly smiling photograph, one seldom seen in later years, was printed and edged in black:

> This Waldemar publication is printed in memory of Miss Ora Johnson and dedicated to the Spirit of Waldemar which she exemplified in her daily life.

The following list of advisory council members, devoted counselors, had been published in the catalog for the 1932 season: W. T. Johnson, manager; Doris Johnson, assistant director; and Ann Miller Crockett, Beatrice Lytle, Ida Mehr, Margaret Gladney, Emma Sealy, Florence Wolkewitz, Laura Wallace, and Carmen Crain, council members.

The council agreed, along with Doris and the Johnson family, that in order to bridge the transition between the older, experienced Miss Ora and young Doris, an older woman should be employed to serve as director for a year or two, with Doris serving as assistant director.

Thus the newspaper, *The Spirit of Waldemar*, announced the selection of Josephine Bell, a well-known and highly regarded educator, as Waldemar's director, and Anna Hiss, head of the department of Women's Physical Education at the University of Texas, as advisory director.

Josephine Bell was principal of Blackwell High School, Blackwell, Oklahoma, when she came to Waldemar. She held many offices in Oklahoma educational circles, was a director of the National Council of Teachers of English, and was much in demand as a speaker throughout Oklahoma.

Anna Hiss had allowed Miss Ora Johnson to use her name as a member of Waldemar's Advisory Council in 1926, the camp's first year, and now she was invited to serve as advisory director. In addition to her prestigious position as head of Women's Physical Education at the University of Texas, she was especially qualified for the Waldemar work because of her early association with Aloha Camps, well-known camps of that era in New Hampshire and Vermont. According to "the old guard," she was an advisor in name only.

A more precise title for Doris Johnson during the off-season would have been "acting director" because it was she who recruited counselors, worked with representatives in signing up campers, and made daily decisions. She was teaching at Harris Junior High School in San Antonio.

If Waldemar can be said to have had a truly pivotal year in its history, it would have to be 1932. The Great Depression was beginning to reach into the pockets of all Americans just at the time the founder and guiding spirit had died. Enrollment figures were reported fuzzily in the *War Whoop*, but the new director announced in the dining room that the enrollment was "practically normal for such a time of economic depression."

Certainly the depression was hitting the camping industry in Texas as well as in the entire United States. An unofficial count from Waldemar address directories shows that 237 girls were enrolled in 1929, 271 in 1930, 251 in 1931, and 107 in 1932, the year following Miss Ora's death. (Of these 107, seven were also listed as junior counselors.)

Many camps did not survive. In later years Doris Johnson was to give credit to the East Texas oil boom for helping fill Waldemar's bunks at this critical time of world depression, and fortunately Mrs. Wolkewitz was strategically located in Tyler in the heart of the oil field to encourage parents to send their daughters to Waldemar.

The 1932 Waldemar staff, thirty-three strong according to the *War Whoop*, was imbued with a renewed desire for excellence and innovation and a driving determination to make the founder's dream a reality. Their activities were well recorded by a *War Whoop* editor trained in journalism at Baylor College,

Belton, Georgia S. "Dimp" Allen, who set the standard for the camp newspaper for many years to come. "Dimp's" early association with the legendary Mrs. W. A. Salter, matriarch of the *Kerrville Mountain Sun*, helped make for excellence in the camp's publication.

The editor and her staff had plenty to write about, not all of it pleasant. A flood of such gigantic proportions that it has not since been matched by the Guadalupe (the fall flood of 1959 approached it) occurred July 1, 1932, less than three weeks after the first camp session without Miss Ora opened.

Only one article about the flood appears in the camp newspaper. It is not the lead story of that issue, perhaps because it was "old news" by July 10 or more likely because a flood is not the most desirable camp publicity. However, nearly four columns on page three are devoted to the telling of the story (written in the style of Advisory Board member Florence Wolkewitz). Because this was Waldemar's first and largest flood, and because the story's word pictures evoke memories of other less devastating rises on the Guadalupe, it is reprinted in its entirety here:

> After lying asleep thirty-two years, the quiet Guadalupe suddenly awakened with an enormous start to carry in its violent current—down its winding course, over hills and through ravines—livestock, villages, people, leaving behind devastation, wrecked homes, ruined crops and deserted villages. . . . Up near the head, smaller streams had swollen and fed the larger, causing the enraged water to gain speed in its rush down the hillsides with a velocity inconceivable. Not taking time to follow its natural course, the stream, rising approximately 10 feet per hour and cutting across fields and lowlands, soon reached Waldemar.
>
> Realizing the danger ahead, the director of the camp, Miss Josephine Bell, summoned her many counselors and co-workers for a brief consultation and assigned definite work for each instructor. Directly their work began. On the waterfront, where the colorful canoe pageant was planned for July 4, the counselors began their work in a cloudburst of wind and rain. Some were dressed in bathing suits, others in regulation camp clothing, and still others in highboots and slickers. Only they alone can tell a story of awe that will startle listeners who will doubt the truth of their related experiences and what they witnessed. Everything movable on the pier was moved, not once or twice but four or five times, for no sooner was equipment placed in one position than the river, like some treacherous serpent, crept quickly upon its prey. From the waterfront to buildings those counselors tramped, their muscles aching from lifting heavy loads and climbing hills.

Already the water had risen 21 feet. Covering the athletic field it pushed inward toward the hillside. The only threatening danger so far as damage was concerned was the possibility of the water rising in the Fine Arts Building [Rippling Waters], which is now in use. The younger campers were high and dry in the camp hotel and hospital. Their games continued as if there were no high water at all. The seniors were even higher, but perhaps not quite as dry in their "kampongs" on the hill duly protected and counseled by a camp instructor.

Thirty-two years ago, old cowboys in the area say, the Guadalupe once rose as high. Certainly the gods the Comanche Indians worshiped long ago were ill-pleased about something! Only the day before, where campers so gleefully played soccer, baseball, volley ball and other sports, water now rushed and heavy soaked logs took their positions on the field of play. Campers saw their pier washed away; their new diving board whirled over tops of trees, enormous uprooted pecan trees swept down in boiling water. They saw their crib and rafts play submarine then crash into a thousand splinters against trees. They heard a part of their dam give way and the powerful roar of raging water as it fell over rocks pressing down on its way to camps below. Later the prized diving board was found lodged in a pecan tree approximately a mile south of camp.

Receding as fast as it rose, the river began its way back to bed for another quiet sleep. Within three hours after the stream reached its highest, it had fallen low enough to permit workers to commence work, removing mud, logs, and debris from around the many different buildings and on the athletic field. Spiders and snakes hurried away at the approach of many spades, hoes, rakes, brooms, and mops. Just before night, with its blackness, the clouds in the west broke enough to allow a faint beam of sunlight to peep through.

The second dawn with more rain and wind found Waldemar cut off from the rest of the outside world. With telephone wire down and all roads leading in and out impassable, she, even then, had no reason for fear. In her pantries and ice boxes was stored enough food to last 20 days. There were enough candles for light, wood enough for fires, and water enough for drinking purposes. Nothing halted the camp program. With the exception of actual swimming and canoeing in the water, classes went on as usual. Fun and play were never lacking! In two old-fashioned fireplaces in the senior dining hall bright and cheery fires burned night and day. The sweet odor of sizzling cedar logs saturated the atmosphere! There was always singing. Even a play-day was held indoors. Ping-pong, bridge, dancing and various other sports were in order throughout the entire time. The piano was a suggestion of what perpetual motion might be. Workers in the slime and mud kept up the Waldemar "plus-spirit" as they hummed and sang "River, Stay 'Way from My Door." Camp life was never so filled with humorous remarks and witty sayings!

Night had brought another cloudburst. Irritated, the river rose another 15 feet. Saturday morning, July 2, saw more rain. Knowing that somewhere in the outside world parents were seeking information as to the safety of their daughters, officials set to work to write a message on the athletic field for any scouting or observation planes that might happen to fly over camp. In 10-foot letters, made from sheets, an "O.K." was made. As an answer to hopeful prayers, in the afternoon some daring pilot risked his life to penetrate the heavy clouds that hung so low, and to sweep between narrow hills for the message. Immediately the only male guest in camp, Rex Beach of Houston, a well-known author, painted on the concrete slab volley ball court, "Don't Land. All O.K. Waldemar." Campers are confident that the flier read their message for he banked, turned, came lower and waved. This salute was answered with loud shouts and cheers from many campers who in turn waved their sweat shirts and coats to wish their friend in the clouds a happy journey! Later over the radio, Waldemar listeners heard their message read out over the air to hundreds of mothers and fathers over the United States!

Anxious for news from neighboring camps and the little village, Hunt, where her assistant director, Miss Doris Johnson, business manager and three counselors had gone the day before on business and for mail, the Waldemar director was glad to welcome instructors from Camp Stewart for Boys who came through on horses. From them came the word that Hunt was no more. Theirs was a pitiful tale. They told the story of how boys were forced from their cabins up the hill. They also told Waldemarites that Stewart's sister camp, Mystic, was practically demolished. Waldemar might have helped and would have been glad to have shared her lot with others, but the river was too swift for transportation.

Across the way, much to the joy of the campers, representatives who were off from camp appeared on the other side of the river. They had spent the night in Hunt. Without food for 24 hours, footsore, tired and wet, they had walked four hours in a steady downpour of rain over slippery hill trails, through ravines of water. Now they were near exhaustion from exposure. Later in the day the current of the river slackened enough to allow their passage across to camp in a war canoe. The following is a "snatch" of their conversation as they sipped hot coffee in the hospital where they were taken for immediate medical attention:

"We were not afraid at first, that is until the water began to rise so fast. The river was very high, but did not look dangerous. Sitting there on one of the store counters in Hunt, we looked up to see houses coming down the river. Immediately we ran out in time to see people running in all directions. We hunted for the road but it looked just like one more river closing in on us. When the waters from the South and North Forks met—well, that was all. Hunt went in 15 minutes. Stone stores and filling stations folded up like corrugated boxes when the two forces met. We chose a home for comfort rather than safety for the night. Had the river again risen, we would have been long gone. At dawn there wasn't anything left to do but try to hike home."

Only a trip around and over the same trail these refugees plodded, slipped and fell will awaken listeners of their story to the realization that it was a dangerous hike.

Today the Guadalupe again is pursuing its quiet and subdued sleep—perhaps for another 32 years. Today Waldemar is basking in the sunshine, happy, dry and none the worse for an experience with a mighty river that swept so close to the doors threatening to enter unasked and unwanted.

Old-timers are said to have warned Ora Johnson that she was placing her Fine Arts Building (Rippling Waters) in the path of a river that flooded violently on occasion, but she assured them that she would "build it to stay." In 1932 the water is said to have "reached to the rooftop with water lines in the tower attic of Rippling Waters," but, true to her word, the redoubtable Ora Johnson had built her building to stay. Campers made service points by digging mud from its honeycomb interior walls.

A few flood-related stories appeared in the same issue of the newspaper, but not many. A new concrete pier was being constructed "to replace the wooden one lost in the flood" and an extra stone step was being added to the pier "to accommodate more spectators."

The crib washed away by the flood will not be replaced as instructors have found that "cribbers" seem to swim just as well in the shallow water of the river as in the old crib.

Pictures of "the crib" show it to be something like a giant play-pen tethered to a tree. Emma Sealy, specialist in beginning swimming and by then a member of the Advisory Council, evidently changed her mind because the use of the crib was continued for a few years.

Mr. and Mrs. Rex Beach, Houston, parents of Betty, have been guests in Waldemar during the past two weeks. Mr. Beach has been proclaimed the father of all Waldemar girls, who are indebted to his sound judgment and advice during the flood.

Perhaps it was Mr. Beach's sound advice that caused authorities to send a War Canoe across the river for "the refugees" rather than standard canoes.

The record-making flood had postponed a visit to Waldemar by the Simmons University Cowboy Band from Abilene, scheduled for July 4. The famous musical group was associated with Colonel Johnson's Madison Square Garden Rodeo, and their eagerly awaited appearance at camp was rescheduled for July 18.

In 1929, when Col. W. T. Johnson took the Waldemar horses to Madison Square Garden for a "New York Charity Horse Show," he called his group the "World's Championship Rodeo," as confirmed by a picture in the catalog for 1931 which shows the Colonel riding "King Waldemar, a prize winner in the World Champion Rodeo, Madison Square Garden, New York, October 1929." Waldemar has no way to validate his success in the 1930 and 1931 seasons, but by 1932 the "Camp Manager" had put together an organization that Madison Square Garden bosses were proud to present.

It was not surprising that the nationally known Simmons University Cowboy Band of Abilene had found another showplace for their talents with the Colonel at Madison Square Garden. The band, under the direction of D. O. Riley and business manager G. B. (Gib) Sandefer, son of the illustrious president of Simmons, the up-and-coming Baptist College which would later become Hardin-Simmons, "had traveled over a quarter of a million miles during the past six years," according to the issue of the War Whoop which announced its coming. In 1930 they had taken a concert tour of Europe which lasted eight weeks; they had played at the inauguration of Herbert Hoover; and they were on their way to perform at the 1932 Olympic Games in California when they stopped at Waldemar at the request of their friend and show business buddy, W. T. Johnson. Gib Sandefer, as colorful as the Colonel, was to bring his group to Madison Square Garden in October for the rodeo.

Waldemar is indebted to Mary Ellen Kirven (Marchman) for a rodeo "Prize List" for 1932. It describes the upcoming rodeo as the "Seventh Annual" which implies that someone before the Colonel had attempted to "bring West to East." Madison Square Garden called it the "World Series Rodeo," with winners receiving large cash prizes and being named champions of the world—all under the direction of Col. W. T. Johnson.

Bronc riding, bareback riding, steer riding, steer wrestling, calf roping, cowgirls' bronc riding, trick and fancy riding were all a part of the rodeo, and cowboys came from all parts of the world to share in the glory and the prize money. Rules were strict.

SPECIAL NOTICE

Every contestant must ride in all parades and every Grand Entry.

If you are not willing to dress in highly colored shirts, boots and big hat every performance— DON'T COME!

Strikers will not be tolerated.

If you are a real cowboy or cowgirl HERE IS THE PLACE TO PROVE IT.

All stock that will be used for this contest is contracted from Col. W. T. Johnson of San Antonio, Texas, and he will also be in charge and manage all Arena events.

Mary Ellen Kirven was a prolific letter writer, and her mother saved those written in 1932 by her low-senior daughter, a top horseback rider and obviously a favorite of Colonel W. T.'s. He had acquired two spectacular mares to lead the rodeo's Grand Entry.

I've been riding with W. T. this a.m. He let me ride Sun Down (one of the two sisters), and is going to take me out again at about 4:30 to ride both of 'em, and that gorgeous white-maned chocolate-colored creature. I had more fun than I've had in ages, and he also said to Mr. Oliver [stable manager] (while I was standing there!) "Let this girl come up to the stable any time she wants to and take out either Sun Up or Sun Down." I was so thrilled I could hardly stand there. It's almost too good to be true, but since he spoke to Miss Bell about it too, I s'pose it must be.

Jane Reid (later Tait), a teacher at Kincaid School in Houston, joined Anita "Pat" Patterson in Waldemar's horseback department in 1932 and continued to add strength to that department for at least a dozen summers. At the first-term horse show:

The fifth event of the show will be pair riding, the riding of the famous twin horses, "Sun Up" and "Sun Down," by Miss Anita Patterson, instructor in English riding, and Miss Jane Reid, instructor in Western riding.

Later correspondence with Mary Ellen confirms that "the mares" were half-sisters—"one's mane falling to the left and one's falling to the right."

Pictures of Waldemar's string of paint ponies in 1932 are impressive and it is possible that the beauty of the animals eclipsed the skill of the riders. Without fanfare, the names of the first-term 1932 Waldemar quadrille riders appear in the camp newspaper of July 22, 1932:

In the quadrille which was led by Buster Boyle and Ernestine Hill the following riders took part: Gretta Connally, Josephine Newberry, Bess Rayford, Mary Ellen Kirven, Ruth Potts, Jane Long, Narcille Gouger, Margaret Manor, Mary Johnson and Gwendolyn Smith.

Mike Hastings, five-time world champion "bull dogger," spent much time at Waldemar and was a favorite with campers and counselors alike. A *War Whoop* story of July 31, 1932, reported that there were "about 80 horses at the stables including quadrille horses, polo ponies, rodeo ponies, and any kind of horse one might name except nags." Cowboys named were Jack [Reeves], Sikes, Chris, Chet and Slim with Mr. Oliver overseeing when the Colonel wasn't around. Experienced drop-in help was welcomed.

We had a grand time during rest hour yesterday. Slim and Chet, a new Scotch cowboy, were out here by the kampong raking up leaves, and they certainly did entertain us. The Scotchman said he wanted to go home, that he had started to go last year but didn't have the money. He also said "he's been a cowboy 5 years, and never seen a cow." They were very indignant at their occupation, and once Slim said, "Madison Square Garden performers raking leaves!" They spoke of the various rodeos they'd taken part in, and all about the championship cowboys.

Mary Ellen was looking forward to the arrival of the Cowboy Band on July 18 (delayed by the flood) because she was one of the "skilled riders" chosen to greet them. According to the camp newspaper, when the colorfully attired band arrived from Abilene, they were greeted by

34 of Waldemar's skilled riders on horseback led by Colonel W.T. Johnson, manager of camp, Miss Anita Patterson, instructor in English riding, and Miss Jane Reid, instructor in Western riding. The internationally famous band circled the athletic field followed by Sheriff Watson of the band and Mike Hastings who carried the flags of the United States of America and the state of Texas. They were followed by the grand parade of Waldemar riders and by Colonel Johnson. The parade ended at the volleyball court where the band played "The Eyes of Texas."

A canoe pageant preceded the Cowboy Band concert presented that evening at the pier "before a crowd of approximately 300 guests." The pageant, featuring extravagantly decorated canoes carrying costumed camper-actors, was musically accompanied by the Waldemar Glee Club "singing from a war canoe decorated with a musical staff running its full length quietly anchored near a raft."

All of this occurred less than three weeks after the river had raged uncontrollably. The resiliency of the Spirit of Waldemar was becoming more evident.

There were other excitements to be reported in Dimp Allen's 1932 *Waldemar War Whoop*. No doubt in order to boost enrollment, a trip to Mexico—including Monterrey, Saltillo, and Lake Don Martin—was awarded to all twelve-week campers, and six- or eight-week campers could make the six-day tour for "a nominal fee of approximately $15 or $20." The tour was to be personally conducted by Miss Josephine Bell as well as by Col. W. T. Johnson, "who will go with them in his private car."

> During the absence of Miss Bell from camp, Miss Doris Johnson will serve as director. . . . Lucille Smith will accompany the party to supervise the cooking on the lake camping trip.

But Doris had seen to it that the camp program held more for the girls than rodeos, canoe pageants, and Mexico trips. She had presented to her campers in concert Walter Gilewicz, widely acclaimed pianist and head of the Fine Arts Conservatory at Baylor College for Women, Belton. Gilewicz was a popular and inspiring guest artist at Waldemar for several summers, and often he brought some of his talented students with him to perform.

Mrs. J. M. Dawson, wife of the pastor of the First Baptist Church of Waco, was a nationally known speaker who was invited to spend several days at Waldemar each summer and speak to the girls in a series of talks. A good friend of the camp mother, Mrs. Wolkewitz, Mrs. Dawson was the premier speaker for young people in the South and Southwest, and her visits were anticipated by both campers and counselors.

Waldemar's tribes were undergoing subtle changes in 1932 which were making them more than just pep organizations. Perhaps one of the most important and lasting innovations of the 1932 season was the appointment of counselor "sponsors" for the tribes. They now met separately on their hills, and hints of the beginning of rituals were disclosed. The Tejas reported early in the second term:

> By the consent of the entire tribe, a formal ritual will be performed at the beginning of every meeting hereafter.

At the last meeting of the second term 1932, the Comanches

> buried a treasure on our campground which will remain under rocks and soil through snow, rain, and sleet . . . until next year when the new Comanche chief and his braves will scale the hilltops to regain the treasure. The directions will be left in the office in the care of Miss Doris Johnson, assistant camp director.

Fencing was first added to the Waldemar program in 1932. It was introduced by handsome Trueman O'Quinn, holder of a law degree from the University of Texas, whose professional ambitions were momentarily limited by the depression. Trueman, whose young wife came to visit on occasion, also taught riflery and campcraft and he found himself playing leading roles in camp dramas. The agreeable fencing master was at Waldemar only one summer.

A game of polo was first played at Waldemar in 1932. The Waldemar cowboys, captained by "Little Tom" Johnson, W. T.'s son, were challenged by the team from Camp Stewart headed by the captain of the University of Arizona's polo team.

The faithful Mary Ellen wrote her mother:

> We watched a polo game yesterday. Our cowboys played some men, and we got beaten only 4-3. I think that's pretty good as one of the rivals was captain of the University of Arizona polo team and the others were pretty well-known too. Jack, Sikes, Chris and Little Tom Johnson played for us.

Tribal dances honoring the members of the rival tribe were presented in 1932 and for many summers thereafter. Oftentimes Kerrville's "Bobby Schmerbeck and His Bluebonnet Hotel Orchestra" played for dancing. The theme program, interspersed with the dancing, showed off the talents of both campers and counselors, and decorations and favors were elaborate and time-consuming in the making.

> Manor [Tejas tribal leader] and I [Tejas cheerleader] have some work to do. . . . We had to address all those dance bids (to old campers) and it really takes some work. We also have to cut up bushels of confetti and put it up in socks, or somethin'!

Much is made in the camp newspaper first term of 1932 of a secret organization known only as the "S.A. Club," and Waldemar campers of that day will be happy to know that Mary Ellen's letters clear up that mystery. There were only five members—all Tejas and in the same kampong—and the name was not related to "sex appeal," "social aristocrats," or "secret assurance," as guessed by inquisitive reporters. The name was "Sweet Affinity," the motto was "it must have been something we et," and the colors were "true blue and blood red."

> Miss Bell told us our S.A. Club was causing discontent and we had better shut up about it a bit. We're all terribly mad . . . but I guess it would be better to shut up a little!

The controversial club died a natural death when two of its five members stayed only one term, but before leaving they were feted with a watermelon feast by their S.A. sisters.

Miss Ora Johnson had obviously been hesitant about banning all eating between meals at her camp "except as served by the camp." The "health rules" of 1930 read:

> No eating between meals except fresh fruit or milk
> and
> No candy except within 15 minutes after meals

Mary Ellen's letters to Mrs. Kirven thanked her for cake, tostados and other goodies and begged her for more, always assuring her mother "we can eat 15 minutes after meals, you know."

It wasn't until 1937 and 1938 that the "no food rule, except as served by the dietitian," became truly a part of Waldemar.

The Awards Banquet of the 1932 season was a "Grand Round-Up" with Miss Bell playing the Texas Ranger, Colonel W. T. playing the rancher, Doris Johnson as the "dark-eyed heroine," and Margaret Gladney as the foreman. It was at this program that the modern version of the "Legend of the Guadalupe" received Waldemar's cachet. Mary Johnson, young cousin of Miss Ora and an outstanding camper, told the story of Guada and Lupe and said that this version of the legend was the favorite of Miss Ora Johnson.

The first memorial service honoring the woman whose ideals so strongly influenced the lives of Waldemar girls was held the last Sunday of the 1932 camping season. The "Vesper Memoriam" began with the entrance on the pier of all Waldemar campers and counselors in double line singing "Waldemar, Sea of Woods." Mr. R. F. Grant, editor of the *San Antonio Express*, came from San Antonio to speak of his esteem for the late teacher and camping pioneer, and Mrs. Wolkewitz and others spoke briefly.

It was at this memorial service that "Waldemar, Waldemar (Carry On)" was introduced. It was written by Harriet Booker "Totsy" Stokes of Temple, a former camper and then a junior counselor, in commemoration of the life and in celebration of the spirit of the former director.

Appearing on the program was Mrs. Fannie Pierce Goodwin, a frequent visitor from San Antonio. Mrs. Goodwin was the talented doll maker whose creations had decorated the earlier Waldemar Doll House, and her cowboy dolls advertising Colonel Johnson's rodeo had received acclaim in New York City. In 1932 she had a studio in Hollywood and made "life-size humanettes of movie stars." (The Waldemar Museum has one of her cowboy dolls advertising the rodeo.)

The last paragraph of the Vesper Memoriam news story reads:

> Mrs. Fannie Goodwin then paid her respects to Miss Johnson by presenting a plan to the campers by which the camp might build a memorial to Miss Johnson. On a table, Mrs. Goodwin had a miniature statue she called "Perfect Girlhood" standing on page eighteen of the Book of Life. This girl was the perfect American girl, the Ideal Waldemar camper as Miss Ora Johnson would have her be.

The miniature model for the suggested statue was lovely and inspiring as was the poem which was to be engraved upon it. But was a statue right for honoring their vigorous founder? Would she have chosen something more spiritual and personal?

They thought about how best to honor their good friend during the winter months.

1933

From the *Waldemar War Whoop*, June 15, 1933:

Waldemar started its eighth annual camp season with 36 councillors and three Junior Councillors. There is an improvement in the number of campers of last summer which proves that people in spite of the depression are becoming more camp-minded and realize that it is not a luxury but a necessity.

The increase also proved that the summer of 1932, Waldemar's first without the warmth and security of Ora Johnson, had been a rousing success despite the flood.

The summers just after her aunt's death were

times of high purpose for Doris Cherry Johnson. She was twenty-six years old in August of 1932, and she had committed her life to her aunt's camp project. She was constantly reminded that each summer Waldemar had grown and developed dramatically under "Aunt Ora's" stewardship and, fed by the love and admiration she had for her aunt and her own growing love for Waldemar, she embraced the project with the same constant flame burning within her that had inspired and motivated her aunt.

Although church and vesper services had been in the forefront of Miss Ora's Waldemar, and ministers and inspirational speakers had been frequent guest speakers, Doris Johnson and her superior staff recognized that an obvious platform for building character and teaching moral values had been overlooked. The tribes should not be simply pep clubs organized to stimulate enthusiasm for field meet activities. True, competition was important to the success of Waldemar's sports program and the building of strong bodies, but the weekly meetings of the Tejas and Comanches around their campfires should stimulate inspirational and spiritual growth in Waldemar girls.

The first step toward that goal had been the introduction in 1932 of counselor sponsors for the tribes. Downs Lander, a counselor from Little Rock, Arkansas, had suggested the idea of sponsors to Doris in 1932, and that year she became the first Comanche sponsor, with "Totsy" Stokes, composer of "Carry On," as her assistant. The first Tejas sponsors were Betty Lynn Hoskins, Knoxville, Tennessee, and Augusta (Buster) Boyle, San Antonio, an outstanding former camper and by this time a junior counselor, and a particular hometown favorite of Miss Ora Johnson.

As a girl, Downs Lander had enjoyed camping experiences at Camp Junaluska for Girls in North Carolina, "the oldest girls' camp in the South." She had been both camper and counselor, and she had been awarded their highest honor, "The Lady of the Cup." The award and the ideals surrounding it meant so much to Downs that when she located what she called a "ready-made" trophy in San Antonio (the same trophy Waldemar awards today), she suggested to the Comanche tribe that they sponsor a "Spirit of Waldemar" award in memory of Miss Ora Johnson. She privately revealed her plan to Doris, who embraced it wholeheartedly, and on the first Sunday evening of camp, in 1933, the Comanches presented a vesper which echoes resonantly at Waldemar today.

The Comanches came down the twin stairways of the senior dining room marching in twos and singing "Waldemar, Sea of Woods," which the news story

labeled "rather an alma mater song of Camp Waldemar." (Miss Ora herself had decreed that this song should always be sung out of doors, but the Comanches were forgiven because of the "nature of their program.")

Then Mrs. Wolkewitz spoke of Miss Ora's ideals and hopes for Waldemar girls and announced that the Comanches were going to present, in the founder's memory, a trophy symbolizing the perfect girl. The honored girl was to be chosen by the counselors in secret ballot at the end of the term.

She then summed up the ideals which she knew Miss Johnson would want a Waldemar girl to have. Her criteria, written and presented in 1933 and still quoted today, follow:

The award, which is not to be consciously sought for, will be a trophy which will be given to the girl who has lived up to these traits:

The one who has made the best use of the faculties which God has given her . . . the one with as fine a body as right living and right thinking can make it . . . the girl with a beauty of soul which will shine in her face . . . the girl with fairness of spirit in all phases of life with honesty of self and honesty of words . . . one who is kind and considerate of others, whose life has a definite aim and purpose, who enters into work or play with a will to accomplish something . . . one who is willing to sacrifice pleasure when necessary and is satisfied with herself only when she has done her best . . . the girl who can take advice or admit an error . . . who has appreciation of others . . . who is never spoiled by success . . . the girl who is individual, who thinks for herself and has the courage to stand alone if necessary for the right . . . a girl with wholesome sensible ideas of having a good time . . .

To this girl would Ora Johnson entrust the good name of her beloved camp—to her would she hand the torch to be held aloft in the name of Waldemar's perfect girl.

After Mrs. Wolkewitz's talk and an affirming one by Margaret Gladney, the Comanches rose and sang a new song, "The Spirit of Waldemar Girl," written by Downs Lander especially for the occasion and secretly taught to the excited Comanches by the song writer. This is the same song sung to the Ideal Waldemar Girl today. "The service ended with everyone feeling a bit finer and bigger having heard these qualities of the perfect Waldemar girl," concluded the reporter.

There was no special ceremony for the bestowing of the honor the first year of the award. A printed program for the "Final Banquet" of first term 1933 is in the Waldemar archives, and the last award on the program is the presentation of "the Comanche Trophy Award" and the singing of the "Song to the Ideal Camper." The counselors had selected Margaret Manor of San Angelo; Margaret had received recognition as the Best All-Round high senior, elected by both counselors and campers, in 1932 and again in 1933, thus affirming the validity of the counselors' choice.

The lack of ceremony that year did not diminish the importance of Downs Lander's award. The editorial page of the *War Whoop* frequently reprinted Mrs. Wolkewitz's criteria, and editorial writers often chose the "Spirit of Waldemar Girl" as their subject. So well accepted was the award that Doris asked Downs and the Comanches to relinquish it to the camp, which they did. For many years the Comanche sponsors directed the program, but when their tribal load became heavier, they were relieved of this responsibility. Still the Comanches help in any way they can and take pride in the program and the award.

A counselor came to Waldemar in 1933 whose positive influence was so immediate that she quickly became a camp favorite. She was Cobby de Stivers, director of music at Waco High School, but Cobby was more than a fine musician. Her enthusiasm for camp was so great that "one would think she was a veteran camper by the way she fell into the scheme of things from the beginning."

She later became Comanche sponsor and her contributions to hill programs and to Waldemar's vesper services and special programs were tremendous. Her place in Waldemar history was assured when she helped Downs Lander develop the Spirit of Waldemar program which is still used today.

In an early catalog, Doris Johnson wrote of the Spirit of Waldemar award:

> Throughout eleven years of outstanding achievement, Waldemar looks upon the establishment of this ideal in the lives of the campers as its greatest accomplishment.

Ernestine Hill of Auburn, Alabama (Anita "Pat" Patterson's niece) was asked to sponsor the Tejas tribe second term of 1933. Ernestine, a junior counselor in 1931 and 1932, knew and loved "Aunt Ora" and wanted the Tejas to honor her in some tangible way.

So if the Tejas had felt left out when the Comanches conceived the Spirit of Waldemar award in Miss Ora's memory, they quickly overcame it early in the second term when Ernestine announced that the Tejas tribe was presenting to camp a life-sized portrait of the founder and that it would be unveiled

with proper ceremony at the last vesper service of the summer.

That dramatic unveiling vesper service began at twilight with an outdoor program produced by the junior department in which the juniors built "Waldemar's Ideal Tree of Life." Then all went to the senior dining room single-file, Tejas leading. Ann Miller (Crockett) paid tribute to the founder by saying, "No portrait painted could ever depict her dynamic personality filled with essence of every quality of kindness and love." As the violinist played "The Rosary," Doris Johnson unveiled the portrait and campers sang "Waldemar, Waldemar (Carry On)" to close the emotional service.

The portrait was painted "by Wolfe," a Louisiana artist, from a photograph. It hung first in the Pioneer Room and then over the west fireplace of the Dining Hall until it was moved to Cedar Lodge and its place for many years above the mantle. Although the portrait was always controversial, with those who knew "Aunt Ora" feeling that it portrayed her as being stern and unbending rather than compassionate and jolly, it was always displayed at the pier during the Ideal Waldemar Girl Ceremony, dedicated to her memory. The portrait was a part of Waldemar until the mid-'70s when it was replaced by the current portrait, painted by Houston artist Allison Joy, which hangs in the office. Allison studied all of the existing photographs of Miss Ora Johnson and created what she called "an illusion" which Doris and Billie Johnson considered a faithful and happy representation of their aunt.

Downs Lander and Ernestine Hill worked closely together, establishing rituals and traditions for their hills and emphasizing good sportsmanship and high ideals. Cobby de Stivers and Ann Miller (Crockett) were equally concerned and imaginative, and so traditions were burgeoning at Waldemar in 1933—traditions that have continued to enrich camp life through the years.

"The tribes have agreed to make their tribal meetings more serious and reverent," began an article about a Comanche meeting. Work toward this goal had begun in 1932 and was now furthered when the sponsors, at their separate meetings, ceremoniously presented the surprised leaders with Indian headdresses which, like the "bracelet treasures" buried at the end of the 1932 season, are still the symbols of their office.

Although the tradition which climaxes Comanche hill programs was not reported in 1932 as having been established, at a Comanche meeting second term of 1933 Ann Miller (Crockett), whose brainchild it was, spoke about the "Comanche Rockpile," sometimes referred to in early days as the "Comanche Cairn," because it is "a heap of stones set up as a landmark or monument."

"This tradition, begun only last year," Ann told the Comanches, "has attached to it a sentiment unsurpassed." Each year thereafter the Rockpile Ceremony has been explained to new Comanches, and all take inspiration from the sense of continuity and communion with past Comanches which grows within them as the Rockpile grows.

The early tribes had only a leader and a cheerleader or two, but the first-term Comanches elected "squad leaders" in 1933, offices corresponding to the division leaders of a later day. The second-term Tejas saw the need for a "scribe" whose duty it was "to keep an accurate and detailed record of all events in which the Tejas take part" and to pass it on to new tribal members year after year.

According to the only issue of the *War Whoop* published in 1928, the two tribes often held joint campfires on the riverbank to the south of "Junior Rec" (Waldemar Lodge). By 1931 they had their separate campfire spots, with the Comanches probably meeting on the present Comanche Hill. But the Tejas evidently had difficulty satisfying their needs. In July of 1933 a news story read, "Walled in by a high cliff, beside a running stream of water, the Tejas tribe met last Friday night . . ."

And then in mid-August of 1933:

Because of threatening rain clouds last Friday evening, the Tejas were forced to have their tribal meeting indoors rather than at their new campfire grounds. The Tejas have changed their campfire spot to their former grounds of 1931 because of dangerous hazards met in approaching the place of the past year.

It is not known exactly when the present Tejas Hill became their meeting place.

Grades on table manners were given as early as 1930 or before when they counted as "optional points" toward the winning of the plaque or high point honors but were not mandatory. Drawing for places at table was begun early in 1932 with places being changed by lot every two weeks. But evidently Doris and her advisory board members saw the need for upgrading the table manners of Waldemar girls, and they knew that it could be done best through the tribal system and the girls themselves. Thus in 1933

this headline and subhead appeared in the camp newspaper:

COMMITTEE OF GIRLS DRAWS UP OWN CODE OF TABLE MANNERS

Comanches and Tejas Combine
To Set New Tradition
In History of Waldemar

A committee consisting of members from the Comanche and Tejas tribes has been appointed to draw up a code of table manners to be used throughout the remaining weeks of camp.

This committee, names to be announced later, has in its power the right to draw up rules and regulations by which their fellow tribesmen are judged. This is the first time in the history of Waldemar that campers have undertaken this type of work.

There is no follow-up story in the *War Whoop* about the committee or its code, but Waldemar has one copy of a flyer entitled "TABLE-ETT-I-KATE" that was probably the work of "Kat" Frazer Gannon, dietitian in 1933 and for several years thereafter. Clever stick figures illustrate the following doggerel which describes the Waldemar Way yesterday and today:

You can get to breakfast on time
If you rise on the dot.
Your food will be waiting—
We know you want it hot!!!

When first "soupy" blows, each of you
Should start to gather near,
But do not enter the dining room
Until "second" sounds out clear.

Stand and bow your heads
While the Blessing's being sung—
Don't make a grab for that chicken breast
There's more where it "come frum."

The counselor will serve the food,
With a helper on her left hand;
Be alert to pass the plates
And to help them all you can.

We plan and work so all the food
Will balance exactly right.
If you don't eat some of *everything*
You'll be "out of balance" at night.

Emily Post is "tops" on manners,
As I'm sure you've all observed—

She says not to start eating
Until everyone is served!

Emily also insists—
And we know it's very true
That no one should leave the table
Until everyone is through.

When a dish is empty
And for seconds you're "a-twitchin'"
Ask your counselor—she'll give the order.
There's always more in the kitchen!

Remember the old song about sitting straight
And sit a little straighter.
Siesta isn't now, you know,
It comes a little later.

Our service isn't very formal,
So it's a nice thing to do
To stack the plates and pass them
To help the waitress through.

We dearly love your songs and
Even "lady-like" cheers
But when you yell to "bust a lung,"
We grit our teeth and hold our ears!

If you'll observe these rules
And be as mannerly as you're able
We'll all be very pleased
And you'll make your points at table.

Thus Waldemar's reputation for teaching its campers good table manners and for maintaining a pleasant dining room in which to enjoy its incomparable food was well established by 1933.

While all of these traditions were being established, Doris Johnson was making herself as popular with the campers and counselors as her aunt had been before her. Campers saw the traditions being established as assurances of Waldemar's strength and viability, and they saw Doris' progressive attitude as the source of that strength. She was able to combine a fun-loving and enthusiastic nature with a quiet dignity and reserve which generated confidence, love, and respect. Campers and counselors who also knew Miss Ora were looking forward to the day Doris would assume the directorship of Waldemar. They wanted a director who "had a twinkle in her eye like Aunt Ora," wrote a camper of the era.

During the second term of 1933, the camp newspaper dropped tell-tale hints that perhaps the time was near.

It was Doris who planned and chaperoned a three-day trip to San Antonio for the eight- and twelve-week campers, and it was Doris who offered a free trip to a six-week camper who wrote the best letter about life at Waldemar.

She began to be identified in the paper as "owner of Waldemar" as well as the assistant director, and her father, J. F. Johnson, began to be identified as her advisor.

Thus in the Christmas issue of the 1933 newspaper, Waldemar announced that Miss Doris Johnson "has assumed the directorship of Camp Waldemar and will begin her duties as such immediately. . . . Her father, J. F. Johnson, and her brother Billie will join her in the business management of the camp."

She was not yet twenty-eight years old.

1934

No headlines were splashed across the front page of the *Waldemar War Whoop* when Doris Johnson became director of Waldemar. The change had been happily anticipated and was now firmly applauded. She had enrolled 190 girls from eight states for the first term of 1934 and employed fifty-six counselors to serve as instructors, and she had named Waldemar's long-time friend, Florence Wolkewitz, as Camp Mother. The directory lists 326 girls for both terms.

From the first years of Miss Ora's Waldemar, every counselor was a "Waldemar representative"—that is, she was paid a commission for each girl she enrolled in camp. Since counselors were chosen largely, but not exclusively, from the teaching profession, they were in daily contact with their "prospects," and attractive Waldemar catalogs made their way into the homes of desirable girls.

Thus the "190 girls from eight states" were the result of careful selection of counselors from a wide geographical area, and Waldemar's loyal staff recommended friends and co-workers who would fit happily into the Waldemar situation and enrich its program, thereby giving Doris the time to continue teaching in the San Antonio school system.

She also found the time to confer with Harvey P. Smith, the San Antonio architect who had designed Miss Ora's second Dining Hall. Doris told him she wanted to "do something with that grove of trees between the Fine Arts Building [Rippling Waters] and the Doll House."

Immediately the architect recalled that when he was working on the Dining Hall, Miss Ora had talked with him about the possibility of an open-air theater in that area. It was being used, he remembered, as a miniature golf course in 1930, that craze having swept the country and died at Waldemar in almost one summer. He told Doris of Miss Ora's 1930 concept, and they both recognized that an open-air theater originally envisioned by the founder herself would be a fitting and tangible memorial to her, augmenting and gracing the Spirit of Waldemar award which was dedicated to her memory.

Harvey P. Smith had earlier made a study of existing open-air theaters in this country in preparation for his designing of the Sunken Garden Theater in San Antonio's Brackenridge Park. Now his enthusiasm, in part inspired by his respect and admiration for Miss Ora, was such that

> Doris quickly supplied me with a piece of wrapping paper and, sitting under a liveoak tree, I began to draw the plan for the Memorial Amphitheater.

Under Ferdinand's skillful hand and Harvey Smith's watchful eye, the theater was ready for use when camp opened in 1934. It was not dedicated until the close of the second term.

Johnny Regan, the "English Cowboy" who became a Waldemar institution, came to camp in 1934. Except for one year in the 1930s (1937) and four years during World War II, he brightened the lives of Waldemar girls until 1979 when his health dictated that he stay with his family in London.

"Born in Windsor Cavalry Barracks, this son of a Royal Guardsman left his imminent soldiering to join a circus as an amateur cowboy in a Wild West Show," began many of the news stories and press releases about Johnny. That decision to become a cowboy, disapproved by his parents who wanted him to be a musician, led him to Australia, where he learned to spin a rope and manipulate a bullwhip and become a real horse-loving cowboy. Johnny was a consummate actor and born clown, and with these skills and talents he roped, whip-cracked, and clowned his way through Australia, Europe, Africa, and England.

Practically all Waldemar junior campers enrolled in one of his "trickroping" classes and at the horse-show all would perform, creditably, then gather close around Johnny, who was elevated on a barrel, and allow him to twirl his giant lariat around them all, enclosing them in his magic circle.

His performance with the Australian bullwhip was awesome. After "cracking" it with resounding ferocity, he invited a member of his fascinated audience—sometimes a counselor but usually a camper—to hold a rolled-up paper in her hand, and, taking deadly aim from about twenty feet, Johnny deftly dislodged the paper from her hand. Sometimes he struck a match into flame with his whip, all the while keeping up a patter of pertinent—and sometimes impertinent—remarks. He was able gently to wrap the snaky end of his bullwhip around a willing neck, and he held all spellbound.

Johnny's many evening programs at Waldemar were varied showcases for his talents. He would costume heavily and then peel off pieces in a tasteful and comical strip tease. "At one point he began to take off his trousers and we all held our breath; but Johnny was clad in a second pair of bright orange," wrote a worshipful young reporter.

What lucky turn of fate brought the "English Cowboy," a world traveler, showman, and gentleman to the quiet life of an American girls' camp?

Johnny had returned to England from Australia during World War I to serve his country. After the war was over in 1918, he perfected his act and traveled all of Europe, delighting audiences with his skills and his clowning. For three years in the late 1920s the nomadic performer traveled in Africa, returning to England in 1930 to play engagements in the music halls of his native country.

That was the year the Simmons University Cowboy Band from Abilene made a tour of Europe and England, and included in their itinerary was London, where they were booked to play that city's famous music hall, the Palladium. Sharing the bill with the American band was rope-twirling, whip-snapping, wisecracking Johnny Regan.

G. B. "Gib" Sandefer, business manager and guiding force of the band, was so taken with the young Englishman that he invited him to travel with the Simmons University Band and then join the group in Abilene. It was against the nature of the peripatetic Johnny, who had never been to America, to refuse. Thus through the Colonel's friend "Gib" Sandefer, Johnny Regan became a star of the Madison Square Garden Rodeo and of Camp Waldemar. It is not known if Johnny visited the camp with the band in 1932.

In addition to trickroping, Johnny taught horseback riding to delighted junior campers, whom he called his "Little Squeakers," and they truly loved this Englishman who was a part of their Waldemar lives. The slightly built Johnny was little more than five feet tall, but his erect carriage and bouncing verve changed him into a seven-foot Pied Piper to Waldemar's junior campers. The arena near Ora Johnson Theater where Johnny taught, long known as the "trickroping arena," is now designated "Johnny Regan Arena."

The tribal sponsor plan, inaugurated in 1932, had proven so successful that in 1934 Doris decided to increase its influence by assigning certain qualified junior counselors to serve as advisory staff members to the senior sponsors.

Original ideas flowed freely from these talented coalitions. Tribal hill meetings became platforms for orienting new campers to the customs and traditions of their tribes and of Waldemar. They inspired the members to practice good sportsmanship in the friendly rivalry between the two tribes, and inspirational talks, prayers and poems about friendship, leadership, strength and God enhanced the meetings and stimulated the moral growth of the girls. The natural beauty of the hills, the stars, and the campfires combined to make the weekly meetings reverent and the campfire ground sacred.

In 1933 each tribe had produced a Sunday evening vesper service, the Comanches inaugurating the Spirit of Waldemar award and the Tejas unveiling their gift, the founder's portrait. In 1934 it was called "traditional" for the tribes to present a vesper, and they planned their upcoming services with enthusiasm. Thus another lasting tradition was born, the Tribal Vespers. Of special interest is the fact that "My Creed," which later became a cherished part of the Spirit of Waldemar Ceremony, and "Touching Shoulders," long a favorite poem on Comanche Hill, were first used in the second-term Comanche vesper service of 1934.

An important and coveted award was added to Waldemar's list of honors in 1934 when a Tejas junior camper, Eileen Becker of Houston, provided a cup to be presented to the girl voted by her tribesmen the "Best All-Round Tejas." The first recipient was Bess Rayford, who was tribal leader that year. Later it was agreed that henceforth the tribal leader, whose excellence had been rewarded by her office, would be ineligible for the award. The Comanches followed the pace-setting Tejas by electing their first Best All-Round Comanche in 1936.

(The Ideal Waldemar Girl is also ineligible for the Best All-Round tribesman honor. Sponsors, who tally their tribe's votes, are asked by the camp director to give the tribal honor to the second-place camper should the first choice receive the Spirit of Waldemar award.)

Still another treasured tradition was established in 1934: the first Sunday vesper service was dedicated to Miss Ora Johnson and the Spirit of Waldemar and to the ideals which go to make up the character of the Ideal Girl. That year prominent campers spoke on the ideals, and Doris, Laura Wallace, and Mrs. Wolkewitz, all of whom knew Miss Ora Johnson well, spoke on the merits of the founder and her desires for her camp. "The Legend of the Guadalupe," either in word or in action, soon became a part of Waldemar's initial vesper service.

Supervising this 1934 vesper was Cobby de Stivers from Waco, where she was director of music at Waco High School. Cobby was well known throughout the state because her orchestra and glee clubs had won first place in state competition several years in a row. There is no record of her having directed an orchestra at Waldemar in 1933, but in 1934 she assembled and directed a group of nineteen musicians made up of campers and counselors, the first since Ann Miller (Crockett), an accomplished violinist along with her other talents, directed an orchestra as early as 1930. (Ann's predecessor was Otto Zoeller, director of music in the San Antonio schools and staff member at Lone Star Camp, who was at Waldemar for the first two summers.)

In 1935 Doris asked Cobby to select talented young high school musicians from throughout the state and bring them to Waldemar on scholarships. Cobby assembled an outstanding orchestra composed of two violinists, two cornetists (one doubling on drums), a trombonist, three saxophonists, a clarinetist (Johnny Regan), a pianist and a string bassist—Cobby herself. The group played superior music for every type program, from church and vesper services to musicales and dances. Their excellence was recognized and appreciated throughout the area, and they were much in demand. By 1935 they wore white shirts, black trousers, black ties, and white mess jackets, and Waldemar's reputation for excellence was enhanced by this talented group.

From that time on, Waldemar had either an orchestra or the "Waldemar Band," the name change from orchestra to band taking place in the 1960s. Assembling talented performers is more difficult in this last of the twentieth century, but there are still camp musicians who play dinner music in the dining room twice weekly, as inaugurated by Cobby, and serve as accompanists for drama programs.

One of Cobby's cornetists who came to Waldemar in 1934 was Emmie Craddock, a junior counselor from Houston who attended Rice Institute. Emmie's talents were quickly recognized, and she was named a member of the newly formed Tejas advisory staff, even though she had not been a Waldemar camper. Like Cobby, she is remembered for many contributions other than her musicianship. Campers gained confidence and grew in character from Emmie's challenging talks at church, at vesper services, and on Tejas Hill, and later she was Cobby's capable successor as director of the orchestra.

But it is Emmie's trumpet sounding "taps" which echoed softly through the Waldemar hills for which she is probably best remembered. A camper reporter once called taps "Emmie's sweet clear 'Amen.'" Another called it "the final diamond in the setting of a Waldemar day." Emmie left a more tangible musical legacy: she made vocal arrangements in three-part harmony for many of Waldemar's most beautiful songs, some of which she composed, and a few of her penciled originals are in the Waldemar archives.

The orchestra was by no means the only musical organization at camp in 1934. Remembering that to her aunt the love and appreciation of music was a part of the education of young people, as early as 1932 Doris had lured Oklahoma City's most prestigious piano instructor, one trained in the teaching of ensemble piano work, to Waldemar, and she often presented her piano ensembles in concert on the patio of the Fine Arts Building. In 1934 such programs were interspersed with selections by vocalists, violin trios and classical dancers, each of whom had been trained by specially selected Waldemar counselors at no extra fee for private lessons.

Drama teachers presented plays every two weeks or so, and the "Legend of the Guadalupe" was at last dramatized in its approved form and presented in the second term of 1934. Strangely, even though Mary Johnson had told the story in 1932 with "Guada and Lupe" as the ill-starred lovers, this early dramatization called the Tejas brave "Grey Lance" and the Comanche maiden "Night Faun."

The craft department was enlarging its offerings. Pottery was first on the Waldemar schedule in 1934, with the campers' projects being fired in San Antonio. "Kodakery" was offered for the first time, and if a work was judged worthy, it was enlarged by Mr. Cleveland Wheelus of Kerrville, long-time camp photographer, and then the proud camper tinted it with "photo-oil" paints. Sketching was popular, with many of the artists choosing as their subject the rustic footbridge which spanned the river over the dam which had been replaced after the flood. Mary Strange's leather department was more popular than ever, and girls taking an unusual craft called "campcraft" started a museum in the Fine Arts Building which fea-

tured a collection of rocks, wildflowers, mounted leaves and butterflies.

"Corrective Posture" was on the Waldemar curriculum for the first time in 1934. It was supervised by a counselor whose training included "some time spent at the Warm Springs Foundation in Georgia," and its presence in the curriculum showed Doris Johnson's early concern for posture training and body fitness for Waldemar girls.

Interest in marksmanship had begun with Major Reilly of San Antonio's ROTC in 1927, and there is evidence that Waldemar had become a member of the National Rifle Association by 1929 or 1930. In 1932, according to Trueman O'Quinn, whose patience with the girls was such that editorials were written commending him, "25 National awards were given first term and we expect as many second term." So popular had marksmanship become by 1933 that a story in the War Whoop states that "64 percent of the campers eligible to take riflery second term are doing so."

Thus in 1934, Doris deemed it advisable to update the rifle range. The War Whoop reporter wrote:

The new rifle range, one of the featured improvements at Waldemar for the summer, has an added attraction in the new concrete floor and gun cabinets.

The use of cabinets saves time and effort for the girls taking riflery in that it eliminates the necessary walking from the camp store room, where equipment was kept, to the range.

There are also new firing points with a well-constructed backboard.

New Springfield automatic rifles, recently added to the equipment, are an asset to this department and have increased the popularity of this sport among Waldemar's riflemen. Although these new rifles are used and recommended by Miss Evelyn Baird, instructor in riflery, some students still prefer the old style Winchester 22 single shot rifles and are allowed to use them.

There was fun and frolic in 1934. The Tejas entertained the Comanches with a Circus Dance preceded by a parade, and the Comanches entertained with "a moonlight cruise on the Good Ship Comanche" honoring the Tejas tribe. There was a Masked Mexican Cabaret Banquet on the tennis court and a Funny Paper Banquet for which all costumed as cartoon characters. The usual free San Antonio trip for girls staying eight or twelve weeks had so many girls eligible that it was taken in three groups. A hilarious mock wedding, taking off on the soon-to-be-married director of activities, good sport Margaret Gladney, was presented by the drama department.

A water pageant presented on the evening of the Fourth of July was staged both on land and in water with a reported 500 guests in attendance. Its theme was the "King" crowning his "Queen of the Guadalupe" and then presenting an "entertainment" for her. The royal couple, the Lord High Chancellor, the many dukes and duchesses, the princes and princesses of the tribes—all elaborately and ingeniously costumed in paraffined splendor—entered the water either treading or swimming, and the show's finale was the famous fire dive by Hannah More Frazer, followed by a fireworks display staged by Billie Johnson featuring a spectacular "Welcome to Waldemar."

It was deemed appropriate this second year of the "Ideal Camper" award to combine the annual canoe pageant, presented on the night before the awards program, with the presentation of the Spirit of Waldemar trophy which had been given at the awards program the year before. The pageant, under the direction of Dolly Downes, featured canoes representing the four seasons, each elaborately and appropriately decorated.

The ceremony which followed was the first Spirit of Waldemar ceremony and is of special interest because the roots from which the later-day program grew were firmly planted there on the river in 1934. A reporter wrote:

> Then the two tribal war canoes filled with girls dressed as Indians came down the river, and as they reached the pier area the orchestra played the tribal songs, "We're the Fair and Square Comanches" and "Tejas Forever."
>
> Forming beside a raft on the west [sic] bank of the river, which also served as a stage, the two tribal chiefs, Elaine Markham, Comanche, and Bess Rayford, Tejas, stepped from the bows of their respective canoes to make their farewell speeches to the camp and to their tribes, after which the audience, acknowledging their salutes, answered singing the tribal songs.
>
> The orchestra played the Ideal Waldemar's Camper song as a canoe of white and silver, "The Spirit of Waldemar," appeared. In it sat Margaret Manor and Marjorie Jane Denman, who are the only two girls to be selected Waldemar's Ideal Girls in the past. Margaret was in the stern of the canoe. After this canoe docked and after Marjorie Jane made her charge to all past, present and future Waldemar campers, with a response by Winifred Hill, Elaine was taken from her tribal canoe, placed in the "Spirit of Waldemar," and as this canoe departed into the darkness, the audience sang "Waldemar's Ideal Song," after which they sang the special song dedicated to Miss Ora Johnson, and "Waldemar Sea of Woods."

"Taps," sounded by Emmie Craddock, ended the program.

Waldemar's eventful first summer under Doris Johnson's full direction was climaxed by the dedication of the Ora Johnson Memorial Theater August 26, 1934. Dean E. G. Townsend of Baylor College for Women, Miss Ora's alma mater, spoke of "Ora Johnson, the Woman" and Harvey P. Smith, Waldemar's architect, spoke of "Ora Johnson, the Builder." After musical numbers performed by Waldemar's Glee Club and its orchestra, Doris unveiled the bronze plaque on the west proscenium pillar which dedicates the theater to her aunt.

The theater became known through the years simply as the "Amphitheater," and it was frequently mispronounced over the loud speaker as "ampitheater." In the 1970s an effort was made to teach campers and counselors to call it "Ora Johnson Theater," and it has been successful.

1935

It was a happy milestone—this tenth summer of Waldemar's operation. During those ten years the camp had weathered a disastrous fire, the premature death of its charismatic founder, a record-setting, devastating flood, and although there were still many vestiges of the Great Depression, it had weathered that too. Waldemar—and Doris Johnson, bolstered by her experienced advisory council—had triumphed.

In the Easter edition of the *Waldemar War Whoop* dated April 21, 1935, Doris wrote that camp was being limited to 200 campers for each term for the coming summer:

> It appears now that May 15 will find 200 girls enrolled for the first term and no one else will be accommodated after that date unless a cancellation occurs.

In explaining the reason for her decision, the director wrote of the season before, 1934:

> Last year no late cancellations came in and yet about 50 girls, most of them old campers, arrived for the opening without making reservations. The management felt an obligation to those who came without reservations because no advance notice of a closed enrollment had been given. Such notice has now been sent to all campers and counselors and no application will be considered after the capacity number has been re-

ceived. Waldemar's organization and equipment make it possible to care properly for 75 juniors and 125 seniors.

Camp opened on June 9, but it wasn't until June 23 that a *War Whoop* was issued. There was no mention of a flood, but handwritten in the upper right hand corner of the file copy is "No *War Whoop* was given the first week on account of the flood."

The issue of June 25 had a small story about the enrollment:

More than a dozen girls who had not made advance reservations were unable to be accommodated.

In the July 7 issue:

Eighteen girls have enrolled for the eight weeks term and have either already arrived or will come in today. Since the camp is already full to capacity, a new kampong was erected to take care of part of the new girls during the two weeks that overlap in the first six weeks term, and the others will be placed in various kampongs where room can be found.

Doris remembered that she had smiled indulgently behind Aunt Ora's back in 1928 when the older woman had mused aloud: "Some day Camp Waldemar will be turning girls away!"

Was her prediction beginning to come true?

The building of the Ora Johnson Memorial Amphitheater in 1934 was satisfying to Doris and it had whetted her appetite for construction. Thus she embarked upon a building program that was to continue until the early 1970s, when her last big project was the construction of courts numbers 5 and 6 of the large tennis court complex known as Casa Courts.

Although the Doll House was an attractive wooden ranch-type structure, built only five years before, Doris chose to replace it because of its highly visible location between the Dining Hall and the Fine Arts Building and its promise of complementing the Memorial Amphitheater. (She never considered this new Doll House a "kampong," always calling French Chateau, not built until 1938, "the first rock kampong.")

The charm of the new building, which was ready for the 1935 season, brought many visitors to Waldemar. Each rock, each piece of wood, each antique wrought-iron lighting fixture had been thoughtfully chosen and/or approved either by Ferdinand, Harvey P. Smith, Doris Johnson, or her father and advisor, J. F. Johnson, and the finished building was their collective pride.

Except for the later removal of the fish pond from the living room, the building has remained as it was in 1935, when it was considered a showplace and this news story appeared:

The outside walls of the building are made of river rock which was found several miles up the Guadalupe. Mingled in with that for effect are many black rocks, most of them are the shape of cannon balls, giving an interesting appearance to the whole. Several are double, looking like dumbbells. Back on Mr. J. F. Johnson's ranch there is a spring surrounded by Indian mounds, and it is here that these unusual rocks were found. They were brought out by horseback.

The roof is made of tile, ordered especially for the building from Peru, Illinois. Five lovely colors harmonize in the roofing. Under the tile is pecky cypress, interesting because of the process by which it is made. A certain species of bug is put into the tree, and it sets about to disease the wood. When a certain stage is reached, the tree is cut, and the diseasing process stops. [This process is now disputed.]

Where the electric wires meet the walls on the exterior, the wires, which are in a steel cable, run into a steel pipe, which carries all wires throughout the building. The rocks were laid around the piping, thus making fire from the wiring an impossibility.

All of the screens are made of copper, and the doors of red cedar were made especially for the Doll House. The rocks in the downstairs room came from Elemendorf, and are of the type as those used in the buildings at Randolph Field, the West Point of the Air. The two-story living room, with its beamed ceiling and its round conservatory is the center of interest to all visitors, and they are always carried away with the circular seat of sweet smelling cedar, looking as if it were just made for a story-telling group. The niches holding potted plants, the fern beds, and the fish pool, presided over by a big green frog are features of the conservatory.

This pool is made of stalactite and stalagmite formations coming from a cave on Mr. Johnson's ranch. Ferdinand Rehbeger, who is responsible for the beautiful rock work and the finding of many of the lovely stones which went into the structure, got these formations 1100 feet back into the cave, and has been back as far as 2400 feet. Lining the pool are pieces of crystallized calcite, and the green and yellow frog spouting a steady stream of water from its mouth, first made his appearance in Germany. . . .

Fish-net, adorned with corks, provides unique curtains for the living room. The chandelier is fashioned of wrought iron and genuine old oil lamps wired for electricity. Reading and desk lamps light the room with soft and attractive light, and all are old oil lamps, modernized and equipped with shades. All the lamps were found among the old German families of Fredericksburg.

Set deep in the wall is a mammoth fireplace. Rocks in the chimney were found in caves nearby, and the petrified wood was found near Fredericksburg and Leakey. On each side of the fireplace, concealed by the living room wall, are seats, forming an inglenook. The cedar benches found here were brought from the Old Colonel Brackenridge home. In keeping with the character of the room are the shovel and fork hanging before the fireplace.

The red rock in the interior walls is very rare. In each piece are many sea shells, giving proof to the fact that this country was under sea many years ago. This rock had to be hunted out, and there is very little of it left. It was found in a canyon and was brought out by pack horses for nine miles. The huge boulders were then dynamited, exposing the surface containing the shells. They were then brought over a hundred miles to Waldemar. . . .

An outstanding feature, for which Mr. Johnson himself is responsible, is the type of windows used. The frame is of steel, and was set into the wall, and the rocks built around it. There are two windows to each opening, and may be opened only from the inside. . . .

Harvey P. Smith of San Antonio was the architect for the Doll House, as he also was for the Dining Hall. All the iron work and the collecting of the lamps and their transformation into modern electric lamps was done by Mr. Coop of Fredericksburg.

The former Doll House, still in excellent condition, was moved up the hill to the north and slightly east of the new Doll House and turned into the Academic Building

where classes are held by day and counselors are housed by night. The small cabin formerly occupying this site has been moved up the hill and over on a ledge, overhanging the trees of the ravine, and has been christened "Hangover Lodge."

Waldemar was constantly enlarging its curriculum as well as its physical plant. In her small green booklet distributed before her 1926 opening season, Miss Ora had written: "An eighteen-hole golf course with natural hazards is another of the attractions of Camp Waldemar." This dream did not materialize, but a four-hole course, "laid out to the right of the entrance gate," was ready for the 1935 season. The camp was furnishing "Brassies, putters, niblicks and the like," but girls owning clubs were urged to bring them. Their parents were invited to play the course.

Jewelry making, wood carving, and basketry were added to the crafts program, the offerings of that department depending upon the varied talents of the competent artists on the staff. "Kodakery" was less commercially renamed "Photography."

Since the tribes were formed in 1928, some campers had come for six, some for eight, and some for twelve weeks. Because of the large number of "carry-overs" from first to second term, the tribal plaque, Waldemar's prestigious symbol of tribal supremacy, was awarded only at the end of the second term. Even though the points of "first-term-only" girls counted in the ultimate tally, unless they returned to visit they were not on hand to enjoy "the thrill of victory or the agony of defeat," always a special moment in the lives of Waldemar girls whether they win or lose.

Thus, in 1935 the decision was made to award the plaque each term upon the basis of points earned by the girls of that particular term. It was won that first term by the Comanches—perhaps their sweetest victory ever.

Just why this change is not noted until 1939 on the engraved plaque which hangs in the office is a mystery since it is clearly pointed out in the *War Whoop.*

The present-day Spirit of Waldemar ceremony began to emerge in 1935. Instead of a canoe pageant with decorated canoes, Dolly Downes created a canoe drill using six canoes. Having built confidence that first term, she directed ten canoes in intricate patterns and formations for the second-term event. The War Canoes and the white Ideal Girl Canoe came down the river very much as they do today, and the white-clad girls stood in the form of a "W" and made speeches delineating the attributes of the girl who would be singled out and taken to the waiting white canoe.

The Spirit of Waldemar urn, an Italian vase from Miss Ora's collection, mercilessly painted white, was used for the first time during the second term of 1935:

Standing before an urn in which burned a steady blue flame, Jeannette Johnson as master of ceremonies explained the symbolism of the flame as burning away the dross in our characters and leaving only the fine and lovely things.

Research indicates that the speakers did not light candles from the urn until second term of 1936. Although others may have contributed to the writing of the ceremony, it is believed that since both Downs Lander and Cobby de Stivers were at camp in 1935, they collaborated in the planning and writing. In the July 13, 1935, issue of the *Waldemar War Whoop,* an editorial appears called "The Spirit of Waldemar." It carries the by-line "Downs Lander," and it is the opening speech of the master of ceremonies practically word for word.

The Fourth of July water pageant of 1935 brought together in directorial collaboration two of Waldemar's talented entertainers: Bertha Lacey of Corpus Christi and Marion Woodward of Dallas.

"Lacey" had come to Waldemar in 1933 to head a department of four dancing teachers. Her "Studio of Dance" in Corpus Christi was considered one of the most outstanding in the state, and at Waldemar "Lacey" taught ballet, tap, ballroom, character, and any other type for which there was demand. She had danced her way to Europe teaching the tango on the *Ile de France*, perhaps the most luxurious of the ocean liners of the day, and she and her students were exciting performers on many Waldemar programs.

The summer of 1935 was Marion Woodward's first at Waldemar. This never-tiring thespian taught at the Woodrow School of Drama in Dallas, and she had studied at the American Laboratory of Dramatics in New York City and received her degree from the University of California.

"A Romance of the Sea" was the title of the 1935 pageant which Marion wrote and directed and Lacey choreographed. Every camper appeared in the story of a dashing pirate captain who wooed and won the Sea Princess.

Hats were properly doffed to the team of counselors who devised costumes for the pageant and whose creations were, in some cases, worn into the water:

> The princess was appropriately gowned in a sea green satin covered with a scale design in sequins. Her long glittering train further carried out the deep sea theme, following the contours of a fish tail.
> The two sea nymphs, in floating green draperies, danced around a sea shell, opening it at the end of their dance to reveal four more dancers within.

Doris had surmised that the team of Lacey and Woodward would present a tremendous pageant, and she had employed the professional lighting company of Crowell and Crowell of San Antonio to work with her directors.

In a humor column, a backstage observer had written:

WHAT THE AUDIENCE DIDN'T SEE OF THE PAGEANT—(we hope)—Ida's and Dolly's taxi system . . . Downs and Bess Richards pumping talcum powder from behind Neptune's throne to make the scene stormy . . . the shoes and socks swimming around the raft . . . Baird lighting torches . . . Lacey, Ro and Duffy lining up the dancers . . . the downfall of Betty Berlowitz's frog outfit . . . and Billie running across the river.

A most important camper came to Waldemar in 1935. She was Bertha Whattacamper, an imaginary friend of Tid Compere and Bess Rayford, and she wore the color "purplish orange." According to Tid and Bess, "she can swim the river eight times under water, beat both war canoes down the river without anyone to help her, shoot fifty-one out of a possible fifty in riflery, and Bertha always rides two horses at once."

Bertha Whattacamper stayed around well into the 1950s. Early on she wrote an advice column, "Bertha's Bane for Broken Hearts," she judged contests through the years, and she explained just how to clean a kampong. Her table manners were impeccable, and, in a strange way, Bertha Whattacamper became a yardstick by which campers measured their progress, their attitude, and their Waldemar "Plus Spirit."

The requirement of an early morning "dip" in the Guadalupe or "set ups" (exercises) on the Athletic Field had been a part of Waldemar from the beginning. At first participating in either of these activities netted a camper one-half point, and by 1935 one point, toward her quest for high-point camper honors.

The daily schedule in 1935 marked it "optional," a modification that promptly caused the demise of the early-morning activity.

In 1939, when Dolly Downes was being interviewed by a camp reporter, she said: "Waldemar ain't what it used to be—thanks for small favors. I used to have to get up before the bust of dawn and lead sleepy campers in their daily dozen set-ups."

From the time of Miss Ora, each camper was weighed upon entrance, and those who were underweight were encouraged to gain and those who were overweight were encouraged to lose weight. (Tables at which fewer calories were served were furnished for the overweight girls as early as 1933.) An incentive for conforming was the promise of extra points, and careful records were kept. The term "nourishment" is derived from the serving of milk and crackers to the "underweights."

The Tejas of 1935 entertained the Comanches with a Futuristic Dance featuring a spaceship on their invitation, and the Comanches created a Disneyland for the Tejas long before Walt Disney began using his characters in that fashion.

Lucille Smith had baked a five-tiered birthday cake large enough to serve everybody in camp at noon on Sunday, July 7, in celebration of Waldemar's tenth birthday. Each of the ten large candles was lighted separately by a counselor who had been a part of Waldemar during the year her candle represented, and the sentimental and loyal counselors made Waldemar's first birthday party a joyous and festive affair.

Del Rio with Villa Acuna thrown in was the free trip offered to eight- and twelve-week campers, and the Dolls received from Doris their first pony cart within which the Waldemar cowboys hauled them around on request; the Monterrey trip was resumed, still given free to eight- and twelve-week campers; rates for a room in the "hotel" were $2.50 for one person and $4 for two in a room; all meals for patrons were fifty cents except Sunday dinner, the price of which advanced to seventy-five cents; a new baking room had been added to the kitchen and the "back porch" was enclosed to create a preparation room and hold "tables for the cowboys"; and the Commissioners Court of Kerr County had authorized the spending of $5,000 for the construction of low-water bridges at "Camp Lone Star and Hope fords," both between Hunt and Waldemar, and they were completed by June 1, 1936.

The pageant had been called "The Romance of the Sea," but Waldemar girls had been enjoying their own "Romance of the Guadalupe" for quite a few summers. Margaret Gladney of Beaumont and Camp Waldemar married Buddy Savage of Beaumont and Camp Stewart on August 12 in Pine Hill, New York.

1936

Dallas had its Texas Centennial Exposition, Fort Worth its Casa Manana, and Camp Waldemar its "Heritage of Glory" in honor of the 100th birthday of the Lone Star State. This pageant, written and directed by Marion Woodward and choreographed by Bertha Lacey like the one in 1935, replaced the annual Fourth of July water carnival and attracted a large patriotic audience from the area as well as many enthusiastic patrons.

The ambitious scope of the pageant was described by its author:

It represents in dramatics, music and dancing, the events of Texas history from time of Indian occupation through French and Spanish invasion, with their consequent effects on the customs and standards of the people, to frontier times and the beginnings of Texas' growth as an empire state of world prominence.

The "stage" was the east end of the Athletic Field, and every camper had a role to play. There were Indian chiefs, braves, squaws, medicine men, and scouts; there were LaSalle's dashing Frenchmen; there were Spanish *señoritas* and *caballeros*; there were Mexican soldiers and there were frontiersmen and their ladies. A touching love story ensued, and after the marriage of the protagonists, there were tableaux depicting events that were still to come in Texas history.

The love story did not emerge until Part Three of the pageant, when "Richard," a handsome frontiersman, fell in love with "Ellen," the daughter of a frontier family. Preceding their wedding, the following bit of spirited action took place on the Waldemar Athletic Field:

During the dancing, a lone Indian entered the circle of wagons and stole a horse tethered nearby. Frightened, the group scattered, some giving chase to the thief, leaving the future bride unguarded for the moment and open to the attack of two more Indians who seized her and placed her upon the mount of their chieftain.

Frontier riders immediately galloped after the escaping kidnappers and Richard heroically rescued his bride from the fleeing Indians as the chieftain jumped from his galloping horse in a mad attempt for his life and escaped into the darkness.

The sets for this extravaganza, appropriately scaled for the area and for the vigorous action, were professionally made in San Antonio by Crowell and Crowell, who also brought out the lighting equipment as they had done in 1935. (Two large portable floodlights which have "Crowell and Crowell" embossed on them are still in use at Waldemar.)

A column called "Pageant Pranks," an insider's humorous report, appeared in the next issue of the newspaper:

The poor besieged electrician on the dining room porch went into complete delirium when he blew out both spotlight bulbs at the same moment. The other technician sat calmly behind the scenery on the field and pulled this wire and that trying to help out his partner—by remote control, we suppose. And said partner was worrying whether to replace the bulbs because they cost three fifty each! Don't they know this is Waldemar?

Kentucky enjoyed the pageant—nipping at the mules, howling at the orchestra, and chasing frogs across the Athletic Field. [Kentucky Boy was Billie Johnson's beloved wire-haired terrier and a camp favorite despite his irreverent behavior at camp programs.]

Ellen the bride almost got stood up for her kidnapping date, but a little staggering around the stage filled up the time until Tommie Espy remembered she was an Indian horse thief.

The thrill of the Wild West show was wasted on a darkened audience, but Tommie slid off her horse on the right foot (putting her best foot forward again!), made a perfect three-point landing, and escaped her pursuers even if her art wasn't appreciated. [Tommie Espy (later Williams) was spending her first of several summers at Waldemar as a member of the horseback department. The popular Tommie had been reared on a ranch in the Big Bend Country of Texas and was more than equal to the rigors of the Wild West show.]

Tommy Beard's part in the pageant: The Firebringer-onner, the Fire-putter-outer, and the Firetaker-offer. Playin' with fire.

One befuddled camper wanted to know just HOW the *War Whoop* could carry the complete story of the Fourth in the Sunday edition. My dear, this is WALDEMAR.

Cried an alarmed camper, carried away by the spirit of the-show-must-go-on: "Don't look over there—they're stealing the horses!"

The Torch Dance of the pageant was unique in that no one laughed when the Lanes used a Johnny Jr. (wrapped to resemble an earthen jar) to put out the fire, but we doubt the historical accuracy of the useful water carrier. [The Lanes were Charlotte and Charline, identical twins from Houston, who came to Waldemar as young campers in 1928. They held the distinction of having been chosen Best All-Round low senior campers three years in a row and then, when eligible, were voted Best All-Round high senior campers. These talented and loyal Comanches, who were tribal sponsors in 1936, answered to the nicknames of "Chaw" and "Chawin."]

Many of the dance and drama rehearsals for this pageant no doubt took place in the newly remodeled Junior Rec, originally Waldemar Lodge. Hardwood floors had been laid in 1935, but the building was now made twice its original size, and the new addition contained a stage with a costume room and a dressing room on each side.

Striking features of the room are the Mexican pottery chandeliers hung from wrought iron bars. The lights are nestled in small pots suspended from these bars. One of the disadvantages of the old building has been removed, with the installation of many windows providing adequate ventilation for all occasions, including dances.

In remodeling the front of the building [the south side of the building, facing the river, was called the front] Miss Johnson and Mr. Harvey P. Smith have kept in mind the church services. New circular rock steps have replaced the old wooden ones. The new steps are arranged so that the choir or orchestra can be seated on them. The old rock terrace has been replaced with one large enough to accommodate the entire camp.

Efforts to stir up interest in renaming the building by offering prizes failed.

Wanted: A Name. Junior Rec is no more. Choice of a new name for the remodeled building will be made by a committee from those submitted to the office by Saturday. The excellent suggestion has been made that the building should bear Doris's name.

Evidently Doris' refusal caused the contest to bog down. News stories called it the "Poor Nameless Building" and it was not until 1937 that the name "Cactus Lodge" was chosen—because of the little Mexican pots designed for growing cacti in the chandeliers.

The cowboys played a special role in the lives of Waldemar girls. All could sing a little and dance a little and most could tell tall tales; occasionally they shared these talents with campers and counselors at evening programs. Everyone sat around a campfire on the banks of the Guadalupe and basked in the flavor of the true west which emanated from these friends.

Of necessity the cowboys had played roles in the pageant first term—what with wagons to be circled and uncircled and horses to be mounted and dismounted; and Jack Reeves and Ox Sultenfuss had shared Indian rider duties with Tommie Espy and a few other experienced riders.

There was no Fourth of July pageant to engage them second term, and so the boys decided to present a rodeo—a private rodeo—and a reporter's write-up follows:

The cowboys truly whooped it up Saturday afternoon. Each in his Sunday-go-to-meeting clothes, they showed us the real way to ride and rope.

The show started off with a bang by Ralph Alexander bringing in a huge bull. Everyone grabbed for his red colors, and did a few Comanches wish they were Tejas when they practically had to get rid of the orange that so closely resembled red.

After the bull and the many little calves were in the ring, Mangum Sikes gave an idea of how a calf should be roped. This stunt was followed by a series of ropings by Jack Reeves and Ralph Alexander.

"Kentuck" was then called to the rescue to make the bull mad, and proceeded to bark at his heels. Kentucky, by the way, had a tooth knocked out, but the show must go on so he continued to bark. Henry (Ox to you) then climbed aboard the bull and rode him around the ring. Oh, me, was the bull mad. It was the first time in the history of camp that an ox had ridden a bull.

But girls, while all this was going on, Johnny Regan, our own Johnny Regan, was flirting with the cutest little bull you ever saw. That bull seemed to be watching Johnny so hard that he forgot to mind the red shirt that Johnny seemed to be so proud of. When the bull was finally roped, he must have thought Johnny was the pony cart, for he certainly took him for a ride.

After the riding of the bull and the roping of the calves, the rodeo then progressed to the outside of the ring where goats were turned loose and roped. Here is where the gallant Hayden Smith came to the rescue. When a goat ran out of the enclosure Hayden jumped on his trusty steed and was off like Paul Revere to warn the goat that he was coming. Did he bring the goat back alive? He must have because all the goats were there at the end of the rodeo, thanks to Hayden.

Ida Mehr was first listed as a Waldemar camper from Houston in Miss Ora's original mimeographed directory for 1929; in the 1930 directory she is listed as a junior counselor, and in 1931 as a senior counselor. She and young Doris found themselves working together, with the store and the mail as areas of responsibility. Their "shenanigans," as their stunts were often labeled, were well publicized, and Ida ruled the office with a firm hand and gruff charm for ten years. Although her talents were exceptional, perhaps her chief legacy to the camp did not come through her skill in organizing Waldemar's early-day office; instead it evolved from a comic episode typical of the irrepressible Waldemar staff.

During the second term of 1936, it was announced in the newspaper that a group of eleven counselors, including the athletic Ida, would meet the winners of the scheduled camper tribal Field Day in contest on the following day. The challenge was accepted but the action was postponed two days, probably so that the counselors could become better organized and dig up ridiculous costumes.

Many more than the original eleven took part in what turned out to be a hilarious day, with the counselors being victorious. When a slip of the announcer's tongue caused Ida to be called to participate in the swimming meet as "Iza," she quipped through the laughter, "Iza Buzzard."

At dinner that night Frances McCluskey announced that the field meet had been Doris' way of finding out which counselors would not be invited back next year. Any who lost could not return. Ann Miller Crockett and B. J. Sehman had lost the canoeing disrobing race, and they left the dining room weeping and clinging to each other dejectedly and saying they were going to Mystic. Soon they returned announcing that Mystic would not have them either without "Iza Buzzard."

Thus the Waldemar counselors became known as the Buzzards, but the name was slow in catching on, especially first term, and was used only for occasional field meets or softball games. It became commonly used in the late 1940s, when black and blue were chosen as their colors and the Buzzard song was written.

Doris, popular with both campers and counselors, was the subject of many news stories.

> She drives the new blue bus with pride, but she also has a snappy red car, which counselors call "The Fire Wagon."

Feeling that the girls needed a little more quiet time, Doris started the Waldemar Library in 1936.

1937

The summer just past had been the fifth without the founder, Ora Johnson. Camp was filled, according to the first *Waldemar War Whoop* of 1936, and valuable counselors were returning year after year to strengthen the camp program and add a sense of continuity to the girls' traditions and memories of Waldemar.

Now, in 1937, the enrollment picture was encouraging indeed. Because nineteen first-term girls were staying over for eight weeks, thus taking them two weeks into the second term, it was necessary to house eleven of them for two weeks in W. T. Johnson Ballroom.

> The counselor deluxe in W. T. is Maggie Savage. The elite have been for two weeks privileged to hang their shirts on wrought-iron lamps, dispense with mopping, and practice their chop sticks on their own piano. The group will be missed immensely. As old girls, they helped the new girls get adjusted. . . .

Four campers were living in Rippling Waters, and Waldemar was bulging at the seams. Although there were thirty-six wooden kampongs, accommodating varying numbers of campers, plus the Doll House, it was clearly time to think about more housing.

A sure sign that the enrollment picture was bright in 1937 was that the Monterrey trip, free to eight-week campers in 1936, was announced as costing $25 for six-week campers and $15 for eight-week campers. Inducements to come to Camp Waldemar were becoming less important as the program grew and enthusiastic campers themselves became the best advertisement.

The 1937 architectural improvement was not intended for camper housing; still it would ease the bed situation by serving as the summer home for a few counselors. During the construction of the Doll House in 1935, Doris had joined Ferdinand Rehbeger in having no reservations about the talent and imagination of architect Harvey P. Smith. Whereas Miss Ora's buildings had established the overall geographical plan for the camp, it was now the privilege of Doris and Harvey Smith to embellish that plan with buildings designed to grace the landscape and complement the activities of the campers.

Casa del Monte, to be used as a craft house, was the worthy 1937 embellishment. Two years before, the wooden Doll House had been moved to the top of the hill just north of the new stone Doll House, and now that frame structure was moved again, this time higher on the hill joining Hangover Lodge on what came to be known as Counselor Hill. Ironically, the Counselor Bunkhouse, haven for counselors and off-limits to campers, began life as the home of Waldemar's youngest campers.

Harvey Smith considered Casa del Monte a distinct departure in design because the existing Waldemar buildings were of the "rustic, mountain lodge" type. According to the architect, Casa del Monte is designed along the lines of early Texas ranch houses of the Southwest with Spanish provincial accents. Horizontal lines predominate because of the long flat stone used, and heavy wood timber lintels over the openings accentuate the sturdy ranch house feel of the architecture.

The building is one-story on two different levels except for the round tower rising two full stories high, the dominant architectural feature of the house. The tower room can be reached by winding stairways from both inside and out, the outside one curving gracefully around the tower offering photographers an unusual setting.

A large fireplace with built-in seats on each side of the fire opening and bookcases and rustic storage cabinets around and above it, a huge circle-head window facing southward, and the inside stairway to the tower, its treads adorned with decorative Mexican tile, make the living room uniquely beautiful. Behind the living room to the north, set at a forty-five-degree angle from it and a half-floor above it, are two rooms connected by a short hall from which two colorful tile bathrooms are entered. Both of these large rooms open onto the long, low covered porch which faces east.

The contest to name the remodeled "Junior Wreck" having been a fiasco alerted Doris to the difficulty, as well as the importance, of choosing appropriate names for her buildings. "Casa del Monte," literally "house of the mountain" in Spanish, came naturally; the "Doll House" had inherited its name; and "Cactus Lodge" was finally settled upon for old Junior Rec. The Fine Arts Building begged a more inspired name as well as a more flexible one, and in 1937 "Rippling Waters" was chosen because of the nearby Guadalupe River, which ripples and murmurs soothingly as it enters the shallows. These names were carefully spelled out on page one of the first *War Whoop* of the 1937 season, and a wise-cracking reporter wrote: "It was the 'Dining Hall' when we went to bed one night and 'Cypress Inn' when we arrived for breakfast." She called the new name "a fitting change," but as several decades of campers know, the "Dining Hall" won out in the end.

Civilization was slowly edging closer to Waldemar. The construction of low water crossings the year before had made the camp more accessible, and now the installation of an electric power line made a number of electrical improvements possible.

> Frigidaire drinking fountains have been placed in Cactus and Cedar Lodges . . . The infirmary has its own Frigidaire equipment . . . The kitchen has been modernized by the addition of various electrical appliances now that the electric current is stronger. [These included an electrical refrigeration plant and a giant free-standing Hobart Mixer "for Lucille's bakery." The mixer finally made its last revolution in 1987, 50 years later.]

One of Waldemar's indispensable tools over the years and one requiring electrical power was installed in the second term of 1937 and, surprisingly, didn't rate a front-page story: Waldemar acquired its first public address system. A tongue-in-cheek article evaluated the new gadget:

> The programs vary from the deep bass of "Waldemar testing 1, 2, 3, 4" to the lyric soprano of the prima

donna, Rollin Hunter. In a recent audition Ida Mehr won honorable mention for diction and Bertha Lacey was chosen Miss Personality of '37 with her "Are ya listnen?"

The only drawback to this newest example of Waldemar's collection of the mosta of the besta is expressed by the swimming instructors, who watch aghast while struggling "tadpoles" halt their labored strokes at the sharp command of "Attention, please" . . . and promptly sink.

Seriously, campers, the amplifying system was brought here for your convenience, as is everything else in Waldemar; and you'll add to your popularity by answering its summons immediately.

Later in a gossip column: "Attention, attention, please! Please, Amplifier, we're tired to playing soldier. Give us a rest."

But by August of 1937 one of the plusses of the amplifying system was embraced with enthusiasm. A free night had been declared after a strenuous Field Day.

Some of Waldemar's best dancers tripped the light fantastic to the tune of the nation's best orchestras in Rippling Waters. Others, preferring songs of mosquitoes, sat star-gazing and serenading on the athletic field until Ida's voice of experience announced suddenly from station W-A-L-D-E-M-A-R that a recorded program would follow.

Thanks to Gene Hunt, who furnished the records, and to Doris, who likes the canned music as much as we, the evening lullabies will be continued.

And in that same issue:

Ida, after playing the "Taps" record: "My lips are so puckered from blowing that bugle I can't talk straight."

"Live" camp buglers still played "taps" at the end of tribal hill programs and other traditional camp programs, and it was always a nostalgic moment when the amplifier failed for some reason and the tones from the horn of a live bugler echoed through the hills.

On Tuesday, July 15, 1937, Waldemar got a taste —albeit a disappointing one—of the movies that were soon to become a twice-weekly feature of the camp program. The article is entitled "So You Won't Talk?"

Actors and actresses of Hollywood have the reputation of being temperamental when their feelings are stepped upon. The movie-going public of camp has learned that Tuesday night "they wouldn't talk."

This was spoken of as a foolish error, but the truth is that the sound cable was trampled by those too anxious to hear and be heard to look underfoot.

Mr. and Mrs. E. E. Dyess of Fort Worth will be back with their movie machine on Monday, June 21, and again on Wednesday, June 30. Mr. Dyess is principal of one of the Fort Worth Schools, and is spending the summer close by so that he might show pictures to several of the camps in this vicinity. Bill James, director of Stewart, asked him to make these arrangements.

Other movies were shown first term, but the reviews were less than enthusiastic. Evidently there was little choice of product. Somehow Doris discovered one for the second-term girls that was passable enough to encourage them to thank her for "bringing us this interesting entertainment."

Waldemar had a menagerie and two gigantic bird cages filled with exotic birds in 1937.

Have you been down behind the stables into the deer park yet? Did you know three grown deer and two baby antelopes spend their summers here too? The three grown deer are the same small ones that ran around camp with bells on their necks last summer.

Waldemar has other pets of its own. No doubt most of you have seen the large cage situated in the trees by the Doll House. Seventy-five parakeets, cockateels, and lovebirds can be seen flying around most of the time.

Eight colorful pheasants occupy a beautiful newly-built cage near the new Casa del Monte. These birds were bought in San Antonio.

Another *War Whoop* article reported:

Badminton crashed the gate of Waldemar sports second term this summer when the never-ceasing fount of equipment under Doris's bed yielded new racquets and new shuttlecocks.

The sport was described as "this new form of aerial tennis" and it was suggested that if the shuttlecocks didn't hold up, the pheasants might be called upon "to lend a little color to the occasion."

Even though Waldemar was known as "The Texas Horseback Camp," the performing arts were also flourishing. During the first term the archery and tennis departments had two counselors each while the dancing department boasted four instructors and two accompanists, the dramatics had four counselors, and "nearly forty campers" were taking private lessons on a musical instrument.

The song "To Doris" was first performed at a vesper service second term of 1937 by "the camp trio of Emmie Craddock, Margaret Thomas, and Ruth Wright." According to Doris, the song was introduced "by a counselor from Kansas in 1936," and it expressed the love and respect which all campers and counselors felt for their young director. The song was sung spontaneously by admiring groups of campers and counselors through the years thereafter, and Doris' gracious and poised reception of the loving tribute wherever she might be was appreciated by the singers, and those moments became treasures.

Dedicated sponsors continued to make the tribal hill programs inspiring and unifying, and the division "captains," like the chieftain, now wore bracelets signifying their offices. To the horror of the campers, kampong inspections, heretofore scheduled only for mornings, now took place twice a day.

The Tejas entertained the Comanches with a racing meet at "Upsand Downs," and the Comanches had a gala opening of the "Waldemar Airport," dropping invitations in the form of parachutes from the porch of the Dining Hall to their Tejas guests. An elaborate "Gay Nineties" party for which everyone costumed kept the social scene lively.

A "Spanish Gypsy Tribal Combat" was the theme of the 1937 Fourth of July pageant featuring swimming, dancing, and horseback riding, with the dancing and riding taking place on both sides of the river. At one point—in the darkness and on the south side of the river—the horses were turned loose.

> Some of the girls had been warned that the horses were going to be turned loose, but no one had warned the swimmers. They almost jumped in for an impromptu part when they heard the approaching hoofs.
>
> No one had warned Connie Douglas either, and she thought of every possible danger when she heard horses running. Evidently she thought she could catch them if they were bearing riders for she started running in the direction of the ford as hard as she could go.

Perhaps 1937 can be considered a watershed year as far as the counselor staff is concerned because two counselors joined the staff that summer who gave so unstintingly of their talents that they became central to the success of the Doris Johnson organization.

Doris had finally enticed Constance Douglas, by this time a recognized horsewoman in San Antonio, to Waldemar—the same Miss Douglas whom her aunt had mistakenly advertised as being Waldemar's counselor of dramatics for the opening year of 1926.

By this time Connie, a teacher of public speaking at San Antonio's Thomas Jefferson High School (where she was having phenomenal success with the girls' pep squad called the "Lassoes"), owned thirty horses at her own "Oak Hill Stables" where she raised, trained, and showed saddle-bred horses, both three, and five-gaited. She joined Jane Reid (Tait) and Tommie Espy (Williams), Waldemar veterans, in

rounding out an exceptionally strong horseback department.

Doris realized that Constance Douglas was a "natural" for the Waldemar situation, and she congratulated herself upon securing for her camp an equestrienne of such fine reputation and unlimited talent. She had no way of knowing then that in 1943 Connie and Jack Reeves, head of the Waldemar cowboy staff who lived and worked on a Johnson ranch in the winter, would marry, thus cementing their association with Waldemar. Jack died in 1985. Connie, an amazing nonagenarian in the 1990s, was the capable and revered head of Waldemar's horseback department until 1996.

Ellen Easley, whose positive influence on the success of Camp Waldemar is second only to that of Doris Johnson, first came to Waldemar in 1937 as director of camp publicity. In the performance of her duties she sent pictures of girls engaged in camp activities along with news stories about their achievements at Waldemar to their hometown newspapers. Her quick mind, her fervor for perfection, her broad range of interests and talents did not go unmarked, and in 1939 Doris invited her to become a year-round employee and resident of Camp Waldemar.

Except for two years in the late 1940s, Ellen lived at Waldemar from 1939 on, becoming Doris' "right hand" as well as the camp's assistant director. There are few areas of organization at Waldemar which she did not improve, either by setting up a new and better system for accomplishing a task or by upgrading an existing one. The efficiency of the office staff grew under her supervision, but Ellen Easley always found the time to sponsor a tribe or direct the junior department or teach a class if the need arose.

For campers and counselors, the two names "Doris and Ellen" became naturally linked, and when Doris moved from the camp in 1979, Ellen moved with her a mile downriver and lived with the "doyenne of Hill Country girls' camps," as *Texas Monthly* had dubbed her, until her death in 1985. Ellen then retired in Denton, Texas. She died in 1995.

The catalog promoting Waldemar's 1937 camping season had two distinctions: it displayed for the first time the Comanche and Tejas tribal crests, artfully placed on a two-page pictorial of Field Day; and it published for the first time the poem written in tribute to the Ideal Girl. The "Tribute to the Spirit of Waldemar," popularly known as "Lovely Sunbrowned Girl," was written by Florence Mai Albrecht of Houston when she was a fifteen-year-old camper. The popular "Flossie," later a counselor, was honored by her contemporaries for diving triumphs, and it is her swan dive which the photographer "caught" so stunningly in early-day catalogs. However, she will be remembered longest at Waldemar for her contribution to the Ideal Girl ceremony—her poem which captures the essence of the girl herself and which Doris thought worthy of an entire page in the 1937 catalog:

Lovely sun-browned girl
With flying hair,
Laughing for sheer delight
At Nature's beauty;
Stretching your eager hands
For stars that hide within
The murmuring cypress;
Filling with gentle memories
And kind thoughts your sincere heart;
Playing—losing and winning;
Sharing your dreamy soul
With those who have no dreams;
Lovely sun-browned girl,
Guard these, your ideals,
For they are the honor . . .
THE SPIRIT OF WALDEMAR.
—Florence Mai Albrecht

Even with the wonderful help of her representatives and staff, Doris had now discovered the time and the work involved in running her girls' camp to be incompatible with teaching school in San Antonio. So the fall of 1937 found her relaxing a bit, first in New Mexico and then in New York City.

Our Doris would a-roaming go, and so when all the conventions were over during the three weeks after the campers went home, Doris, Ida and Dolly set out for New Mexico.

Doris was planning an excursion for campers to Carlsbad Caverns in 1938, and she thought a trial run advisable.

After this adventure, Doris and Billie took a well-deserved trip to New York City, Billie to attend the World Series and Doris to enjoy the new plays on Broadway. All of Waldemar was happy for the two vacationers who gave so much of themselves to others during the summer.

1938

A major change was about to take place along the banks of the Guadalupe, a change that would be accomplished so quietly and smoothly that campers and counselors would be unaware of it.

Beginning second term of 1933, the second and last year of Josephine Bell's directorship, Doris had sometimes been referred to in the columns of the *War Whoop* as the owner of Waldemar. True, she owned the handsome Waldemar buildings, but she did not own the land upon which they rested until 1938. With the blessing of her father, J. F. Johnson, and her brother, Billie Johnson, she bought the land from Mr. and Mrs. T. V. Lawson of Cleburne, Texas. The sale was not publicized and there was no perceptible change, but it was the final commitment of the young woman's life to her aunt's dream. In 1938 her address in the camp directory changed from the St. Anthony Hotel, San Antonio, to Camp Waldemar, Hunt, Texas.

Having learned from her aunt, the ultimate publicist, during her years at Waldemar, Doris had not overlooked a single recruiting or publicity opportunity. Aunt Ora had published her first *Christmas War Whoop* in 1929, and Doris had continued that practice. This issue, which served as a Christmas greeting card, told of the annual improvements at Waldemar and was filled with chatty news of the doings, goings and comings of campers and counselors. More often than not, an Easter issue arrived at the homes of campers and prospective campers.

The camp's professionally designed Valentines were unique, and examples of them are in the Waldemar archives. Thanksgiving greetings and clever mailing pieces designed simply to say "Hurry" or "Welcome" were sent regularly to campers and counselors. Hometown newspapers were eager to publish pictures of prominent local girls engaged in camp activities, and a bunk at Waldemar had become prestigious and sought after.

Doris' representatives and counselors were also prestigious in their communities, and they were proud of the girls they enrolled at Camp Waldemar and happy that they could make this summer educational institution available to their communities. Doris encouraged enrollment "races" among cities and towns, and picnics and breakfast cookouts gave the groups identity.

On the front page of the Christmas issue of the *War Whoop* preceding the 1938 season appeared a boxed story intended to encourage early enrollment:

The early bird gets to go to camp. Last year more than 100 girls were turned away from Waldemar because the enrollment was swollen to capacity long before the opening of camp, and every indication points toward a similar situation this year.

Doris announces that there are already more enrollments than ever before in the history of the camp at this early date. Allene Clower from Eunice, N.M., was the very earliest "early bird." She left her application before leaving camp last summer. So don't wait too long, all you Comanches and Tejas.

In that same issue an article appeared warning that "Waldemar cannot give its campers a new building every year" and explaining that Waldemar's improvements for 1938 would include extensive landscaping and new kitchen equipment, an electric dishwasher, and a bake oven.

Despite the disclaimer, a handsome new building greeted campers upon their arrival in 1938. The two-unit kampong was temporarily designated "the rock cottage."

It replaces the old triple 19-20-21 and is the first step in the replacement of all kampongs with rock structures. . . . Many a senior, born six years too soon, envies the little sisters of camp who romp in their "advanced Doll House."

No more was written about the attractive building styled after a French farm house and simply labeled "Rock. No. 1" and "Rock No. 2," but when campers arrived they found that the building, which clings to the hill between Cedar Lodge and the Dining Hall, had been aptly christened "French Chateau."

"Real" motion pictures, current and popular ones, came to Waldemar in 1938, being shown on Tuesday and Saturday nights. A curious camper-reporter, inquiring about the "movies" that the girls so much enjoyed, found that a Mr. Gene Farley brought the projector and sound machine to Waldemar, that he received the film "from the exchange in Dallas," and that many of the pictures were seen at Waldemar before they were taken to the city of San Antonio for showing.

Commented Johnny Regan in his unforgettable British accent:

This is really the most extraordinary cinema audience in the world—what with pajamas and blankets and hair rolling and dancing.

Something else was new on the Guadalupe when the campers arrived in 1938—something more thrilling for eager tribesmen than new kampongs and motion pictures: Doris had bought two new War Canoes.

And it was not a moment too soon. Evidently Doris had put off this expenditure, not an inconsiderable one, as long as she dared. As long ago as 1935, a columnist wrote: "We Nominate for the Hall of Fame"—

BLUE CANOE, which can hold more water and still keep afloat than Ripley would believe possible. We can understand the phenomenon of the floating sieve now. Observation: bathing suits are the safest canoeing costumes.

While both canoes had been serving the tribes since 1928, the Comanche canoe was in fairly good condition; but everyone knew that it would be ill-advised for Doris to buy just one new War Canoe. On Field Days the year before, 1937, the tribes had drawn straws to see "who had to race in the Tejas canoe and take on all that water. Now there will be no more purple suits in the orange canoe and vice versa . . . no more alibis, no handicaps of any kind."

Two smaller canoes in tribal colors were purchased at the same time from the Old Towne canoe factory in Maine, bringing the number of canoes at Waldemar to "approximately 25 boats."

In 1931 the campers of a boys' camp, defunct by 1938, had carved and presented to Waldemar a totem pole which was placed in front of Cedar Lodge. Waldemar's original flagpole, fashioned from an East Texas pine tree and standing near the original camp building, now seemed outdated and misplaced, and the Tejas tribe decided, in 1938, with Doris' approval, to replace the totem pole with a new flagpole.

Oh, say have you seen from the hill that new flagpole rearing its silvered shaft high into the heavens? It stands in front of Cedar Lodge in place of the old Totem Pole which has watched over Waldemar campers for the past eight years.

This handsome flagstaff is the gift of the Tejas tribe to the camp. A color guard composed of the tribal chiefs, cheer leaders, and color bearers (Betty Boyles, Comanche, and Jane Simmon, Tejas) will raise the flag at 7:15 each morning and lower it at sunset. Campers who are in sight of the flag at these hours will always stand at respectful attention as it is being raised or lowered.

In a second-term newspaper: "Thanks, Comanches, for the Waldemar flag." This outsized purple and orange flag displaying a huge W still exists in the Waldemar archives.

The Fourth of July celebration stretched over three days in 1938. On Saturday night, July 2, campers and their guests enjoyed a Patriotic Dance on the tennis court featuring a gala floor show. Costumes and decorations were ingenious and extravagant.

On Sunday, July 3, rifle and tennis exhibitions preceded the evening "Water Exhibition" in which every advanced swimmer in camp participated. Their formations, performed to the strains of the Waldemar orchestra, were soon to be characterized as "water ballet."

One group of advanced swimmers will perform with lights which will reflect in the water as they move rhythmically through their formations. [The lights, battery operated, were strapped to the swimmers' arms.]

The finale of the Aquacade will be formed by girls from the two tribes, the Tejas and the Comanches, who in their tribal colored bathing suits will swim into their own letters. Each swimmer will hold a lighted sparkler in her hand to form the complete outline of the letter. Then the entire group will unite to form a W to represent the true spirit of Waldemar. In celebration of this unification there will be an array of beautiful fireworks across the river as the Aquacade ends.

There is no report of the success or failure of these aquatic maneuvers in the next issue of the paper except: "Flash! Swimmers wear lights—did you want to give the fish a sight of the bright lights?"

Monday morning at 10:30 the annual Fourth of July Horse Show, under the supervision of Jane Reid Tait, Tommie Espy Williams, and Johnny Regan will be presented. Resplendent in shining white and special costumes, riders will stage drills and novelty stunts, including the exciting quadrille. . . .

Waldemar's stables, owned and operated by Mr. J. F. Johnson [Doris' father], boasts many fine horses, Pure Gold and Sonny being among the best. When these gaited ponies, under the elaborately tooled fine leather saddles that Waldemar girls ride, go on parade tomorrow, there'll be no doubt in the minds of the spectators why the "South's Finest Camp for Girls" also takes pride in being the "Texas Horseback Camp."

And in the same issue of the newspaper:

To the top of the Empire State Building on all fours—that's the record of one Waldemarite. His name is Billy Sunday, and if you doubt his marvelous record, he's liable to get horsey about it and reveal even more information concerning his stable companions.

Six of the handsome Arabian paints to be used in the Quadrille tomorrow are of the original string used by Col. W. T. Johnson in staging the same formation

riding at his famous rodeos in Madison Square Garden, New York City. Here professional cowboys cavorted to "Turkey in the Straw" on the same mounts that Waldemar girls whoop it up in the climaxing event of the Horse Show. Sport, Teddy, Partner, Curley, and Spanish can practically dance the quadrille without riders, but it takes a skilled horsewoman to stay on them when they start racing through the snappy formations and abrupt turns of the Quadrille.

The trip for which Billy Sunday is famous was made in 1930 when he was starring in the rodeo. [The trip, made by elevator, was a publicity stunt advertising the rodeo.]

A newspaper clipping, part of Johnson family memorabilia from the files of Sarah Jayne Johnson Manning, Billie Johnson's daughter, states that Col. W. T. Johnson sold his rodeo in 1937 but not to Gene Autry, cowboy singer, as often reported. Autry bought it a few years later before the death of the Colonel in September 1943.

The Fourth of July guests were barely out the gates when forty campers left by chartered bus and the Blue Bus for Carlsbad Caverns on a three-day excursion. A patron in Ozona feted them with a barbecue lunch in an Ozona park; the superintendent of the Caverns "adopted" the entire party as his personal charges; a police escort met them on the outskirts of Del Rio on the return trip and led them into town, where the mayor presented the chaperone, Mrs. Hill, Waldemar's charming and gracious hostess, with a six-foot golden key to the city; and a military escort from Villa Acuna took them across the International Bridge to "Mrs. Crosby's," long the best known of Acuna's restaurants.

There were changes in the camp schedule in 1938 which were applauded by campers and counselors alike. The onerous "morning dip and set-ups" had been abandoned in 1935, but "organized after supper games" from 7:00 to 8:00 P.M. on Monday-Wednesday-Friday were still scheduled but no longer popular.

"Hobby Hour," created in the middle 1930s and usually scheduled from 7:00 to 8:00 P.M. on Tuesday-Thursday-Saturday, was more acceptable because it was more flexible. A camper could use that time to write letters if she pleased; perhaps she preferred modern dance; or she could join her fellow War Canoe crew and have a run down the river; or she could rehearse her role in a drama production or a hill program.

To the delight of campers, evening games were disbanded in 1938, and every evening included a

Hobby Hour after dinner before the evening program. "Cooperative counselors are on duty to help any group which wants to do something special; they will take you on hikes out of the campgrounds or for strolls in the fields," a reporter assured her readers. It was mandatory that the girls be "off the hill," and "90 percent of them enrolled in letter-writing," wrote the reporter.

Doris made a small but significant change in the 1938 schedule that drew unanimous praise from counselors and campers alike: Heretofore "Reveille" had blown at 6:15 A.M., and now a columnist thanked Doris for not "getting us up at the bust of dawn this year and letting us sleep until 7 o'clock!"

Whereas these schedule changes were making camp life a bit more relaxed physically, Doris decided to "tighten up" on Miss Ora's early-day candy rules.

Even though the candy ban had been first listed as a "health rule" in 1930, the "bible" had read: "Health Rules to be kept for 3 consecutive weeks for any honors" and among them was "No candy except within 15 minutes after meals." Early on, however, "no candy" was listed under "optional points" where "keeping the candy rule" earned 50 points. But there were so many optional points available and so few required for All-Star that many girls didn't "keep candy rules," preferring to make their optional points in other less pleasure-depriving areas.

In 1937 a small story had appeared:

There are certain advantages to being employed in the post office. Sealy and Bobbie [counselors] got candy Wednesday because they were on hand when it arrived for a camper who was keeping candy rules.

But in 1938 the picture changed, and a gossip columnist wrote:

Is it true that . . . A box of candy received through the mails for a camper was really confiscated in accordance with the new ruling?

The "new ruling" was not spelled out in the newspaper, but since "no candy" was not a source of optional points the next year, 1939, it can be assumed that in 1938 eating candy at Waldemar, except that which was camp supplied, was "breaking candy rules." Obviously, it was not mandatory that a camper abstain from candy, but "keeping candy rules" was a source of points toward the tribal plaque.

Surprisingly, "no chewing gum for six weeks" still earned 15 optional points. An editor's note read: "Keeping the gum rule helps keep the hill clean of gum wrappers." The proper disposal of "chewed gum" was not mentioned.

Here and There in 1938: A dark room for developing film was provided for photography classes . . . Tribal "little sisters" were first mentioned in print in 1938 when "each Comanche old girl lighted a candle for her new girl Little Sister" . . . Doris' wardrobe was admired editorially . . . On their hill the Tejas participated in a "wish ceremony" in which they filed past their fire and placed on it a written wish . . . and the following story proved two things: first, the flag, now in its place in the center of camp, was not lowered until after dinner and second, Waldemar's director was a good sport:

D.J.'s p.j.'s
Reward: For information leading to the capture and arrest (dead or alive) of the scoundrel, outlaws, rascals, who strung the director's pajamas up on the flagpole under the stars and stripes during dinner Wednesday night. Communicate with D.J., station H-U-N-T, Search, Texas. (Comanche editor's note: And they were Purple, too!)

1939

Architect Harvey P. Smith, Contractor Ferdinand Rehbeger, and Doris of the Magic Wand have joined hands this winter to produce a miracle change in the way of kampongs, two new buildings that will fairly take your breath when you arrive in camp. They are native stone buildings erected on the sites of Kampongs 11 and 12.

So wrote the editor of the *Christmas War Whoop*, dated December 22, 1938, of the new Swiss Chalet and Ranch House which were to house five groups of campers. Photographs were not yet available, but the architect's drawings were reproduced in the paper and the completed buildings were faithful to them.

The entire junior department can now be housed in rock kampongs since these new buildings, plus the French Chateau, which was built last year, and the doll house will accommodate approximately 60 juniors.

The buildings were already named "Swiss Chalet" and "Ranch House" in keeping with their architectural styles. Swiss Chalet was the first to get under way.

It contains two separate bunk rooms to accommodate two kampong groups (in other words, it's a double) and in each there is a large stone fireplace, attractive built-in dressing tables and nick-nack *[sic]* corners, and private adjoining bath facilities. From the upper bunk room—for they are on different floor levels—is a circular stairway in a tower leading to the bath which is on the level with the rest of the building. . . .

The second new building is designed after the typical American ranch house and contains three bunk rooms with private bath for each.

This issue of the newspaper does not mention Swiss Chalet's most enchanting feature, the decorative brightly painted woodwork which sets it apart and makes it a fairy land from out of the Swiss Alps.

The spring issue of the 1939 *War Whoop* added late information about Ranch House. The headline proclaimed: "COWBOY JACK MODELS FOR ARTIST PAINTING MURALS IN RANCH HOUSE."

Imagine Cowboy Jack [Reeves] being an artist's model! That's exactly what happened this spring, and although the artist said he was a good model, Jack said it was the hardest work he ever did. He was posing for Herbert Barnard of San Antonio who painted murals above the fireplaces in the new Ranch House.

Juniors in that new building this summer will live ever in the presence of the real western atmosphere portrayed through these murals which are the outstanding features of the three rooms. In one room there is a calf-roping scene, and the cowboy has just finished tying the struggling calf's legs together. Tommie's [Espy Williams] horse, Pumpkin, did the posing for this, but he will be turned into a paint in order to show up better on the white wall.

In another room the mural shows the picturesque chuck wagon scene with the cowboys busy around the campfire. Here's where Jack did his stuff, and we daresay you'll recognize him this summer holding out his plate for more beans.

The third room shows a cowboy on a bucking horse, and the only reason Jack didn't pose for this picture was because he and Pumpkin couldn't "hold it" long enough. The artist, however, has depicted the real bronc riding action which we have seen so often in the rodeos.

Barnard is an artist from a long line of artists, father and grandfather before him. For some years he has been located in San Antonio, although he began his career doing art work for theatres in the East. He draws and paints with a very realistic style, and it was fortunate for Waldemar that he was able to visualize exactly what was needed to make the ranch house complete.

During the years since 1939 the interior walls of Ranch House have been painted many times, with the painter carefully avoiding the western scenes. Some flaking of paint had occurred, and in 1986, Marsha asked Barbara Tyson, long-time counselor and artist on the Waldemar staff, to retouch the colorful murals and restore them to their original freshness. Barbara researched the kind of paints the artist might have used in 1939, and under her talented hand and eye, Mr. Barnard's western scenes live again.

In the same Christmas issue of the *War Whoop* which described the new junior kampongs, Doris asked for suggestions for a new name for "the doll house." She explained that some young campers did not like to be known as "dolls" and would prefer to be thought of and treated as members of the junior group. Thus on June 18, 1939, the *Waldemar War Whoop* announced that the dolls were now promoted to low juniors, that they had assumed kampong duties, and that they were living in "Happy Haven." The name change was difficult to master, but "Happy Haven" eventually caught on. However, it was a much longer time before the occupants of Happy Haven ceased to be known as "dolls."

Other improvements listed in the *War Whoop* of June 11, 1939, included "a canoe pier and three new rafts for the waterfront," and "a terrace adjoining the dining room for refreshment period." It may have been an uncovered terrace at first but it was quickly covered. Harvey Smith designed an attractive screened porch with stone pillars compatible with those of the Dining Hall, and it became "the Junior Dining Room Porch." Nourishment was served here for many years, with waiters or waitresses delaying the setting of the porch tables until after nourishment was served.

The room held four tables, each seating ten, thus allowing Waldemar to accommodate more girls.

And the indefatigable Doris Johnson wanted just that—more girls—and she and her representatives were getting them.

Approximately 225 campers are at Waldemar this term with 40 percent of them having attended Camp Waldemar before. . . .

For 14 years this "Shangri La" situated 17 miles from Kerrville has been an ideal vacation spot for girls, and Miss Doris Johnson, director and niece of the founder, Ora Johnson, continues to improve and expand the camp each year. . . .

North Texas, with Wichita Falls as a center, sends a record crowd of 27 campers this year. [Wichita Falls had also been first in number of campers first term of the previous year.]

The interest in Waldemar among West Texans in

the late 1930s was not just happenstance. Waldemar had strong followings throughout the South, in Oklahoma, and in most areas of Texas, the result of the work of enthusiastic, socially prominent, and well-respected representatives, and although there were some girls from the western part of the state of Texas who were campers, Doris felt that Waldemar could be more popular west of Wichita Falls if she worked at it.

So she appointed a "field representative," Mrs. Talbot Williams of Tyler, to "open up" West Texas. Mrs. Williams was well known in musical circles throughout the state as chairman of "Student Groups of the Texas Federation of Music Clubs" and her work with those groups took her to West Texas:

> Mrs. Talbot Williams, field representative of Waldemar in West Texas, has returned to her home in Tyler after a brief visit in camp. . . . She will return to camp in a few weeks to plan a picnic for the West Texas girls.

The Wichita Falls representative, dynamic wife of one of the city's leading physicians, was on hand often to take her girls on a fried chicken picnic, and she saw to it that the parents of her girls got proper recognition in the *War Whoop* when they brought their daughters to camp.

Doris' springtime was taken up with parties given in her honor by "Waldemar Clubs" in the various cities and at which she showed the Waldemar movie. Counselor-representatives who were geographically close enough (Frances McCluskey of Waco and Ann Miller of Austin) brought campers and prospective campers to Waldemar for a day of horseback riding, canoeing, and ping-pong playing, a day climaxed by a hearty picnic.

The introduction of motion pictures two nights a week into the camp schedule meant that instead of counselors scrambling for ways to entertain the girls during evening program time, Margaret Savage was scrambling for places on the calendar to put programs that were long-time camp favorites.

"Charm," under the guise of "Posture, Poise and Personality," was added to the Waldemar offerings when Doris was able to obtain the services of Mrs. Virginia Roser, a drama teacher at Kincaid School in Houston, whose resumé included work in radio, in motion pictures, and on the professional stage. It was with good nature that the campers referred to her popular charm class as "poison personality."

A new nature study class was described in the *War Whoop* of June 11, 1939:

> In addition to one daily class, the activities will be extra-curricular in form, and five points will be given toward the all-star award for participation in each trip. These activities will include short hikes and overnight trips for the purpose of experimenting with and observing various forms of the outdoor life of this section.

The nature counselor (sometimes accompanied by Ellen Easley, life-long nature enthusiast) took the girls enrolled in her classes on overnights or on canoe trips up the river, and a "Nature Cabin," located three miles from camp, was popular with overnighters who left camp "carrying knapsacks and field books."

"Picnics, Overnight Rides and Nature Trips" was the heading for a full page of news about out-of-camp excursions to the various "picnic grounds" which Waldemar had acquired. They were variously labeled by reporters as "old," "new," "first," "second," or "camp" picnic grounds. The "Smith Place," about five miles distant, was popular, and Honey Creek was a favorite location for overnight horseback rides. The excursions required careful scheduling to keep the horseback riders from trampling the nature lovers. Steak and watermelon were popular menu items.

Trips to San Antonio and to Monterrey were still well patronized by the girls. Sixty campers spent four days, June 27-30, on a Monterrey trip and still participated in the glorious Fourth of July celebration at Waldemar.

> . . . . It will be colorful and eventful as it will be a joint Field Day and Horse Show. Activities will begin the night before with a swimming and canoeing exhibition followed by a brilliant display of fireworks along the banks of the river.
>
> The Horse Show will begin with a grand entry followed by various horseback contests and the quadrille. . . .

A "swimming exhibition" was presented the night before the Field Day and Horse Show.

> It will be witnessed from the pier and will show the skill of swimmers as they rhythmically go through various formations to music furnished by the camp orchestra.
>
> Fifty-five Tadpoles with balloons on their arms will form a human "WELCOME" in the water.
>
> Juniors will go through elaborate formations using flutter boards.
>
> Using a side stroke the Frogs will swim in a huge butterfly formation.
>
> Rivaling Billy Rose's Aquacade, the Fish with tiny light bulbs on their fingers, arms, and head will go through a number of interesting formations including: the double swim, double porpoise, the wheel and circle, barrel roll and the new Waldemar stroke which is

a combination of a crawl and side stroke. A comic surprise awaits the onlookers which is to be something in the Gay Nineties' spirit.

A grand finale will include a display of the American flag and swimmers spelling out Comanche and Tejas. Fireworks across the river will flare for a final good night signal to Minnie Maude's big show.

"Minnie Maude" was popular, hard-working, gregarious Minnie Maude Harlow, originally from Texas City and then from Houston (where she taught), who had joined the Waldemar waterfront staff in 1936. In 1939 she became head of that department and continued to "run the waterfront" for several years. "Min" also made a big contribution to camp by serving the Tejas tribe as sponsor for several terms.

The Tejas tribe's most treasured and lasting traditions were born first term of 1939, although it wasn't until early in the second term that they were described in the *War Whoop* dated July 23, 1939:

The new shrine, built of rocks to house the relics of the tribe, contains behind a glass door the Tejas will bequeathing the hill and all tribal tradition to successive members; the peace pipe, from which each Tejas removed a leather tag for a last term member, and a candle, lighted in dedication to all Tejas not present. Each week a girl will be chosen to light the candle who has done, without outside suggestion or hope of reward, some unselfish service of outstanding merit. . . . Each Tejas will, at the end of the term, place her own tag on the peace pipe, to be preserved in the shrine for years to come.

Tribesmen will remember this night as the beginning of an influence which will make them deeper and finer long after Thursday campfires burn no more.

Another tradition was established at Christmastime in 1939:

. . . at the final campfire on Tejas Hill Doris lighted the original "Memory Candle" in the shrine, and each girl took her light from it, with a pledge to burn her candle again on Christmas Eve to renew the friendships formed in the Tejas Circle.

At the appointed time the candle again burned brightly on Tejas Hill, surrounded only by the far off whispered loyalty to all the Tejas hearts. Thus, a tradition was born.

In 1932 the first-term tradition of each tribe's entertaining the other at theme dance had been born, and time, money, and effort were not spared in trying to make "our dance" the best, the most fun, the most original, and most glamorous of all time.

The affair began as a tribute to their friendly rivals, but it was impossible for a competitiveness not to surface, and tribal sponsors were harried and exhausted after days of preparation.

Members of the arts and crafts department found themselves designing decorations and favors and making them during class time—and then until the wee hours. Their efforts were appreciated by the girls, and seldom did an issue of the camp newspaper appear that Lalla Lay, "the whittler," did not come in for praise for her originality, her craftsmanship, and her willingness. Lalla had come to Waldemar from Austin in the second term of 1935, and she stayed through 1939 strengthening the arts and crafts department and enlivening camp with her inimitable personality.

In the spring issue of the 1939 *War Whoop*, a story under the heading "Brewing" appeared, warning the girls of things to come:

There's something brewing in the air, and it has to do with Tejas and Comanche dances. There's a rumor going around this year that the warriors and chieftains will lay down their war drums and tomahawks and come together in one big pow-wow at Waldemar, an occasion on which colorful costumes and decorations will outdo anything ever before seen on the tennis court.

This is only a rumor, of course, but some rather convincing arguments have been coming forth from the tepees of some of the leaders. Big Chief Crockett [Ann Miller], for instance, mutters words like these: "Dances interest few . . . Lalla [Lay] and sponsors do all work . . . one dance and heap big costumes would be swell."

Over in a Tejas tepee squats Squaw Stengl [Sunny] grunting short syllables, "Ugh . . . let brown-faced campers do the work . . . turn young warriors loose with own ideas . . . one big dance, matters no . . . maybe so, maybe no. . . . campers should have their say so."

Tejas Min [Harlow] she nod head and say she for it, too, one big dance where Tejas and Comanches join the hands while pale face musicians beat tom-toms.

Squaw Everett [Libby Lou] claps hands and nods, "Yah, yah . . . one big dance she make my warriors stop their nagging with their friends . . . she make my warriors be real friends with yonder tribe, the Tejas . . . and one big dance, she give me more sleep."

The wisdom of the sponsors prevailed and a joint dance was the result. The theme was patterned after the New York World's Fair of that year with its "trylon and perisphere."

In 1940 an imaginary voyage to the Hawaiian Islands began with dinner aboard "the Good Ship Waldemar," the Dining Hall, and after dinner, the tribesmen were escorted down the gang plank and taken to the entertainment the natives had planned in their honor (at the tennis courts). Second term, the theme was "Playmates," and the party was held in the new playhouse.

In 1941 the money that would have been spent on decorations was given instead to "Bundles for Britain," and all Waldemar girls proudly signed the letter which accompanied the $25 donation. The Playhouse was inexpensively decorated with Waldemar-owned flags and bunting, and the girls wore red, white, and blue. By 1942 tribal dances were gone from the camp calendar.

A former camper and counselor who became a Waldemar institution was back in 1939 as an "honorary counselor," the first and perhaps the only one to achieve that title. In 1926 one of Miss Ora's campers was her niece Laura Jean Johnson, Doris' cousin, and although she could not be at camp every summer, she visited often and had close ties with her Aunt Ora and later with Doris. Her impersonations, her gift for clowning, and her penchant for devising outlandish costumes made her a welcome visitor and evoked this feature story in 1939:

> Don't look now, but under that derby hat and moldy hay and behind those missing teeth is Laura Jean Johnson, not the father but the cousin of Doris (both of them have equal right to be proud) who is in Waldemar as honorary counselor, and chief mingler and cheerer-upper this term. Laura Jean puts everybody in good spirits the minute she appears with some dopey act, complimentary conversation, or quaint observation on camp life.
>
> With a TSCW [now TWU] college education to live down, she is also an experienced comptometer operator and secretary, and ranks with professionals in her knowledge of photography. Besides that, she never has to be told a person's name twice; and she can tell you more about what's happening in camp than the *War Whoop*. Welcome home, Laura Jean.

Laura Jean later worked for IBM for many years and often spent her vacation time helping Doris and Ellen get ready for the opening of camp each summer. Since 1979 she has stayed at camp all summer. Marsha has depended on her for pre-opening help, and she has stayed both terms each summer as a valuable assistant. One of her principal tasks has been "kampong inspector," and she is loved by the campers.

Posing for publicity pictures had long since ceased to thrill busy Waldemar girls, but on July 1, 1939, an opportunity arose which was exciting to those invited to participate and fun for those who watched.

"Newsreels," a short moving picture digest of events of the time, and a forerunner of television news, were shown in theaters before the scheduled film, and they oftentimes included a "feature story" in addition to the regular news. The headline read:

UNIVERSAL NEWS CAMERAMAN
"STRIKES A WALDEMAR SET"
FEATURING DIVING, TRICK ROPING,
WATER ARCHERY

Graham McNamee to Supply Narration for Pictures of Number One United States Girls Camp, Which Will Be Shown over the World Before 30 Million People

Activities at Waldemar became international news as Jimmie Lederer, cameraman of Universal Newsreel, made action shots at the waterfront, flash shots at the entrance to the camp, and various views of the entire camp yesterday. There is a possibility that the pictures may also be shown by Paramount News and March of Time.

Feature shots were of a dive through three twirling ropes from a specially constructed diving board which seemed to extend from the spreading branches of a giant cypress tree across the river.

Lederer filmed a new game of water archery in which girls standing in canoes shot arrows at a target in the middle of the river. The spills and thrills of this stunt were as exciting to girls in camp as they will be to millions of theatergoers all over the world.

The Hollywood cameraman pictured Camp Waldemar as a village inhabited by 250 lovely girls who are governed by an adored mayor, Doris Johnson. Lederer characterizes Doris as being, "a demure little damsel who has the law on one side of her face and a smile of contentment on the other."

Lederer states, "If Graham McNamee doesn't have something good to say about this camp, we will send a gang of these Waldemar girls to Universal Studios in Hollywood and 'strike a set' there."

Whether Universal Studios distributed Mr. Lederer's Guadalupe masterpiece to theaters "over the world" is not known, but the memories were in the making of it. The questionable use by the headline writer of the drama term "to strike a set" added to the fun.

In August of 1928, Miss Ora Johnson had announced in her first issue of the *Waldemar War Whoop* that after her dismissal from San Antonio schools she had conceived "the unique idea of opening a camp for adults after the close of the present camping season." If the experiment proved successful, she planned to make the adult camp a permanent feature of Waldemar.

Obviously, the experiment did not prove enormously successful since no more was written about it until ten years later, when in 1939 Doris, becoming prouder each year of Waldemar's buildings and facilities for recreation, decided to try a "September Camp."

For several years people acquainted with Waldemar have been requesting a post-summer camp for families and selected groups. This year Doris Johnson, Waldemar's Director, is offering such a camp from Aug. 28 to Oct. 15.

The "September Camp" is open to any desirable person, family or party. The rate is $4.50 per day, an all-inclusive fee. Special rates will be given to parties of four or more people who remain for more than a week.

The Christmas issue of the camp newspaper reported:

The Adult Camp made ardent horseback riders out of the numerous guests with two or three rides a day, showed them the thrills of swimming in the Guadalupe . . . and took them in the blue bus to dances at Mountain Home. Best of all, the adult campers went by horseback and station wagon to a chicken barbecue up the river.

The venture led to the establishment of the Waldemar Guest Ranch, which flourished from the winter of 1939 to 1952. At first the season was advertised as being from October to May, but soon brochures modified those dates to read "from December 1 until April 1." Later the season was shortened to January, February, and March.

Tables and benches were removed from the senior dining room and sofas, easy chairs, card tables, a ping-pong table, and a pool table transformed the room, with its large fireplaces, into an attractive lounge. The Pioneer Room became the guest ranch office. Meals were served in the junior dining room. Rock kampongs were stripped of all but two lower bunks, curtains were hung at the windows, loveseat-type sofas were moved in, rugs were scattered here and there, and Ferdinand Rehbeger, a favorite card partner of the guests, quietly appeared each morning to light fires in the fireplaces. The rooms above the dining hall were also much in demand.

The guest list was never lengthy at one time, which was the way the devoted clientele wanted it, many guests confessing that they didn't want to tell too many people about the great vacation spot they had found. If it can be said there was a drawback to the Guest Ranch operation, it would have to be the weather at Waldemar during January and February, which was unreliable.

The increasing need to devote her time and energy to the burgeoning girls' camp caused Doris to discontinue the guest ranch activity at the end of the 1952 season with reluctance and regret.

Insurance men's conventions had been coming to Waldemar immediately after camp closed since 1932, and they were scheduled early so that U. S. and Lucille Smith could stay over and prepare "those good Waldemar meals." Later, there were other groups who enjoyed Waldemar and its facilities, including social workers and doctors. Doris discontinued conventions in 1952 in order that she and Ellen could travel during the off-season.

Chapter 3

1940s

1940

It can be argued that Waldemar's fifteenth season, the summer of 1940, was not really the beginning of the decade of the "war-torn forties," but rather the exciting end of Waldemar's formative years which had begun so positively under Ora Johnson's inspired hand in 1926. The summer was Janus-like in that looking back on Waldemar's history and phenomenal progress was almost as satisfying to campers and counselors as looking ahead to its future challenges. Camp was old enough that many counselors could reminisce about "the good ole days," and a strong sense of history pervaded the pages of the *Waldemar War Whoop.*

Certainly a strong sense of optimism for the future was present in the columns of the newspaper. A headline announced that over fifty campers were turned away first term "in order that the enrollment for this term might not become too large to keep every girl from receiving individual attention," and a capacity enrollment was announced for second term.

In keeping with Doris' plan to replace Waldemar's wooden kampongs with attractive rock buildings, "Bella Vista" (Spanish for "beautiful view") and "Skyline" were ready for occupancy in 1940.

Bella Vista, clinging to the hillside just north of Cactus Lodge (Waldemar Lodge), was inspired by the houses of Taxco, Mexico, and its three units, each on a different level and linked by uniquely designed balcony-like porches and stairways, were romantically beautiful. The imagination of Harvey Smith and the skill of Ferdinand Rehbeger were epitomized in this building. Large colorful Mexican plates and handsome, big, almost-flat bowls were set into the walls for unusual decoration, and brightly colored inlaid tiles

of serape design were laid into the floors in front of each door.

Skyline, a two-unit building with a common porch area, was aptly named because for many years it was the highest of Waldemar's rock kampongs, the only one "across the road" which meanders up the Waldemar hill. Its elevation and its "exclusiveness" added to its charm.

Almost as enriching as these two new buildings was the transformation of the old volleyball court, often unesthetically called "the concrete slab," into the "Playhouse." A huge metal frame was installed and covered with a large canvas canopy edged with colorful scallops. From the June 9, 1940, issue of the *Waldemar War Whoop:*

> . . . and this will be used for dancing and games. Tribal dances and weekly dances are being planned for this spot. The floor is being made very slick in order to make dancing more enjoyable . . . A small hedge is to be planted around the entire playhouse, and colored lights will be used for decorating. Those not desiring to dance will be able to play any sort of game on the field and at the same time enjoy the music of the orchestra. This has been one of the most popular places around camp since this term began.

The "slab" held nostalgic memories for old-timers. It was upon its surface that Rex Beach had written the words "Don't Land—All OK at Waldemar" for scouting airplanes to see during the flood of 1932, and it was less than three weeks thereafter that the famous Simmons Cowboy Band had climaxed its parade around the Athletic Field by assembling on the "slab" and playing a stirring "The Eyes of Texas." The "small hedge" was never planted around the Playhouse, for obvious reasons.

Doris' enthusiasm for music and musicians

matched her aunt's. The first issue of each term's newspaper inevitably carried a front-page story about the Waldemar orchestra, with biographies of each performer and kudos for her musicianship. Everyone in camp appreciated the girls' willingness to play or to sing or otherwise perform when asked, and these entertainers held a special place in the hearts of Waldemar campers. Emmie Craddock, she of the unforgettable "taps," who came to Waldemar in 1934, had succeeded Cobby de Stivers as the director of the orchestra. Ruth Wright (later Green), saxophonist and vocalist, and Mary Edna Norris, pianist extraordinaire, were long-time members of Emmie's orchestra, and campers in the dining room stopped eating to listen to Mary Edna's sophisticated piano work or to beg Ruth to sing "Playmates." These talented performers were also valuable to Waldemar as long-time tribal sponsors and vesper authors.

Libby Lou Everett, former camper from Houston and later *War Whoop* editor and tribal sponsor, wrote of Emmie: "As a trumpeter, she can hit more notes per second than the hills have rocks." A *War Whoop* reader of that era could well have remarked that humorous lines and quips, strung together descriptively, flowed from Libby Lou's typewriter like notes from Emmie's trumpet. A typical "Libby Lou" two-line "filler" in the *War Whoop* of August 4, 1940, delighted "kampong housekeepers":

We're broom-mates, we is. We sweeps together. Dust us two.

Libby Lou's 1940 paean to Billie Johnson attests to Billie's unselfish contribution to Waldemar and to Libby Lou's writing talent.

ORCHIDS TO . . .
Billie Johnson

Whose broad shoulders have proved big enough to carry either some camper's heavy trunk or the weighty title of Purchasing Agent for Camp Waldemar. Billie pilots a big red truck into town every morning and returns laden with store supplies, lost laundry, a pair of bathing-shoes-size-7-for-the-doll-with-athlete's-foot, ice for the siesta pitchers, hay for the horses and cereal for the campers, party favors, and most anything else that somebody's mama forgot to pack in somebody's trunk.

He pokes around in vegetable counters and fruit stands, demanding the best foods, he stands in line for hours mailing your slack suit home to be altered since you gained, and he never growls about it. Not Billie.

A stocky figure ambling between the office and the kitchen for orders, driving up the hill in a rattling station wagon followed by a dusty but devoted pup, playing chauffeur and chief entertainer to carloads of spring-breaking campers on town trips, picnics or church . . . ever with a jolly greeting and a helpful hand—that's Billie. And though he may not like orchids, exactly, it's our way of telling him "Thanks."

Billie Johnson was never too tired or too busy to drive a busload of campers to a picnic (or to Carlsbad Cavern for that matter), to build a campfire, or do whatever needed to be done to effect a smooth-running and happy camp. His willing spirit, his good humor, his smile, his devotion to duty and his dedication to Waldemar make him a shining star in the Waldemar story.

In 1939, Naomi McClendon, a nurse from Hamilton, Texas, joined the Waldemar staff, and in 1940 Billie and "Mac" were married.

Even though Waldemar had seemed just about perfect at the beginning of its fifteenth summer, its program continued to expand and evolve. The camp newspaper of July 7, 1940, displayed a banner headline proclaiming an upcoming event that thrilled and excited the campers: Waldemar girls were to be hostesses to the boys of Camp Stewart at a dance!

DANCES TO BE HELD AT TENNIS COURT

Waldemar for the first time in its history is going to play hostess to Camp Stewart. On both Tuesday and Wednesday nights the boys from Camp Stewart will be guests of the Waldemar girls for a big party. Dancing with Emmie's orchestra will be the featured entertainment of both evenings. On Tuesday night the Seniors will be entertained and the Juniors will have the dance floor all to themselves on Wednesday night.

With all the plans that are being made for both of these parties it is certain that both will be gala affairs. Informality is the keynote to be stressed and the girls are to wear their smartest slack suits or their "snappiest" looking shorts. Dresses will be "taboo" for these occasions. The floor show is to be furnished by both camps. The Waldemar dance department is working up our part of the floor shows and we are all anxious to know what the Stewart boys are going to do.

Bertha Lacey is going to be the mistress of ceremonies for the parties. She will give the instructions for the folk dances, as American folk dances will be featured that night. There will be couple dances, Cinderella dances, Lucky Number dances and a Lemon Tag dance. These will all help keep the crowd mixed so you can each one be assured that you will dance with everyone of the Stewart lads. Dancing, eating and playing will continue from eight to ten.

So from here on it will be up to Waldemar girls to show that they are the perfect hostesses in order that we may have more of these entertainments. The song need no longer be "and when I get to Stewart, I don't want no more . . . " for we are going to have Stewart here at Waldemar! So press your slack suits, gals, and curl your hair for Tuesday and Wednesday are going to be your big nights.

The success of this first Stewart dance was virtually assured with Bertha Lacey acting as mistress of ceremonies and Emmie's orchestra exhibiting its musicianship and showmanship. Lacey's talent for organizing mixers was recognized by Waldemarites, Corpus Christi socialites, and patrons of the *Ile de France.*

The Stewart Dance has continued to be a social highlight of the camp term. When older boys lost interest in going to summer camp, the senior girls were divided, and half went on one night and the rest on another. It was finally decided that Waldemar's "intermediates" (seventh graders) should be the oldest girls to participate, and they defied the 1940 rules by bringing their best dresses to wear to the heralded Stewart Dance.

Proof that it was no longer necessary for Waldemar to offer as many enticements for girls to become campers as it had in the early years was apparent in a story appearing in the July 7 issue of the *War Whoop,* with this headline:

FEWER AWARDS TO BE GIVEN CAMPERS
FOR ACHIEVEMENTS
New Policy to Take Effect This Term

Waldemar's silver loving cups, whose number had grown by 1940 to "about 50" through the generosity of patrons and business friends, had become a burden to the administration and the cups had lost some of their charm through sheer numbers. The winner of a cup took it home for the winter, had her name engraved thereon, and brought it back to be awarded again. If the same girl won the cup three times, she "retired" it—that is, it became hers. But if a one- or two-time winner was not returning to camp, it was oftentimes difficult and frustrating to try to get the cup back. In addition, the gradual separation of the two terms made it necessary to have two separate sets of cups.

Finding a place to display the collection during the summer was difficult, too, with the Pioneer Room usually being the setting of choice. The cups were of varying sizes and shapes and made an effective focal point on the tennis court at the Final Banquet, where they were displayed on a large, three-tiered, sheet-covered stand that resembled an oversized birthday cake. This display stood conveniently behind the table of counselors who were to make the awards. Long tables radiated like spokes from one side of this "loving cup hub."

The cups, which were soon to disappear completely from the Waldemar awards system, were not all discontinued in 1940, but their number was greatly decreased.

Waldemar's riflery department had been affiliated with the National Rifle Association since 1933, and NRA medals were now given to attest to each camper's skill and individual progress. The archery department became affiliated with the National Camp Archery Association during the second term of 1940, and their pins were awarded campers who qualified.

The year 1940 marked the first time "regulation horseshow ribbons such as are given in large horse shows over the country" were awarded at Waldemar.

The Waldemar waterfront had been associated with the American Red Cross since the camp's founding. In 1940 progress in swimming "will be rewarded by the American Red Cross swimming certificates and by Life-Saving pins and emblems. These awards will be presented at breakfast on the morning of the Final Banquet in 1940." (In earlier years, they had been presented at the "Swimmer's Banquet" or between acts of drama productions!)

With the reduction of the number of Waldemar's cups and medals, the winning of them became a prestigious achievement, and it has remained so throughout the years.

The girls of 1940 thoroughly approved of the awards changes, but they did not approve one change that the administration had thought would please them:

First year campers gaining their all stars will be given bronze pins bearing the Waldemar seal instead of the Waldemar felt W and star.

Now what could one do with a bronze pin? The sporty felt and chenille W in a tribal color, which identified a girl as a Waldemar camper, could adorn a shirt or a sweater and the felt star could be worn with pride somewhere near it. So very soon, Doris went back to Aunt Ora's original award.

Almost from the first, Waldemar's swimmers were evaluated at the first of camp and classified as pool swimmers, tadpoles, frogs, or fish. Later the Flying Fish classification was added and achieving that high mark was so difficult that few girls made it.

Qualifications to take the half-day test included being a Red Cross Life Saver and performing all Waldemar strokes, including the surface dive, to the satisfaction of the strict examiners. Ordinarily no more than a half dozen girls were recognized at the awards program as being Flying Fish.

The Best All-Round Tejas award, begun in 1934, and the Best All-Round Comanche award, which followed in 1936, had proved so popular that the Best All-Round Senior, Low Senior, and Junior awards had been discontinued after the 1938 season. In the early days, these coveted honors had been selected by popular vote of all campers and counselors, but now it was agreed that camp was becoming so large that a fair selection was difficult. Also discontinued after the 1938 season were "high point" awards which rewarded girls whose individual record cards were enhanced by keeping Waldemar's rules, even optional ones, and making an inappropriately large number of service points.

But the Spirit of Waldemar award, begun only eight years earlier, continued to grow in prestige, and its edifying influence enveloped and warmed the hearts of Waldemar girls, whose understanding of beauty of character, of fair play, and of loyalty was confirmed and strengthened by the intangible Spirit of Waldemar.

"Monkey drill" was first introduced at Waldemar's second term of 1940, and the ten girls who learned to charge around the Athletic Field standing up on horseback were the idols of campers young and old. Emmie's orchestra furnished the music and the daredevils, wearing gaily striped boys' pajamas, entertained campers and guests at the closing horse-show. Marilou "Moey" Rutledge rode "Roman" with "each foot planted on a separate horse."

These accomplished riders who performed in Waldemar's first monkey drill were Marilou "Moey" Rutledge, Angilee Davis, Carol Liebman, Dot Hilker, Anne Gentry, Gay Noe, Mary Kathryn Castle, Elizabeth Gates, Midge O'Brien, and Jane Bingman.

Second-term campers of 1940 were understandably jealous and disappointed when they discovered that first-term girls had entertained the boys of Camp Stewart at a dance and there was no such affair scheduled for second-term campers. But being at Waldemar on August 9, 1940, more than made up for missing out on the "Stewart men."

It was the custom for the director's birthday to be celebrated in the dining room each August 9 with everyone sharing in the birthday cake which Lucille Smith took joy in baking. Because the camp's birthday was a momentous one, the fifteenth in 1940, the two occasions were combined and close counselor friends of Doris provided comic historical notes as they lighted candles on a giant birthday cake to be shared by all.

At the end of this fifteenth camping season, the birthday party was a time for Janus, whose face had been forward-looking all summer, to look backward over those fifteen years and cause campers and counselors to spend a hilarious evening reveling in happy nostalgia.

From Libby Lou Everett's *War Whoop* of August 11, two days after the party:

SOCIETY ITEM: Miss Doris Johnson entertained Friday night with a birthday party honoring her daughter, Waldemar, who was 15 years old this summer. The occasion was also the "21st" anniversary of the hostess.

Pink and blue paper caps, birthday napkins, and souvenir programs recounting the history of Waldemar marked each cover. The main feature of the banquet menu was the speckled trout broiled whole and served complete with head and tail and olive eye.

After a clever program, the huge four-tiered cake, lighted by 15 multi-colored candles, was cut by the hostess and served with ice cream.

. . . . The honoree was enthroned with a lap-full of bluebells in the Pioneer Room, where the entire Johnson family posed for toothpaste portraits before the meal. Both Doris and Brother Billie were charmingly gowned in blue.

In celebration of Waldemar's anniversary, Mrs. Wolkewitz had prepared a printed program and she introduced counselors and others associated with Waldemar who have been connected with the camp over a period of 10 years or more. A candle for each year of Waldemar's growth was lighted as these told in rhyme some event in the camp's history or some detail (uncensored) of the director's life. While campers hung on every word, the director herself spent quite a squirmy evening. The toasts, printed elsewhere in this issue, may tell the reason. . . .

OLD-TIMERS ENLIGHTEN
CAMPERS WITH RECOLLECTIONS
OF WALDEMAR, D.J. IN 1926

These notable events, dusted off from the attic of Doris's and Waldemar's past and presented in verse by Emmie Craddock, were remembered as candles celebrating Waldemar's fifteenth anniversary were lighted by Billie Johnson, Ann Crockett, Laura Wallace, Carmen Crain, Margaret Savage, Flossie Mai Fullinwider, Libby Lou Everett, Frances McCluskey, Laura Jean Johnson, Geane Brogniez [mother of Geane Brogniez the camper], Jack Reeves, Mrs. Burdah Adams, Dolly Downes, Ferdinand Rehbeger, and Mrs. Gannon.

Doris probably won't recall the year that she was
    born in,
Because for quite some time now, her birthdays
    she's been scorning;
But people over Mt. Pleasant way have not forgot
    the day
For whistles blew, and horses neighed when the
    stork flew over that day.

The stork brought a lovely bundle—all wrapped in
    baby clothes
And conducted her first interview and photo-
    graphed a pose.
And when he asked the cute little trick why she was
    always ravin',
"Why," she replied, "I'm practicing up to live in
    Happy Haven."

Now, Doris grew and grew and grew, into a
    mischievous lass
And so Aunt Ora brought her to camp—to cure her
    of her sass.
But Doris had her own ideas of how to act out here,
And soon Aunt Ora was asking all if her brains
    would ever appear.

In the year of 1929, D. J. gave out the mail
And she was very popular handing letters out over
    the rail,
And later on she kept the store and was a huge
    success
Her hours were quite indefinite, but she liked it
    none the less.

In the year of 1930, the dining hall burned down
And the buckets from the johnnies helped to bring
    the water round.
Although they did not save the building, they did
    not miss a meal
They just built some extra tables and ate out in the
    field.

D. J. ain't no hick; that gal has been around,
She went with Johnson's rodeo, to New York and
    other towns.
She rode in the grand parade and rode a bronc or
    two
And showed those city boys some things they
    couldn't do.

Now girls, one night we were having a dance, so to
    Stewart goes our Dolly
To borrow one of Bill James' goats, to make the
    night more jolly.
She dressed him up in Doris's clothes and placed
    him in her shower.

He ate the soap and chewed the towels and was sick
    for many an hour.

I give a toast to the outdoor girl, champion of them
    all;
She rides and swims and roller skates and never
    takes a fall.
She's good at ping-pong, liverpool, and paddles a
    mean canoe,
Her life has only just begun; wait 'til she's twenty-
    two.

More doggerel, most about Doris and her youthful antics, enlivened the evening. Those who knew Doris Johnson well knew her to be a "super good sport," and indeed she accepted the hilarity of the disclosures about her "escapades" with grace and good humor. But perhaps the incongruity of her birthday's being celebrated with Waldemar's and the inappropriateness of her life's story being told at all struck her as lacking taste and compromising the dignity a director of Camp Waldemar should project.

Although Lucille continued to bake a cake for Doris' birthday, this was the last time that such a party was held. Doris' birthday was never completely ignored, as she wished it would be, but it was never again so roundly celebrated.

FASHION

Miss Ora Johnson heard only one complaint about summer camping from her patrons: suitable camp togs for their daughters were not available at any store at any price.

She attempted to rectify this situation in 1928 by appointing Wolff & Marx Company of San Antonio "official outfitters." Patrons were directed to get order and measurement blanks from "Miss Josephine Gastringer of that establishment who will personally supervise all camp mail orders."

Either this system didn't work out too well or the resourceful Miss Johnson felt that she now had time to supervise the apparel business herself because in the catalog promoting the 1929 season she announced she was going to sell camp clothes at the Waldemar store, then located in the office.

The suggested list of items needed and available from the camp store was listed in the catalog, but Miss Johnson was careful to make it clear that it was not necessary that these items be bought at Waldemar, that she was simply making them available if the patron wished to buy them from Waldemar, and that Waldemar had no uniform.

   5 pairs of knickers—2 colored, 3 white
   5 shirts or middy blouses—2 colored, 3 white
   1 pair black bloomers, 1 pair black zips
   1 wool bathing suit (orange or purple according to
        tribe assigned)
   1 bathing cap
   1 pair of brown cotton whipcord riding breeches,
        or colored long trousers for everyday riding
   1 long purple or orange tie
   1 large straw hat

Note that this 1929 list contains no shorts (although "gymnasium zips" were first cousins) and that long white trousers were not required.

The popular "Let 'er Buck" silk kerchief in purple or orange made its appearance in the store in 1929 or 1930. The colorful silk squares featured a camper on a bucking horse. From the *War Whoop* of June 22, 1930, comes this bit of fashion flaunting:

> . . . After lunch the girls rode five miles beyond Hunt, past the Heart of the Hills Inn and Mystic Camp. The girls were dressed in white riding outfits with the Let 'er Buck handkerchiefs knotted around their collars. They made a very attractive picture as they rode by.

In 1931 progress in American sports fashions suggested to Miss Ora that "bloomers" be dropped from the list and replaced by "two pairs black shorts or zips." At the same time "knickers" were dropped in favor of "long white trousers." All-camp pictures with campers wearing "long whites" and "Let 'er Buck" ties were impressive.

After Miss Ora's death, the selling of clothes at the camp store was gradually eliminated. Up-to-date sportswear became available at hometown stores, and "trendsetters" preferred to set camp fashion rather than follow it. Sailor suits, knickers, and bib overalls continued to be popular for several seasons because of their accessibility, and all kinds and colors of ties added variety and individuality to the camp costume.

In the early 1930s few girls were pictured in the catalogs in shorts, although "gym zips" were common. By 1935 shorts were just as common as zips, but everyone wore long white trousers for dress occasions.

The decade of the 1940s saw Waldemar fashion enter the modern world. Of course, one could wear "long whites" to church, but short whites were just as acceptable and much cooler. As if to place Waldemar's cachet on it, the Ideal Girls of both terms of 1940 are pictured in the catalog wearing white shorts.

1941

Waldemar's first fifteen years—six under the guidance of Ora Johnson and nine under her niece Doris—had produced an organization so joyously workable and so finely tuned that the anniversary might well have been fifty instead of only fifteen. A counselor joining the Waldemar staff in 1941 (this writer for one) was greeted with unrationed helpfulness and instant cameraderie by a knowledgeable and talented staff. Many of the members of the 1932 advisory council were still giving of their expertise to Waldemar, and former campers—tribal leaders and Ideal Girls among them—were adding to the effectiveness of the camp program. The early part of the 1930s had presented Waldemar with one crisis after another over which it had smilingly triumphed and an air of confidence about the future pervaded the thriving girls' camp.

Bring on the challenges of the forties, said the director and her staff. They agreed that the war in Europe was dreadful and frightening, but after all it was far away, and certainly President Roosevelt would keep us out of it.

Doris was continuing to devote as much time as she could to the recruiting of effective representatives. She believed that they were vital to the kind of success she dreamed of for Waldemar. She kept remembering her Aunt Ora's prediction that someday Waldemar would be "turning girls away," and she yearned to make that prediction come true. The Christmas editions of the *War Whoop* told of her travels to show the camp movie and the parties given by patrons and representatives promoting the camp.

Creative enrollment incentives were continued in 1941. A Monterrey trip was given without charge to the Wichita Falls girls because they had the largest number of campers enrolled by Christmas. Houston was coming into its own, sending forty girls first term and thirty-eight second.

The new rock kampong for 1941, by now a given, was built around a tree-filled patio and boasted four units strung together in the artful manner of the camp's architect, San Antonian Harvey P. Smith. The linked verandahs holding the four units together in crescent shape were made cozy and inviting by stone seats and blue tile benches accented by picture tiles of Mexican motif. The white inside walls and red Spanish-tile floors were dramatic, and the handmade red tile roof capped the kampong with artistry and warmth as it nestled against the hillside.

Wooden kampongs 30, 31, and 35 were moved to make room for the building which welcomed visitors to the east side of Waldemar's camper hill. The kampong was originally named "La Alameda," but the name was shortened to "Alameda" because campers referred to it as "La Tomato."

Doris' strong interest in girls building fine bodies resulted in Dr. Felix L. Butte's coming to Waldemar for a few days in 1940. Dr. Butte, an orthopedic surgeon from Dallas, whose daughters were Waldemar campers, examined the posture of Waldemar girls during registration time and recommended remedial exercises for those who needed them. Then he returned at the end of the term to check on their progress. He came again in 1941, and upon his advice, Doris was able to add to the staff the inimitable Roe Johnson, who called her field "corrective gymnastics."

From the *Waldemar War Whoop:*

Demands for Mrs. Johnson's corrective gymnastic courses is so great that nine classes are now in progress. Two classes are offered each period during the third and fourth hours, and a special class has been added during round-up time on Tuesdays, Thursdays and Saturdays.

The article continued:

After deciding that the field of "corrective gymnastics" offered the largest opportunity for her individual work in the field of health, Mrs. Johnson attended Newcomb Normal School of Gymnastics. She was associated with St. Mary's Hall at San Antonio for 25 years both as a student and a teacher. During the winter months Mrs. Johnson works with San Antonio doctors on special corrective cases.

Fortunately the Playhouse had acquired a roof in 1940, because Roe Johnson's classes filled that space. The girls paraded before her, being told to "tuck your tail feathers in," and they sat cross-legged doing shoulder exercises at her command. Despite the large size of her classes, each girl received individual attention for her particular problems, and the campers loved this special woman who walked laboriously with a rolling gait and always dressed in a blue denim skirt. She had a sawed-off chair in which she was comfortable during classes and she was accompanied by a sawed-off dachshund pup named "Minnie Pearl." Roe Johnson reigned at the Waldemar Playhouse every morning for twenty summers. She had a house not far from Waldemar.

Most of Waldemar's 1941 traditions were already established when campers arrived for this sixteenth summer. That these traditions had taken root so firmly was the result of enthusiastic campers returning to Waldemar year after year.

For example, at the end of second term in 1941, eighteen girls received diamond star pins signifying their achievement of all-star rank for four summers, five received five-year awards, one received a six-year award, and one, the seven-year award. These girls became steeped in the lore of Waldemar and they saw to it that the new girls learned the camp's traditions and treasured them. (The seven-year camper was Geane Brogniez, whose mother came to camp in 1931 as counselor for the youngest girls and brought her daughter along. Although young Geane joined in camp activities, she was considered too young to qualify for all-star until 1935.)

As early as 1931 the always optimistic Ora Johnson had become convinced that Waldemar was going to be a real success, and she became concerned about the nature of the award for a girl who came for more than four years. "Should it happen that a girl should come for five, six or even seven years, we will put other diamonds where those three small stars are on the crest."

There is no concrete evidence that this ever happened, and the awards problem was complicated by the fact that a few girls stayed both terms, but in a 1940 *War Whoop* there appears the following paragraph:

As a special award to five, six and seven year girls, a bracelet of exquisite design and craftsmanship is being given. A miniature Waldemar seal in gold is in the center of the design.

After her camp career was over, Geane Brogniez's life took her away from Waldemar for many years, but in 1986 she and her husband moved to Kerrville and she joined the Waldemar staff. One day she brought to camp for show purposes a bracelet which had been awarded her at some point in her camping career. The beauty of the design and the workmanship would have pleased even the meticulous Miss Ora. Geane prized it so much that it was kept in a bank vault because of both its intrinsic and sentimental value.

As early as 1934 it became traditional for the Tejas and Comanches to present tribal vesper services each term. Inspired counselors adapted for presentation material such as *The Prophet* by Kahlil Gibran and well-known biblical stories, and they wove together inspirational poems in advancing a theme which the girls selected. By 1941 each tribe had pretty much settled on a traditional vesper service, the Comanches presenting each term "The Quest for Loveliness" and the Tejas choosing the theme "Candlelight Memories."

As each Tejas spoke of some beautiful memory she would take home from Waldemar, she floated a gleaming candle downriver and created a magical moment of quiet reflection.

The Comanche "Quest for Loveliness" was more dramatic. The audience crossed the bridge over the rapids and was seated opposite the pier, and inspirational poems were read during the hushed stillness. The climax was the enactment of the story of "Michael and the Madonna," and a dance interpretation of the story was carried out across the river by a dozen white-robed dancers on the stone steps of the softly lighted pier. A "stained glass" window crafted of colored theatrical gels stood at the top of the pier steps, and the "Madonna," dressed in pale blue, stood against it to receive "Little Michael."

One tradition begun by Miss Ora and continued by Doris for a few summers was the all-camp pageant, an extravaganza requiring costumes, stage lighting, music, dancing, and the cooperation of campers and counselors alike. The rehearsals oftentimes interfered with class time, and instead of a pageant in 1941 a Field Day and a horse show were planned for the Fourth of July to which parents and guests were invited as they had been to the camp's pageant. The horse show was a spectacle in itself.

From the *War Whoop:*

Waldemar campers dressed in their best riding outfits, Western and English, will enter the athletic field arena at 10:30. Immediately following the grand entry Johnny Regan and Waldemar campers will present an exhibition of trick and fancy roping.

A flag drill, horseback jumping, Western flag race, English bareback team race, and junior Western exhibition will follow in that order. The highlight of the show will be the quadrille.

From that same issue of the *War Whoop,* there was a story entitled "Waldemar Rides Again":

"Ride 'em cowboys" and don your loudest shirt, fanciest boots, your biggest Stetson hat and get ready to go to Kerrville's Seventh Annual Hill Country Championship Rodeo the night of July the 4th. The WHOLE camp is going en masse in trucks, station wagons, busses, and a couple of the counselors' jalopies.

At the rodeo, besides all health rules being suspended, campers will see calf roping, steer riding, bronc busting and bull-dogging. Two of Waldemar's

top cowboys, the Sultenfuss brothers, Leon and Ox, are planning to enter the bull-dogging and bronc busting contests. With all this and no health rules too everybody can celebrate the Fourth with a bang.

And from the next issue of the newspaper:

The Waldemar section [at the rodeo] yelled itself hoarse because Connie Douglas, Mildred Acton [counselor] and the quadrille girls all rode in the rodeo, and Red, Ox and Leon (Waldemar cowboys) performed. The customary pageant was certainly not missed.

This was not the first time the whole camp had gone to the rodeo. In 1937 Doris had chartered buses to take the entire camp to the Third Annual Hill Country Rodeo, but neither the counselors nor the quadrille performed.

1942

The architect's drawing of "Doris' 1942 Christmas gift to campers" was pictured in the Christmas issue of the 1941 *War Whoop.* It was "La Estrella," a three-unit kampong located uphill and to the west of French Chateau. The cutline under the picture read:

A swinging gate gives entrance to a low-walled patio from which steps lead upward to the verandah which serves all three rooms. In the rooms are copper light fixtures from Taxco, Mexico, and on the verandah are three large copper lanterns in the shape of stars—thus the name "La Estrella," Spanish for "star!"

(Again the "La" was soon dropped and the struggle through the years has been to keep non-Spanish-speaking campers and counselors from calling the romantic Mexican-style building "Australia.")

The building was begun shortly before the traumatic December 7, 1941, bombing of Pearl Harbor, and was ready for the summer of 1942. The bound file of the camp newspaper of 1942 is missing, but a copy of the Christmas issue is in the camp archives, and it recaps some of the summer's agenda.

Again it had been decided that Waldemar would "carry on" despite the country's having been drawn into World War II. The relief that campers felt that there would be camp in 1942 was expressed in letters to Doris promising complete cooperation in any necessary adjustments for war time, and they were true to their word.

The war escalated during the summer, and twenty-four older campers of second term volunteered to help out with some menial tasks to keep Waldemar beautiful.

From the Christmas newspaper:

When Waldemar suddenly found itself without some of the yard men, gardeners, etc., a fine group of girls known as the "Victory Girls" came through with flying colors. They arose by alarm clock an hour before reveille and set to work cleaning the Play House, the pier, the grounds around the cabins, the terrace in front of the office, etc. Some watered flowers, some picked up papers, some swept and mopped, and everyone did it in a wonderful spirit.

Waldemar owes a real debt of gratitude to these girls, and next year if camp goes along as usual there must be more and more "Victory Girls" because there will be more and more patriotic tasks that must be performed—We cannot expect to use men laborers at camp when those men can serve Uncle Sam better by working elsewhere.

The article suggested that "other patriotic tasks" might be in the making for 1943:

You may be called upon to be a Nurse's Aid in the infirmary. You may be on a committee to flatten the tin cans that come out of the kitchen, or you may chop weeds in a Victory garden.

You would do these things to help make Waldemar as interesting and lovely a place as ever, wouldn't you? And perhaps you have your own ideas about what Waldemar can do to serve the country in war time. If so, write to Doris and tell her what you would be willing to do as a "Victory Girl."

This Christmas issue of 1942 also told of the Waldemar girls who were helping Uncle Sam during the winter, some by forming war stamp clubs in their various schools, and some by volunteering their services for the gasoline registration. Most had taken first aid courses, and the girls of the Rio Grande Valley wrote:

And scrap iron? Why, the Edinburg girls say there isn't a single rusty nail left lying around in the whole county.

A scrap iron drive was conducted up and down the Guadalupe, and Waldemar contributed at least ten truckloads, according to Doris and Ellen. Included in these loads were rusty garbage cans, dozens of old beds and cots, and the kitchen equipment ruined in the Dining Hall fire of 1930. "We hope these are already on their way to the bomb factories and for once something good has come out of the dump heap."

A Wichita Falls camper sold $131,000 worth of bonds in one week and another sold $115,000 worth in a similar contest, according to the paper.

There was news of former Waldemar counselors who were making their mark in the WAACS, the WAVES, and the Red Cross. Their educational qualifications and their physical education majors made them particularly suited to such military tasks as developing training schools as soon as they received their commissions.

1943

Perhaps Mr. and Mrs. America wanted to ensure some sense of normalcy in their daughters' lives in this time of worldwide upheaval known as World War II; perhaps the hard work done by Doris Johnson and her representatives in publicizing Camp Waldemar was paying off; or perhaps it was the excellence of the camp in all areas. Whatever the reason, requests for space in the 1943 summer camping season came flooding in, and it appeared that there would be at least a hundred more girls in camp each term than in 1942. Doris had no doubt that she could find beds for the increased number, but she was concerned about giving each of them the individual attention for which Waldemar was by now famous.

As early as 1927 Miss Ora Johnson had recognized the need for leadership opportunities for the younger girls as well as the older ones, and beginning in 1928 much of that leadership training became the responsibility of the Comanche and Tejas tribes. Already there had been concerns in 1942 that the tribes were too large, and tribal sponsors regretted that they couldn't get to know each of their tribesmen as well as they would like. Nor was it possible for each girl to have a speaking part on a tribal hill program, a coveted privilege, and certainly an agent for personal growth and development.

The solution seemed simple, but it was almost heresy to contemplate it: Waldemar needed a third tribe.

The advantages of a third tribe were obvious. Competition on Field Day would be enhanced and another full slate of tribal leaders would be elected each term. Doris knew that her present-day campers and former campers as well would find the whole idea of a third tribe unacceptable because they wanted new campers from their hometown to choose to belong to their tribe. After all, Longview was known as a "Comanche" town, and Oklahoma City was a "Tejas town." Could the new girls be cajoled into joining a new tribe after they had been "rushed" by their hometown friends?

A survey of the applications of the new girls showed that there were older more mature girls coming to Waldemar for 1943 who could supply leadership for a new tribe, and after much consideration, Doris and her advisors decided that the fairest thing to do was try to persuade all the new girls to be pioneers in this momentous undertaking, the forming of a new tribe at Waldemar.

In the mid-1980s, Marsha received a letter from the first-term Aztec tribal leader of 1943 telling of her feelings thirty-five years earlier. She had been graduated from high school the spring before camp opened, she had friends in both Waldemar tribes, and she was distressed about having to choose between these friends.

> So all the way down on the bus, I prayed that something would work out. Well, the first night Doris called a meeting of all the new campers and explained why she thought we needed a new tribe, but she wanted us to decide. She told us how the camp had grown and all the reasons she thought it was a good idea. Several of us expressed our feelings. (Of course, I wanted it!) As I remember it was a unanimous decision. Then we elected officers. . . . I was so thrilled to be elected tribal leader . . . when I came out of that meeting I felt my prayers had been answered. . . . Half the camp was waiting outside wondering what was going on . . . they were dumbfounded over what had happened.

Seven girls were chosen to assist in the creation of the tribe, and this founding committee, together with tribal sponsors Genevieve "Penel" Stack and Ruth Wright Green, chose the name, the color, the hillsite, and designed the flag. Excitement ran high. The girls had been told that if they didn't like this experiment they could give it up the following summer and affiliate with either the Tejas or Comanches. It had always been the privilege of new campers to choose their tribal affiliation and part of the fun was being sought after, but it wasn't long before these girls knew in their hearts they were Aztecs!

The very first decision was choosing a name. They considered Navajo, Apache, Sioux and others, but Aztec "seemed right." Choosing a color was easy: wasn't green the symbol of growth and strength as well as the third secondary color on the art color wheel, the other two being purple and orange? Then the two sponsors explored the surrounding area on horseback, looking for a suitable site for Aztec hill ceremonies and, when they found it, they marveled that such a fine hillsite had not been chosen for such purpose fifteen years earlier.

The seven girls of the founding committee designed the Aztec flag with all its symbolism, and an accommodating counselor named Rosemary Atkinson made the first one. Miraculously it was ready to fly on the first Field Day in which the new tribe participated.

The enthusiasm and determination of these brand new tribesmen was such that they didn't do so poorly on their very first Field Day. They were the predictable third, but on second Field Day—even though they lost—they beat one of the "Big Two."

By the end of the term, the consensus was that the experiment was a success. But the new girls of second term were given the option of perpetuating the fledgling tribe or going back to the old two-tribe system. They, too, enthusiastically embraced Aztec and approved all the ideas and traditions proposed by the first-term girls.

Because Ruth Wright Green was not in camp second term, Ann Miller Crockett, whose original ideas had sparked so many traditions of the Comanches in early days, became an Aztec sponsor. She saw that the Aztecs needed a ritual to parallel the Comanche Rockpile Leader (which she had conceived in the early years) and the Tejas Memory Candle Girl, and she suggested "The Girl of the Cypress Bower," which soon became known simply as "The Cypress Girl." The ceremony honors three girls, two who hold cypress branches to form a bower under which the chosen "Cypress Girl" of the week stands.

It was impossible for Doris to get a War Canoe shipped for use by the Aztecs that first summer—and besides, no one knew what the outcome of this experiment would be. The War Canoe races were run in sections, with the Aztecs using the Tejas Canoe when they raced the Comanches and vice versa. On Field Day a race in the morning between two of the tribes determined which two canoes would race in the afternoon.

There was still another consideration: "The Legend of the Guadalupe" must be revised. By this time "Night Fawn" and "Grey Lance," hero and heroine of the traditional "Legend of the Guadalupe," presented the first of each term, had become "Guada" and "Lupe," and it was now necessary to add the Aztec tribe to the familiar story. There were three tribes instead of two, and they had lived happily and peacefully by the beautiful river, but when one tribe, the Aztecs, chose to move away, the Tejas and Comanches became unhappy and quarrelsome. How the Aztecs returned and helped solve the problem between their old friends enriched the ancient legend.

First-term Aztecs presented a timely patriotic vesper, and the second-term girls chose to present to the camp the plans for an Aztec library. Each charter member donated a book or contributed to the purchase of the more valuable books, and Mary Strange designed an appropriate bookplate. The presentation was dramatic and thrilling.

A counselor came to Waldemar in 1943 who would share of her many talents for forty-five summers. Margaret Shannon (later Harber) came to teach Western horseback riding, and for fourteen summers she was enjoyed at the stables by campers, counselors, and cowboys alike. In 1957 Doris recruited her to serve as program director, a demanding post also known as director of activities and first filled at Waldemar by Margaret Gladney Savage. Shannon's name will surface often during Waldemar's upcoming forty years. Her contributions to the smooth running of Waldemar are incalculable.

There was no building project at Waldemar in 1943, a concession to the war, but the excitement of the founding of the Aztec tribe and its gracious acceptance by the two older tribes made the summer of 1943 a memorable one. From the June 27 issue of the *War Whoop:*

> The Aztec tribe was given a royal welcome to Waldemar last Tuesday night by the older Comanche and Tejas tribes. After being driven ceremoniously to the dining room steps right before dinner in Cappie Collier's sports job, the Aztec leaders dismounted and were received by the leaders of the other tribes, who made welcoming speeches and presented them with the keys to all doors at Waldemar.

Cappie Collier, owner of the snappy-looking convertible, was a petite blonde former camper who joined the counselor staff in 1943.

1944

It was no doubt trying for Doris Johnson to see a year go by without Waldemar's physical plant being enhanced by a wonderful new building, but the restrictions of war could not keep her from improving the first floor of Cedar Lodge, built in 1927, which housed the office. The transformation accomplished by the elbow grease of Doris and Ellen, who "antiqued" the walls, was a welcome sight for campers of 1944.

> Everybody misses some of the old things . . . that swinging squeaking gate that always made chills run up and down your spine, the counter where names could be carved without fear of ruining the finish, and the old telephone booth . . .

The war dragged on, but Doris and her staff saw to it that Waldemar's 1944 camping season was just as exciting as the peacetime summers had been. Some valuable counselors had joined the Wacs or Waves or the Red Cross, but there were other capable women who opted to spend the time on the banks of the Guadalupe River in Texas while their husbands were in the service.

Billie Johnson met the critical challenge of keeping the Waldemar larder supplied, and Ripple Frazer's menus and U.S. Smith's translation of those menus into Waldemar food pleased campers' palates as much as ever.

There were shortages, of course. Perhaps the most limiting for Waldemar was gasoline. One reporter was looking forward to the day

> When we can go to San Antonio sightseeing and buy out the Buckhorn Saloon.
> When a chartered bus can meet any train at any hour and move girls and baggage directly to Waldemar.
> When Doris will let us use the station wagons for kampong picnics instead of making us hoof it.
> When we all get to go to the Fourth of July rodeo in Kerrville.
> When we get that delicious Waldemar ice cream . . . 16 per cent butterfat and made with sugar instead of honey.
> When tennis balls, golf balls and Kodak film will be on sale in the store.
> When we can get blue jeans for riding classes.

When dude ranch guests from Minnesota hinted to Doris that they might be able to send her some butter, she took them up on it immediately. The Waldemar deep freeze held a bountiful supply, and J. F. Johnson, Doris' rancher father, saw to it that Ripple's menus didn't lack meat.

Both terms the Aztec vesper service was "The Book of Books," a presentation which enabled the tribe not only to make its gifts of books to camp for the new Aztec library but also to dramatize in tableaux the books of the Bible. The Comanche and Tejas continued their traditional vesper services.

Gasoline rationing kept parents from visiting their daughters on the Fourth of July, but a carnival on the tennis court was designed by counselors to keep campers from missing them. Campers proclaimed this Fourth of July the best ever.

The "red letter day" of the summer, not only for the Aztecs but for all campers, was Friday, August 3, when a truck rolled in at 11:00 in the morning carrying the new Aztec War Canoe.

> The news spread like wild fire, and soon it was the talk of the camp from the river to the stables to the rifle range and all over the hill. Gleaming brilliantly green in the sunlight, it was truly a thing of beauty.
>
> Friday right after noon campers and counselors thronged to the canoe dock to witness the christening.
>
> Doris named the craft "The Aztec Angel" and poured water from the Guadalupe on the stern as she said "Win or lose, may uprightness always prevail among crew and members." To add fuel to the fire of excitement, a photographer put in his appearance at the exact psychological correct moment and snapped a picture of "The Angel" as it glided into the waters of the river for the first time manned by its crew.
>
> The Tejas and Comanche crews put their canoes in the water for a tryout race. History was being made, and everyone recognized the importance of the moment.

Field Day was the following day. A reporter wrote:

> There just couldn't have been a more thrilling race ever to take place. The three canoes came down the river straight and true, and bow to bow for many yards. The Tejas jumped ahead, and then the Comanches were in the lead. Just before the end of the race the new green "Aztec Angel" sprouted wings and shot ahead of the other two, but a final burst of speed by the Comanche crew assured them victory.

Fanny Bolinger, Dublin, whose name became synonymous at Waldemar with gentleness, kindness, and Christian goodness, first came to Waldemar second term of 1944 as a member of the academic department. It wasn't until 1946 that she became the permanent Happy Haven "Mama," where her patience, warmth and love made her the idol of Waldemar's youngest campers. Fanny's religious background made her the perfect choice for director of Sunday services, and her love of beauty caused her to take over the flower arrangements for the tables in the dining room when Doris decided that fresh flowers or fresh greens should grace the Waldemar dining room.

1945

The arrival of Waldemar's first "daughter of a former camper" added to the sense of maturity the camp was experiencing in this, its twentieth summer. Margaret Lowery of Victoria, a second-term camper, was determined to surpass the fine record her mother, Ginger Crain, had made in the early days of camp. Gazers in the crystal ball knew that Margaret was the first of many "legacies" who would add strength to Camp Waldemar.

This was the first summer since 1929 that Margaret Gladney Savage hadn't been at Waldemar. She wrote: "Greetings to everyone who is lucky enough to be at Camp Waldemar this summer. There is no place in the world quite like it and I am missing everyone. Nothing but MY BUDDY would keep me away." She had been able to join Buddy in Oklahoma during this phase of the war.

Sue Garrison, who came to Waldemar in 1941, took over Maggie's job as director of activities in 1945, only the second director of activities in Waldemar's history. She was from Palestine but taught school in Houston and became a full-fledged Houstonian when she was named director of physical education at Houston University. She was proficient in all sports, and she had had previous camp experience. At Waldemar she taught hiking and sponsored the Comanche tribe, and it was generally agreed that "Sue can do anything!"

This was the year Doris decided that perhaps the tribes needed some new vesper programs because a few mischievous campers, becoming bored with the "traditional" vespers, were "cutting" them and hiding on the hill. The Aztecs presented an Indian "prayer stick" vesper in which colored feathers, each carrying a prayer, were floated in the air from the curving outdoor stairway at Casa del Monte. Led ceremoniously from the Dining Hall by Indian braves holding aloft flaming torches, the audience was seated just to the east of Casa. The impressive ceremony was enhanced by the Hiawatha costumes of 1930.

Sue Van Noy became the Aztec sponsor in 1945.

She had come to Waldemar in 1941 to edit the camp newspaper, and was on hand in 1942 but missed the summers of 1943 and 1944 to work at an air base. The popular "Penel" Stack, one of the founding sponsors of the young Aztec tribe, rejoined her serviceman husband in 1945, and Sue became head Aztec sponsor. She was universally known as "Squish," a name which evolved from the more esthetic sounding "Tish" (from her hometown of Tishomingo, Oklahoma), and the sound made by feet encased in waterlogged tennis shoes.

The Tejas sponsor was Mary Edna "Eddie" Norris, musician extraordinaire, director of the Waldemar orchestra and director of the camp chorus. Eddie's entire chorus joined the Tejas when they presented in song and costumed scenes the forms of worship practiced by America's ethnic mix.

Tribal unity was the theme of the Comanche vesper service held on the athletic field near the pier area. Tribal friendship was epitomized by the presentation of a totem pole featuring the tribal crests carved from mahogany by tribal sponsor (and director of activities) Sue Garrison. Regrettably the handsome marker was not finished in time for first-term campers to see and enjoy. This challenge proved again that "Sue can do anything."

Just as Doris had hoped, these three outstanding vesper services filled tribal members with pride and convinced them that missing a vesper service was not in their own best interest. From this time on, staging an inspiring vesper service has been a priority for tribal sponsors.

Because a polio epidemic was gripping Texas, trips out of camp were curtailed and girls were "kept within the gates of Waldemar." An imaginative counselor staff took the sting out of this restriction by creating hilarious evening programs which were anticipated from week to week.

Radio station KTCW (Kum to Camp Waldemar) was a weekly parody of popular radio programs of the era. "Fannie Faces the Future," the tear-jerking story of Fannie Featherock, was eagerly awaited each week, as was "Wilbur Wides the Wasteland." Waltermar Winchell revealed many secrets, and there were question and answer shows that involved the audience and offered prizes galore.

The Waldemar carnival, for which counselors transformed the lower tennis courts into a fun-filled arena with many of the same "booths" which have been continued through the years, was a night of revelry, and the popular doll raffle featured unique dolls made by talented Geneva McGaugh, second-term

craft counselor from Arkansas who had come to camp in 1941.

Since their founding in 1943, the Aztec tribe had not experienced a victory of any kind, but second Field Day of second term 1945 found them winning the War Canoe race, and by virtue of that win, Field Day. The green canoe led all the way. The emotional crew stayed downriver facing the dam until they composed themselves and with tears streaming down their faces, they returned to the pier to accept the congratulations of their rivals. The margin of victory for the Field Day was one-half point, but it was as good as a thousand. A prominent Comanche remarked as that tribe was lifting its canoe out of the water, "Girls, a new era has begun."

Comanche sponsor Sue Garrison and Tejas sponsor Eddie Norris wore green to dinner that night, a gesture which caused Aztec sponsor Squish to shed a few more tears of joy.

"News Lights" was the name of a column compiled by old-timer Carmen Crain which appeared each week in the *War Whoop*. News of the war was especially appreciated by campers and counselors who had fathers, brothers, and husbands serving their country. In August of 1945 the Japanese surrendered. When peace was declared, all of Waldemar met at the flagpole at sundown to listen to the ceremonial proclamation of peace on radio and to celebrate that peace and rejoice that the four-year war was over. Waldemar had its own memorable ceremony, a program which included patriotic poems, prayer, and song led by the camp chorus dressed in white, standing on the porch of Cedar Lodge. As the retreat bugle rang out, the three tribal leaders lowered the flag while campers and counselors stood in hushed attention, some with tears in their eyes and all with patriotic reverence.

In her column of August 19, Carmen wrote: "Many wartime controls have already been lifted and it is expected that many more will follow. An end has come to the rationing of gasoline, fuel oil, stoves, canned fruits, vegetables, catsup and grape juice."

1946

World War II, that second worldwide conflict which changed maps, peoples and attitudes, and scattered Americans around the globe, had failed to suppress the wonderful Spirit of Waldemar which had been commemorated since 1933 but celebrated since Ora Johnson founded the camp in 1926.

As the war ended, Waldemar completed its first twenty years of operation, and Doris, with well-deserved pride, reviewed the successes of those twenty years. It was no longer necessary to "beat the bushes" for campers. As Ora Johnson had predicted long ago, they were beginning to "stand in line" for a bunk at Camp Waldemar. Doris had assembled a network of representatives who helped promote the camp and the Waldemar representative position had increased in prestige as the quality of the camp became known.

The 1940s were the years when the enrollment all but outgrew Doris' vision of the camp, and soon it became necessary to apportion space to the representatives so that the camper group would not be made up of girls from only a few areas. Representative lists for the decade of the forties have been preserved and the 1943 list includes some eighty names, among them counselors and mothers of campers. By 1947 the list had been pared considerably, and a well-worn working list of that year boasts names of women prominent in their communities whose daughters eventually became representatives themselves, some serving into the 1990s. The hereditary nature of the representative posts paralleled the camper legacy tradition.

Through the years "junior counselors," usually former campers, had been listed in the directory as a part of the staff, and the years from the middle 1930s to the early 1940s were enriched by these enthusiastic ex-campers. However, the demand for beds for campers curtailed that practice in 1943. Now Waldemar was able to add to its staff former campers fully qualified for counselorship by virtue of having earned a college degree.

Talented and dependable counselors helped the camp run smoothly during the 1940s. Stalwarts like Bess Richards, San Antonio, whose name became synonymous with the rifle range, and Louise Jeter, Kilgore, who headed the tennis department and sponsored the Comanche tribe, had come to Waldemar in the late 1930s. Versatile Floy Hume, San Angelo, joined the staff in 1943 as did Margaret Shannon (Harber). Elizabeth Hull, Fort Worth, piano-playing head of the waterfront staff, spent the decade of the 1940s entertaining all with her sharp wit and the writing and directing of such radio masterpieces as "Wilbur Wides the Wastelands." Annette Duval, owner of a dance studio in Austin, came in 1945 and was a proper replacement for the dynamic "Lacey." Often

Annette brought stars of her dance studio from Austin to present in recital to Waldemar campers.

Tid Compere, Susie Wells, Jane Douglass, Winnie Hill, all former Ideal Girls, Bess Rayford, the first Best All-Round Tejas, Angilee Davis, fencer extraordinaire and all-round athlete, diminutive blonde "Cappie" Collier and Virginia "Gigi" Jones, the first Aztec on the counselor staff, and many others lent of their talents and know-how during these years.

Ruth Wright Green, arguably the most versatile counselor ever to serve at Waldemar, first came in 1935 to teach "basketry." Through the years she taught swimming, golf, tennis, art, played saxophone with the orchestra which she sometimes directed, sponsored tribes, acted as tribal coordinator, sang "that difficult middle part" in every counselor trio (including the one that introduced the "Song to Doris"), emceed many a "Counselor Cut-ups," helped write vesper services and final banquet programs, and was considered the ideal kampong counselor by her senior girls.

Excavation work for enlarging the kitchen was begun during the summer of 1945, and the new kitchen was ready for the 1946 season. The bakery and the "back porch" were enlarged, and a new "walk-in" refrigerator and deep freeze meant that "Billie won't have to 'fudge' on the milk cooler at watermelon time." Stainless steel cabinets, shelves and work tables and wonderful appliances graced U.S.' domain. The row of new fountains attached to the wall just outside the kitchen was well patronized by returning horseback riders. It was a tribute to Ferdinand's skill as a stone mason that a reporter wrote: "No one can tell where the old building ends and the new one begins."

The tribal song contest for plaque points was begun in 1946, no doubt instigated by "Eddie" Norris. When Sue Garrison took the Houston University position, she and Eddie decided that they couldn't stay at camp second term, and Squish reluctantly became director of activities until a suitable replacement for Sue surfaced.

Bettye Meyers, a native of Heavener, Oklahoma, joined the Waldemar staff second term 1946 as a member of the tennis department. In the late 1940s this TSCW graduate (now TWU) became director of activities, a position she enhanced and upgraded until 1957. Bettye was a badminton specialist as was Shannon, and their Sunday afternoon matches were highlights of the week. Another Sunday afternoon diversion was the Buzzard softball match between the "waterfront and the landlubbers," and "Birdlegs"

Shannon's pitching for the landlubbers usually ensured victory for that group. The waterfront's Tessie Schexnaidre and Shannon often entertained with a pitching duel.

The Aztecs were firmly established in 1946 with the first-term Aztecs winning a War Canoe race and the second termers winning both War Canoe races, both Field Days and the plaque, and for the first time the Ideal Girl was an Aztec. The "Big Two" had become the "Big Three."

Radio station KTCW continued to broadcast weekly, and singing commercials written and performed by counselors for such products as "Stifle Deodorant" and "Squish's Squash" sent both campers and counselors into spasms of convulsive merriment.

Counselor theatrical talent with gleeful abandonment of dignity was displayed each term in the much anticipated "Counselor Cut-ups." The production took many forms, but it was always a memorable evening for the "ham" counselors as well as the campers.

1947

Trying to keep the tribes balanced in numbers had always been a hit-or-miss proposition, with new campers choosing the group with which they wanted to affiliate. During enrollment day, Laura Wallace or some equally persuasive counselor sat at a table in the Playhouse and signed up new girls for the tribe of their choice. If the Comanches, for example, got too far ahead, Laura surreptitiously sent word to the Tejas and Aztecs that they needed to recruit, and vice versa. At the end of this process, uneven numbers and age groups presented tribal sponsors with a dilemma: How could they make Field Day line-ups that were fair and equitable when their numbers were staggeringly incompatible?

There was a solution, unpopular though it might be, and the plan was instigated first term of 1947. With no fanfare, the new Waldemar campers drew by lot for their tribal affiliation. The outcry from former campers who had sisters coming to camp (and might someday have daughters) and present-day campers who had little sisters coming to Waldemar was difficult for Doris to ignore, but she stood firm, knowing that the formula developed for the drawing, with the tribes and ages of returning campers as the determining ingredient, would mean that each of the three tribes would have approximately the same number of

juniors, low seniors, and high seniors. Critics of the drawing saw its advantages and recognized that it would improve all areas of camper life.

In 1947, Ripple Frazer recommended as dietitian her friend and colleague in the Dallas school system Idabel Cabaniss. Idabel came in time for second term and stayed twenty years. The responsibilities of the dietitian at Camp Waldemar were more than simply planning the delicious, imaginative, and bountiful meals that U.S. Smith and his staff produced for Waldemar girls three times a day: she worked closely with Billie Johnson, purchasing agent, to be sure supplies were on hand when needed; she was the overseer of the numerous picnic baskets which were carried from the kitchen each day at noon; she planned the guest day menus which U.S. and the kitchen staff executed so flawlessly; and she planned and usually prepared herself the after-taps surprises which campers won at the quiz show contests and other fun endeavors. In addition she supervised the dining room and the two nourishment periods.

Waldemar's often remarked success in the food department was credited to the organizational ability and dedication of U.S. and Lucille Smith and to the expertise and loyalty of its dietitians through the years. Ripple Frazer had come to Waldemar as dietitian in 1927, the second year of the young camp's operation. Her equally qualified older sister, Katherine Frazer Gannon (known as "Kat" or "Mrs. G.") took over for much of the 1930s, and it was Ripple again in the 1940s until 1947, when Idabel came. According to old records, the Frazer sisters missed 1932 only, and later Polly Bowlby—counselor, mother of a camper and Dallas representative—pinch-hit for the first term of 1947.

Through the 1950s Ripple and Idabel alternated, with Ripple's coming first term and Idabel second (except for second term in 1953). The two friends continued this practice until Idabel began coming both terms in 1963.

In 1967, when Idabel's health precluded her coming to Waldemar, Doris persuaded her sister-in-law "Mac" Johnson, Billie Johnson's wife, to take over the demanding dietitian's post. As Naomi McClendon, registered nurse, Mac had first come to Waldemar in the late 1930s. Since her marriage to Billie in 1940, Mac had not been on the Waldemar staff until she returned in 1968. She stayed until 1979. So it can be said that for its first 54 years, Waldemar had only four dietitians. Their longevity of service, their continuity, and their loyalty to Doris and to Waldemar made them important keys to Waldemar's success.

Johnny Regan, Waldemar's rope-twirling cowboy and Pied Piper of the juniors, had left Waldemar after the 1942 season to return to England, rejoin his old regiment, and entertain English soldiers on several battle fronts. His return to Waldemar in 1947 was a celebrated event. Johnny came each summer until 1979, when his health dictated that he return to his native London.

In describing Ellen Easley's position at Waldemar, a *War Whoop* editor wrote in 1947:

Ellen Easley: institutional secretary and Jill of all trades. She's the one who tells you what to do when, where and how. Technically, Ellen's job is to run the office, which she does. But add about forty million other sundry tasks to that and you'll get a picture of what she does for Waldemar.

When it was discovered that Ellen would leave Waldemar at the end of the second term in 1947 to pursue an advanced degree in sociology at the University of Minnesota, the first reaction of campers and counselors alike was dismay and the second was self-pity. "How will we get along without her?" was the question posed by all Waldemarites. Ellen had come to Waldemar ten years earlier in 1937, and since 1939 she had lived at the camp year-round. Waldemar Guest Ranch and the convention season were now running smoothly, and Doris decided to ask Squish, whom she knew to be lukewarm about a college teaching position in Oklahoma, to become a year-round employee so that Ellen could achieve her long-held ambition.

It was agreed that Ellen would forsake Minnesota and spend the summer of 1948 at camp. She missed the summers of 1949 and 1950, but returned in 1951, thus enabling Squish to opt for marriage at the end of the 1952 season.

The large number of campers which now seemed assured called for more teaching space at the pier, and after the 1946 season, Ferdinand enlarged it. Wrote a reporter: "The two trees now in the pier formerly marked its boundaries." At this time, Ferdinand also raised the "theater" steps to the present level.

1948

The geography of Camp Waldemar's physical plant changed as improvements and additions were made. In 1928 an Oklahoma City friend of Ora Johnson's asked her why she was building her dining hall "so far from the center of camp" which was then considered the area around Waldemar Lodge.

In the 1927 brochure promoting the camp, Aunt Ora wrote that "the tennis, volleyball and baseball courts are located on the athletic field and new tennis courts are being added." In 1928 she wrote: "The camp has four tennis courts, one cement, two of clay and gravel, and one of natural soil."

At some point a cement court was built on the east side of camper hill, and through the years wooden kampongs were moved around it as they were displaced by rock kampongs. The court continued in use for many years. After the large new tennis courts near the dining hall were built in 1930, they were identified as "lower courts" and the earlier one was called "upper court."

For this reason the two fine new tennis courts which greeted campers and counselors in 1948 were dubbed "Casa Courts" because of their proximity to Casa del Monte. In the *War Whoop* dated December 24, 1947, the announcement was made that the stables were being moved to make way for the tennis courts.

What about the stables? we hear you yell. What about Jimmy Dear? [a favorite mount] Where in the world is Doris going to keep him?

The answer was that the new stables were being built on the site of the old deer park.

In 1948 the site for pep rallies was moved from the "front drive and athletic field" to the riding field where the tribes met at separate campfires to generate Field Day enthusiasm and hear the reading of their line-ups. At the appointed time tribal leaders lit torches and led a snake dance "across the field and back to the front drive." Second-term girls were enthusiastic about the new meeting place for the pep rallies.

Groups of parents sat on the outer circle of each rally learning in what activities their daughters would participate the following day and hearing their daughters' inspiring lesson in teamwork.

By this time snake dancing into the dining room at lunch time was an old and revered custom. Members of the War Canoe crews had specially decorated tables, and the dining room was festooned with colored streamers. Waiters and waitresses found it a dangerous procedure to serve the girls during the ensuing pep rallies and inevitable "mini-snake dances," and dietitians deplored the condition of the dining room after it was all over! Never liking to impose rules that inhibited the fun of camp life, Doris Johnson condoned this custom for many years but finally ruled that "Field Day will not be carried into the dining room."

KTCW was still on the air in 1948, and a fun-loving and talented orchestra group began another radio show called "The Breakfast Club," which started each week off with a bang. The orchestra played, singers sang, and actresses acted on the stage of the dining hall each Monday morning. Tables made requests for their favorite numbers and the "Music Makers," as they were soon to be called, signed on and off with their appropriate theme song, "The Johnson Rag."

1949

The fall of 1948 was another busy one for Ferdinand Rehbeger. The campers were barely out the gate when he and Doris got their heads together and decided that a new diving pier was a worthy project. The twenty-eight-foot-long concrete structure which resulted carried two diving boards, a high and a low, which enabled twice as many girls to enroll in each class.

This little project was completed in September, but there was a bigger one for Ferd to tackle. He decided he wanted more water in the river! It took him over a month of hard labor, but he built a new dam that raised the water level two feet. When that project was complete, Ferdinand rested for thirty minutes. Then he went up the hill to the new tennis courts and started building a rock retaining wall on that northwest side that looked so new and bare last summer.

So wrote the *War Whoop* editor for the Christmas issue.

Cedar Lodge, second floor of the office building and known as Senior Rec when it was built in 1927, at last was newly decorated for the 1949 season. Paneled walls and handsome cabinets, some for storing books making up the growing Aztec library, and others for camp supplies and keepsakes, were

enhanced by a handsome hardwood parquet floor. The north wall displayed a collection of "horse brasses," antique decorations that were strung all over the harness of a horse in England, and the design of the brass usually depicted the occupation of the owner. They were collected and given to Doris by Doris "Dusty" Dustin, a long-time Waldemar counselor who spent the war years in England with the Red Cross.

The tribal drawing had been in place for two summers—four terms—when in 1949 Doris realized that a ceremony could surround the drawing which would enable the tribes to introduce some of their traditions to the new campers on their first night at Waldemar. The ceremony devised in 1949 has changed little since it was initiated, and another Waldemar tradition was born.

The eventful 1940s saw Waldemar continue to accommodate itself to the changes brought on by the larger number of campers who came back year after year and the eager new girls who were knocking at the door. "Quotas" had been placed on representatives (who were constantly crying for more space) and on the "office list" too; and the facilities, the staff and the curriculum had been enlarged to meet the challenge of giving each of the 300 or so campers the personal attention for which Waldemar was famous.

Billie Johnson, Doris' younger brother, served primarily as Waldemar's purchasing agent, but he was much more than that. He stood ready to do anything that needed to be done, and counselors and campers, knowing that his duties took him to town every day, asked shopping favors of him which his prodigious memory and happy disposition allowed him to accommodate. His kindness, generosity, and willingness made him an example of the Spirit of Waldemar.

Just as Aunt Ora had been buttressed by her brother, Colonel W. T. Johnson, so Doris was advised and sustained by her father, the Colonel's brother, J. F. Johnson. "Joshie," as he was affectionately called by family and Doris' close friends, lived during the 1940s in Rippling Waters with his wife, Adell, Doris' stepmother, who kept the account books for the camp, his ranches, and his various other business enterprises.

J. F. Johnson kept his daughter's stables "populated" with fine horses, saw to it that they were properly "wintered" at one of his ranches, advised her on the physical additions to Waldemar, and shared his innate Johnson wisdom with her throughout his lifetime.

In the summer season Doris lived in the small east room off the main office which served as her office in the daytime. It boasted a desk, a studio couch and a sunken bathtub—sunken not for esthetic purposes but because the tub and the bather had to fit under the sharp slant of the east steps leading up to Cedar Lodge.

A large, old-fashioned dresser was secreted in the east end of the crowded storeroom just behind her living space, and from these spartan quarters a meticulously groomed director emerged daily with a "smile on her face and a gleam in her eye." During the winter Doris lived in Room Number 2 over the dining room. Either Ellen or Squish lived in Number 5.

Chapter 4

1950s

The decade of the 1950s began with Waldemar's celebrating its twenty-fifth anniversary culminating in a final banquet program titled "Waldemar Then and Now." Camp clothes of past eras were featured to the delight of the camper audience and their parents, and they gave all a sense of historical significance.

When Squish became assistant director in 1948, young Bettye Myers, eminently qualified and loved by all, became director of activities, a title which soon evolved into "program director and guidance counselor." She also became Comanche sponsor, and her salutary influence in both these positions is felt to the present day.

The "lower hill" ceremony was begun by Bettye and the Comanches in the second term of 1951. This innovative concept has been retained because it allows mundane but necessary tribal business to be transacted on lower hill rather than intruding on the inspirational moments of upper hill. The other two tribes soon followed the Comanche lead.

One of the priorities of the new program director was to make Field Days as equitable as possible, and Bettye began her progress in this area by promoting a change in War Canoe points on Field Day, a move which had long been considered but not acted upon. Because of the number of girls involved and the importance of the race, it was agreed in 1950 that first place in the race would count 10 points as before but second place would earn five points and third place three. This meant that on closely contested Field Days, the ultimate victor of the day would not necessarily be the winner of the War Canoe race. This action paved the way for still more modification in 1957 to ten points for first, seven for second, and four for third, the scoring which has been in place since that year.

In order for each camper to be entered in some

activity for Field Day (unathletic though she might be) it had long been necessary for Field Day line-ups to include such activities as relays and games not represented on the camper's daily class schedule, and it was incumbent upon sponsors to try to make running in a relay on Field Day as important in the eyes of the camper involved as riding the most popular horse in the stable. "Junior baseball," soon to be known correctly as "softball," was another "catchall" activity for which there was no organized time for tribal practice but for which spirited seniors sent out frantic calls over the office P.A. system, most often unsuccessfully because of the uncertainty of the practice hour.

In 1951 a story appeared in the *War Whoop* saying there would be no junior baseball that year because "13-year-olds are now seniors," an important structural change that wasn't chronicled elsewhere in the paper. Missing the fun of the game, in 1953 Bettye adjusted the schedule so that each tribe could have a softball class period of its own for which team points would be given, thus making softball an important Field Day event. In 1958 it was agreed that "fourteen-year-olds can play on the soft-ball team because they are too small for War Canoe and they want to participate in a competitive group effort." Thus "junior baseball" grew into an exciting team sport under the tutelage of an experienced counselor and an elected tribal softball manager.

Turning her attention to the evening program schedule, Bettye formed a "senior camp council" made up of two elected and three appointed members from each tribe who were to meet with her weekly, discuss camp situations, and help plan the "senior choice nights" which Bettye was initiating. The council's input was tremendous, and under Bettye's guidance they tackled and approved such ideas as giving plaque points only for medals in the arts (drama, dance, crafts, etc.) which were not credited to a tribe by Field Day participation.

On choice nights seniors could choose to go on hay rides, skating trips to Ingram or practice for any of the activities requiring it, and decorating committees for Field Day could spend their choice night planning their "themes" and executing them. The program council members suggested choice night activities, lined up counselors to oversee them, and even performed the onerous task of "checking the hill" to be sure that all girls were profitably engaged.

Later on, in 1956, the council promoted senior "Kampong Kut-Ups," the forerunner of kampong skit night which gained in importance when an out-of-camp holiday became the prize, besting the after-taps surprise of 1956. Also in that year the council took on the task of compiling a much-needed new camp songbook.

War Canoe Day, begun as a regular picnic in the early days, expanded each year in the 1950s. By 1956 it included a skating party at Ingram, lunch at Mrs. Torres' Mexican restaurant in Kerrville, a thirty-minute shopping spree in downtown Kerrville, and ended with a watermelon feast at the overnight site.

First term of 1951 the tribes returned from their pep rallies to Cedar Lodge, but second term they stopped at the dining hall and the balcony became the drama-filled scene of the hanging of banners and the drawing for flag positions on the flagpole and War Canoe positions on the river as it has been ever since. The hanging of the banners indicates to all that Field Day, that most exciting of days, is only a few hours away.

The Buzzard tribe was "obnoxiously active" in the 1950s, and there are indications that their flag was developed in the mid-fifties. However, the handsome black and blue ensign with its intriguing device —that rare and regal bird cherished for decades—was not pictured in the *Waldemar War Whoop* until 1959.

The outstanding counselor staff during the decade of the 1950s was the result of Doris' constant search for excellence, and the counselors themselves recommended friends they knew to be worthy of Waldemar. Many of these personable specialists returned year after year to enjoy and be enjoyed by Waldemar's campers. Those selected to serve as tribal sponsors felt highly honored and were dedicated to their tribes. Tribal vesper services were inspirational and elaborate, and imaginative drama teachers often gave of their limited time to help direct memorable productions. In 1956 Doris agreed that each tribe

needed three sponsors. Field Day competitions were directed by department heads specially trained in their fields, many of them teachers with several teaching at the university level. They were skillful, versatile, and energetic.

Margaret Shannon Harber had come to Waldemar in 1943 to teach horseback, and ten years later, she added sponsoring the Aztec tribe to her duties. She continued sponsoring the Aztecs through 1960. When Bettye Myers elected to pursue her educational ambitions in 1957, Doris asked Shannon to leave the horseback department and take over the duties of program director, a position she held until her death in 1989, a span of three decades. Maggie Savage, Sue Garrison, Squish (who served only in an interim capacity and so doesn't count) and Bettye Myers were Shannon's predecessors, which means that Waldemar had only four program directors for some sixty years. Although many campers will remember Shannon as the "schedule changer lady" or the consummate "boss of Field Day," there are those from 1943 to 1957 who remember her best as the "fun leader of the singing on the horseback trail."

Kay Mitchell (later Estes), a physical education professor at Baylor University, joined the Waldemar staff in 1954. At first she assisted Shannon as an Aztec sponsor, but when Bettye Myers left Waldemar, Kay became head Comanche sponsor, a post she held for twenty years along with supervising the junior department. Kay was so versatile that early in her Waldemar career, she was called "PT" because she served in many departments on a "part time" basis. No vocal trio performed without Kay's rich alto, and she led singing in the dining room with spirit and verve. Kay brought many religious and folk songs to camp including "Jacob's Ladder," Waldemar's "gathering song."

The war had slowed Doris' building program a bit, but after the kitchen was enlarged, it was agreed that a new rock storeroom and the cowboy dining room were the proper construction goals for 1950. In 1951 a sleek-looking four-unit dwelling of modern architecture named "Greystone" was added to the list of rock kampongs. Greystone was described by a reporter as

so modern it has tinted walls. . . .
If you want to know what happened to K6, K8 and K9, K9 is now the Waldorf on counselor hill and either K6 or K8 is the leather room.

Three units of Monterrey were ready for the

1952 season, and when campers arrived in 1953, they were surprised to find numbers 4 and 5 attached to the beautiful building high on the hill and slightly to the west of Cedar Lodge. Its placement and its size make its name "Monterrey," which translates from Spanish as "King of the Mountain," appropriate.

"Casita," the "little house" pavilion where horseback riders assemble for roll call, was built in 1955. In 1956 a "new modern garage," with airy and functional craft rooms above it, was welcomed by craft counselors, and close by, tucked between Doris' greenhouse and the garage, and almost abutting the lower tennis courts, were two modern bedroom units for Ferdinand and Johnny Regan, later named "Hacienda." Ferdinand's workshop was below them.

Of more interest to campers was the new bus gleaming inside the new garage, but of most importance to visiting fathers was the restroom for men located in the south end of the garage, the first such amenity provided for long suffering dear old Dad.

Ferdinand fulfilled the dream Aztec sponsors had held since the birth of the tribe by building the pyramid on their hill during the winter of 1951, following the design of a clay model sculpted by sponsor Floy Hume. In that same year the Tejas, under the sponsorship of Ellen Easley, proposed a new performance area to be called "Tejas Theater" and subsidized by members of the tribe for five years. The outdoor theater was to be located where most of the very first Waldemar programs and campfires took place between the original Waldemar Lodge and the river. The Tejas suggested terraced steps covered with grass, and this long anticipated project was accomplished as planned by 1957—except that it became known as "Tejas Chapel." The chapel was dedicated to Ferdinand on June 23, 1957, against the wishes of the builder who called it "inappropriate."

Sarah Jayne Johnson, daughter of Billie and Mac, gave the new chapel a Hammond organ. It was housed in Round-Up Lodge but ingeniously moved to the top of the building's outside circular stairway during church services.

Older campers had long eschewed living in "the fancy new rock kampongs" with their tile floors and their window screens upon which finger-nail-polish graffiti was prohibited. Leaving your name and your tribe and the date of your occupancy of the kampong assured you a sort of "permanency" in this camp that was, after all, really yours.

In 1958 this negative feeling began to change when Doris assigned the oldest and most prominent campers to new kampongs 12 and 14. Built on the east hill just above the lower tennis courts, these simple but attractive kampongs boasted welcoming porches and wonderful bath and dressing rooms which precluded trips to the shower houses. Kampongs 11 (later 9) and 15 were ready in 1959, and older campers, enjoying the privacy their quarters afforded, gladly gave up their graffiti.

Potpourri of the 1950s: In 1950 the name of Cactus Lodge was changed again to "Round Up Lodge," largely because "all camp Round-Ups" were held there. From the original Waldemar Lodge to Junior Rec to Cactus Lodge, the new "Round-Up Lodge" represented many remodelings and years of service. The dark walls were now painted a light cream color, blue denim curtains decorated with red bandannas hung at the windows and the stage opening, and the old building was ready for another 40 years of service . . . The Tejas and Comanches got new War Canoes in 1953 . . . In 1955 the original Comanche song, written to the tune of "The Eyes of Texas," was replaced by the present song, a substitution bemoaned by old-timers . . . In that same year Doris presented each tribe with four new tribal bracelets for the tribal leaders, low senior leaders, scribes and program council members. The old tribal leader bracelets, still in excellent condition, were moved down to the high senior leaders. All the bracelets were designed and made by Taller Borda Silversmiths of Taxco, Mexico . . . A trampoline was added to the camp's equipment list in 1956 and the sport proved so popular under the tutelage of a University of Texas state champion, that Doris bought a second one in 1958 . . . A new riding ring, built to Connie Reeves' specifications, was ready for riding classes in 1956 . . . In 1958 "Miracle Man Ferdinand" added two rows of seating to the pier steps so skillfully that only those who had previously had to sit behind trees on Field Days were aware of them . . . And in 1959 the Aztecs adopted the name "Zuma" for their War Canoe, feeling that the name "Angel" (which Doris had hurriedly christened it in mock ceremony upon its arrival in 1944) was entirely too "angelic" for a War Canoe competing against the likes of Comanche "Ben" and Tejas "Big Blue."

In late June of 1959, the largest flood during the camping season since 1932 raised the Guadalupe fifteen feet. A call from Mo Ranch had alerted Doris and Ellen, and counselors moved canoes and waterfront equipment to high ground. Ferdinand and his crew removed the diving boards from their pier to higher ground, but not high enough to save them. Campers were in awe of a talented neighbor downstream who "saw the boards and lassoed them." Waldemar's main losses were the floating pool piers and damage to fences.

Former campers continued to return as counselors during the decade of the 1950s "to give back some of what Waldemar has given me." The July 5, 1959, *War Whoop* (the same issue that chronicled the June flood) pictured a former camper on horseback who had joined the riding department. She was Marsha English from Beaumont, a camper from 1950 through 1954, the year she was named Best All-Round Tejas. Since her camping days, Marsha had been a counselor at a Campfire Girls' camp, she had headed the English riding department at Camp Mystic in 1958, and she spent 1959 and 1960 under the tutelage of Connie Douglas Reeves at the Waldemar stables.

The popular Connie, in addition to her horseback duties since 1937, had distinguished herself as an inspiring speaker at church and tribal hill services. Such tributes as this from a *War Whoop* of 1951 were frequent:

> Connie Reeves gave an inspiring talk [at church service] on "God's Beautiful World." Editor's note: Not only has Connie spent much time riding around in God's beautiful world, but she has keenly observed the life therein. This experience has, therefore, given her a sound understanding of the subject upon which she spoke.

One of the most important and lasting pieces of work accomplished during the 1950s took place between the summers of 1955 and 1956. The registration cards of each camper had been carefully preserved, bundled by years, and stashed on a shelf in Cedar Lodge. The enormous task of assembling the cards in useful order was tackled in the mid-fifties by Doris and Ellen, who spent the winter filing the last registration card of each camper in alphabetical order. If a girl came seven years, she had seven registration cards, and they filed her last one after having noted the years she attended in the upper left-hand corner. The card contains her kampong requests for her last year, her tribe, and other significant information. This master file, kept up-to-date from that time on, is kept as current as possible with married names and addresses carefully noted. When a former camper who knows no one at camp visits Waldemar and is

shown this card, a symbol of her happy camping days, she knows that she is not just a number at Camp Waldemar—her roots are here.

Because Doris' father and his wife had moved downriver to their new home early in the decade of the 1950s, Doris and Ellen were now living year-round in Rippling Waters. When Ora Johnson chose the location for her Fine Arts Building in 1930 (known as Rippling Waters since 1937), she was warned by old-timers in the Hill Country that her building was going to be mighty vulnerable to a beautiful but fickle Guadalupe River which flooded ferociously on occasion. She assured them that her building would be constructed to withstand the occasional fury of the river, and shortly after her death her confidence was affirmed. The "great flood of '32" filled the building with mud and debris, left water marks in the tower attic, but the building suffered no structural damage.

On October 8, 1959, Rippling Waters was threatened again, this time by a mammoth flash flood caused by a cloudburst. Ferdinand had commented on an ominous black cloud which hovered over the horizon all afternoon, but because the camp had had no rain and because rises on the river customarily follow several days of rain, Doris, Ellen, Doris' father, Shannon Harber, and Kay Mitchell went to a Saturday night movie in Kerrville. A few hours later they left Kerrville in a driving rainstorm and were soon stopped by a highway patrolman who told them they could go no farther—there was "a 10-foot rise at Camp Stewart." The moviegoers spent a nervous night in Kerrville.

The next morning the Waldemarites learned there had been an estimated "30 foot rise in Kerrville." No communication was possible with Ferdinand, the only person at Waldemar, and their apprehension grew. On Monday morning, when they were finally able to return to camp, they learned from Ferdinand that water had risen all the way to the road in front of the office, five feet had stood in the living room of Happy Haven, the water was waist deep in the Amphitheater, Rippling Waters had stood six to eight feet deep in churning water, and black mud was everywhere. The water had receded by 2:00 A.M.

Before the flood reached its peak, Ferdinand opened all the windows and doors in Rippling Waters to let the raging water go through, and some of Doris' prized antiques were carried down-stream with it. Once again Miss Ora's building suffered no structural damage, but repairing, cleaning and redecorating the house took two months. Doris and Ellen lived downstream with Mr. Johnson during those two trying months.

Because all camp equipment was stored for the winter months, trees were Waldemar's greatest loss. Two giant cypress trees on the Rippling Waters side of the pool were carried away, and smaller trees below the dam went with the raging water. The two large cypress trees at the pier were undamaged but a big shade tree by the golf course was swept away as was a huge pecan tree by the gates "estimated to be over a hundred years old."

Although this flood of October 1959 was compared to the "big flood of '32," it differed in several ways, not the least of which was that camp was not in session.

Chapter 5

1960s

Florence Wolkewitz, confidante of Ora Johnson, wrote in her 1932 serialized history of Waldemar that Aunt Ora believed the success of her endeavor on the banks of the Guadalupe was dependent upon the quality of her counselor staff. Later her niece Doris subscribed to the same dictum and indeed through the years since the camp's founding, Waldemar had been able to attract superior women and men whose character, talents, personalities, and enthusiasms made them worthy of positions on the Waldemar staff. Just as their predecessors had embraced the camp and loyally returned year after year, eager to make their contributions and put their personal stamps upon such a remarkable institution, so did the counselors of the '50s and '60s return for many summers and give of their best to campers for whom they were both role models and friends.

Waldemar observed its fortieth birthday in 1965 as a smoothly running machine powered by caring and experienced counselors who took joy in creativity and perfection. Why shouldn't a Field Day—that fun-filled but complicated tribal contest in which Waldemar strives to make stars of each of some 300 or so campers—work perfectly with Shannon Harber as coordinator and department heads of many years' experience teaming to promote fairness and fun?

A partial list of the "longevity honor roll" for the '50s and '60s (based on service of at least ten years) was headed by Laura Wallace, who joined the Waldemar staff in 1928, became a close friend of Ora Johnson, and stayed forty years; Ripple Frazer, who became dietitian in 1927 and who, along with her friend Idabel Cabaniss, saw to it that this post was filled until 1968 (their contributions have been discussed earlier); Jack Reeves, who began his work at the Waldemar stables in 1930 under the hand of the legendary Colonel W. T. Johnson; Johnny Regan, who first twirled a rope and snapped a bullwhip at Waldemar in 1934 and stayed forty-five years; Bess Rayford, who began her Waldemar career as a camper in 1932, then returned as a counselor in 1941 heading the canoeing department and sponsoring the Tejas tribe for many summers; saxophonist Ruth Wright (later Green), who joined the Waldemar staff as an art counselor in 1935 and whose musicianship, athletic ability and originality enhanced Waldemar for some thirty summers; Connie Douglas Reeves, a 1937 arrival, whose name is synonymous with horseback riding at Waldemar and continues to be as she and the century move into the '90s; Ellen Easley, crucial to Waldemar's success, who came in 1937 and stayed until Doris sold the camp; Roe Johnson, who kept campers' "tail feathers tucked in" from 1941 to 1959; Reba Holcomb, who joined the academic department in 1941 and later became a member of the office staff until 1958; Margaret Shannon Harber, who wore a Stetson in the horseback department from 1943 to 1957, then laid it aside for the program director's hat and wore it until her death in 1989; Floy Hume, who spent from 1943 to 1955 heading the riflery department and sometimes sponsoring Aztecs; Agnes "Aggie" Talley, who spent from 1946 to 1956 teaching badminton or swimming; Reba Lacey, who headed either the waterfront staff or the canoeing department from 1951 to 1962; Helen McCoy, who came in the late '40s and spent the decade of the '50s and well into the '60s teaching canoeing, fencing, swimming, diving or horseback riding and sponsoring the Tejas tribe; Kay "Gib" Gibson, who first came from Kentucky in 1948 to teach swimming and wound up teaching diving into the 1970s and stayed on the staff until the '80s; Elois "Sis" Elliott, who nurtured and perpetuated the tribal song contest throughout the '50s; Millie von Tungeln, who first arrived in 1948 as an accompanist, followed "Sis" Elliott as choral director, became Sunday service director, and in the early '60s took over Fannie Bolinger's position as "Happy Haven Mama" first term; Fannie herself, the Dublin, Texas, grade school principal, who was as at home arranging flowers for the thirty-four dining room tables or playing comedienne as a Buzzard cheerleader as she was with the youngest campers; Mary Kelley, representative for the Alexandria, Louisiana, area, who was second-term "Happy Haven Mama" ("Rise and shine, my proud beauties: Time to do your kampong duties!"), dining room flower arranger and contract bridge maven from 1942 to 1972; Ruth "Red" Lindsey, who arrived in the late '40s, headed the archery department, and sponsored Aztecs through much of the '50s.

La Neal "Tank" Tankersley, who served on the waterfront staff and played drums with the band for at least twelve summers, beginning in 1955; Barbara Tyson, who came to Waldemar in 1955 to teach horseback, later taught English and art to U.S. Army dependents in the Azores Islands and in Japan, returned to Waldemar to teach horseback and art in the '60s, skipped the '70s but returned in the '80s to teach art and reclaim the Ranch House murals; Emma Jeanne "Cookie" Cook, who arrived in 1948 and soon became head of the first-term waterfront staff, a post she held for eighteen summers; Ruth "Tate" Tatum, a 1948 arrival, who headed the junior department, originated the "Adventure Hour" class, and sponsored the Tejas tribe for fifteen years; Carolyn "Bunny" Blankenship, who taught riflery and sponsored Comanches during much of the '50s; Betty Blakely, who joined the first-term waterfront staff in 1958, became its head when Cookie left, and sponsored first-term Tejas from 1959 to 1964; Kay Mitchell (later Estes), who arrived in 1954, became one of the "Big Four" decision makers (Doris, Ellen, Shannon, Kay) as head counselor, junior director, and Comanche sponsor for twenty years; Jan Cannon, whose proficiency in teaching tennis, canoeing, horseback riding (and every other sport) together with her knowledge of music and her beautiful singing voice she so graciously shared, and her years of sponsoring Tejas made her invaluable as a member of the staff from the '50s through the '90s; Marguerite Clawson, who joined the waterfront staff in 1944 and later succeeded Roe Johnson as correctives specialist through the '70s ("Grace comes from pushing from the earth and rolling on the balls of your feet!"); Bettye Myers, who came in 1946 and soon became Comanche sponsor and program director, staying until 1957; Joyce

Jordan, who joined the first-term archery staff in 1959, soon headed the department, later became an Aztec sponsor, and continues to add strength to the staff in the '90s; "Jackie" Toman, drama teacher extraordinaire, who first arrived in 1955, was erratic in attendance (even spending a year abroad) but served for fifteen summers; Jill Johnson, camper of the '40s, who returned second-term of 1959, became head of the archery department and the Tejas tribe and continues to add her expertise to Waldemar in the '90s; Barbara Keller, who joined the first-term waterfront staff in 1962, became its head in 1966, and continues to head Waldemar's largest department into the '90s; Janice Ward, a 1962 arrival who taught archery and sponsored Tejas into the '70s.

B. J. Gray, who came to teach badminton in 1963 and remained to teach softball and archery and sponsor Comanches through the '70s, '80s and on into the '90s; Waneen Wyrick, who in 1956 was strongly recommended as a fencing master by the University of Texas physical education department despite her youth and stayed to teach fencing, canoeing, trampoline, and swimming and sponsor the Aztec tribe until she became a part of UT's physical education department; Kay Alderman, who joined the waterfront in 1957 and stayed for eleven summers; Sue Vaughan, former camper, who returned second-term 1966 to join the waterfront staff, soon headed that department second term, taught horseback riding first term and sponsored the Aztec tribe both terms, a regimen she continued until she opted for law school in 1984.

From 1958 through 1967, the *Waldemar War Whoop* was edited by Marjorie Menefee, who challenged campers to write for the newspaper by giving medals for excellence at the awards program beginning in 1960. With Shannon's approval, one gold and three silver medals were awarded, each carrying points toward the tribal plaque. Heretofore ambitious tribesmen struggled to "make a team" in *War Whoop*, which many campers interpreted as requiring quantity of published articles rather than quality. The new plan gained immediate acceptance and encouraged excellence in writing. Marjorie and Mary Anna Branson taught a course in creative writing when it was desired.

The 1960s could well be called "The Decade of the Drama." Jacqueline "Jackie" Toman, Mary Anna Branson and Helen Schafer, drama counselors, chose to present hits from the Broadway stage adapted for the Waldemar situation. "My Fair Lady," "The Crucible," "Our Town," "Stage Door," and "The Sound of Music" were among the choices of the ambitious directors and camper actors who were assisted by set design art majors from the craft department.

The drama counselors found time to help direct tribal vesper services, many from the pen of Marjorie Menefee. Marjorie, a Comanche sponsor, also wrote the scripts for some of the awards programs and Memorial Vespers during the 1960s.

Perhaps the most welcome news for all campers and counselors arriving in the year 1960 warmed more than their hearts. A reporter wrote:

> Doris felt that Waldemar should step forward from the stone age and have hot water, so all the kampongs on the hill are now living in the lap of luxury—except Shower House 3.

It is unclear what the problem was, but a protest group, later to become a symbol of the 1960s, marched to the office, and the girls who used Shower House 3 soon knew the wonders of a warm shower and shampoo.

Putting Waldemar back in operating condition after the flood of October 1959 had taken most of the winter and spring before the 1960 season, but the building of a new rifle range, for which plans had already been drawn, was now imperative because of the ravages of the flood. The new range, enlarged and slightly repositioned because of the sometimes blinding afternoon sun, not only improved safety but allowed more girls to shoot at the same time and provided much needed storage space. The range, designed by former camper Frankie Kelly, later received national recognition when the National Rifle Association used pictures of it in its literature.

When Camp LaJunta for Boys wanted to buy two of Waldemar's used War Canoes, it was necessary for Doris to decide which of the three was in the best condition and so should be kept. The Aztec canoe had been in service since 1944 and by 1960 was badly in need of replacement. The Comanche and Tejas canoes had been new in 1953, but the years of competition had not dealt kindly with the Comanche canoe, and Doris decided that the Tejas canoe was the one to keep. Ellen Easley, a Tejas sponsor in the 1950s, concurred in this assessment. Although "Big Blue" did not fare well in races first term 1960, the second-term Tejas canoe either won or tied for first place both Field Days, dispelling any notion that a new canoe is faster than an old canoe!

Connie and Jack Reeves, who lived on the Johnson Ranch where the Waldemar horses spent the winter and enjoyed the Reeves' tender loving care, began breeding Waldemar's own horses for use at camp late in the 1950s. Doris bought six mares for breeding purposes, and a registered quarterhorse owned by Jack was used as the sire. By 1960 nine colts had been born, and "Bonita," a little buckskin mare with a black mane and four black stockings, was stabled at Waldemar in 1960. It was with pride that Connie announced that presentation of the little mare, Waldemar's own, and her official christening would be made at the horse show at the end of camp.

By 1962 there were sixteen colts of Waldemar's own stock at the ranch, and four were brought to camp that year. Camp did not depend solely upon its home-bred stock, however, because in 1963 a reporter wrote that "Jack and Mr. Johnson [Doris' father] have knowledgeable scouts on the look-out for horses suited to the Waldemar situation."

In 1962 Connie announced there would be no "monkey drill" because "the horses aren't right." Horses trained for Colonel W. T. Johnson's Madison Square Garden rodeo had made the spectacular event possible, but time had taken its toll on these grand horses that had served Waldemar so well.

The "choice night" concept, begun in 1953 by Bettye Myers, was embraced by Shannon, who worked closely with the program council, now made up of two elected seniors from each tribe, to give the senior campers a selection of activities. An evening of skating at the Ingram skating rink had been a popular choice through the years, but when the Hill Country Arts Foundation was established in 1958 on the property where Johnson Creek meets the Guadalupe just west of Ingram, the skating rink had been converted into a "building for art classes."

A stage was built on the slope to the river, the land in front was cleared and terraced for chairs for an audience, and the "Point Theater" was born. Directors and actors for the theater's productions were often from Houston's prestigious Alley Theater, and the theatrical fare presented made an excellent choice night selection. Another alternative was offered when Doris made arrangements for the Heart of the Hills bowling alley in Kerrville to close its doors to all customers except Waldemar girls on selected nights, and although the bowling skills of the campers were not noteworthy, their performance at the snack bar became legendary.

Another popular choice night activity in the '60s was the kampong overnight trip. In 1954 the site known as the Smith place had been enhanced by the building of two dams to make swimming and canoeing possible, by the discovery of three springs to furnish water for dishwashing and such, and by the efforts of counselors knowledgeable in the needs and joys of outdoor life.

Despite all these tempting trips out of camp, choice nights were still used by tribal committees for executing Field Day decorations, and vesper rehearsals were sandwiched in somehow by busy campers.

Second-term campers of 1960 had heard many stories of the big flood of the fall of 1959, but on August 15, 1960, they saw one of their own.

It had rained hard for two days and nights and the notes of Reveille that Monday morning were immediately followed by the announcement: "Attention campers. Please stay in your kampong and keep dry. All counselors report to the canoe docks now."

The counselors, Ferdinand and his staff, and the cowboys soon had all waterfront equipment moved to high ground, and Doris and Ellen, recent victims of the October flood of 1959, decided to move the furniture and their personal belongings from Rippling Waters. The counselor staff reacted swiftly to the challenge.

It is estimated that the water rose about five inches an hour reaching about 16 feet in all. About 4:30 Monday afternoon the flood crested and water covered half the steps in Tejas chapel and rose to the level of the higher steps of the pier.

Then the receding period started. The water went down so fast it looked like someone had pulled the plug out of a bathtub. High seniors were used as links in a chain to return the furniture to Rippling Waters. Everyone wanted to help not only as a good deed, but also to get a peek in Rippling Waters.

When it was all over, Waldemar had suffered more inconvenience than damage.

Second-term campers of 1964 saw many of their end-of-camp activities rained out, and their disappointment was chronicled in the 1965 *War Whoop*. "Hectic, Hurried, Tearful, Traumatic" were words used in a headline to describe those last few days. The song contest was moved to Round-Up Lodge, and counselor musicians acted as judges because the Kerrville judges could not get there. Miraculously, despite the ugliness of the muddy river water, the Ideal Girl program was held as usual, and afterwards determined campers trudged and slipped up their muddy tribal hills, "taking one step forward and slipping back two." The next day the Quadrille girls rode broomsticks instead of horses as Shannon gave the familiar square dance call; awards and medals were

given out in a hurriedly called assembly on the Athletic Field; and the plaque winner was announced without ceremony. The flood which resulted from all the rain, both at Waldemar and upstream, was classed as "minor." Counselors had moved all imperiled equipment to safety during the song contest, but fathers who came out in big highway trucks to gather trunks and campers will not forget the closing of Camp Waldemar of second term 1964.

Two years later, on August 13, 1966, second-term girls again experienced a swollen Guadalupe. A fierce electrical and thunder storm the night before preceded a cloudburst. Counselors, awakened on Saturday morning by the roar of the river, were able to save all equipment except the pool platforms and the diving boards. This fifteen-foot rise was disruptive, but Waldemar rebounded for a smooth closing some ten days later.

Thus in the 1960s Waldemar suffered three floods, all during second term. Counting the first-term flood of 1959, and the disastrous October flood of that year, the camp endured five floods in eight years.

By 1961 Doris was ready to resume building the single unit kampongs now so popular with the older girls. Four had been built in the late 1950s: K-12 and K-14 in 1958 and K-11 and K-15 in 1959. (This original K-11 was soon renumbered K-9.) Before building could continue, the old, deteriorating badminton courts which intruded upon the site to become known as "Rivery Oaks" had to be moved to another location. A site between the golf course and the riding ring just to the north of the winding back entrance road was chosen for the four new courts. It wasn't until 1963 that the windscreen was installed.

In 1961, Alameda, now twenty years old, gave up its picturesque but leaking mission tile roof for one of cedar shakes; an archery cabinet was built to preclude the toting of bows and arrows to and from Cedar Lodge every morning and night, an improvement deplored by some as eliminating service point jobs; the Tejas tribe decided to replace the flagpole they had given to the camp in the 1930s after it was necessary for Frankie Parker, former camper now head of the riflery department, to stand dramatically on the porch of Cedar Lodge and shoot down Old Glory entrapped at the top of the pole since the end of first term; the new flagpole was dedicated in appropriate ceremony by the Tejas on July 4, 1962; and the Comanches announced their plan to commission an artist to paint a portrait of Doris to hang beside the portrait of Aunt Ora. (Just as Ora Johnson had told

Ora Johnson

Doris Johnson

Mrs. Florence Wolkewitz

Carmen Crain

Margaret Gladney

Laura Wallace

Ann Miller Crockett

Emma Sealy

ADVISORY BOARD

Mrs. Florence Wolkewitz
Camp Mother
Margaret Gladney
Ann Miller Crockett
Emma Sealy
Laura Wallace
Carmen Crain

W. T. Johnson

J. F. "Josh" Johnson

J. F. "Billie" Johnson

 2A

 2B

 2C

 2E

 2D

 2F

A—Billie, Ora, and Doris Johnson
B—Josephine Bell
C—Doris Johnson
D—Harvey Smith
E—Ferdinand Rehbeger
F—Lucille and U. S. Smith
G—W. T. Johnson
H—Ora Johnson

 2H

 2G

3A

3B

3C

3D

3E

3F

3G

3I

Lovely sun-browned girl
With flying hair,
Laughing for sheer delight
At Nature's beauty;
Stretching your eager hands
For stars that hide within
The murmuring cypress;
Filling with gentle memories
And kind thoughts your sincere heart;
Playing, and losing, and winning
Sharing your dreamy soul
With those who have no dreams;
Lovely sun-browned girl,
Guard these, your ideals,
For they are the honor . . .
THE SPIRIT OF WALDEMAR.
—BY FLORENCE MAI ALBRECHT.

3J

3O

3K

3N

3L

3M

3H

4A

4B

4C

4D

4G

4H

4I

4J

4K

4M

4L

4O

4Q

4P

4N

5A

5B

5C

5D

5E

5F

5G

5H

5J

5T

5K

5I

5O

5R

5N

5Q

5P

5M

5W

5V

5S

5X

5Y

5U

6D

6F

6G

6J

6K

6M

6P

6L

6O

6Q

6R

7L

7D

7I

7M 7H

7N

7R 7S

7W WALDEMAR 7X 7Y

9A
9B
9F
9G
9J
9L
9P
9K
9Q
9S
9W
9R
9M
9X
9EE
9CC
9Y
9II
9JJ
9KK
9FF

9C

9D

9E

9I

9N

9H

9U

9Z

9BB

9T

9O

9HH

9GG

9V

9LL

9AA

9MM

9NN

A—Three Indians (Squish, Carolyn, Marsha)
B—Carolyn Wheat and Squish Willett
C—Connie Reeves
D—Susan Gordy
E—Marsha Elmore
F—Ellen Easley
G—Jan Cannon
H—Squish Willett and Laura Jean Johnson
J—Marsha Elmore
K—Dale Elmore
L—Marsha Elmore
M—Swans
N—Dale Elmore
O—Marsha Elmore
P—Marsha Elmore
Q—Dale Elmore
R—Marsha Elmore
S—Roxie
T—Yankee Doodle Dandy
U—Wuki
V—Happy Jack

Marsha English Elmore

Meg Elmore Clark

Waldemar Family

the campers of 1929 she would sit for a portrait "when she had time," so Doris accepted the Comanche plan with grace and warm appreciation but procrastinated a decade and a half in its execution.)

"We miss Jack Reeves' rushing from the stables to the office in his rattling old pick-up to find out why a camper is holding up the horseback class," wrote a reporter when in 1963 the camp communication system was upgraded by the addition of battery-powered crank telephones.

Ellen had seen the old-fashioned equipment used at a small camp in New Hampshire and recognized the system's usefulness for Waldemar. The camp installed a five-party line serving the office, the infirmary, the kitchen, the bunkhouse, and the stables, each with a distinctive ring.

No one doubted the improved efficiency, but service point girls were distressed because "technology was taking over their jobs."

The crank telephones are still a part of Waldemar thirty years later.

The new single-unit kampong which rose on the site of the old badminton court was ready for the 1962 season. It was pictured in the *War Whoop* as K-7, but before the printer's ink was dry, it became K-10. The numbering of the new kampongs and the tearing down or moving of the old woodens was so confusing that the new K-10 became known as "This is K-10" for several summers, a title which was perhaps easier to perpetuate because the Kampong Mama was the *War Whoop* editor. When present-day K-11 was built in 1963, it took the number away from one previously named K-11 built in 1959 along with K-15, and that kampong became K-9.

A double kampong, K-7 and K-8, each with a little more floor space than those built earlier and featuring spacious bathroom counters with two lavatories, was built in 1964, and K-6, the highest kampong on the hill, was ready for the 1966 season. Three of the wooden kampongs that were replaced were moved to the gully behind the lower tennis courts leading to the rifle range during the shuffle and became the "tribal decorating shacks."

Newspaper articles continued to lament the passing of the wooden kampongs to which so many girls were sentimentally attached. Finding one's mother's name on a kampong rafter was an exhilarating experience, and young journalists proclaimed the woodens "a part of the Spirit of Waldemar." By 1966 five wooden kampongs remained on the Waldemar hill—K-1 through K-5—and although it was possible to attend Waldemar for seven or eight summers without

living in one, Doris did her best to see that every girl had the experience of spending one summer in a kampong of Miss Ora's original design. The experience became "a rite of passage."

The older girls were now reveling in the comfort and convenience of the rock kampongs which encircled the area they called "Rivery Oaks" after the River Oaks section of Houston.

"Blakely and the Sweet Sixteens" usually opened the tongue-in-cheek social season with a Christmas party in K-15 to which the occupants of K-6 through K-14 were invited. Improvised Christmas decorations festooned the kampong and although the party was short on time, it was long on originality. Marjorie Menefee of "This is K-10" responded with a party introducing her debutantes to society. In 1967 "Cookie," long-time first-term waterfront director, willed that important post to Betty Blakely, who consequently moved from K-15 because of the workload, and the social whirl was over. (Betty Blakely was so dedicated a Tejas sponsor that she was referred to in the War Whoop as "Big Purple Mama.")

K-10 was the last kampong built by the remarkable Ferdinand Rehbeger, whose death on February 2, 1963, was deeply mourned by the Waldemar community. Mrs. Wolkewitz had called Ora Johnson's death in 1931 "Waldemar's darkest hour," but this hour thirty-two years later was just about as dark. Ferdinand had built all of Waldemar's buildings, all show places except Round-up Lodge and Cedar Lodge, and he had added restorative touches to those landmarks through the years. He was admired for his strength and abilities but loved for himself. (The fascinating story of how this German artist came to Waldemar from his native Russia is told earlier in the 1920s.)

Ferdinand had built Tejas Chapel in 1957 at the request of the Tejas tribe and its sponsor, Ellen Easley, who was probably his closest friend. Recognizing his immeasurable contribution to Waldemar, the tribe had wanted to dedicate the chapel to him at that time. Ferdinand deemed that "inappropriate," but this did not keep the Tejas from dedicating the chapel to him after their vesper service first term of 1963. A bronze plaque was placed at the corner of the rock wall separating the chapel from Round-Up Lodge. It reads:

Tejas Chapel
Dedicated to the Builder
Ferdinand Rehbeger
A part of Waldemar 1928-1963

"Blessed is the man who has found his work."—Carlyle

The ashes of Waldemar's miracle man rest behind the simple marker.

Two years after Ferdinand's death, Harvey P. Smith, the San Antonio architect with whom Ferdinand had worked so closely since 1930, was drawing plans for a new Waldemar gate to be given to the camp by the Aztec tribe. The celebrated architect, who had restored many of San Antonio's famous missions, had designed all of Waldemar's picturesque buildings except Round-Up Lodge, Cedar Lodge and Rippling Waters, and the team of Rehbeger and Smith, which Ora Johnson had put together in 1930 and Doris Johnson had nurtured through the years, was remarkable in the consistency of its happy productions for the beauty of Waldemar. While he was designing the new gate, Harvey Smith died, and the deaths of the two artists, so close together, marked the end of a symbiotic relationship of over thirty years' duration.

Both terms of 1965 the Aztecs dedicated the handsome new gate, with its huge black block letters proudly spelling out the name "Waldemar," to Harvey P. Smith. In a candlelight service after a tribal hill program, a bronze plaque commemorating the dedication was placed in a waiting niche, and in tribute to Waldemar's architect it read, "A thing of beauty is a joy forever," a quotation from John Keats.

At Doris' invitation, her longtime friend, the architect's widow, and his son, Harvey P. Smith, Jr., attended the second term dedication.

J. F. Johnson, Doris' father, died February 8, 1966. Thus in the span of three years, Waldemar lost three men whose contributions to the camp had been incalculable. J. F., younger brother of Ora Johnson, had served Doris as advisor and staunch supporter since she assumed full directorship in 1934.

K-11, K-7 and 8, and K-6, their plans drawn and their sites chosen by the time of Ferdinand's death, were the work of a father-son combination from Fredericksburg who had sometimes helped Ferdinand, and of Reyes Morua-Pina, an important part of Waldemar since 1957. Reyes had learned the art of stone masonry from the master, and he is still serving Waldemar in the 1990s. Known as Reyes to all campers and counselors, this loyal, thoughtful man has helped make Waldemar the wonderful place it is for almost forty years.

Eladio Renteria came to Waldemar in 1970. He soon became Doris' "right-hand man" in caring for Waldemar's flower beds and the greenhouse along with many other chores necessary to the maintenance of Waldemar and the operation of the camp. Eladio's happy disposition and willing spirit made him a favorite with both campers and counselors, and he too is still serving Waldemar in the 1990s.

James Rathke, an Ingram carpenter whose ingenuity and skills were well suited to Waldemar's needs, became head of maintenance in 1964. In addition to his duties of supervising building maintenance and care of the grounds, James took over Ferdinand's on-season duties such as assuring campers that their tribal hill ceremonial fires would be built as requested, building vesper, drama and awards programs sets, and rescuing dental retainers and jewels from kampong plumbing traps. James was known for his patience and tolerance, and he continued his Waldemar work through the decade of the seventies.

Throughout the years probably the most onerous kampong duty had been the ice detail. Ice for the kampong was required twice daily, at siesta and bedtime. The heavy-even-when-empty aluminum pitcher was filled with ice laboriously chipped with a lethal looking ice pick from the huge chunk in a box near the kitchen door, the ice was then covered with water from a nearby faucet (because water in the shower houses was not potable), and the hapless camper trudged back uphill to her kampong. The practice of carrying the empty pitcher to the evening program to save steps after the program was discouraged because inevitably some restless camper would kick the metal pitcher, which would clank resoundingly against a stone step during a solemn moment in the program.

The upgrading of this kampong duty began in 1964, when Doris decided to buy one newfangled ice machine to be placed on the porch of Round-Up Lodge on a trial basis. Juniors and low seniors lived in position to benefit most from the machine, which proved so popular that two more were installed in 1965, one by the kitchen and another in the Rivery Oaks area between K-14 and K-15.

Billie Johnson, who had hauled ice from Kerrville all the years of the camp's life, joined a camper journalist in proclaiming

"Now we are left without a care
On account of a machine—by Frigidaire."

In 1967 water wells were drilled which supplied the entire hill with potable water, and lightweight ice buckets replaced the old pitchers.

In 1965 another departmental improvement greeted arriving campers. A small closet opening on the outside of the lower tower of Casa del Monte had been the inadequate repository of golf equipment which was hand lugged at class time to the tee on a mound just outside and slightly north of the Happy Haven gate. The placement of the tee imperiled counselors' cars parked along the fence, and in 1964 a new tee was placed some forty yards east of the old one. By 1965 a "clubhouse," so named because it was literally used to house golf clubs, complemented the tee and it included storage space for equipment, benches for early arrivals, and a sheltering roof.

Square archery targets, touted by equipment vendors as longer lasting, made their debut in 1965, but their popularity proved to be short-lived when they were found to be too heavy for service point girls to turn and too tough for arrows to penetrate easily. So much for progress.

The age structure of Waldemar's divisions—junior, low senior, and high senior—was about to undergo revision. In 1966 it was tentatively announced that "perhaps next summer an intermediate department will be initiated," but it was second term of 1968 before the new department became a reality. It was made up of twelve-year-olds going into the seventh grade who were considered too mature to participate in junior activities and too young to compete with seniors. A director of intermediate activities saw to it that their calendar was full, and among their special treats was a dance with Camp Stewart's boys, who were the right age to make the evening enjoyable for Waldemar's intermediates.

Recognizing that Waldemar's eighth- and ninth-graders needed "something of their own," Shannon inaugurated the "Low Senior Track and Field Tournament" in 1966. Her careful planning and the enthusiasm of the counselors whose kampongs were involved made the weeklong event a tremendous success, with kampongs vying for group honors and individuals winning trophies as well as accolades. Records were established and Waldemar's thirteen- and fourteen-year-olds indeed had "something of their own." Because there was no audience as such, a Tejas who established a record in broad jump, for example, was honored on Tejas hill, and the *Waldemar War Whoop* was liberal in its coverage. Working the events into the free time of the campers' crowded schedule required the cooperation of many counselor judges and time keepers, and the event became almost (but not quite!) as important as Field Day.

Doris' decision in 1967 to set the upper age limit of eligibility for camp enrollment as "entering the eleventh grade next fall" was controversial. Explained Ellen: "Each year there are girls who have gone all the way through camp with their grade level, but because of the way their birthdays fall, they have an extra year of eligibility they don't really want because their close friends won't be back. We have decided that these campers and Waldemar will be best served by following the new rule."

Tribal decorating shacks served as a "private club house" for the execution of clever decorations which carried out the tribe's Field Day theme. Until 1964 there was no limitation on the number of signs and "props" a tribe could display, and excited, competitive-minded committees frantically adorned every available Waldemar inch with their tribal color.

To end this mad competition (and the clutter), Doris limited decorations to the banners over the dining hall, a large decoration in front of the office, individual motifs worn or carried by tribal members, and one portable decoration to be used both at the Playhouse and the pier.

Tribal themes were jealously guarded until their unveiling the night before Field Day. "Sock 'em, Aztecs" was the theme when Aztecs wore green socks; Comanches, self-appointed marshals of the Old West, featured a sign reading "Wanted: A Field Day Victory" with an orange jail decorating the Playhouse; and the Tejas proclaimed that the purple T was the "hottest brand going," a play on the popular Conoco commercial.

Throughout the years parents who came to enjoy Field Day with their daughter had worn some bit of her tribal color to prove their solidarity with her and her tribe. With the drawing by lot for tribal affiliation in 1947, this custom became more complicated because some parents now had daughters in all three tribes. By 1965 their costumes had become highly personalized, with a mother's white "shift" tastefully decorated with purple, orange and green ric-rac and a father's orange trousers topped by a green shirt with a purple tie receiving complimentary editorial comment. The enthusiastic father who dyed his white mustache orange was immediately recognized as a Comanche father and applauded by all.

The canvas canopy, festive but fragile, which had topped the Playhouse since 1940, required replacement about every five years even though it was removed and stored in the off-season. In 1967 a fiberglass alternative was offered to Doris, and although it was not as attractive as the original scallop-edged canopy, the fact that it might last at least twenty years justified the change.

"Howdy Day," the brainchild of B. J. Gray's Kampong-9, was initiated in 1967. Shortly after Reveille,

Ellen, in a twangy Western voice, announced that this was "Howdy Day" and asked that everyone wear some bit of Western garb and a smile. At breakfast the enthusiastic members of K-9 passed out sheriff's stars or some equally appropriate motif and announced there would be an election at afternoon nourishment time to find out who was acclaimed the friendliest junior, senior, and counselor at Camp Waldemar. Winners were feted in the dining room at dinner time and pictured in the next week's *War Whoop,* and the fun of the day and the enthusiasm of K-9 perpetuated it for four summers.

Waldemar took note of the country's changing mores during the 1960s by welcoming flower children—hippies—to the stage of the Farewell Banquet. (They were protesting because Doris said they had arrived too late to join a tribe and participate in the contests for Waldemar's medals.) Counselors protested the wearing of giant hair rollers at the dinner table even though they were concealed by ruffled "boudoir caps," which Connie banned from the stables. The campers' good-natured acceptance of her ultimatum resulted in their bringing her an especially gorgeous one when they returned from a War Canoe trip.

Instead of protests, the *Waldemar War Whoop* of the 1960s was filled with personal testimonies of the love the girls felt for Waldemar, for their tribes, and for the privilege of establishing and honing their lifetime values guided by Doris and her carefully chosen staff.

In the 1980s a long-time Waldemar counselor was asked to name something about which she would expect to read in a story of Waldemar. She unhesitatingly replied, "Oh, the story of the disappearance of the 'Saturday' record!"

Just who originally brought the "Saturday" record to Waldemar in 1952 was a secret until 1976. "Shine, Shave and Shower" was its proper name, and the record had made many a revolution on a turntable by the time it made its debut at Waldemar. Each Saturday morning immediately following Reveille, a scratchy, jazzy voice announced "Oh, it's Saturday—yes, it's Saturday." Some listeners declared it an intrusion upon their early morning reveries but secretly enjoyed participating in a Waldemar tradition no matter how raucous the sound of it.

One Saturday morning during second term of 1962, the controversial record was missing from it usual storage place. An inquisition turned up no clues, and the intriguing mystery very nearly disrupted Camp Waldemar. Doris tried to replace the record only to find that it was "out of press."

During first term 1963, a package postmarked from Houston arrived addressed to "Doris Johnson et al at Waldemar," and there was the treasured record. There was no note, but Doris received threats mailed from New York, California, Pennsylvania, and Florida to beware if "Oh, It's Saturday" wasn't well treated!

The mystery of the missing record is still unsolved, but every camper and counselor of second term 1962 remains suspect—except perhaps Happy Haven girls.

In 1976, thirteen years after it disappeared, two former campers claimed the dubious honor of bringing the "Saturday" record to camp second term 1952. Sissy George, Shreveport, and Cindy Beattie, New Orleans, were sixteen-year-olds that year. Sissy's cousin, who owned a radio station in Shreveport, gave the well-worn record to the girls, and the first Saturday morning of second term they were able to slip into the office and play their treasure right after Reveille to the consternation of listeners on the Waldemar hill. Of such stuff are traditions made!

Chapter 6

1970s

Throughout Waldemar's years, fast approaching fifty, "banquets" had been a popular form of entertainment. Costuming for the annual "Mexican," "funny paper" or "movie star" banquet was part of the fun, and prizes were given for the most original and most beautiful costumes, chosen during the grand march into the dining hall. Artists in the craft department decorated the tables, and individual favors carrying out the banquet's theme helped make the evening memorable. A program featuring talented campers, counselors, and the Waldemar orchestra made these banquets special, and the dietitian and kitchen staff saw to it that the food was delectable and served with a flair.

As the camp calendar became more crowded, these banquets were gradually dropped, but one remained—the so-called "final" banquet at which awards earned in classes were bestowed and that grandest award of all, the tribal plaque, was presented to the winning tribal leader for her and her exuberant tribesmen to fondle and cherish for the few more minutes they remained at camp.

Parents attended this banquet held on the lower tennis court, and Waldemar waiters and waitresses, under the watchful eye of first U.S. and then Lucille, served delicious food to patrons and campers, sometimes numbering almost a thousand.

A "filler" in a 1968 *Waldemar War Whoop* read: "We can quit worrying about the drought in the Hill Country. Next Saturday is Final Banquet."

Certainly the author of this cryptic remark spoke with the voice of experience. Too often the rains came, charitably avoiding the Spirit of Waldemar program the night before but focusing on the awards banquet. Oftentimes money for tickets sold to patrons had to be refunded, a time-consuming process, and Waldemar was left with mountains of broiled chicken and potfuls of its accompaniments. Or perhaps the food had just been served when the heavens opened, and parents and campers, sometimes gnawing a chicken leg, crouched under sheltering tables unsure whether to laugh or to cry. The crowd for the popular event was growing yearly, and Doris decided in 1970 it was time to discontinue this tradition of forty-five years, serve the campers an early special meal in the dining hall, and later welcome their parents to the awards program on the tennis court where chairs would be arranged in theater fashion in front of the stage. Waldemar's campers, always traditionalists, were disappointed but sympathetic with Doris, who had to make the tradition-breaking decision.

The Waldemar curriculum had not remained static through the years. Doris and Ellen were never content to let Waldemar rest on its laurels, and Shannon was always eager to have new courses to offer the girls. If interest in an activity waned, that course was dropped and another found to replace it. In 1970 Doris acquired the necessary equipment to offer a course in gymnastics, a sport which had received much media attention during the 1968 Olympic Games. When campers arrived that summer, a balance beam, uneven bars and tumbling mats were at the Playhouse, and skilled gymnasts were on hand to teach the sport.

Among other courses added in the '70s was self-defense, open only to the older girls, and taught by dynamic Kit Boesch from the staff of Ohio State University. "Slimnastics," a combination of yoga, aerobics, jogging and rope-jumping, was another of Kit's offerings in the mid-seventies which took the older girls by storm, and dance, so popular in Waldemar's early days and reluctantly given up in the sixties, was reintroduced in 1976. Basketball and cheerleading were new to the curriculum in 1978.

In 1972 Doris answered the increased enthusiasm for tennis, experienced nationally, by moving the hay barn and building two more tennis courts adjoining Casa Courts.

The first third-generation camper came to Waldemar second term 1970. When Lauren Kenzie's name was called at the tribal drawing and the announcement of her third-generation status was made, it was enthusiastically cheered, and to Doris it was further testimony to the "rightness" of her lifelong commitment to her aunt's dream.

Another tradition was broken in 1971, this time of necessity rather than by choice. In Waldemar's first summer, 1926, there was one term of eight weeks, but the following summer Miss Ora offered twelve weeks of camping. Even though campers could attend for six, eight or even twelve weeks, the rule of two separate six-week terms was soon established.

In the late 1960s and early 1970s, public school openings and closings became sporadic, and in 1971 Waldemar was forced to shorten its terms to five weeks each so that both campers and school-teaching counselors could meet the deadlines of school openings and closings.

Clearly, losing a week of camp meant that some evening programs had to be dropped from the calendar. Doris, Ellen, Shannon, and Kay decided that as hilarious an evening as the counselor cut-ups provided, it must be discontinued. The kitchen staff concert would be given up, regretfully, and another beautiful tradition, "The Legend of the Guadalupe," usually presented on a Sunday night early in the term, would be dropped from the calendar. In deference to the camp's history, the "Legend" has henceforth been presented occasionally by one of the tribes.

Because of the shortened term, as well as her desire to interrupt class time as little as possible and thus ensure that her campers gained as much as they could from her always talented counselor staff, Doris decided in 1971 that parents should no longer be invited to First Field Day, a move that many patrons applauded.

The first of three floods to bedevil Waldemar during the decade of the '70s came some ten days before the end of the second term of 1971. There were three major rises, and the first one, very early in the morning, resulted in the loss of five canoes, the rafts at the pier and the pool platforms. When word came from upstream that another rise was on its way, Doris and Ellen decided to make it an educational experience: the rest hour bugle was delayed and campers were invited to watch their beautiful river "show its dark side."

The second flood of the '70s occurred in early August 1974, and ten canoes were lost in this one, some broken in half. The river, fed by the flooding Bear Creek and not by the Waldemar fork of the Guadalupe, quietly rose to flood proportions about 9:30 P.M., and when counselors were called to the waterfront, darkness and blinding rain hampered their efforts. Cindy Salser, long-time head of the riflery department and Aztec sponsor, good-naturedly chided her good friend and fellow sponsor Sue Vaughan, head of the waterfront, saying, "The waterfront panicked. All they could think of were their precious rafts." It wasn't long before the North Fork joined Bear Creek in flooding, thus imperiling the rifle range gully, a backwash from the Guadalupe, and Sue was heard to mutter, "My precious waterfront went to check on Cindy's precious rifles." No rifles were damaged.

A reporter suggested that floods came every four years, and as if to prove her right, the river rose twelve feet in early August 1978. The excitement of this one was enhanced by the landing of four "Good Samaritan" helicopters, three on the golf course and one on the athletic field, which so excited counselor Debbie Norton she had her picture taken at the controls.

Debbie, proficient in all sports but especially golf and swimming, had come to Waldemar in 1976. She soon headed the second-term waterfront staff, and before the decade was over she added endurance and speed swimming as an adjunct to the form swimming for which Waldemar was famous. Records were kept on the number of river "laps" a camper had swum during the term, racing starts were practiced for Field Day performance, and if interest in swimming had waned, it was quickly revived. Debbie became a long-time Comanche sponsor and is still serving Waldemar in the 1990s.

"Squish" returned to Waldemar in 1972 after a twenty-year absence. Because she had written and directed the farewell awards programs before she left in 1952, it was understood that this would be one of her assignments and that she would direct the Ideal Girl program. In addition Doris and Ellen asked her to try to solve a thorny problem which had plagued Waldemar since the tribes were formed in 1928 and continued to get more out-of-hand each year.

Miss Ora Johnson invented the service point system as soon as she founded the camp not only to teach her girls to give of themselves and serve their community but also to "get the peas shelled, the flies in the dining room swatted and the rock removed from the athletic field." The "service points" issued by the counselor who supervised the duty were recorded by the kampong counselor on the camper's individual record card and counted toward the winning of the tribal plaque. In the early days there was no limit to the number of points a camper could earn each week, and enthusiastic tribesmen constantly bedeviled counselors who, not having proper paper at hand, scared up unmanageable little scraps upon which to issue two or three points much to the kampong counselor's annoyance.

As the years went by, the number of points a camper could earn each week was limited, and every camper wanted to earn the maximum else her tribesmen would frown upon her. Each hoped to get a "permanent" job, one in which she did the same duty each week, and to that end immediately upon arrival at camp she rushed to the porch of Cedar Lodge, where some counselor sat with a chart, to get first choice of the popular jobs. Obviously, the "savvy" camper had a decided advantage over a new girl.

This cumbersome and oftentimes ineffective system had not been abandoned because many of the duties performed were vital to the smooth operation of the camp. Others relieved counselors of chores campers could very well do, and the discipline the system taught was a part of Waldemar's training.

In 1972 the system was overhauled in that a camper did not get her job until *after* her schedule was arranged, and the service point job she was assigned was compatible with that schedule. For example, if a camper's duty was to help put away supplies after fourth-period pottery class, she must be enrolled in that class, a requirement which made it easy for her neither to forget her duty nor detain the counselor. If the camper changed her schedule, a practice with which Shannon was patient to the end that all campers were happy with their schedules, oftentimes it was necessary to change her service point job.

Department heads cooperated in establishing this new centralized system, and although it was tedious for the counselor in charge to set up, by the end of the first week, every camper had a permanent job she considered worthwhile and for which she alone was responsible.

Kampong inspection rules had not been updated in many years, only amended by inspectors. They were aimed at wooden kampong living when all but the youngest campers used shower houses and carried pitchers of chopped ice up the hill. During the first term of 1972, a small committee of campers and counselors met for several sessions bringing inspection rules up-to-date, and these rules were inaugurated second term of 1972. Kampong duties were adjusted to the needs of rock kampong living as well as the new five-week term, and the duty of "swing girl," a term borrowed from Lucille's kitchen staff, was added to take over duties when a kampong mate was in the infirmary or involved in a rehearsal.

A change in camp nomenclature made its debut in the second term of 1972. Alice Arnold, Aztec leader, found the appellation "Sweet Sixteen" for a sixteen-year-old camper cloying and inappropriate, and she didn't like "graduating senior" much better. She set her mind to the problem and came up with the term "Hilltoppers" for the girls who were spending their last year of eligibility at camp. Although many name changes at Waldemar have proven difficult to establish, this one was so apt and so needed that it caught on immediately with both campers and counselors, and "Rivery Oaks" of the '60s became "Hilltopper Courtyard" in the '70s. The first-term Hilltoppers of 1974 set a record by having forty-two members.

Julie Menges came to Waldemar in 1972 as office manager. Julie, who lived with her husband and seven-year-old son Wade on a neighboring ranch, had been a part of the Kerrville business community before her marriage, and now that Wade was in school, she was free to pursue her career at Waldemar. Her tenure was interrupted by the birth of daughter Suzanne, but she returned in 1983 and is still Waldemar's secretary and office manager into the 1990s.

The "winds of change," gentle breezes really, had been softly buffeting Waldemar since the decade of the '70s began. Small changes they were, progressive for the most part, but a change in 1974 was a traumatic one. Lucille Bishop Smith, a Waldemar tradition herself since 1928, was unable to return to camp, her second home. Campers did not have to be prompted to "Cheer for Lucille"—they did it spontaneously when her "monkey bread" (so named because those to whom it was served pulled round sections of delicious bread with their hands "monkey fashion" from a huge round loaf) or "chili biscuits" or "blarney stones and coffee ice cream" were served. Before they realized that Lucille's days at Waldemar were numbered, the girls of both terms celebrated "Lucille B. Smith Day" just as her home city of Fort Worth had done. She was driven around the oval in a convertible as her subjects cheered lustily. "Lucille's Treasure Chest of Recipes" became a prized possession in many Waldemar homes.

Not the least of Lucille Smith's triumphs during her forty-five years at Waldemar were the love she received from Waldemar girls and the esteem in which she was held by them and their families.

Lucille was succeeded in 1974 by capable Fort Worth cateress Bessie Williams Munson, and Robert Munson, her husband, directed the dining room service.

At the tribal drawing ceremony in 1975, Doris welcomed all campers and counselors to Waldemar's Golden Anniversary year, and during the summer a great interest in "the olden days" was revealed in the pages of the *War Whoop*. Pride in the accomplishments of Ora Johnson, in all the campers who had gone before them, and in Doris filled the hearts of current Waldemar girls, and even counselors new to the camp felt a strong sense of purpose and a desire to make this year a memorable one.

Doris invited all former Ideal Girls she was able to contact to the second-term Ideal Girl program, and twenty-seven of them came to participate in the ceremony, some from long distances. At the pier each came from offstage when her name, term, year and hometown were announced, and joined the expanded honor guard to hold high her lighted candle in tribute to the 1975 Ideal Girl. All were invited to attend their tribal hills after the ceremony.

Mary Brooke Oliphint (Casad), Ideal Girl of second term 1971, was editor of the *War Whoop* in 1975 and participated in this historic ceremony. She remembers that these former Ideal Girls were deeply touched by the beauty of the ceremony and grateful for the privilege of hearing again the ideals of Ora Johnson upon which the camp was founded.

The farewell awards program the following night portrayed the history of Waldemar. Opening with a spirited Charleston dance, setting the time of the founding as the 1920s, it progressed by decades to the 1970s. Billie Johnson was especially honored as the only person who had been at Waldemar all fifty years, and wearing trousers with one orange and one purple leg topped by a green shirt, he accepted a huge fifty-year all-star, elegantly constructed of gold painted cardboard with a large diamond twinkling in its center.

From the time of its founding in 1943, the Aztec tribe had sponsored the Aztec library, later renamed the "Somers Matthews Memorial Library" perpetuating the memory of a young Aztec from Little Rock, Arkansas. In 1976 the tribe added to its admirable cache of books in Cedar Lodge the "Betty Ruth Mitchell Memorial Library of Inspirational Books," which is housed in a section identified by a brass plaque. These are especially useful to campers and counselors in preparing talks for tribal hills and vesper and church services.

It was Betty Mitchell who, as a Hilltopper second term of 1972, stepped from her farewell serenade group to give her candle, used to light the words of the songs, to a fifteen-year-old whose tear-stained face spoke of her love for the departing Hilltoppers and for Waldemar. This spontaneous gesture established the tradition of each Hilltopper "passing her candle" to a fifteen-year-old at the end of the serenade.

Johnny Regan, Waldemar's beloved English cowboy who lassoed the hearts of all Waldemar girls through four decades, was above all a showman, and in 1977 he suggested that Waldemar's annual carnival needed a queen. Thus Queenie Fourteeny, chosen from among the fourteen-year-olds by an all-camp vote, was heralded each term with homage and exaggerated obeisances from her devoted subjects. Wearing cape and crown, she reigned over the carnival and received free admission to all events.

Johnny, in his familiar clown suit, always led the grand march onto the tennis court on carnival night, and younger girls were thrilled by a ride on the wooden horse on wheels he pulled around the tennis court. Johnny had come to Waldemar in 1934, and in 1937 Marilou "Moey" Rutledge, Dallas, became a second-term camper. Moey's contributions to camp through the years were many: She was Comanche tribal leader in 1941, an "aide" in 1942, a counselor for several years beginning in 1950, and a frequent horseshow judge. Later she established "Merriwood," a highly successful day camp, in Plano, Texas, telling Doris "monkey see—monkey do," and when Johnny Regan was not at Waldemar or in London, he was at Merriwood with his friend Moey.

Sadly, 1978 was Johnny's final summer at Waldemar. The 1979 carnival was dedicated to this charismatic showman whose story is told in an earlier chapter (1930s). The trick roping arena was renamed "Johnny Regan Arena."

The real name of Waldemar's Johnny Regan was Walter Alexandre.

The oil portrait of Doris, so long awaited by all but especially by the Comanches who had contributed to the project from 1961 to 1970, became a reality in 1978. Doris' innate modesty had caused her to put off sitting for the portrait until friends convinced her she owed this gesture to Waldemar as well as the Comanches. In 1974 a patron and former Waldemar camper asked Houston artist Allison Joy, daughter of renowned portrait painter Robert Joy, to come to Waldemar and discuss the painting with Doris. The two were immediately congenial and it was agreed that Allison would come from Houston each fall and spring when her commissions there allowed and that the sittings would take place under the trees just west of Johnny Regan Arena.

During these sittings Doris asked Allison if perhaps she could "do something" to soften the expression on Aunt Ora's face in the old portrait. The artist demurred but agreed to paint a new one. She studied numerous photographs of Miss Ora, and the portrait, called "an illusion" by the artist, was unveiled at the 1977 Memorial Vesper. At this vesper the Hilltoppers challenged campers and counselors to call the amphitheater by its correct name, Ora Johnson Theater.

The surprise presentation of the portrait of Doris was the highlight of the 1978 Memorial Vesper. Kay Mitchell Estes, long-time Comanche sponsor who had suggested to the receptive Comanches that Waldemar needed a portrait of Doris, had continued to urge Doris to choose an artist. She returned second term to unveil the portrait, and counselors on the staff who as campers had contributed to the fund, considered adequate by 1970, participated in the ceremony.

Conjecture about the future of Waldemar without Doris, an unwelcome thought but persistent topic of conversation among Waldemar lovers, was increasing as the years passed. It was generally agreed that Doris Johnson, the realist, would know when it was time for her to choose her successor. Perhaps the process began when Marsha English Elmore returned as a counselor in 1976.

Marsha English from Beaumont had drawn Tejas when she came to Camp Waldemar as a twelve-year-old in 1950, and in 1954, her final summer of eligibility, she was named "Best All-Round Tejas."

Marsha chose Southern Methodist University for her college career, and during the summers, while awaiting eligibility for counselorship at Waldemar, she honed her camping skills, first as a counselor at a Campfire Girls' camp and in 1958 as the head of the English riding department at Camp Mystic. In 1959 Doris invited her to join Connie's horseback department, and she returned in 1960.

After graduating from SMU, Marsha married Dale Elmore, a graduate of Texas A&M from Silsbee, and they settled down in Beaumont, had three children, and Marsha pursued her art career while rearing them.

The Elmores began returning to Waldemar for field days and closing activities when their daughter Meg became a first-term camper in 1974. Marsha found the "soul" of camp to be as inspiring as it had been during her camping days in the 1950s, and discovered that she was still exhilarated by it. The dream of owning and directing this Shangri-La of her youth began to take shape.

In order to be sure she wanted to commit her life to such an awesome responsibility, Marsha again joined the counselor staff in 1976 and 1977. Certain that Waldemar was their future, in 1978 she and Dale spent the summer next door at Camp Sequoia auditing activities and becoming better acquainted with campers and counselors. Thus they were ready to assume directorship in 1979.

In the announcement of the new ownership sent to all patrons after the 1978 season, Doris wrote: "Waldemar must be directed by those whose primary purpose is to perpetuate the principles, ideals and policies established by Miss Ora Johnson and cherished by campers and patrons throughout the years. Marsha and Dale Elmore meet that criterion. They are dedicated to camping in general and to Waldemar in particular."

Dr. Dudley M. English, Marsha's father, gave up his medical practice in Beaumont and moved with the Elmores to Waldemar. "Dr. E." quickly became a favorite, dispensing grandfatherly love and advice along with medication. In 1979 Marsha, Dale, and "Dr. E." moved to Rippling Waters, built by Ora Johnson forty-nine years earlier, and Doris and Ellen moved to the large house built by Doris' father one mile downriver.

The camp newspaper is filled with glowing tributes to Waldemar written by grateful sixteen-year-olds who have spent their childhood at this camp for girls on the Guadalupe, but none captures the essence of Waldemar better than a few simple lines written by a thirteen-year-old in 1969:

A Feeling

There you are, walking along on a bright sunny day, carrying the absentee report. You look around. What do you see? Friends and familiar, beautiful surroundings. You smile and take a deep breath. You feel as though you're going to burst. You want to shout out to the world how you feel, but what words can express such a warm feeling? Then you throw back your head and laugh. It's great to be alive, young and happy—at Waldemar.

"THE NEW ERA"
1979

As Doris and Ellen were settling into the large stone house her father had built on his ranch a mile east of Waldemar, an excited young family began to make plans to embark on the greatest adventure of their lives so far. Marsha English Elmore and her husband Dale prepared to move from the three-story home she'd grown up in and still shared with her husband, father, and three children. Dr. English closed his medical practice to the sadness of his many patients. Teak (seventeen), Meg (fifteen), and Josh (twelve) bid their childhood friends goodbye, and when the school terms ended in Beaumont, Texas, the Elmore/English family "went west" to Waldemar.

What a change it was! And what a challenge! Marsha and Dale were now the owners/directors of Camp Waldemar. Happy and thrilled to have been chosen, and hesitant to even think they might ever fill Doris Johnson's shoes, they were comforted by Ellen Easley's presence as advisor that first year. Rippling Waters, their new home, housed Marsha and Dale with a wing for Dr. English. Meg took her place as a first-term Waldemar camper, and Josh and Teak were regulars at Camp Stewart's first term. Most of their belongings were hastily stacked in warehouses, and the new directors gave Camp Waldemar their full attention.

Traditions at Waldemar are unchanging, and the Elmores were determined to keep the high ideals, superior staff, and outstanding camper program strong and intact. They brought to Waldemar new attitudes—that of a couple whose main priorities in life were their family, and whose favorite pastimes reflected a love of nature and the outdoors. They brought to Waldemar campers a family—a loving grandfather, a sister, and two brothers. (BOYS! And good looking ones too!) And the family brought their pets, making it even more like a home away from home for the girls.

The "old guard" remained to work with the newcomers. Squish Willett continued to do her unparalleled job with the Hilltoppers—perfecting their performances in "The Tribute" (a vesper she wrote to commemorate Ora Johnson, founder of the camp, and when Doris retired, rewrote to include Doris Johnson's many rich years as director), and writing and directing both of the two camp closing programs. Shannon Harber continued to apply her sharp mind

and inspired leadership as program director, scheduling each camper's activities, assigning counselors their classes, masterminding Waldemar's complicated Tribal Field Days. Shannon's energetic presence was appreciated and applauded by everyone. Connie Reeves, still regal and tall in her saddle, presided over the Waldemar Horseback Program as she had for so many years. Barking out commands in her strong voice, she prepared to teach another summer of young girls to ride—as she'd taught so many of their mothers to do.

The first summer under the new directors was very successful. Much fun was had, much was learned, and not just by the campers. The Elmores were full of enthusiasm—and offered several new ideas to enhance the girls' summer camp term. The Hilltoppers were treated to a special field trip to the famous Y-O Ranch, and enjoyed a tour, swim, cookout, and overnight adventure. New tan songbooks appeared in the Dining Hall to be used enthusiastically. The camp store offered campers and counselors tribal tee shirts for the first time. The lines were long at the "Hill Country Neiman Marcus" beside the office until everyone had their proper colored shirt.

The outdoor picnic suppers, previously held twice weekly on Thursdays and Sundays, were changed to coordinate with the camp movies on Wednesday and Saturday evenings, thus giving the staff a more reasonable time-off period to enjoy the Hill Country. Wednesday and Saturday evenings became easy, lazy outdoor times for everyone—having a picnic supper on the grass, and then waiting for the sky to darken and fill with stars as the girls enjoyed a movie together in Ora Johnson Theater.

The camp program was much the same as always—sunny, class-filled days, and warm summer evenings filled with laughter and challenging activities. A new class called "Adventure Hour" was added for the youngest girls, with the intent of allowing them to learn more about their camp with visits to the kitchen and senior hill, fun activities such as hayrides and river tubing, and always a visit down the road to meet Doris. All senior girls were taken on an overnight campout, all intermediates on a cookout, and juniors to a S'mores campfire by the enthusiastic new outdoor counselor, Carolyn Wheat. The infirmary was a popular place to stop in and visit with "Dr. E."—who dispensed both medical advice and love in equal measure. And soccer, experiencing a national renewal of interest, was added to the Waldemar program.

At summer's end, the Elmore family began their new life in the Hill Country community of Hunt. The children lived in Casa—unheated though it was—and enrolled in local schools. They began the process of making new friends and a place for themselves. And Marsha and Dale turned their attention to the part of Camp Waldemar they'd never experienced: "What do you do for the other nine months?"

The answer wasn't long in coming. They were soon busy planning the next summer season. The enrollment of new campers, a carefully fair process, took about a month or more each November. Build-ings and equipment must be repaired and winterized. The horse herd was moved to winter pasture. Plans for improvements were discussed, drawn up, and begun. And the all important schedule to visit colleges to interview counselors during February was prepared. The days were full, and everyone in the Elmore family busy and healthy. Their new life as camp-owners and Hill Country residents was in full gear, and 1980 was the new year. The new era had begun!

Chapter 7

1980s

(The following years are covered in somewhat of an outline form so as not to distract from the main body of this history of Waldemar. The years to come brought changes to camp; as time must surely do. Some were happy and positive changes; some saddened, as beloved camp friends slipped away from this world. The Elmores made Waldemar their home, and as such, it received their personal touches and absorbed their personalities slowly. Touching on some of the milestones from their life there, here are some of the highlights of those years.)

In the spring of 1980, Marsha and Dale commissioned the design and installation of special outdoor lighting throughout the camp and on the river front. Designed by John Watson, Dallas, the moonlight effect cast by the lights hidden in trees, eaves of buildings, and flowerbeds illuminated the camp as the enchanted playground it truly is. On the riverbank, the cypress trees and river glowed softly as if a full moon were rising.

From their kampong the girls could look out the windows beside their bunks after taps and perhaps see a deer or an armadillo rustling the leaves. On the athletic field, the solidarity of Cedar Lodge and the Dining Hall could be seen standing guard nightly, their classic designs illuminated by the "moonlights." A ceremony was held for campers during each term, dedicating the beautiful new outdoor lighting to Doris Johnson, with the new lights being first turned on for the girls of each term as Marsha read this dedication:

"The Special Outdoor Lighting of Waldemar is dedicated with love and gratitude to Doris Johnson for the light that she has brought into our lives"
1980

A brass plaque with this inscription was duly installed beside the front door of the office in Cedar Lodge.

The Waldemar Dining Room had a handsome new face. Roy Spears was hired as director of food services—and to become in the following years anoth-er Waldemar legend, as he earned his Master-Chef, 5* rating, and CCP standings. (CCP is the designation for Certified Culinary Professionals, a level of proficiency held by less than 120 chefs in America.) During Roy's fifteen years at Waldemar, the food would become even grander, and even more healthful, as the public knowledge of nutrition increased; and while old favorites like blarney stones and cherry squares were always cheered, the lights might dim in the dining room, and the waiters march in with a special treat—a flaming dessert! Chef Roy's youth and enthusiasm were inspiring to all who worked with him, and to all who received the culinary blessings of his many talents. Among the changes Roy would inspire at Waldemar were "Breakfast in Bed" for kampongs on Sundays, the revival of the "Field Day Picnic" for campers and parents in a beautiful tented setting with a gourmet luncheon, the publication of *The Waldemar Cookbook,* and two lady chefs from London's famous Cordon Bleu came to work in the Waldemar kitchen. (They were friends made by Roy when he trained at the Cordon Bleu.)

The campers of 1980 were treated to "new wheels" as the Waldemar fleet added two Ford vans, and told to "smile" as kampong group photos in living color were taken to memorialize the 1980 summer cabin-mates. First term was treated to an Arabian horse show in full costume to broaden their knowledge of horsemanship and equine history. With signs

98

of satisfaction, the Elmores completed their second summer.

Convinced that the many pleasures of Waldemar life would be great fun for adults, Marsha and Adm. Asst. Carolyn Wheat began Waldemar Women's Week in September. Special guests were WWW "Golden Girls" Squish Willett, Bess Rayford, Ruth Green, Ellen Easley, Moey Rutledge, Shannon Harber, and Kay Mitchell Estes. Designed as a program for the whole woman—mind, body, and spirit— Carolyn would serve as WWW director for the next thirteen years. Sports, crafts, seminars, spa services, theme dinners each evening—a program of excitement, relaxation, and education was offered to all women compatible with Waldemar. Only thirty-five "campers" attended the first WWW session, but it was to grow in future years into an eagerly looked forward to and well attended event each autumn.

1981

The mighty Guadalupe rose fourteen feet during the first term, causing first Field Day to be held two days late. Campers and counselors alike watched excitedly as the water level rose to the top step of the pier before cresting. Squish and Jeanne McKay, the camp secretary, were caught in town and prevented from returning to camp for several days. The dam and many fences were damaged, but the waterfront equipment was all saved, and camp continued as normally as possible when the flood waters receded.

Campers enjoyed the new Arabian filly, "Quita," who had been born at Waldemar during the winter. The canoe paddles were organized into a special new rack built that spring. An exciting addition to camp life was the "Tree House" built by Teak on camp land beyond the stables. Constructed around a towering tree, its three levels provided a perfect place for picnics and cookouts. The sound of construction was constant during the spring, as Marsha and Dale added a large new wing to Rippling Waters.

Waldemar campers were photographed and interviewed on every occasion, and the first summer yearbook in many years was produced and published. It was appropriately titled *The Tradition*. The books were mailed to eager campers at Christmastime. Another exciting change was the presence of the *"Gringos"*—Josh and Teak and occasionally their friends,

hired to help out during the summer. The *Gringos* were kept busy with the many chores camp required, and all eyes were upon them as they went about their jobs.

During second term, portable field lights were designed and installed around the central athletic field by Danny Wheat of Beaumont. They could be removed and stored on a trailer when not in use. This grand addition allowed games and activities formerly sandwiched into already full days to be held in the cooler evenings—and the lights would find their way into many evening events in coming years.

1982

Campers arriving at Waldemar in 1982 entered camp through handsome new iron front gates designed and built during the winter. The camper program offered a new craft class called "Creative Crafts," which filled to capacity immediately. Senior drama classes were treated to an evening field trip to a Hill Country Arts Foundation summer theater production. And tickets replaced the coins traditionally used by campers at their evening Carnival event. New booths and games were added to the Carnival—making it more fun than ever.

Connie and Jack were still presiding over the horseback program, although, having suffered a stroke, Jack's role was greatly diminished. For the first time, the Waldemar wranglers were Wranglerettes! Capable girls were hired to fill the jobs held by boys in the past, and were soon seen to fit into the camp program very well. Among those first Wranglerettes was Liz Pipkin from Houston, Marsha's oldest niece.

The loyalty and great contributions of long-time staff members were recognized by Marsha and Dale, and the counselor staff tenure pin award began that summer. Designed by Marsha and created by James Avery, gold W pins were awarded to permanent staff members and all serving ten years. The same pin in silver was awarded after five years.

Among the building projects accomplished during the winter months, one in particular excited the campers. They found a larger new Post Office and Camp Store building awaiting them between Swiss Chalet II and Cedar Lodge. The project was the work of the Waldemar crew, headed by Reyes Morua-Pina.

1983

Slipping easily into their roles, Marsha and Dale accomplished many projects to update the camp buildings, equipment, and program. The kitchen staff found their kampongs rebuilt and modernized. Their job was made easier with a new Hobart commercial mixer, five feet tall and large enough to turn out recipes big enough to feed all 450 people! The Dining Room wait staff was composed for the first time of Vietnamese and Cambodian boys from Houston. Their cheerful good manners and strong work ethic proved an inspiration to everyone in camp.

To the delight of everyone who knew her, Julie Menges returned to work in the Waldemar office in the fall of 1983. Having worked at camp from January of 1971 to March of 1976, Julie knew the requirements and traditions of Waldemar and slipped easily back into the thick of things. With her young family just a few miles up the road, she was perfect for the job. Her intelligence and cheerful good nature were a great addition to the team. For the years to come, Julie would be a source of strength and accurate information—a loyal and trusted friend to help carry the load!

Laura Jean Johnson, who came each spring from her job and home in Dallas to help Doris prepare for first term, retired from IBM and came to work all summer at Waldemar. She took the job as kampong inspector and covered the camper hill twice daily, doing her difficult job with such good spirits that campers and counselors both revised their opinion of "The Inspector" to a more favorable one. She also stocked and operated the Camp Store, aided by campers earning service points. She also enlivened the carnival with her clown act, and led the Carnival Parade each summer. (At this 1997 writing, Laura Jean is eighty-three, and her energy, warmth, and enthusiasm are still a cherished presence each summer!)

Waldemar's physical property showed many changes with new trees at the chapel, stables, and the athletic field. Cedar cross fencing replaced the old wire fences, and outlined the entire Waldemar property. The road from the Rippling Waters gate to the stables and to Counselor Hill was asphalted. The dam, which had been weakened by the flood the previous year, was strengthened and rebuilt. A modern telephone system was installed in the office, making the stables, infirmary, kitchen, and Rippling Waters easily reached. The camp was coordinated with a Master-Lock system, ending the frustration of individual locks, lost keys, and unavailable key holders.

In the summer terms, campers were invited to increase their knowledge and enjoyment of the outdoors with a new class. "Outdoor Skills" was its title, and senior girls enrolled to gain proficiency in camping, hiking, and cooking over an open fire. Safety and survival techniques were included in their class activities. Another activity was again added to the schedule—"Meal Rides." Horseback classes now rode out into the Hill Country to be treated to a campfire breakfast, lunch, or dinner.

The new purchases for Waldemar included several Arabian horses, and a blue trailer/truck rig capable of transporting ten horses. A colorful "HEX" sign, painted in tribal colors by Marsha and her sister Linda, warded off all "bad luck" at the stables. The riding ring was rebuilt and a stall added to house lucky horses penned there.

For church services in Tejas Chapel, Teak built a large cypress cross which Josh hung in the trees above the stage. And from wide pecky cypress boards Teak designed and built a speaker's stand. The addition of an electric piano to the Waldemar musical equipment meant the end to moving the heavy "Tom Thumb" piano about the camp. Used at church services, vespers, drama productions, and band concerts, this purchase made music a much "lighter" subject!

The three tribes found new aspen log drums awaiting their use on tribal hills. Each drum had an original design including the tribe's name and colors—the designs and painting the original artwork of Carolyn. The summer of 1983 ended without mishap, and Waldemar closed another successful summer—fifty-eight years since Ora Johnson's dream became a reality.

1984

With the grass mowed and flowers blooming along the many walkways, Camp Waldemar was ready and waiting for the 1984 campers with several surprises. Their daily Guadalupe River swim class had a new program, designed by Debbie Norton as a project she had done for a master's degree at North Texas State University. It offered campers a choice of three "tracks": (1) Endurance/Fitness Swim, (2) Aerobic Exercise Swimming (incorporating water aerobics, synchronized swim, and water games), and (3) traditional "Waldemar Strokes and Form." Every girl would learn her basic strokes, and becoming proficient in them have a choice of one of the three tracks for that term. This new approach allowed for more variety and pleasure in swim classes, for *every* Waldemar camper still swims *every* day.

In addition to the new swim program, there were big changes IN the river! The piers at the pool area had been redesigned. Removable steel pipe frames were driven into the river bottom at a right angle to the dam, and wooden docks were placed on them extending out about twenty-five feet. Attached to the pipe structures, these platforms could be quickly removed when the river rose. From this improvement on through the coming years, Waldemar lost no more swim docks. Also, Dale had a special invention he'd prepared for the campers that spring: Upriver from the pier, three strange triangular towers rose out of the water. First Field Day demonstrated their use as canoe starting gates for competition. Gone were the days of free floating canoes handled by staff members trying mightily to line up three tribal contestants! Especially impressive was the historical War Canoe Race—when the gates' solidarity allowed each tribe to align their canoe and remain in position. And on the river, a pair of snowy white swans swam in silent patrol. Their names were "Guada" and "Lupe," and their beauty added a special grace to the deep green river of Waldemar.

Rippling Waters now had a four-stall carport with a sundeck above it fenced with cedar in the same design of the Dining Hall's upper porch. Campers would be invited to its lofty height on special occasions and for special after-taps treats on starry nights.

The mostly Texas accents heard at Waldemar were blended for the first time with the international accents of staff members from England. Hired through an organization specializing in placing highly skilled girls from other countries in camping jobs for the summer, the three quickly learned to be at home in Texas, and made a noteworthy record as good counselors. Future years would see girls from all parts of the globe arrive to share the knowledge of their country with Waldemar campers and gain a new appreciation of Texas and its people.

Casa Courts had a major facelift during the spring. They were resurfaced and painted green. But the major change there was the replacement of the rusted wire mesh fencing with vinyl-coated cyclone fencing! The lower courts, while concrete for heavier use such as the Carnival, also received new fencing. Though not apparent to campers and staff, the

kitchen was completely renovated during the winter months. Two stainless steel commercial ranges, warming ovens, a large grill, two new deep fryers, and a convection oven were proudly installed to increase safety and ease of food preparation. A sprinkler system was also installed to ensure greater safety of the beautiful and historically important Waldemar Dining Hall and the Waldemar campers.

Returning to the Waldemar scene were paint horses, famous in the camp herd since the days of W. T. Johnson. Marsha began to add more "paints" to her herd each year, and this summer found eight new ones added to the riding department's care.

And in May of 1984, the first of the Elmore children, Teak, became a graduate of the University of Texas. He remained in the area and took his new status in the real estate world. That summer Meg was an Aztec sponsor and counselor, and Josh was head *Gringo*.

1985

Waldemar celebrated its sixtieth anniversary with a special twilight vesper on the pier. Written by Squish Willett, it celebrated and honored its three directors, Ora and Doris Johnson, and Marsha Elmore. It told of the many significant milestones Waldemar had encountered over the sixty years. Many former campers and staff members were able to return for the sentimental evening, and many former Ideal Waldemar Girls were present also. Following the beautiful riverside vesper the staff, campers, and guests shared an enormous birthday cake in the Playhouse. However, this sixtieth year would end on a sad note in November, when Jack Reeves died after fifty-five years at Waldemar, and Doris Johnson died two weeks later. She had slipped quietly away after a lengthy illness. Doris' death saddened the many, many women whose lives were made richer by her lifework—Camp Waldemar.

Lured by the current boom in Texas real estate, Dale hung up his clipboard at camp and returned to his professional element—real estate development and sales. Entering into partnership with two local friends, he made Kerrville his home office, while traveling, when the need arose to develop other deals and properties. His arrival home at camp at night was always greeted with shouts and waves from the campers who missed his jokes and good humor. On weekends he resumed his role in camp administration and as Waldemar's "Daddy."

Meanwhile, the usual improvements and additions awaited the opening of camp in June. The grounds were improved with the planting of fifteen new live oak and pecan trees. A fine new ice-machine and two soft drink machines stood grandly on the Bunkhouse porch. A large heavy-duty smoker/cooker stood proudly outside the kitchen, waiting to smoke chickens or beef briskets for 450—or to be hooked to a truck and moved to the Tree House for steaks on a cookout evening.

Movie nights were greatly improved by the purchase of a powerful new projector to show videos, and a new movie screen for Ora Johnson Theater. No more sudden breaks in the film, to the pleasure and delight of all viewers! The former projection shack was moved to the golf clubhouse area to serve as storage for equipment of activities such as soccer. And Josh and Teak were released from captivity in the projection shack, where they had served bravely until this new marvel was added to Waldemar's equipment.

The Guadalupe River always required spring cleaning, and often Marsha would be inspired to add improvements and new equipment. The year 1985 was no exception, and six shiny new canoes rested on their racks in readiness for campers' use. A large cypress tree halfway between the pool and the pier, offering a perfect place for a "Zip-Line," stretched invitingly across the river. Girls on kampong picnics zipped across daily with shrieks of delight and swam slowly back to take their places in line for another thrilling ride.

The Tree House area became the site of the Waldemar Ropes Course. The challenge course would be used by trained Waldemar staff members and the Outdoor Skills classes. The Hilltoppers were treated to an exciting new experience one day of each term by professional personnel trained in Ropes Course Management. In future years, conference groups attending workshops at Waldemar would use the course as a personal growth and team-building experience.

Chorus membership had been in decline for several years, with tribes having difficulty in enrolling a chorus. For the first time an All-Camp Chorus was made up of musically interested campers to perform at church services each Sunday morning and sing on other occasions. First Field Day, the last year's graduates were invited back for "Hilltopper Day"—sharing the excitement of tribal competition and inspiring and cheering on their tribe. Also new on the camper

schedule first term was an old-fashioned Fourth of July celebration; a parade in the morning ended at the flagpole with the singing of "God Bless America" and other patriotic songs. The evening meal was an All-American picnic—hot dogs and watermelon, followed by elaborate fireworks ignited from the field across the river. Roy had to attend a special fire marshal school to be licensed to light the colorful collection of skyrockets. A similar day was added to the second-term schedule.

Barbara Tyson, on staff for numerous summers in the craft house, spent a part of her summer restoring the cowboy murals in Ranch House 1, 2 and 3. Connie Reeves, on the Waldemar staff continously since 1937, was presented with a golden W pin studded with diamonds. As August ended, all staff and campers agreed: Waldemar's sixtieth summer was "a very good year."

1986

A builder by nature, Marsha continued to add improvements and new features to Waldemar. At the first evening vesper of each 1986 term, plans were unveiled for a grand new building to replace the old wooden Round-Up Lodge, which was now too small to house the entire camp when bad weather prevented use of the many outdoor meeting sites. To be named Doris Johnson Lodge, it would stand at the west end of the athletic field and include a small kitchen, the costume room, two restrooms, and a stage with a dressing area on each side.

Tribal chorus was restored to the camper's choice of classes, and a special field trip to town for pizza was promised as a reward for singing participants. Plenty of fresh water was always available from the new 75,000-gallon tank that replaced the old 49,000-gallon one used previously. Drama students found the grassy (and sometimes muddy) stage of Tejas Chapel replaced with flagstone. The stage arched gracefully out in a complementary half round shape from the curved amphitheater steps.

Part of the lawns and the floor of Ora Johnson Theater received St. Augustine sod in the spring, and were ready for campers by June 1. Marsha bought new and better rifles for the range, and added two miles of new cedar fencing. Eight new horses swelled the size of the Waldemar herd to eighty. But the least expensive addition to camp proved to be everyone's favorite: a popcorn machine! The staff of the kitchen surprised campers with popcorn at many movies, and the pig-out privilege of Carnival night now also included popcorn.

Waldemar camper and counselor since 1949, Jan Cannon retired as coach of the Texas A&M women's tennis team to move to the Hill Country permanently. She joined the camp year-round group as an adminstrative assistant, blending her vast knowledge and endless energy with the other talented Waldemar staff. Geane Jeffery returned to Waldemar as a waterfront staff member after an absence of forty-four years since her camper days. Geane's life at Waldemar began when she was just four and a half, and continued for ten years while her mother was "Doll-House Mama."

Roy rewarded counselors and campers with Sunday breakfast delivered to their kampong doors for keeping the campgrounds free of litter from nourishment and picnic suppers. The imaginative first-term Hilltoppers in "Rivery Oaks" held an elegant social affair, the Hilltopper Ball, on the lawn between their cabins. Invitations were very exclusive—only "debutantes" graduating together that summer term were invited. Much care was lavished on hair, make-up, and costumes—with music and dancing under the stars lasting until taps!

Becky Burkhardt, the very talented Waldemar band leader, composed a beautiful song to Marsha which was privately practiced by each tribe. They combined their numbers on the athletic field to surprise her with their tribute as she stood on the balcony porch of Cedar Lodge. In the years since 1979, Marsha had grown quietly more confident in her role as director, and the words of the song reflect the love, appreciation, and admiration the campers and staff hold for her.

SONG TO MARSHA

To you we sing this melody
To let you know the way we feel.

Your gentle smile and giving ways
have helped us through some trying days.

Our lives were touched, our hearts renewed
from moments that we spent with you.

Your love your strength and all you are
Dear Marsha we take with us from Waldemar.
Dear Marsha with love from us at Waldemar.

As 1986 brought the excitement of a fine new house for Teak and Josh east of the stables, it also brought a great sadness with the death of Dr. English in June. Having lived a long and productive ninety-three years, Dr. English had begun a new career as camp physician at eighty-four. He was missed sorely by family, old friends, and his new Waldemar friends, young and old. Marsha and Dale announced a $1,000 memorial scholarship to be given in his name each year to a Waldemar staff member needing help in gaining a college education. "Dr. E." will always be remembered as a strong, quiet, and gentle man with a twinkle in his eye and love in his heart.

1987

In one of their largest and most ambitious projects to date, Marsha and Dale rewired the entire camp, adding much needed additional voltage to replace the somewhat dangerous and outdated wiring. Conscious of the safety of campers and staff, and of the timeless and irreplaceable beauty of some of the older buildings, they considered the financial investment a necessity. By June, every kampong had enough voltage to support several hair dryers and sets of hot rollers simultaneously; and to the astonished delight of arriving campers and staff, thirty-six-inch fans were in place to cool every single kampong!

The many flowerbeds on the Waldemar grounds helped make them lush with native Texas wildflowers and plants, most of which the deer disliked and left to bloom all summer. An underground sprinkler system now watered all the many flowerbeds, and large stones created an artful impression of natural beauty in the beds along the athletic field walks. Each kampong had a new ceramic nameplate created by the ceramics classes the previous summer.

The stone steps that served to seat the audience at Tejas Chapel were only one stone wide, and filled with St. Augustine grass to the next step up. This grass required frequent watering resulting in muddy wet seating, and the shade trees slowed growth of the grass. Marsha decided to fill in the grassy portion with stonework, which was a definite improvement to the comfort of spectators at events held there.

A beloved and familiar face was missing that summer: Squish retired as rheumetoid arthritis finally made the effort too great for her. Her wit and warmth and unequaled talents left a large void. In the years after 1980, foreseeing the day when she would no longer pack her bags for summers at Waldemar, Squish had carefully prepared Carolyn Wheat, assistant director, to "carry on" in her place. The classic vespers, the drama and *War Whoop* files, and the clever final programs she had written and directed for so many years were all filed with copious notes for her chosen successor. The Ideal Waldemar Girl script was marked with notes from every year that she had directed its beautiful and moving speeches. The legacy of Sue Willett's talents and love of Waldemar remained alive in her absence. Carolyn added Squish's duties to her already full days as assistant director, and called upon the knowledge she had gained working alongside this talented lady from Kansas to guide her in producing the traditional end of camp programs for Waldemar each summer.

On a more physical level, a new parking shed was added across the driveway from the garage—spacious enough to shelter eight of the camp's ever growing fleet of vehicles. A double portion of the existing garage was enclosed and power tools installed to carry out the many ambitious projects undertaken each season.

Camp concluded in August. The Elmore family made the long drive to their East Texas home on Lake Rayburn to rest for two weeks, and the leaves at Waldemar turned from green to golden browns. Adult conferences occupied the days and kampongs during the fall and winter months, extending the magic of the Waldemar experience to many from other backgrounds seeking life-changing experiences. The income from using the camp for adult education and enrichment provided for the employment of many talented personnel on a year-round basis—and funded many of the ambitious building projects.

Among the Elmore family milestones, the University of Texas gained another alumni, as Meg graduated that spring. Dallas, and eventually New York City, would claim her talents for the next few years. (Meg's eight years as a camper, her several years of counseling and sponsoring the Aztec tribe, and her unending love for Waldemar would bring her "home" in the future to begin her training under Marsha to become the next director of Camp Waldemar.)

1988

One gigantic and major project outshown all others for 1988! The construction of the new Doris John-

son Lodge, to replace Round-Up Lodge at the west end of the oval athletic field, was the most impressive addition to Waldemar since the majestic Dining Hall arose in 1932. The sentimental demolition of the old lodge was accomplished in the fall, with timbers and boards saved to be used whenever possible in future construction projects, serving as a bridge between Waldemar's past and future. The construction spanned the summer months, and all of Marsha's many talents and Dale's construction abilities were called upon, as every decision required their artistic vision and guidance. The building must rise majestically and compatibly with the older grand structure of the Dining Hall. It must be new and modern, and yet look as if it had always been there. This task was given to Richardson Robertson III, a talented, top-of-his-class University of Texas graduate in architecture. Rick did a masterful job blending all the original custom designs that Harvey P. Smith, Sr., so beautifully created for Waldemar in the Doris Johnson Lodge. Rick Robertson has continued his award-winning design career from Highland Park in Dallas, Hollywood and Bel Air, California, to New York.

In the new lodge, naturally stacked river stone buttresses braced stone walls as heavy timber trusses held up a massive roof which peaked at about twenty-four feet. The two walls of glass doors would open to covered porches overlooking the camp and the Guadalupe. Danny Wheat, long-time friend and professional civil engineer, oversaw and guided the construction of the grand new building as it arose majestically. John Pipkin, brother-in-law to the Elmores, acted as an experienced advisor, with many frequent trips from his construction business in Houston. The Wheats were newly converted Hill Country residents, although Carolyn had added her considerable capabilities to the Waldemar staff each summer since 1979.

Upon completion, the new lodge was named and dedicated as the Doris Johnson Lodge. The motorized movie screen, new sound system, much needed bathrooms, kitchen space, and costume closet were immediately in heavy use as campers and staff gratefully occupied the beautiful new building and enjoyed the modern improvements it offered! A stone fireplace at the southwest end of the room included special stones chosen to echo the geodes and quartz crystals of the Dining Room fireplaces. Amethyst crystals, orange fossil rocks, and green malachite were included to commemorate the tribal colors. The tribal history and significance was painted by Marsha and Carolyn on an authentic buffalo skin and hung to the right of the fireplace. Original cedar sofas were designed and built by Tom Haines, head of maintenance and wood worker, and cushioned with pillows of Kilim rugs from Santa Fe. The soaring ceiling was illuminated with large chandeliers Teak constructed from antlers. Mexican tilework ornamented the stage steps, bathrooms, and kitchen, and quaint wall paintings were added to complete the effect. A joint effort of Marsha and Dale—and the talents of local craftsmen of the Hill Country like metal craftsman Bill Givens, stone mason Dean Mitchell, master roofer Ben Weber, Rick Robertson's design, John Pipkin and Danny Wheat as superior and dedicated construction experts, Teak as a young and talented artist in furniture and fixtures, and Carolyn as an inspired and enthusiastic interior designer—the new lodge rose to take its place as one of the most beautiful buildings of Camp Waldemar.

Other projects were accomplished during this year, but fire extinguishers, new water fountains, the construction of a stone gatehouse, the resurfacing of Johnny Regan Arena and the stage of Ora Johnson Theater all take a backseat to the addition of Doris Johnson Lodge to Waldemar.

1989

As the new year opened, Camp Waldemar projects began with a much needed "facelift" for the Dining Hall. Rotten cedar trim was replaced with new, and old doors and window frames were rebuilt and refitted. Trucks delivered many new hickory tables and chairs for use in the Dining Hall and kampongs. Workers on the grounds of Waldemar now communicated with "walkie talkies," and everyone was connected with the command center—the office. The enlarged horse herd had several colts among its numbers, and Danny Pate, head wrangler and year-round employee, built a round ring for their training. Danny, in residence on the Furrs' property next door to Waldemar's east boundary, was on hand to manage the feeding and welfare of the Waldemar horses, who stayed at home for the winter months.

As the spring bloomed forth, the sudden illness

and death of Margaret "Shannon" Harber was a shattering loss to the Waldemar staff. As a young teacher at Ward Belmont College, Shannon came to Waldemar in 1944. Her energy, intelligence, and talents filled many staff positions in her early years. She ultimately became Waldemar's program director, serving in that capacity until her untimely death in 1989. Her warm interest in every camper's happiness and progress was sincere. Her genius in scheduling the complicated tribal Field Days, her joyful participation in the counselor-camper softball contests, her painstaking attention to excellence in all camp activities—these rare and admirable qualities were the essence of Shannon Harber. The camp mourned her passing, especially as the first class registration was held in the new lodge first term.

Long-time and experienced staff members were reassigned to fill the position she left open, although never to take her place in Waldemar history. Debbie Norton, a veteran of fourteen years, ably handled the program director's job first term while Joyce Jordan, with twenty-nine years experience, assumed the job of scheduling all extracurricular camp activities. Since each served as a head tribal sponsor during opposite terms, they simply exchanged jobs first and second terms. Shannon's habit of making notes about everything, every year, furnished an extensive and comforting guideline for both Joyce and Debbie their first summer in this administrative position. Shannon's gift of forty-four years (1944-1988) of service was honored by Marsha with the Shannon Harber "Best Counselor Award." Her picture and a plaque listing those honored by the award hang in the Waldemar office. A stone bench was constructed by the flagpole on the athletic field, where Shannon often stood, watching camper activities. It, too, is marked by a brass plaque, reminding past and future generations of this talented and special woman, who set an example of excellence in all ways with her life.

The past eleven years had seen the three Elmore children grow up at Waldemar and leave to pursue their educations and careers as young adults. In 1989 Teak returned to the family business of camping as business director, Meg enjoyed the challenge of a career in New York City, and Josh entered his final year of college at UT. Marsha and Dale were "empty nesters," but there was no time to notice it as they went about their full days.

Chapter 8

1990s

1990

The Texas wildflowers lasted beautifully into June of 1990. Another idyllic summer in the Hill Country began as busloads of campers from all directions rolled toward the Kerrville area. Waldemar was full to capacity as usual. The summer would see several exciting changes in the girls' activities and programs. The horseback classes offered "polocrosse"—polo played on horseback with lacrosse bats. To introduce the new sport to the girls, a polocrosse demonstration clinic was held at Waldemar. A note of interest here: A local polocrosse team would be formed by Teak Elmore during this year, competing as the Texas T-Bones in national competitions. A number of area riders, including Teak and Jeepers Ragsdale from Stewart, would be regulars on the polocrosse circuit. In 1995 the national meet would take place in Kerrville.

Also in the horseback department, Marsha honored Connie again with the formation of "Reeves' Riders" first term and "Connie's Cowgirls" second term. Each term, outstanding riders would be invited to become members and the group rewarded with a visit to town for supper with Liz and Connie at each term's end.

The traditional "Camp Stewart Dance" was exclusively for the sixth- and seventh-grade intermediates for many years. It was such an envied event—allowing girls to dress up in a dress, curl their hair, and wear make-up—that a happy compromise was made in the 1990 first All-Camp Dance. All campers and staff of both camps shared in the informal fun on the Waldemar tennis courts. A band blared the required rock music, plentiful refreshments refreshed the hot and happy dancers, and the staff of the com-

bined camps served as hosts, youth directors, and chaperones.

The Fourth of July festivities first term included a parade around the athletic field, led by Marsha and "Happy Jack"—a thirty-one-inch high miniature donkey, and "Y. D. Dandy," a llama she'd just purchased. Happy Jack and Y. D. (for Yankee Doodle) Dandy were the beginning of the camp's petting zoo. Soon they were joined by Murphy Brown, a goat, and Gucci, a pot-bellied pig. The campers enjoyed their antics in their special pen behind the golf shack.

Both terms the War Canoe teams and Hilltoppers were treated to a field trip to San Antonio's newest recreational site—Sea World. Also begun during this summer were the kampong "Mini Olympics." This light-hearted event was held the first week of each term—a great way to help new campers and staff get in the swing of things and make new friends. The competitive events were limited only by the imagination of the counselors in charge, and included a tug-of-war for seniors over a mud hole Marsha allowed on the athletic field (temporarily, of course).

Josh graduated from the University of Texas in the spring, completing the family's days of education in Austin. One more goal reached for the Elmores! All their children grown, educated, and doing well, Marsha and Dale looked back over the years with wonderful memories of their family life. The mountains of Colorado would soon call to Josh, a talented skier and climber.

One more change took place in 1990: Carolyn Wheat retired after twelve years as Marsha's "right-hand woman," in order to spend more time with husband and family, including grandchildren. Louise Bivins, Waldemar camper, counselor, and Aztec sponsor, was tapped to become assistant director and take on its many jobs.

106

1991

Although Waldemar had seen many changes since Marsha and Dale took over in 1979, the program changes had been mostly the addition of new classes or activities for campers. The summer of 1991 provided a noteworthy new addition—a III Term! It was an eight-day short term for girls in first through fifth grades, and was held at the end of August. Carolyn came back to serve as the first director of III Term. Rather than have tribes with Indian names, the girls were divided by age into groups called Armadillos, Jackrabbits, and Coyotes. It was a resounding success; strangely, the youngest campers experienced less homesickness than the older girls normally did, and fun and laughter filled the air. Waldemar's Hilltopper graduates were summoned back to work as C-2s (Counselors, Too). They helped their young charges to dress and get to the proper classes, do their kampong duties, and assisted with classes while passing on the joys of camp.

Late in the summer a singular event occurred for both Marsha and Waldemar: two life-size bronze sculptures were delivered and duly installed to the left of the Dining Hall. They were the work of a promising new sculptress, Marsha English Elmore. The figures are a pretty young counselor and a camper sitting and talking. Titled "The Girls," the older model was her own daughter, Meg, and Heidi Neusel of Beaumont modeled for the camper.

A truly significant event occurred in 1991. The *Waldemar Cookbook*, long a dream, became a published reality. Roy collected the best loved recipes of U.S. and Lucille's and Bessie and Robert's years in the camp kitchen, and added the special recipes he'd introduced into the camp menus. The handsome blue looseleaf notebook-style book included many pictures and recipes, bringing happy memories to all who acquired a copy.

Waldemar's horse herd had increased by now to more than ninety, including several mares ready to produce colts, so Marsha built a "mare's dorm" barn across the street in the camp's south pasture.

* * * * *

Author's Note:

I pause here in recounting the progress and the necessary modernization of Waldemar to make a truthful and very profound point. Many years have gone by since "the good old days of Waldemar." Civilization has crept relentlessly closer and closer to our gate. While I proudly write of the new buildings and program changes that the passage of time has brought, I even more proudly must make this statement: The courageous defender of good sportsmanship and high ideals who timidly stepped into the role of director in 1979 has truly become a champion of wholesomeness—no small feat in the contemporary world. Each year, the changes of our culture have made it more difficult for Americans to hear the silent message of the wind and the soft whisper of peace in the river. Leaving TV, cars, telephones, rock music, and the frantic pace of our society for even a few weeks can be a life-changing experience for our children—and Waldemar is perhaps one of the few places left that will absolutely not abandon its commitment to excellence for the momentary pursuit of temporary pleasures. Good sportsmanship, good citizenship, good stewardship, the fitness of body and fineness of spirit that were the original inspiration are the strength of Waldemar yet today. Time has brought many, many changes to camp and campers. But on summer nights, when the lights go out, the notes of taps finally die away, and in the peaceful darkness of the kampongs, each camper is, after all, still a little girl. And she is safe at Waldemar.

1992

In early November of 1991, Marsha began her process of enrollment for the coming summer. Due to the installation of a computer system at camp during the past few years, Waldemar's waiting list could now be summoned up quickly. The list, though updated and current, was still long. By Christmas, all the lucky new campers had been invited and were busy making plans.

Many projects were planned for 1992, but one of special beauty and joy took place in October. In flower-filled Tejas Chapel at twilight, Meg Elmore and Clayton Clark joined their hearts and lives in marriage. Friends and family wished the new couple every happiness and fond congratulations. They would soon begin their married life in the Houston area.

Waldemar added 200 more acres of land to its property, purchasing part of what had been a ranch just across its north fenceline. This opened up many new trails for the horseback department and provided a wonderful high mountaintop site for cookouts.

The trampolines were sunken into pits, with the tramp bed at ground level, sides securely padded. This safety feature made it much easier to teach the youngest campers with greater "hands-on" safety.

The All-Tribe Council was formed by Marsha in 1992—a more complete way for all three tribes to communicate about events of camp life. This council would also be the "voice of the campers," sharing the feelings and opinions of tribal sisters with Marsha. Good communiction led to even greater harmony in camp life.

The third floor of the Dining Hall, long ago titled "W. T. Johnson Ballroom," had been in disrepair for some years—used only for storage of furniture. During the winter, the walls were replastered and painted. Ceiling fans were installed, and the room cleared for summer use. Exercise equipment was placed in the west end for staff use, and the editors of the *Tradition* (yearbook) and the *War Whoop* (newspaper) were officed in the remaining space.

The presses rolled in spring with another publication for camp: *The Waldemar Coloring Book,* by Barbara Tyson. It was an instant success with campers, and crayons and markers had to be added to the store inventory for all inspired young Waldemar artists. Louise Bivins and Allison Kerr developed and recorded the Waldemar cassette tape of songs sung by Allison.

The age span of III Term girls was narrowed slightly—it was deemed wise for the girls to have completed the first grade before attending camp. So the Armadillos were dropped, and the girls divided into Jackrabbits (second and third-graders) and Coyotes (fourth and fifth graders). The final program of III Term signaled the ending of the happy summer of '92.

1993

When camp opened in June of 1993, all Waldemar's grounds and kitchen staff were proudly dressed in the new staff shirts designed just for their department. They were hard at work as always: The grounds staff was unloading and delivering luggage and the new wait staff was preparing for the traditional first night hamburger supper. Plus, the Hispanic men and women who had worked at Waldemar for ten years wore their new silver belt buckles awarded for a decade of service. They were Reyes Morua-Pina, Eladio and Aurora Renteria, Amando Renteria, Noel and Tomasa Quinones, Gabriel Garcia, and Carlos de la Torre. Waldemar could not "carry on" without the dedication and loyalty of these wonderful men and women.

The Waldemar grounds crew had a young new foreman, for Josh had returned from the lofty mountains of Colorado to rejoin his family at Waldemar. Loving the outdoors, he spent his days attending to projects on the camp, cycling the country roads, and building original furniture. His ease and skill with computers fit into the picture also. He began writing and publishing materials for camp, such as the *Waldemar Newsletter,* which is mailed several times a year now.

Campers soon discovered new tilework in many bathrooms, and new plumbing fixtures gleamed in the same bath and dressing rooms. Slowly but surely the beautiful old buildings were getting a much needed facelift. Much of the modernization didn't really show—rewiring, new plumbing and sewer lines, new water tanks, and other background improvements like septic tanks—but the overall effect was certainly noticeable. Toilets overflowed rarely now; there was plenty of electric current for teens' ever-present appliances; fans cooled the cabins; and everyone could hear every announcement over the powerful new public address system. Waldemar looked better than ever. It functioned smoothly year-round now—camp in the summer and as a conference site the rest of the year. Most of the kitchen staff stayed at least through September for Women's Week. Time had brought changes that were needed, and Waldemar remained the proud, grand camp she had always been. Many campers were now the third generation of Waldemar girls in their family. At final programs there were often three women to remember their days at Waldemar—grandmother, mother, and daughter—all seeing the Guadalupe River and stone kampongs through the eyes of a child, and savoring memories of fun and friendships shared there. For many women, Waldemar is an affair of the heart—and a visit to this timelessly beautiful camp awakens their young dreams and feelings once again.

The campers of 1993 had a wonderful summer, and many will return with their daughters in future years to recapture some of the joys of their girlhood.

1994

With all three Elmore children grown and returning to Waldemar as professionals, the ideas were many and action almost instant. Teak as business manager (with a thriving business in custom furniture on the side), Meg as conference marketing director (from her home near Houston), and Josh assuming the role of grounds and building maintenance and publishing a camp newsletter three times a year made an active difference in Waldemar's world.

A major project was the refurbishing and redecoration of the second floor of the Dining Hall. With four baths and five private bedrooms, it offered the perfect accommodations for a bed and breakfast-type inn. Beautiful furniture was designed and built (some bought from special artists) and rugs, linens, and fine artistic accents gathered to set the scene. The second floor of the Dining Hall had newly refinished hardwood floors—so shiny they looked like a dance floor. The change was remarkable! The rugged beauty of the stone building was softened and made comfortable and inviting. Next came Happy Haven and Alameda. Bunks were stored, curtains added, heaters added for winter use. Casa was transformed into a charming four-bedroom villa with a living room—perfect for a large family. A colorful brochure with many pictures carried the news to interested patrons.

Another interesting idea became a reality too. Marsha offered ex-campers, staff, and parents an opportunity to purchase a paving stone with their name, dates, and tribe on it. These pavers will eventually form a three-foot-wide walkway around the athletic field, with the founder, director, and many long-time staff members' names surrounding the flagpole. This sidewalk of memories will enable campers to leave their name permanently at Waldemar.

The Ideal Waldemar Girl statue, always awarded to only one girl each term, was sculpted by Marsha and the small but coveted statue cast now in bronze. It is awarded as it always has been, at the Ideal Girl Ceremony on the pier, with the same profound line: "The trophy is small, but the honor is great!" A beautiful medal was also designed to be awarded to the Ideal Waldemar Girl.

Among the many physical improvements during the spring of 1994, Casa tennis courts received a new surface and the tennis *casita* a new roof. The pavilion on the left of the stable road was completely rebuilt

for use by the Dining Room and kitchen staff, and a television and VCR player added to their leisure hours' pleasure. Television still has not invaded the world of the campers.

Roy Spears decided to try his talents in a new direction and retired from Waldemar. He was lovingly encouraged by his Waldemar family in this new venture. David Johnson, a good friend of Josh and Allison Lee, agreed to take on the enormous task of running the Waldemar food service year-round. David enriched the menus with his own unique style. David was with us for two years.

August drew warmly to a close, America's school bells began to ring, and the summer of 1994 became a memory to be cherished for 750 girls.

1995

Camp Waldemar had never looked better than it did when June arrived in 1995. During the year, the imaginative and industrious Elmores had further updated the kitchen by completely rebuilding both walk-in iceboxes and the walk-in freezer. Estrella's three cabins all had newly tiled showers to thrill campers and counselors. The room and bath beneath the craft house was transformed into "The Oasis," painted and furnished with southwestern decor. Laura Jean would soon be its honored guest. And miracle of miracles—the bathrooms under the craft house were updated in fixtures and decor. Fathers were especially impressed when they found the men's room elevated to a place of beauty. The small bathroom in the garage was now welcoming with a steer skull on the door and comfortable bench on the porch.

Campers raised their voices in song with the brand new songbooks published in the spring. The spiral notebook had every song Waldemar campers had loved over many years. It was dedicated to Jan Cannon, whose love of singing had enhanced many occasions at camp. Also during this eventful year, Jim Carey brought Hollywood to Waldemar, where parts of his latest movie were filmed. Everyone signed on as "extras" to be in the movie, but the finished product showed only a small amount of Waldemar.

The Waldemar bed and breakfast was a great success, and many who had been children there were delighted to be able to return as adults. The young Elmores, at ease in the computer generation, designed and launched a B and B page on the Internet. This wonderful renovation and the successful "B and B" business at Waldemar is credited mostly to Lori Appleton, Josh, and Allison Lee, his fiancé. Their originality, talent, and efforts are amazing.

Waldemar's "off-season" business begun in 1980 is blossoming under the direction and creativity of this younger generation. Large corporations like ATT, American Airlines, DuPont, Microsoft, many churches, professional groups, state organizations, and women's groups make up the regular clients taking advantage of Waldemar's conference facility and bed and breakfast accommodations.

Meg and her husband, Clayton Clark, provided a singular reward for Marsha and Dale. Addison Caroline Clark was born April 15. The first grandchild was a glorious occasion—a tiny, blue-eyed blonde who stole their hearts.

The balance board of life tilted the other direction, however, and Ellen Easley passed away. An era had ended. Doris Johnson had envisioned, and Ellen Easley had carried out the visions for many years. A tireless worker finally rested. Ellen's contribution to Waldemar cannot be measured; her devotion was total and sincere. Plans are under way to replace the utilitarian Playhouse on the athletic field with a beautiful stone pavilion, and it will be called the Ellen Easley Pavilion in her memory.

Never one to refuse a challenge, Marsha began work on a life-size bronze of Connie Reeves. She plans to sculpt Connie in working cowgirl garb, leaning on one of Waldemar's cross fence rails.

1996

Seventy years have passed since Ora Johnson followed her heart to the Hill Country to establish Camp Waldemar. There is no way to measure the happiness, the skills, the wholesome maturity and strong ideals she set in motion in her brief directorship. The camp is a monument built by the efforts of many strong and beautiful women, each of whom believes in the ideals it epitomizes. Each summer, many experienced staff people return to Waldemar for yet another summer. In 1996 the sum of all the staff's years of service was more than 700 years. Many of these men and women have dedicated most of

their summers as adults to Waldemar—taking away with them at summer's end the great satisfaction of being part of an institution of great renown and great worth.

Those women, most of whom have over twenty years of tenure and to whom Waldemar is most deeply grateful in this latest era, are as follows:

Connie Reeves, Laura Jean Johnson, Jan Cannon, Julie Menges, Carolyn Wheat, Jill Johnson, Barbara Keller, Joyce Jordan, Debbie Norton, B. J. Gray, Janice Ward, Louise Bivins, Geane Jeffery, Susan Gordy, Sue Vaughan, Mary Vaughan, Sudie Tannehill, Peaches Stevens, Rita Granberry, Sudie Rowell, Sara Saliba, Berle Van Zandt, Suzanne Norton, Tootie Baker, Allison Ragle, Cindy Robinson, Rhonda Smith, Sharon Swenson, Jaye Sanford, Becky Burkhardt, Mary McFarland, Sheena Powers, Mary Fehl, Millie von Tungeln, Blanche Olsen, Pearl Speakman, Anne Hendrix, Sonya Mikeska, Amy Stewart, Amy Brooke, Laura Dickens, Liz Pipkin.

The family that grew up at Waldemar continues to thrive in its beautiful and wholesome environment. In May of 1996, Teak married George Anne Robinson in a sunset ceremony on a beach in Hawaii. The happy pair returned to Texas in time for the opening of camp. George Anne, a bright and shining spirit with lots of talents, immediately found her niche, and settled into the busy schedule with enthusiasm. Meg and Clayton added another little girl to their family, Emmaline English Clark. "Emmy" arrived May 15, 1996.

As is usual, the physical plant had received lots of exciting improvements during the year. The camp laundry near the stables was torn down, and a new building erected in that spot. The staff retreat, known as "The Bunkhouse," was repaired and refurnished in comfort and style. Washers and dryers were added for counselor use—to the delight of staff members.

The Waldemar office was air-conditioned partially, as was part of Rippling Waters. The noise level in the office was lowered by this improvement, and work more easily completed. Climatic changes have occurred over the years, and the Texas Hill Country has experienced warmer summers. The fans in the girls' kampongs and air conditioning in the office make the warming trend less noticeable.

Because of the ongoing year-round activities at Waldemar, more office space was needed. So a second story named the Billie Johnson Office Center has begun behind the craft house, over the kitchen storerooms and Cowboy Dining Room. Following the lines of the original building, it will add much needed space. More products have been added to the camp store also, and it has moved to larger quarters in the Happy Haven Living Room. George Anne is the buyer and manager for the store. She is developing a catalogue for Waldemar.

The future of Camp Waldemar is unlimited. It is first and foremost a fine Girls Residence Camp, with traditions and memories that will never die. But it is also a place of beauty, serenity, and personal growth for many others in today's world. To spend time at the Waldemar bed and breakfast, at one of the special weekends such as Family Weekend, Mother/Daughter Weekend, or at Waldemar Women's Week is to renew one's connection with nature. It is a chance to leave the modern world behind for a brief respite, and to renew acquaintance with beauty, old world ideals, and craftmanship, and even more important, to find inner peace—however briefly. The groups that come to Waldemar are carefully chosen, for the El-

mores are sharing not only their home with strangers, but also their beliefs and their lifestyle.

Yes, Waldemar is alive and thriving! Unlike many fine institutions of the past, it has continued to change in ways that make it possible to keep the best of the old ideals and practices, while adding the new ones that make it a vital part of today—and of tomorrow. It is carefully maintained by its owners, and like a fine antique wine, just improves with age. From a vision by an extraordinary lady in 1926, to the meeting of like minds at a family conference of the Elmores, Waldemar has become an institution—a part of Texas' colorful history. It will continue to open its arms to young girlhood; its doors to adults seeking life's secrets. Its legacy of laughter and joy will be received by many in coming years. All who enter its gates are changed, however slightly, and renewed.

Waldemar—a blessing to all who experience it! May it continue forever.

Epilogue

Doris Johnson's life was a continuum of choices and decisions, and the fulcrum of each was not what was best for Doris Johnson, but what was best for Camp Waldemar. She was a deliberate decision maker, first being sure that she had studied the situation through all the refracted colors of the Waldemar prism.

Her decision to trust the future of Waldemar to Marsha Elmore has been widely acclaimed as inspired. No one doubts that Waldemar has had the immense good fortune to be led and nurtured by three remarkable women: Ora Johnson, Doris Johnson, and Marsha Elmore.

After twenty years as Waldemar's owner and director, Marsha plans to hand the reins to their only daughter, Meg Elmore Clark, who will assume her rightful place at the helm of this great establishment. Marsha will look back with quiet satisfaction at the kaleidoscope of memories and accomplishments of her years at Waldemar. She looks ahead with excitement as she pursues her new career as a sculptor.

IDEAL WALDEMAR GIRLS

1933
1st Term - Margaret Manor
2nd Term - Marjorie Denman

1934
1st Term - Elaine Markham
2nd Term - Mary Jane Harrell

1935
1st Term - Betty Jane Stewart
2nd Term - Phyllis Childs

1936
1st Term - Tid Compere
2nd Term - Virginia Beall

1937
1st Term - Margaret Harris
2nd Term - Anna Munger

1938
1st Term - Marilyn Harwell
2nd Term - Winnie Hill

1939
1st Term - Jo Sparks
2nd Term - Susanne Wells

1940
1st Term - Jane Douglass
2nd Term - Gay Noe

1941
1st Term - Devereux Smith
2nd Term - Bitsy Carlisle

1942
1st Term - Marilyn Hobart
2nd Term - Jessie Lee Touchstone

1943
1st Term - Martha Vose
2nd Term - Lois Dubose

1944
1st Term - Roberta Murfee
2nd Term - Olive Falvey

1945
1st Term - Marjorie Bintliff
2nd Term - Donna Kennedy

1946
1st Term - Bettye Jo Beuscher
2nd Term - Jo Ann Bennett

1947
1st Term - Jill King
2nd Term - Eloise Cappel

1948
1st Term - Beverly Bintliff
2nd Term - Ella Alford

1949
1st Term - Ann Richards
2nd Term - Ann Duckett

1950
1st Term - Nancy Neuhoff
2nd Term - Peggy Rowland

1951
1st Term - Katherine Cowen
2nd Term - Lila Matthews

1952
1st Term - Norma Matlock
2nd Term - Ruth Knighton

1953
1st Term - Carl Ann Graham
2nd Term - Betsy Ross

1954
1st Term - Charm Miller
2nd Term - Donna Odom

1955
1st Term - Penny Hess
2nd Term - Delrena Conner

1956
1st Term - Mary Sue Hanks
2nd Term - Judy Bartlett

1957
1st Term - Pene Pettit
2nd Term - Eleanor Cook

1958
1st Term - Pat Shannon
2nd Term - Mimi Couch

1959
1st Term - Virginia Price
2nd Term - Kathleen Doherty

1960
1st Term - Fran Morris
2nd Term - Jenny Lewis

1961
1st Term - Prissy Hess
2nd Term - Barbara Stone

1962
1st Term - Lucy Holmes
2nd Term - Fredericka Hunter

1963
1st Term - Joan Frensley
2nd Term - Lynn Loomis

1964
1st Term - Barbara Henry
2nd Term - Patricia Hurd

1965
1st Term - Gene Graham
2nd Term - Ruthie Miller

1966
1st Term - Pamela Pitzer
2nd Term - Jane Sheppard

1967
1st Term - Eve Edwards
2nd Term - Margaret Cameron

1968
1st Term - Martha Hill
2nd Term - Nancy Phillips

1969
1st Term - Lyn Woody
2nd Term - Holly Powell

1970
1st Term - Susie Matthews
2nd Term - Beth Johnston

1971
1st Term - Mary Elizabeth Shotwell
2nd Term - Mary Brooke Oliphint

1972
1st Term - Carol Cogdell
2nd Term - Frances Hopper

1973
1st Term - Elaine Brown
2nd Term - Nancy Smith

1974
1st Term - Nancy Eckert
2nd Term - Ann Jennings

1975
1st Term - Amy Grimes
2nd Term - Susan Arnold

1976
1st Term - Nancy Perot
2nd Term - Martha Tisdale

1977
1st Term - Ellen Peterson
2nd Term - Sudie Tannehill

1978
1st Term - Amy Davenport
2nd Term - Linda Charles

1979
1st Term - Francie Billups
2nd Term - Jeanie Gilliam

1980
1st Term - Meg Elmore
2nd Term - Annette Faubion

1981
1st Term - Maria Shelton
2nd Term - Katie Brock

1982
1st Term - Virginia Thompson
2nd Term - Mary Tannehill

1983
1st Term - Margaret Flanagan
2nd Term - Lyle Hagan

1984
1st Term - Kathleen O'Neill
2nd Term - Kelly Schwing

1985
1st Term - Janna Little
2nd Term - Marion Oliver

1986
1st Term - Morgan Warner
2nd Term - Anna Whorton

1987
1st Term - Elizabeth Oxford
2nd Term - Ann Flannery

1988
1st Term - Sally Hedgecoke
2nd Term - Anna Finley

1989
1st Term - Janet Griffis
2nd Term - Lorin Looney

1990
1st Term - Meg O'Neill
2nd Term - Kate Fullinwider

1991
1st Term - Kathleen Matthew
2nd Term - Carolina Rodriguez

1992
1st Term - Reagan Harris
2nd Term - Noelle Seanor

1993
1st Term - Clary Newton
2nd Term - Lane Dilg

1994
1st Term - Libby Taylor
2nd Term - Ashley Jones

1995
1st Term - Blythe Smith
2nd Term - Sarah Hulsey

1996
1st Term - Lucy Marsh
2nd Term - Angelle Judice

TRIBAL PLAQUE WINNERS

Year	1st Term	2nd Term	Year	1st Term	2nd Term	Year	1st Term	2nd Term
1928	Comanche		1951	Aztec	Comanche	1974	Comanche	Comanche
1929	Comanche		1952	Aztec	Comanche	1975	Tejas	Comanche
1930	Tejas		1953	Tejas	Tejas	1976	Tejas	Comanche
1931	Tejas		1954	Tejas	Aztec	1977	Comanche	Comanche
1932	Tejas		1955	Comanche	Tejas	1978	Comanche	Aztec
1933	Tejas		1956	Aztec	Aztec	1979	Comanche	Tejas
1934	Comanche		1957	Aztec	Aztec	1980	Aztec	Comanche
1935	Comanche		1958	Aztec	Tejas	1981	Comanche	Comanche
1936	Tejas		1959	Comanche	Tejas	1982	Aztec	Comanche
1937	Comanche		1960	Comanche	Tejas	1983	Comanche	Comanche
1938	Tejas		1961	Tejas	Aztec	1984	Aztec	Comanche
1939	Comanche	Tejas	1962	Tejas	Aztec	1985	Tejas	Aztec
1940	Comanche	Comanche	1963	Comanche	Aztec	1986	Tejas	Aztec
1941	Comanche	Tejas	1964	Comanche	Aztec	1987	Tejas	Comanche
1942	Tejas	Tejas	1965	Aztec	Aztec	1988	Tejas	Comanche
1943	Comanche	Tejas	1966	Comanche	Tejas	1989	Aztec	Comanche
1944	Comanche	Tejas	1967	Aztec	Aztec	1990	Aztec	Comanche
1945	Comanche	Tejas	1968	Comanche	Tejas	1991	Tejas	Comanche
1946	Tejas	Aztec	1969	Comanche	Tejas	1992	Aztec	Comanche
1947	Tejas	Tejas	1970	Tejas	Comanche	1993	Comanche	Tejas
1948	Tejas	Aztec	1971	Aztec	Comanche	1994	Comanche	Tejas
1949	Tejas	Comanche	1972	Aztec	Aztec	1995	Comanche	Tejas
1950	Comanche	Comanche	1973	Aztec	Aztec	1996	Aztec	Tejas

MY CREED

THIS IS MY CREED: "To live each day as though I may never see the morrow come; to be strict with myself, but patient and lenient with others; to give the advantage, but never ask for it; to be kind to all, but kinder to the less fortunate; to respect all honest employment; to remember always that my life is made easier and better by the service of others, and to be grateful.

"To be tolerant and never arrogant; to treat all men with equal courtesy; to be true to my own in all things; to make as much as I can of my strength and the day's opportunity; and to meet disappointment without resentment.

"To be friendly and helpful whenever possible; to do without display of temper or bitterness, all that fair conduct demands; to keep my money free from cunning or the shame of a hard bargain; to govern my actions so that I may fear neither reproach nor misunderstanding, nor words of malice or envy; and to maintain, at whatever temporary cost, my own self-respect.

"This is my creed and my philosophy. I have failed it often and shall fail it many times again; but by these teachings I have lived to the best of my ability——laughed often, loved, suffered, grieved, found consolation and prospered. By friendships my life has been enriched, and the home I am building is happy."

Waldemar Campers

Compiled by Karen Turner Harlan

These records were taken from two sources: the Waldemar "bible," which is a handwritten list of campers compiled at the end of each term, and an index card file that contains cards filled out by the parents or campers. The list contains the names, tribes, and years attended, and there are records for 11,982 girls. The yearly list of campers for 1927 was missing, and the only records available for that year were taken from the index file. Also, tribes were not recorded until 1930. There are bits and pieces of missing information for a few campers, but this index represents the most complete record available, and every effort was made to ensure that it is as accurate as possible. We hope that all of the present and former campers who read this book will enjoy the memories!

Name	Tribe	Years
A		
Abbott, Jane	T	1934
Abbott, Mary	T	1930-31
Abbott, Rita	A	1947
Abell, Madeleine	A	1950-53
Abernathy, Claire	C	1989-96
Abernathy, Dorothy	A	1953
Abernathy, Leslie	T	1984-91
Abernathy, Vicke	T	1964-69
Abney, Margaret		1929
Abraham, Carrol	T	1968-71
Abrams, Martha	C	1936-38
Abshier, Ann	C	1937
Aburrow, Kristin	A	1987-94
Acker, Barbara	A	1943-44
Acker, Barbara	T	1948
Acker, Frances		1928
Acker, Kit	A	1952-53
Acker, Virginia		1928
Ackers, Florence	C	1930
Ackley, Penny	C	1955
Acola, Maxine	T	1968-73
Adair, Billie	C	1937,40
Adams, Anne	T	1990-93
Adams, Audrey	T	1936
Adams, Betty	T	1931-34
Adams, Camille	A	1954-57
Adams, Caroline	T	1985
Adams, Catherine	C	1990-95
Adams, Doris	C	1932-33
Adams, Dottie	C	1973
Adams, Eleanor	T	1940-41
Adams, Elise	C	1942
Adams, Evelyn	T	1932-33,35
Adams, Gale	T	1945-49
Adams, Gwen	A	1949
Adams, Jane	T	1939-40
Adams, Jane	T	1930-31
Adams, Janet	A	1952-56
Adams, Katie	A	1995-96
Adams, Kiki	A	1963-66
Adams, Lannette	C	1936-37
Adams, Lisa	C	1973
Adams, Madalyn	T	1930-32
Adams, Margaret	C	1935-39
Adams, Marjorie	A	1948-50
Adams, Martha	A	1972-73
Adams, Mary Margaret	T	1983-85
Adams, Mary	A	1973-78
Adams, Nancy	A	1949-50
Adams, Nita	A	1945-48
Adams, Ruth	T	1933-36
Adams, Wendy	C	1978-84
Adams, Winnifred	T	1932-34, 1937-38
Adamson, Carol	T	1964
Adamson, Sandra	A	1964
Adcock, Diane	A	1943
Addington, Alice	A	1956
Addington, Amy	T	1973-75
Adell, Leila	T	1996
Adger, Bettina	C	1990-96
Adkisson, Somers	A	1969-72
Adler, Peggy	A	1944-46
Adler, Rosemary	A	1969-71
Aertker, Carol	T	1966-68
Aertker, Catherine	T	1970-72
Affleck, Ethel	A	1958-60
Affleck, Linda	T	1981-83
Agee, Mary Frances	C	1945-49
Agee, Nancy	C	1949-53
Agnew, Emily Ann	A	1945-46
Agnew, Jeanette		1928-29
Ahrens, Mary Beth	T	1974-77
Aiken, Katherine	T	1931-32
Aikman, Amy	A	1967-73
Aikman, Lainie	T	1983-86
Aikman, Lucia	A	1968-70
Aikman, Meredith	C	1981-85
Akin, Emily	A	1986-92
Akin, Steve Ann	C	1945
Albert, Cora Frances	T	1936-37
Albrecht, Florence Mae	T	1930-32
Albrecht, Lindsay	T	1991-94
Albright, Jo Ann	C	1959-65
Alcorn, Papoose	C	1934
Aldenhaven, Carol	T	1951-52
Alderdice, Ada Reed	C	1929-30
Alderson, Ann	C	1934,36
Aldredge, Mary Lynn	C	1937-38
Aldridge, Alyson	T	1981-87
Aldridge, Claire	T	1971-78
Ales, Mary Mike	A	1958
Alexander, Ann	C	1965-69
Alexander, Anna Pearl	T	1930
Alexander, Audrey	A	1971-73
Alexander, Bel	T	1963-69
Alexander, Bernice		1928
Alexander, Clint	A	1957-62
Alexander, Dorothy	T	1931
Alexander, Elizabeth Ann	T	1942-44
Alexander, Estelle		1926
Alexander, Fidelia	C	1960-66
Alexander, Frances Ann	T	1945-46
Alexander, Frances Marie	C	1938,40
Alexander, Gigi	A	1975-76
Alexander, Jane	C	1954-59
Alexander, Jean	A	1960-65
Alexander, Joan	A	1964-65
Alexander, Kay	C	1960-66
Alexander, Margaret	T	1937
Alexander, Mark Anne	T	1970-75
Alexander, Mary Olney	T	1940-41
Alexander, Mary Kimball	T	1945
Alexander, Mary Mozelle	T	1935-36
Alexander, Megan	C	1989
Alexander, Nancy	C	1955-59
Alexander, Roslyn	C	1931
Alexander, Sara	A	1952
Alexander, Sunya Ann	T	1953-55

Alexander, Susan W.	A	1964-68	Altgelt, Susan	T	1962-63	Ankenman, Kathy	A	1987
Alexander, Susie	T	1963-65	Altom, Tamara	C	1972-78	Ankenman, Maurie	C	1951-60
Alexander, Tappy	A	1971	Alworth, Ashlea	C	1973-75	Annas, Jennifer	T	1995-96
Alexander, Tex Ann	C	1951-54	Amacker, Elaine	T	1943-44	Anson, Jean Lucy	T	1936
Alexander, Virginia Lee	C	1942-43	Amacker, Jeanne	T	1955-58	Anthis, Anna Claire	A	1943
Alford, Ann	C	1973-79	Amacker, Joan	C	1956,58-61	Anthony, Amy	T	1995-96
Alford, Ella	A	1946-48	Amacker, Judy	C	1960-64	Anthony, Carol	T	1952-54
Alford, L'Moore	A	1954	Amacker, Laura	T	1942-45	Anthony, Dee Ann	A	1958
Alford, Mariwynn	T	1940-43	Ames, Janet	T	1952-56	Anthony, Julie	T	1996
Alford, Mary Elizabeh	T	1937-38	Ames, Olive	T	1938,40	Anthony, Paige	A	1974-78
Alford, Sally	C	1948-49	Amman, Ann	T	1955-56	Antil, Worley	T	1993-96
Allbritton, Allison	T	1981-88	Amman, Dottie	T	1957	Apperson, Ann	T	1937
Allbritton, Ashley	C	1973-76	Amman, Evelyn	A	1955-56	Apperson, Carolyn	C	1945
Allday, Ellie	C	1968-69	Ammerman, Jane		1929	Apple, Jane	C	1974-77
Allday, Jana	A	1968	Anders, Nancy	C	1951-53	Apple, Julie	C	1976-80
Allee, LaRue	A	1968-74	Andersen, Alexa	T	1991-93	Appleby, Alma	C	1941
Allen, Alexee	C	1985-92	Andersen, Elizabeth	T	1985-86	Appleton, Katie	C	1990
Allen, Barbara	A	1946-48	Anderson, Amelia	C	1940-44	Appleton, Tracy	C	1990
Allen, Beth	T	1952-53	Anderson, Andrea	T	1956-57	Arbour, Joan	T	1942
Allen, Betsy	C	1955-57	Anderson, Anita	C	1946-47	Archer, Helen	C	1930
Allen, Betty	C	1948-49	Anderson, Barbara	A	1951-53	Archer, Katherine	C	1930
Allen, Blake	C	1996	Anderson, Barbara	C	1950,53	Archer, Maude	C	1930
Allen, Carol	A	1958-61	Anderson, Carla	C	1954-58	Archibald, Margaret	A	1960
Allen, Cathy	T	1958-61	Anderson, Carol	A	1955	Arledge, Ann	C	1946-47
Allen, Charlotte	C	1933	Anderson, Carol Jane	C	1947	Arledge, Grace	C	1946-47
Allen, Elizabeth	A	1943-44	Anderson, Carol	T	1980-84	Arlitt, Janet	A	1968-69,
Allen, Erika	A	1983-88	Anderson, Carol	C	1956-61			1971-73
Allen, Gayle	T	1947-48	Anderson, Connie	A	1958-60	Arlitt, Sezanne	C	1965-69
Allen, Ginger	T	1970-77	Anderson, Deanne	T	1953-57	Armbrust, Aynsley	A	1994-95
Allen, Jean	T	1944	Anderson, Delores	T	1946	Armer, Juliet	C	1939,41-44
Allen, Jennifer	T	1973-80	Anderson, Delph	C	1953-54	Armistead, Eleanor	T	1952-54
Allen, Katharine	T	1981-87	Anderson, Early	T	1955-56	Armitstead, Brooke	C	1977-80
Allen, Kathryn W.	A	1961-66	Anderson, Gretchen	C	1964-66	Armitstead, Dana	A	1979-82
Allen, Kimberly	T	1971-75	Anderson, Helen Louise	T	1938-39	Armour, Jean	C	1937
Allen, Krystn	A	1996	Anderson, Hollyana	A	1983-84	Armstrong, Aimee	C	1979
Allen, Laura	T	1957-58	Anderson, Jacqueline	C	1940-44	Armstrong, Anne	A	1952-53
Allen, Liz	T	1990-91	Anderson, Jane	T	1959	Armstrong, Carolyn	T	1957
Allen, Lorna	C	1957-62	Anderson, Jean	T	1943-47	Armstrong, Cindy Lou	A	1974-75
Allen, Mary Claudia	T	1944	Anderson, Judy	C	1955	Armstrong, Coble	T	1990-96
Allen, Mary Lynn	C	1942	Anderson, Julie	A	1982-85	Armstrong, Criss	C	1974-75
Allen, Maurine	T	1929-30	Anderson, Julie	A	1967	Armstrong, Downie	A	1985
Allen, Melanie	T	1977-83	Anderson, Katherine	A	1980-84	Armstrong, Elizabeth	T	1972
Allen, Meredith	T	1996	Anderson, Kay	T	1953-57	Armstrong, Katherine	A	1984-89
Allen, Nancy Jane	T	1953	Anderson, Lou Anne	C	1936,38	Armstrong, Linda	T	1954-55
Allen, Rosemary	A	1943-44	Anderson, Margaret	A	1977-81	Armstrong, Mary	T	1933-35
Allen, Ruth		1928-29	Anderson, Martha	T	1947	Catherine		
Allen, Stella	T	1961-62	Anderson, Mary Ellizabeth	A	1946-52	Armstrong, Phelane	C	1959-66
Allen, Susan	T	1973	Anderson, Mary Milt	C	1963	Arnim, Bunny	T	1954-56
Allen, Suzanne	A	1952-54	Anderson, Maxine	T	1934-35	Arnim, Carolyn	T	1953
Allen, Thelma Lee	A	1943	Anderson, Nanette	T	1934,36	Arnim, Crystal	C	1934
Allen, Virginia	A	1952-53	Anderson, Sharon	A	1969-73	Arnim, Jackie	C	1939-40
Allensworth, Grace	T	1955	Anderson, Sheila	A	1943-44	Arnim, Jerry	C	1934-35
Allison, Betty	T	1947-48	Anderson, Susan	C	1955	Arnold, Alice	A	1966-72
Allison, Elva	T	1949-50	Anderson, Tasha	C	1978-81	Arnold, Ann	A	1955-63
Allison, Judy Lee	C	1949-50,53	Andrews, Becky	A	1993-96	Arnold, Ann	C	1944-46
Allison, Judy Ann	A	1961-64	Andrews, Jeannette	C	1936	Arnold, Charlotte	C	1988-93
Allison, Susan	T	1960-62	Andrews, Toni	C	1975-82	Arnold, Ellen	A	1975-82
Allnoch, Helen		1928	Andrus, Eula	T	1936	Arnold, Hilda	C	1938
Almond, Alaine	A	1986-93	Anguish, Ellen	A	1972-75	Arnold, Jane	T	1945-49
Almond, Carolyn Kay	C	1950-51	Anguish, Margaret	C	1975-80	Arnold, Jessie	C	1939-41
Alphin, Martha	T	1960-66	Anguish, Nancy	T	1974-75	Arnold, Julia	T	1936-37
Alsabrook, Maya	T	1987-91	Angus, Charlotte	T	1931	Arnold, Linda	A	1957-58
			Angus, Virginia	T	1931			

Arnold, Lydia	T	1978-81,83
Arnold, Mary Virginia	T	1935,37,39
Arnold, Natalie	T	1995-96
Arnold, Pauline	A	1943-44
Arnold, Susan	C	1969-75
Arnold, Tessye Bell	T	1935
Arnold, Vivian	C	1969-74
Arnot, Corrine	A	1996
Arnot, Lyn	T	1956-63
Arp, Majorie Louise	T	1929-31
Arrington, Daisy Lee	C	1933
Arrington, Elizabeth	T	1993
Arrington, Jane	T	1933
Arrington, Melanie	T	1970-74
Arthur, Carter	C	1945
Arthur, Frances	T	1935
Arthur, Jan	C	1945-46
Arthur, Margaret	C	1933
Ashby, Joe Ann	T	1946-50
Ashby, Kathleen	C	1994-96
Ashby, Laura Lari	C	1977-81
Ashby, Mollie Sue	T	1946-49
Ashby, Nancy Jane	T	1945-49
Ashley, Caroline	A	1980
Ashmore, Rayni	A	1994
Ashorn, Marilyn	T	1939-41
Askew, Marie		1928
Atherton, Annabel	A	1994-96
Athey, Jill	T	1944-45
Atkins, Alison	A	1969-74
Atkins, Caroline	C	1939
Atkins, Dorothy	C	1936
Atkins, Geraldine	T	1936
Atkins, Imogene	T	1936
Atkins, Leslie	C	1967-69
Atkins, Mary	C	1981-84
Atkins, Page	A	1979-83
Atkins, Susanna	T	1970-75
Atkinson, Alice	C	1974-81
Atkinson, Amy	T	1967-73
Atkinson, Anne	T	1968-75
Atkinson, Jane	T	1945-47
Atkinson, Louise	C	1938
Atkinson, Richia	T	1942
Atkinson, Sarah	C	1991-96
Attaway, Sarah	C	1989-91
Attebury, Ann	A	1963-67
Attebury, Elaine	C	1992-96
Attebury, Josephine	T	1966
Attebury, Julie	A	1962-67
Attebury, Libby	C	1970-76
Attebury, Nancy	T	1948-49
Attebury, Nancy	T	1967-74
Attebury, Suzy	A	1971-72
Atwood, Mary Louise	T	1937-39
Aubrey, Adrian	C	1977-84
Aubrey, Camilla	C	1970-77
Aubrey, Christian	C	1975-82
Aubrey, Elizabeth	A	1984
Aubrey, Sarah	T	1982-84
Aubry, Adrian	C	1977-78, 1980-84
Aubry, Camilla	C	1971-76

Aubry, Christian	C	1975-78, 1981-82
Augur, Elizabeth	A	1981-84
Auld, Terressa	T	1939-40
Auler, Mary Ann	C	1949,51-52
Austin, Bailey	A	1994
Austin, Darcy	T	1994
Austin, Eloise	T	1989,91-92
Austin, Joyce	A	1952-53
Austin, Rosemary Speedy	C	1948-51
Austin, Sandy	T	1973
Austin, Susan	A	1974-78
Austin, Tiffany	T	1972-75
Autrey, Amber	T	1984-88
Autrey, Jordan	C	1986-90
Avant, Laura	T	1996
Averill, Jacqueline	A	1944-45
Averill, Josephine	C	1934
Averill, Mary	T	1934
Averyt, Wanda	T	1938
Axford, Lindsay	T	1983-87
Aylesworth, Ann	C	1947-49
Aynesworth, Nancy	T	1948-55
Aynesworth, Susan	T	1947-51
Ayres, Donna Lee	A	1943-46
Ayres, Louise		1928

B

Babb, Betsy	A	1994-96
Babb, Lisa	T	1972
Baccus, Earlane	A	1944
Bachman, Barbara	T	1965-69
Bachman, Marianne	A	1960-63
Bachman, Martha	C	1963-66, 1968-69
Bachman, Mary Anne	A	1960
Bachus, Marietta	A	1949
Backlund, Martha Ann	T	1953
Backrack, Dorothy	C	1933
Bacon, Nancy	A	1952-53
Badgett, Leona	A	1943
Badshaw, Amy	C	1982
Baer, Dorothy Ann	T	1944-45
Baer, Ginger	C	1949-54
Baer, Virginia	C	1949-50
Bagby, Brooke	A	1994-96
Baggett, Catherine	T	1984-96
Baggett, Sally	T	1952
Bagwell, Deanne	C	1973-76
Bagwell, Jan	T	1964-69
Bagwell, Jane	A	1947-48,51
Bagwell, Mary Lou	A	1976-81
Bahan, Katherine	A	1943-44
Bailey, Alicia	C	1984-89
Bailey, Ann	C	1968-69
Bailey, Barbara	A	1946
Bailey, Barbara	T	1959-63
Bailey, Charlene	C	1951-53
Bailey, Christabel	C	1931
Bailey, Jenna	C	1987-93
Bailey, Jo	T	1964-65
Bailey, Kathryn	T	1935
Bailey, Laura	C	1987-92

Bailey, Madeline	T	1975-78
Bailey, Margaret	T	1935
Bailey, Margaret	A	1955-56
Bailey, Mary Maude	C	1963-64
Bailey, Nancy	C	1953-55
Bailey, Rebekah	T	1952-53
Baily, Jo	T	1965
Bain, Frances	C	1955-56
Bain, Tillie	C	1936
Baird, Beth	A	1959-60
Baird, Betty	C	1947-48
Baird, Beverly	A	1948-49
Baird, Beverly	C	1953
Baird, Brittany	T	1987-94
Baird, Catherine	C	1995-96
Baird, Eileen	T	1985
Baird, Elizabeth	T	1992-96
Baird, Maggie	C	1996
Baird, Mary Lou	C	1960-62
Baird, Sujane	T	1948-49
Baird, Virginia Mae	T	1994-96
Baity, Margaret		1926
Baker, Alexandra	A	1995-96
Baker, Ann	T	1941,46
Baker, Ashley	T	1987-90
Baker, Cecile	T	1985
Baker, Elizabeth	A	1969-71
Baker, Emily	C	1991-96
Baker, Gay	T	1951-53
Baker, Georgia	T	1993-96
Baker, Joan	A	1951-52
Baker, Linda Lee	A	1952
Baker, Louise	C	1940-44
Baker, Mary Franke	C	1930
Baker, Mary Clyde	A	1943-44
Baker, Mary Martha	T	1952
Baker, Mercedes	T	1944
Baker, Nancy	C	1973
Baker, Sara Ann	C	1944-45
Baker, Susie	A	1952-59
Bakke, Carol	A	1970-73
Bakke, Cathy	T	1974-79
Bakke, Gail	A	1972-75
Bakke, Isabeth	A	1950-52
Balch, Beverly	T	1945
Baldridge, Carol	A	1959
Baldridge, Ellen	T	1981-85
Baldridge, Margaret	T	1982-87
Baldridge, Martha	T	1950-51
Baldridge, Melissa	A	1973-76
Baldwin, Ellen	C	1972-73
Baldwin, J.J.	C	1987-88
Baldwin, Katherine	A	1971-73
Baldwin, Linda	T	1956-62
Baldwin, Marjorie	T	1936-37
Bales, Jennifer	C	1976-81
Bales, Pam	C	1975-79
Ball, Alice	A	1943-47
Ball, Barbara	A	1955-57
Ball, Betsy	T	1981-88
Ball, Dorothy	C	1937-40
Ball, Emma Jo	T	1935-36
Ball, Katy	A	1980-86

Name	Code	Years
Ball, Leah	T	1983
Ball, Marilyn	A	1955
Ball, Melissa	C	1963-67
Ball, Meredith	T	1957-63
Ball, Oteka	A	1980
Ball, Patricia	T	1957-66
Ball, Sally	T	1962-65
Ballard, Beverly	C	1976-80
Ballard, Eleisha	T	1975-78
Ballard, Jennifer	C	1978-80
Ballard, Leslie	A	1986
Balmer, Carolyn	T	1979-85
Balmer, Elizabeth	A	1971-77
Balph, Carolyn	T	1937-38
Bancroft, Anna	A	1988-92
Bancroft, Arabella	T	1940-41
Bancroft, Becky	T	1965
Bancroft, Holly	A	1989-92
Bander, Nancy	C	1970
Bandy, Betsy	C	1962-67
Bandy, Kathryn	A	1964-69
Bandy, Kimberly	C	1995-96
Banister, Bess	T	1977-80j
Banister, Kara	T	1980-85
Banks, Kim	T	1975-81
Banks, Melissa	A	1979-82
Banks, Mimi	T	1946-47, 1949-51
Bankston, Lacy	A	1992-96
Banner, Martha	T	1935
Bannister, Bess	T	1978
Barbee, Suzanne	C	1951-53
Barbee, Tracy	C	1994-96
Barber, Callie	A	1968-73
Barber, Merle	A	1944
Barbolla, Leigh	T	1995-96
Barbour, Betty	C	1933
Barbour, Patty	C	1936-38
Barbour, Sally Ashe	T	1937-38
Barclay, Janie	A	1975-77
Barcus, Jeannie	A	1956-59
Barcus, Mary Margaret	A	1954-55
Barcus, Sue	C	1943-52
Bardwell, Charlotte	C	1937-38
Barfield, Amanda	C	1967-70
Barfield, CeCe	C	1994-96
Barfield, Deyanne	C	1960-62
Barham, Chandler	T	1955
Barker, Austine		1928
Barker, Cindy	C	1965-68
Barker, Marilyn	A	1943
Barker, Marion	A	1943
Barker, Martha Lou	C	1946-47
Barker, Susan	C	1968-73
Barker, Virginia	A	1950-52
Barkley, Elizabeth	T	1951-56
Barkley, Margaret	A	1961-63
Barkowsky, Annie	A	1987-94
Barksdale, Antoinette	A	1943-44
Barlett, Carol	C	1956
Barlow, Sara Jac	A	1951-53
Barnes, Carol Lee	A	1960-61
Barnes, Georgia	C	1939
Barnes, Janet	C	1950-52
Barnes, Jessica	C	1990-94
Barnes, Jolie	T	1989-90
Barnes, Kelley	T	1979
Barnes, Kerry	C	1957-60
Barnes, Mary Evalyn	T	1947-48
Barnes, Mary		1929
Barnes, Mary Jane	T	1934
Barnes, Maury	A	1993-96
Barnes, Phyllis	T	1936
Barnes, Rebecca Ann	C	1954-57
Barnes, Susan	T	1954
Barnes, Virginia		1928-29
Barnett, Ann	C	1967-71
Barnett, Barbara	A	1947-48
Barnett, Bette	C	1969-74
Barnett, Charlotte	T	1930
Barnett, Frances Mary	T	1936
Barnett, Frances	T	1930
Barnett, Harriett	T	1934-35
Barnett, Martha Ann	C	1936-37
Barnett, Patti	T	1968-71
Barnhart, Claire	C	1966-67
Barnhart, Gina	C	1967-68
Barnhart, Mimi	T	1970-71
Barnhill, Tebbie	C	1981-84
Baron, Sarah	C	1994-96
Barr, Ann	C	1961-64
Barr, Marjorie Sue	C	1941
Barrett, Alison	C	1982-84
Barrett, Anne	T	1937
Barrett, Audrey	C	1990-94
Barrett, Beverly	C	1985-91
Barrett, Charline		1929
Barrett, Chauncey	C	1950-54
Barrett, Elizabeth Ann	C	1942
Barrett, Ellen	A	1958-59
Barrett, Judith	C	1961-62
Barrett, Julie	T	1986-93
Barrett, Lyanne	C	1985-89
Barrettt, Neila	A	1964
Barrier, Anne	C	1940
Barrier, Catherine	T	1939
Barrier, Mary	C	1940
Barringer, Pauline	C	1950
Barron, Ann	A	1954
Barron, Dorothy	C	1939
Barron, Helen Louise	T	1936,38,42
Barron, Marjorie	C	1939
Barrow, Bertha	C	1975-77
Barrow, Dolly	T	1964-69
Barrow, Dorthy	C	1930
Barrow, Gladys		1931
Barstow, Janice	T	1942
Bartholow, Carolyn	A	1952-57
Bartlett, Barbara	A	1950-52
Bartlett, Beverly	C	1949-50
Bartlett, Carol	C	1956
Bartlett, Elizabeth	A	1980-86
Bartlett, Jeanne	A	1975-77
Bartlett, Judy	A	1952-56
Bartlett, Melinda	T	1963-66
Barton, Barbara	C	1946-48
Barton, Billie Kay	T	1938-39
Barton, Nancy Jo	C	1951-52
Barwise, Onah	T	1942
Bashaw, Amy	C	1977-82
Baskin, Mary Kirk	A	1961-62
Bass, Chandler	T	1987-94
Bass, Margaret	T	1990-96
Bass, Marian	T	1938-39, 1941-44
Bassett, Blaire	A	1992-95
Bateman, Keith Ann	C	1959-64
Bates, Belinda	A	1957-60
Bates, Betty	T	1951-55
Bates, Helen	T	1953-54
Bates, Jean	T	1937
Bates, Lynn	C	1968-71
Bates, Mary	T	1941,43
Bates, Melanie	C	1957-59
Bates, Patty	A	1973-74
Bates, Susan	C	1973-74,76
Batson, Amy	C	1981
Batson, Beth	A	1979-81
Battlestein, Renee	C	1936
Batts, Mary	T	1978-79
Baublits, Betty	C	1937-38
Bauchman, Barbara	C	1960-64
Bauchman, Jan	C	1961-64
Bauchman, Janet	A	1964-68
Bauchman, Susan	C	1961-64
Bauchman, Virginia	T	1959-65
Baucum, Doris	C	1935
Baucum, Emily	A	1995-96
Baucum, Jennifer	T	1969-74
Baucum, Julie	C	1967-71
Baucum, Laurie	T	1992-95
Bauer, Emma	T	1934
Bauer, Frances	A	1951-52
Bauer, Mary Blanche	T	1930
Baum, Caroline	C	1994-96
Baum, Cynthia	A	1950-51
Baum, Elizabeth	T	1982-87
Baum, Mary	C	1982
Baum, Pricilla	C	1931-32
Bauman, Jennie	C	1970-74
Baumann, Karen	T	1961-64
Baus, Susan	C	1975
Bawden, Betty	C	1945,47-50
Bawden, Sue	A	1947-51
Baxley, Etta May	A	1945
Baxter, Paula	T	1964-69
Baxter, Virginia	C	1931
Bayless, Janet	T	1944-49
Bayoud, Alexis	C	1991
Bayoud, Natalie	C	1991
Bazzell, June	C	1940-41
Bazzell, Nancy	C	1934
Beach, Betty	C	1932
Beaird, Ann	C	1956-60
Beaird, Barbara	C	1949
Beaird, Beth	C	1986-87
Beaird, Dana	T	1977-84
Beaird, Deborah	T	1949,52, 1955-56

Name	Col	Years
Beaird, Jessica	C	1988
Beaird, Kathryn	T	1972-78
Beaird, Marjorie	T	1956-60, 1962-63
Beaird, Nancy	C	1949,51-52
Beaird, Susan	T	1956
Beal, Becky	A	1969-72
Beal, Elizabeth	C	1979-83
Beall, Betsy	T	1975-81
Beall, Florine	C	1934
Beall, Julia	A	1946
Beall, Martha		1933
Beall, Ruby Lee	C	1934
Beall, Trixie	C	1962-67
Beall, Virginia	C	1936
Beamon, Sharon	A	1973-78
Beamon, Susan	A	1972-76
Bean, Alyce	T	1954
Bean, Amelia	A	1944-47
Bean, Katherine	A	1977-80
Bean, Margaret	C	1977-80
Beard, Ansley	T	1996
Beard, Elizabeth	C	1980
Beard, Jessica	C	1988-92
Beard, Lauren	T	1996
Beard, Shirley	C	1940-41
Beard, Stephanie	C	1986-90
Bearden, Sandra	A	1948-53
Beasley, Ann	T	1935
Beasley, Doris	T	1938
Beasley, Jane	A	1945-46
Beasley, Peggy	C	1964-66
Beaton, Anne	C	1946
Beattie, Cindy	T	1940-52
Beaty, Janice	A	1949-56
Beauchamp, Coleen	T	1942-44,46
Beaumier, Mary Ann	C	1944-46
Bebb, Diane	T	1955-61
Beck, Barry	C	1958-60
Beck, Elna Ruth	T	1938-41
Beck, Margaret	T	1938-40
Beck, Marilyn	T	1938-41
Beck, Mary Margaret	T	1956-57
Beckelhymer, Veronica Babe	T	1938-39
Becker, Aileen	T	1932-34
Becker, Betty	C	1946-53
Becker, Carolyn	C	1945-48
Becker, Diane	T	1971-73
Becker, Jackie	T	1937
Becker, Mary Jo	T	1929-30
Becker, Pamela	A	1969-72
Beckham, Anne	A	1984-87
Beckham, Joan	T	1953-54
Beckman, Mary Marcella		1929
Becknell, Leslie	A	1976
Beckner, Elliotte	C	1932-33
Becko, Debra	A	1967-69
Becko, Denise	T	1968-69
Becko, Dianna	A	1966-69
Beckworth, Allison	C	1986-88
Beckworth, Melissa	C	1979-81, 1983-85

Name	Col	Years
Beddoes, Dollie Bess	T	1931
Bedell, Patty	A	1945
Bedford, Alann	C	1951-55
Bedford, Anna Beth	C	1935
Bedford, Frances	A	1953-57
Bedford, Jeanie	A	1957-61
Bedford, Nell Ruth	C	1936,38-39
Bednar, Lucile	C	1940
Beeler, Madalyn Ann	T	1949-50
Beeley, Becky	T	1954-58
Beeley, Linda	A	1952-57
Beene, Betty Jane	T	1942-43
Beene, Judy	C	1947-50, 1952-56
Beene, Susy	A	1950,52-59
Beery, Barbara	C	1948-52
Behrens, Anne	C	1978-79
Beissner, Sally	T	1959
Belk, Mary	T	1933
Bell, Audrey	A	1992-93,96
Bell, Barbara	C	1939-41
Bell, Betty	C	1941-42, 1944-45
Bell, Beverly	C	1942
Bell, Carolyn	C	1955-60
Bell, Christina	C	1989-91
Bell, Dorothy	C	1934-36
Bell, DAnn	T	1995-96
Bell, Eleanor	T	1938
Bell, Eleanore	C	1930
Bell, Elizabeth	T	1954-57
Bell, Emily	C	1930
Bell, Jane	T	1956-57
Bell, Joan	A	1944-50
Bell, Josephine		1926,29
Bell, Katherine	T	1954
Bell, Kickie	T	1939
Bell, Lendy	A	1987-93
Bell, Margaret		1928
Bell, Marlive	A	1963-64
Bell, Martha	T	1992-95
Bell, Martha Buford	A	1953-56
Bell, Mary Wade	A	1993-96
Bell, Mary Lynn	C	1942,44
Bell, Nancy	T	1954
Bell, Patsy Ann	A	1965-71
Bell, Ruth Lila	T	1938
Bell, Susan	T	1963-65
Bellamy, Anne	T	1990-91
Bellingrath, Elizabeth	T	1941,43-44
Bellingrath, Mary	T	1948-49
Bellingrath, Suzanne	T	1935,37
Bellmont, Margaret		1929
Bellows, Alice	T	1968-71
Bellows, Sarah	A	1964-67
Belstrom, Margaret	T	1938
Belt, Mallory	C	1990-96
Belue, Emily	T	1983-88
Bemis, Taylor	C	1993-96
Benbow, Alafair	C	1944
Benbow, Priss	C	1972-77
Benckenstein, Genevieve	T	1934
Benckenstein, Helen	A	1957-63

Name	Col	Years
Benckenstein, Mary Agnes	C	1949-55
Bender, Ellen	C	1938
Bender, Sybil	C	1934
Benedict, Margaret Ann	T	1937
Benest, Marion		1928
Benjamin, Anne	C	1976-79
Bennett, Beverly	T	1970-73
Bennett, Brooke	C	1985-90
Bennett, Carla Jean	A	1951,53-56
Bennett, Emily	T	1985
Bennett, Ethel		1929
Bennett, Jamee	C	1945
Bennett, Jessica	C	1985
Bennett, Jo Ann	A	1944-46
Bennett, L. Dell	A	1945
Bennett, Lena		1929
Bennett, Lois	C	1930-31
Bennett, Louise Ann	T	1938-40,43
Bennett, Lucia	C	1985-90
Bennett, Mary Jane	C	1932
Bennett, Megan	T	1988-93
Bennett, Nancy Bibb	C	1932
Benson, Barbara	A	1946
Benson, Marian	C	1941-42
Bentley, Camille	C	1954-55
Benton, Caroline	A	1947
Benton, Debbie	A	1975-78
Benton, Donna	T	1967-71
Benton, Georgia	T	1986-87, 1990-92
Benton, Joan	C	1941
Benton, Leslie	T	1983-87
Benton, Lynn	T	1948,50-52
Bentsen, Betty E.	A	1944-45
Bentsen, Karen	A	1973-78
Bentsen, Margo	T	1965-69
Bentsen, Pamela	A	1964-65
Bentsen, Tina	T	1960-67
Berg, Bradford	A	1988-91
Bergfeld, Betty	C	1959-62
Bergfield, Cecile	A	1951-55
Bering, Barbara	C	1943-44
Bering, Bevin	C	1994-95
Bering, Eleanor	C	1943
Bering, Gaile	T	1956-61
Bering, Heather	A	1984-87
Berlowitz, Betty	T	1935
Berly, Betty	C	1929-31
Berman, Phyllis	C	1939
Bernhardt, Katie	C	1995-96
Bernsen, Taylor	A	1992-93
Bernstein, Josephine	T	1934,37
Berry, Ali	T	1996
Berry, Amy	A	1993,95
Berry, Beverly	C	1959-62
Berry, Bremond	T	1980-85
Berry, Catherine	T	1978-83
Berry, Cynthia	C	1976-78
Berry, Jean Marie	T	1942
Berry, Margaret	C	1946-48
Berry, Robin	T	1947-49
Berry, Sarah Jane	T	1942-43
Berry, Sarah	T	1992-95

Berry, Susan	C	1949-50	Birdwell, Catherine	T	1994-96	Blair, Beverly	A	1965-66
Berryman, Kathleen	C	1982-84	Birdwell, Jackie	C	1950-53	Blair, Josephine	C	1937
Berther, Katherine	C	1937	Birdwell, Kimberly	C	1977-81	Blair, Susan Ellen	A	1966-67
Bertron, Sarah	T	1931	Birdwell, Laura	T	1991-96	Blake, Nan	T	1964-70
Beseler, Fern	C	1933-34	Birdwell, Lesley	T	1988-94	Blake, Sharon	T	1963-69
Besselman, Joan	T	1945-47	Birdwell, Mary Beth		1929	Blakeley, Bonnie Louise	C	1930
Bethea, Lona	T	1954-61	Birdwell, Missy	C	1972-73	Blakely, Ruth	C	1939
Bethea, Sally	C	1953-56	Birdwell, Naomi	C	1952	Blakemore, Kathy	C	1968-70
Bethea, Shirley	T	1931	Birdwell, Roxibeth	C	1939-41	Blakemore, Kelly	T	1995
Bethell, Lisa	A	1973-77	Biscup, Barbara	A	1946	Blalock, Brenda	C	1941-43
Bettis, Ann	T	1946	Bishop, Lauren	T	1987-93	Blanchard, Chrisian	T	1989-93
Bettis, Martha Marty	T	1961-65	Bishop, Meredith H.	A	1987	Blanchard, Mary Marshall	C	1935-36,
Bettison, Bette	C	1935	Bishop, Meredith	A	1982-89			1938-39,41
Betz, Barbara Jo	A	1958-59	Bissell, Mary	T	1960-61	Bland, Jimmy	T	1934
Beumier, Mary Ann	C	1945-56	Bitter, Barbara	C	1982-86	Bland, Jo Ann	T	1952-55
Beuscher, Betty Jo	T	1942,44	Bitter, Carol	C	1985-89	Bland, Kay	T	1949-52
Beverly, Margaret		1929	Bitter, Catherine	T	1994-95	Blankenbecker, Betty	C	1934
Bewley, Ruth	C	1931	Bitter, Janet	C	1975-80	Blankenbeckler, Brooke	A	1959-65
Beyer, Bernice		1928	Bitter, Sarah	T	1988-91	Blankenbeckler, Caroline	C	1990-93
Beyer, Laura	A	1988-94	Bitter, Smyth	T	1991-94	Blankenship, Betty	T	1938,40
Beyhan, Rose Ann	T	1935	Bivin, Dorothy		1926,28	Blanks, Gay	C	1944-48
Bickel, Gretchen	C	1955-58	Bivins, Betty	A	1954-58	Blanks, Patricia Ann	A	1949-50
Bickel, Loretta	A	1988-94	Bivins, Dorothy		1928	Blanks, Sophia	A	1977-78
Bickel, Stephanie	T	1986-91	Bivins, June	A	1966-71	Blanks, Virginia	T	1948-50
Bickel, Valerie	A	1991-96	Bivins, Louise	T	1967-71	Blanton, Allison	T	1989-95
Bickley, Lillie Mae		1929	Bivins, Sally	A	1954-58	Blanton, Catherine	T	1980-83
Biddle, Brooke	T	1989-96	Black, Allison	A	1987-89	Blanton, Elizabeth	A	1960-67
Biddle, Susie	T	1994-96	Black, Ann	A	1963-68	Blanton, Jo Ann	A	1943
Bidwell, Barbara Ann	T	1938	Black, Anne	A	1949-52	Blanton, Kathy	C	1962-66
Biedenharn, Aron	A	1986-87	Black, Betty	T	1949-55	Blanton, Mary C.	A	1993-96
Biedenharn, Caroline	C	1994	Black, Betty	C	1932-34	Blanton, Nancy	T	1960-65
Biedenharn, Emily	A	1994	Black, Brandy	C	1975-79	Blass, Ellen	T	1939-40
Biedenharn, Jeanne	C	1950-51	Black, Bretaigne	C	1982-88	Blaylock, Brenda	C	1941
Biedenharn, Jerry	T	1940-44	Black, Elizabeth		1934	Blaylock, Elizabeth	T	1976-78
Biedenharn, Jo Ann	T	1940-42	Black, Elizabeth Betty	T	1949-52	Bleakney, Bonnie	T	1972-78
Biedenharn, Louisa	C	1950-51	Black, Frances	T	1941,43-46	Bleakney, Millicent	A	1949-50
Biel, Irma Katherine	T	1936	Black, Fredda Louise	T	1947-53	Bleakney, Tracy	T	1975-82
Bielstein, Gretchen	C	1957-58	Black, Kathleen	C	1942-44	Bledsoe, Sarah Ann	T	1948-52
Biggs, Electra	T	1953-59	Black, Kathy	A	1967-70	Blevins, Ann	C	1947,49-52
Biggs, Elizabeth	A	1976-83	Black, Melissa	T	1979-85	Blevins, Jaime	A	1979-85
Biggs, Helen	C	1953-60	Black, Michelle	T	1980-84	Blevins, Sue	C	1946-51
Biggs, Mildred	C	1930	Black, Peggy	C	1944	Blieden, Valry	A	1959
Bihn, Agnes		1929	Blackburn, Anne	T	1950	Blinn, Diane	T	1961-66
Bihn, Martha Jean		1929	Blackburn, Brenda	C	1958	Blinn, Susan	T	1956-60
Biles, Elise	A	1949	Blackburn, Lauren	T	1985-89	Blinn, Trudy	A	1958-64
Billings, Doris Louise	C	1935	Blackburn, Lilla	C	1980-86	Blish, Harriet	C	1938
Billingsley, Anne	C	1996	Blackburn, Lynne	T	1957-60	Blish, Kathryn	C	1934-35
Billingsley, Bettye	A	1943-45	Blackburn, Mary	T	1994-96	Blocker, Jean	C	1931
Billingsley, Lucy	A	1989-93	Blackman, Ann	A	1943-44	Bloede, Laura	A	1991
Bills, Eleanor	T	1930-31	Blackman, Ann Elizabeth	A	1950,53	Bloemendal, Katherine	A	1986-92
Billups, Francie	A	1973-74,	Blackman, Carrie	C	1982	Bloodworth, Ann	A	1956-58
		1976-79	Blackmore, Kathlyn	T	1937	Blount, Barbara	C	1954-58
Billups, LeAnn	A	1966-69	Blackshear, Jan	C	1966-68	Blount, Katie	A	1995-96
Billups, Liza	A	1966-69	Blackshear, Mary Margaret		C	Blount, Martha	C	1957-61
Billups, Marci	C	1978-85	1971-74			Bloxsom, Carol	T	1968-75
Billups, Margaret	T	1959-61	Blackwell, Ann	C	1950-51	Bloxsom, Charlotte	T	1983-87
Bingman, Jane	T	1938-40	Blackwell, Harriett	A	1974	Bloxsom, Helen	A	1947-52
Bingman, Nancy	T	1938-40	Blades, Becky	T	1996	Bluestein, Peggy	T	1935-36
Bintliffe, Beverly	C	1942-48	Blades, Medrith	T	1963-70	Boagni, Gladys	T	1941
Bintliffe, Marjorie Ann	C	1941-45	Blades, Murnez	C	1955-62	Boardman, Joan	T	1939-40
Birch, Elizabeth	C	1986-88	Blaik, Katie	T	1985	Boaz, Ann	T	1936-38
Birdsong, Anne	T	1940	Blain, Beverly	T	1935-36	Bobbitt, Barbara	A	1947
Birdsong, Sally	T	1948-49	Blair, Betty	A	1943-44			

Bobo, Betsy	T	1938,40	Boone, Chauncey	C	1977-84	Boyce, Emalie	T	1988-91
Bodman, Joan	A	1946-47	Boone, Helen	T	1933	Boyce, Janie	A	1984-87
Boecking, Caroline	C	1962-64	Boone, Jenny	A	1985-92	Boyce, Katherine	C	1991-94
Boedeker, Paula	T	1942-48	Boone, Mary Nell	C	1983-88	Boyce, Laura	A	1986-89,
Bogel, Berry	A	1993-96	Boone, Sara	T	1981-85			1991-92
Boggs, Ruth Anne	T	1955-56	Booth, Cynthia	C	1961-63,65	Boyce, Sally	T	1996
Bohan, Chandler	T	1971-77	Booth, Martha	T	1958-64	Boyd, Alvin Ann	T	1942-43,
Bohanna, Sidney	A	1953-57	Booth, Mary Lea	C	1948-53			1945-46
Bohlman, Katherine	A	1995	Booth, Nan	A	1951-53	Boyd, Beth	A	1965-67
Bohlman, Marge	T	1962	Booth, Susan	A	1965-66	Boyd, Gloria	A	1956-64
Bohlmann, Genny	A	1957-62	Booth, Vicki	A	1965-67	Boyd, Ina Helen		1929
Bohlmann, Katherine	A	1991-95	Booty, Katherine	T	1933-34	Boyd, Lesli Ann	C	1973-77
Bohlmann, Margo	T	1962-67	Bordages, Allison	C	1967-71	Boyd, Lisa	C	1975-78
Boker, Alice Rhea	C	1942	Bordages, Betty	A	1956-60	Boyd, Patsy	T	1936
Bolch, Camilla	T	1966	Bordages, Kate	C	1972-73	Boyd, Rachel	C	1930
Boldrick, Kelly	A	1986	Boren, Carrie	C	1980-83,85	Boyd, Susan	A	1958-61
Boldrick, Starr	C	1971-78	Boren, Nelva		1928	Boykin, Margaret Ann	C	1949-51
Bole, Julia	A	1969-75	Borger, Barbara	C	1946	Boyle, Augusta Buster	T	1929-30,32
Bolender, Beverly	C	1952	Boring, Caroline	C	1931	Boyles, Bettie	C	1933-36,38
Bolender, Nancy Ann	T	1947-49	Borlaug, Natalie	C	1989-92	Boysen, Stephanie	T	1951
Boles, Kathy	C	1978-82	Borlaug, Tiffany	T	1982-86	Boyter, Casey	C	1992-95
Bolger, Caroline	C	1980-85	Bostick, Barbara	A	1974-80	Brace, Dana	T	1979
Bolger, Catherine	A	1976-83	Bostick, Becky	C	1969-75	Brace, Nancy	A	1944-45
Bolinger, Gigi	T	1987-90	Bostick, Betsy	C	1966-71	Bracewell, Betsy	T	1959-64
Bolton, Fran	A	1943	Boswell, Carrie	C	1987,89	Bracewell, Laynie	T	1994-96
Bolton, Marjorie Cameron	T	1943	Boswell, Gayle	C	1954-59	Bracewell, Mollie	T	1995-96
Bolton, Mary Stanton	A	1948-50	Bosworth, Carolyn	A	1976	Brack, Betty	T	1962
Bolton, Suzanne	T	1957-61,63	Botts, Martha	C	1995-96	Bracken, Alicanne	A	1985-89
Bomar, Patricia	T	1937	Botts, Sarah	C	1995-96	Bracken, Allison	C	1982-88
Bond, Betty	T	1939	Boudreaux, Myrtie	T	1936-37	Bracken, Glenda	A	1950,53-54
Bond, Brenda	T	1949-50	Bourland, Claire	T	1992-93	Bracken, Kay	T	1967-69
Bond, Denise	T	1958	Bourlon, Brooke	A	1978-82	Bracken, Shirley	T	1948-50
Bond, Francis	C	1960-61	Bourne, Bonnie	C	1937	Bracy, Betsy	T	1945-47
Bond, Jane	A	1968-71	Bourne, Elizabeth	T	1979-80	Braden, Mary Laura	T	1937
Bond, Katherine	T	1952-53	Bousquet, Kinta	C	1944-48	Braden, Olive	A	1966-71
Bond, Kathrin	T	1965-68	Bovaird, Mary Florence	T	1942-44	Bradford, Betty	T	1938-42
Bond, Lauren	C	1992-93	Bovaird, Ruth Anna	T	1938-39	Bradford, Jane	C	1939-41
Bond, Lindsay	A	1992	Bowden, Betty Ann	A	1943	Bradford, Lawrie	A	1982-85
Bond, Susan	C	1966-70	Bowen, Betsy	T	1956-61	Bradford, Mary Lou	C	1943-52
Bondurant, Caroline	A	1992-94	Bowen, Betsy	T	1991-96	Bradford, Sallie Ann	A	1943-50
Bondurant, Gladys	T	1944-45,47	Bowen, Cynthia	T	1963-67	Bradley, Adele	T	1940-45
Bondurant, Judy	T	1945	Bowen, Joyce	C	1956-58	Bradley, Alatia	A	1982-83
Bondurant, Laura	A	1976-84	Bowen, Katie	A	1995-96	Bradley, Amy	A	1981
Bondurant, Suzanne	C	1989-92	Bowen, Mary	A	1968-74	Bradley, Peggy	A	1947
Bonebrake, Laurie	A	1981-84	Bowen, Neal	A	1993-96	Bradshaw, Nelle	C	1936,38
Bonebrake, Stephanie	C	1981-84	Bowen, Patty	T	1969-74	Bradshaw, Sally	A	1957
Bonelli, Diana	A	1960-62	Bowen, Sally	C	1953-54	Bradshaw, Shirley	C	1952
Boney, Billie Jean	T	1935,37	Bowen, Sally	A	1972-79	Bradshaw, Susan	C	1959
Bonham, Alisa	T	1982-89	Bowers, Beth	A	1995-96	Brady, Carolyn	T	1953-56
Bonin, Amy	T	1988-89	Bowers, Cleo	T	1935	Brady, Margaret	C	1953-56
Bonneau, Kay	C	1946-51	Bowers, Patricia	T	1953-54	Bragg, Mandy	C	1987-90
Bonnell, Laura	T	1980-81	Bowers, Sara Kell	C	1993-96	Brainard, Helen	C	1934
Bonner, Anne	C	1992-96	Bowers, Susan		1965	Brainard, Jane	C	1934
Bonner, Beth	T	1981-86	Bowes, Ashley	C	1981-88	Brainard, Jane	T	1933
Bonner, Bettye	T	1941	Bowlby, Kathryn	T	1941-47	Brainard, Laura	T	1981-85
Bonner, Carlye	C	1985-89	Bowles, Betty	C	1952-53	Bralley, Peggy	A	1947-49
Bonner, Jeanne	T	1966-69	Bowman, Betty Jo	C	1937	Braly, Jean	T	1939
Bonner, Marion	A	1990-96	Bowman, Carol Ann	C	1960	Brammer, Barbara	T	1942
Bonner, Patricia	C	1944-47	Bowman, Jeanne	A	1952	Branch, La Vynda	T	1941-44,46
Bonner, Robin	T	1958-63	Boxwell, Nancy	A	1948	Branden, Bridget	C	1974
Bonwit, Mildred	T	1930	Boyce, Barbara	T	1941	Brandenberg, Fly	C	1961
Boon, Marjorie	T	1931-32	Boyce, Carol-Sidney	T	1993-96	Brander, Katie	C	1968-71
Boone, Brenda	A	1948	Boyce, Ellis	C	1983-84	Brandon, Betty Lue	C	1938

Name		Year
Brandon, Betty	T	1953-56
Brandon, Bridget	C	1974
Brandon, Kassie	T	1973-74
Brandon, Louisa	C	1955-58
Brandon, Martha Ann	C	1948-51
Brandt, Beverly		1934
Brandt, Mary Helen	C	1958-61,63
Braniff, Jean	T	1930
Brannies, Megan	T	1980-84
Brannies, Melany	T	1979-84
Brannon, Lisa	C	1975-78
Branscomb, Margo	T	1965-67
Bransford, Beth	A	1968-70
Bransford, Cynthia	C	1966-67
Bransford, Vicki	A	1964-67
Branson, Ola Fay	T	1937
Braselton, Linda	T	1961-63
Braselton, Mary Louise	T	1934
Brashear, Betty Jo	C	1941-42
Brasher, Sarah	C	1977-80
Brask, Betty	T	1962-63
Brask, Ginger	T	1954-55
Braswell, Barbara	T	1942-43
Bratton, Dorothy Dale	T	1943-44
Bratton-Price, Ann	C	1989
Brawley, Mary Glenn	A	1947-48
Bray, Nan	C	1943-44
Brazeel, Caroline	A	1996
Brazell, Britney	T	1992-95
Brazell, Colbie	C	1992-95
Brazelton, Jane		1928
Brazelton, Shelley	T	1976-81
Brazzel, Kristen	A	1985-86
Breard, Pauline	T	1941
Breard, Sally	T	1960-62
Breaux, Catherine	T	1941
Breck, Mary		1929
Bredenberg, Nancy Fly	C	1958-61, 1963-64
Breeden, Mabel Claire	T	1929-30
Breeden, Rosemary	T	1929-30
Breeding, Elizabeth	A	1976-79
Breeding, Leanna	A	1964-67
Breeding, Virginia	T	1932
Breedlove, Kay	C	1957-60
Breedlove, Molly	T	1981-82
Breimo, Billye Ann	C	1943-44
Breitzke, Mimi	T	1944
Brelsford, Ann	C	1955-58
Brelsford, Carol	C	1964-65
Brelsford, Susan	T	1958-61
Brennan, Dorothy	T	1944-48
Brennan, Jo Anne	T	1937
Brennan, Lauren	C	1968-69
Brennan, Leslie	T	1966-69
Brennan, Patsy	C	1945-49
Brennan, Shannon	A	1969
Brent, Beth	T	1982-85
Brewer, Frances	C	1947-50
Brewer, Jean	T	1930
Brewster, Ann	C	1950
Brewster, Barbara	C	1956-57
Brewster, Gayle	A	1947-48

Name		Year
Brice, Ann	A	1956-59
Brice, Scotty	C	1941-42
Bridewell, Judy	C	1963-67
Bridewell, Kay	T	1958-59
Bridgeman, Brennan	T	1966-69
Bridwell, Josephine	T	1935-36
Bridwell, Margaret	A	1943
Briggs, Barbara	T	1941-43
Briggs, Charlotte		1929
Briggs, Cheryl	C	1955
Briggs, Josephine	C	1940-42
Briggs, Meredith	T	1982-84
Bright, Carol	A	1959-61
Bright, Elizabeth	C	1992-96
Bright, Margaret	T	1959-61
Bright, Margarite	C	1949-54
Brightbill, Cynthia	C	1981-84
Brindley, Beth	C	1979-84
Brinkoeter, Allyson	T	1991-94,96
Brinsmade, Carol Ann	C	1952-53
Brinsmade, Patricia	T	1952-53
Briscoe, Betty	T	1928,31
Briscoe, Bobbie Ann	C	1940
Bristol, Jean	T	1935-36, 1939-40
Britain, Martha	T	1930,34
Britain, Niski	T	1930
Brite, Antoinette		1929
Brittain, Sally	T	1944-45
Brittain, Sally	T	1950-52
Britton, Marian	T	1963-67
Brizzolara, Mary	T	1942-43
Broaddus, Betty		1967-71
Broaddus, Nancy	A	1967-71
Broadhurst, Alison	T	1980-83
Broadhurst, Michelle	C	1971-72
Broadway, Katherine Frances		1929
Brock, Alexandra	C	1995-96
Brock, Barbara	A	1950
Brock, Betty	T	1985-86
Brock, Carolyn	T	1980-85
Brock, Elizabeth	T	1982-87
Brock, Katie	T	1976-81
Brock, Rachel	A	1985
Brock, Suzannah	C	1975-79
Brockhausen, Helen	C	1933
Brockhousen, Louise	T	1935
Brockhousen, Marion	C	1933
Brockman, Jana	A	1973-74
Brockman, Jennifer	T	1981
Broday, Gayle	T	1950-54
Broe, Eileen	C	1930
Broe, June	C	1930
Brogan, Barbara	A	1943
Brogan, Mary Jane	A	1951
Brogan, Mary Catherine	C	1936-38
Brogniez, Geane	T	1931-38, 1940-42
Brogniez, Martha Ann	T	1946-49
Bromberg, Whitney	T	1984-87
Bronson, Beverly Ann	C	1936-38,40
Bronson, Susan	A	1954-58
Brook, Betty Mae	T	1938

Name		Year
Brook, Francis		1929
Brook, Joe Ann	A	1943-46
Brooke, Amy	T	1976-82
Brooke, Barbara	C	1948
Brooke, Elisabeth	A	1977-84
Brookins, Helen	T	1930
Brooks, Amber	C	1996
Brooks, Carol	A	1956-63
Brooks, Cheryl	A	1991-96
Brooks, Jeanette	C	1954
Brooks, Kathleen	A	1952-57
Brooks, Laura Mae		1929
Brooks, Laura	T	1980-84
Brooks, Ollie Fay	T	1933-34
Brooks, Sue	C	1952-54
Brooks, Susan	A	1982-88
Brooks, Veda	T	1941-44
Brookshire, Amy	A	1984-91
Brookshire, Britt	T	1973-74
Brookshire, Carlye	A	1973-78
Brookshire, Jan	C	1949-50
Brookshire, Karen	T	1968-71
Broome, Barbara	C	1943-46
Brosier, Libby	C	1966-71
Brosier, Sally	A	1969-73
Broughton, Jane	C	1942,44-47
Broussard, Anne	A	1969-75
Broussard, Anne M.	C	1948-54
Broussard, Charlotte	A	1984 -91
Broussard, Cindy	C	1964-69
Broussard, Loretta Tita	T	1942-45
Broussard, Margaret	C	1935
Broussard, Mary Jo	T	1942-45
Broussard, Michelle	A	1978-81
Broussard, Reese	C	1971-76
Brousseau, Alexandra	T	1995-96
Brown, Abby	T	1986-87
Brown, Abby	T	1969-73
Brown, Ann	T	1941-42
Brown, Anna Beth	C	1947-48
Brown, Annabelle	T	1983-87
Brown, Aubyn Maurine	C	1934
Brown, Barbara	A	1960-68
Brown, Barbara Ruth	C	1979-84
Brown, Barbara	C	1936-37
Brown, Belle	C	1982-89
Brown, Beth	C	1967-73
Brown, Betty Lou	T	1963-65
Brown, Betty Lynne	T	1948-51
Brown, Beverly	A	1944
Brown, Beverly	T	1969-76
Brown, Beverly	C	1938-39
Brown, Beverly	T	1934-35
Brown, Billy Margaret	A	1951-52
Brown, Brenda	T	1968-75
Brown, Carol	T	1954-57
Brown, Carolyn Marie	T	1977-82
Brown, Carolyn	T	1964-68
Brown, Carolyn Lee	C	1956,59-60
Brown, Carrie	T	1985-90
Brown, Catherine	A	1955
Brown, Cathy	A	1996
Brown, Cooper	C	1962-65
Brown, Debbie Ann		

Name		Years
Brown, Diane	T	1952-60
Brown, Diane	T	1956-58
Brown, Elaine	T	1967-73
Brown, Elizabeth	T	1991-93
Brown, Frances	C	1948-49
Brown, Franci	A	1980-87
Brown, Garland	C	1931
Brown, Garnett	T	1954
Brown, George Ann	T	1940
Brown, Gladys	A	1951-55
Brown, Gloria Jean	T	1935
Brown, Gloria June	T	1935
Brown, Helen	A	1988-91
Brown, Jacqueline		1939
Brown, Jane	C	1948-49
Brown, Janet		1946
Brown, Joan	C	1950-53
Brown, Joan	T	1945-46
Brown, Joy	T	1942-43
Brown, Kathy	A	1966-69
Brown, Kristen	A	1982-85
Brown, Laura	A	1979-83
Brown, Laura	A	1959-64
Brown, Leah	A	1981-83
Brown, Leigh Ann	T	1972-79
Brown, Margaret	C	1996
Brown, Marianne	A	1943-46
Brown, Marilee	C	1959
Brown, Martha	A	1962-65
Brown, Mary Ellen	A	1988-93
Brown, Mary Jane	C	1940-41
Brown, Mary Ann	C	1962-63
Brown, Mary Frances	C	1941
Brown, Mary Carroll		1929
Brown, Molly	C	1951-58
Brown, Mona	A	1944
Brown, Nan	C	1955-58
Brown, Nancy	C	1947-48
Brown, Nancy Lee	A	1956-60
Brown, Pat	T	1946-51
Brown, Patricia Lee	A	1956-57
Brown, Patti	A	1976-81
Brown, Peggy	T	1952-56
Brown, Phyllis	A	1963-65
Brown, Priscilla	A	1972-74
Brown, Rose Mary	T	1941
Brown, Shirley	C	1947-48,51
Brown, Stanton	T	1973-78
Brown, Sue	A	1953-57
Brown, Susan	T	1964-65
Brown, Susanna	A	1993-96
Brown, Susannah	C	1983-87
Brown, Suzan	A	1956-59
Brown, Suzanne Elizabeth	A	1954-55
Brown, Suzanne	T	1981-87
Brown, Tricia	A	1968-73
Brown, Virginia	A	1949-50
Browne, Bonnie Blue	A	1951-52
Browne, Helen Lee	A	1948
Browne, Kelsey	A	1946-50
Browne, Liza	A	1993
Browne, Susie Ann	C	1939-40
Browning, Christine		1929
Browning, Elizabeth	A	1990-96
Browning, Helen	A	1989
Browning, Jo Deane	C	1950-53
Browning, Kay	A	1957-63
Browning, Roberta	T	1950-52
Brownlee, Lauren	T	1994-95
Broyles, Kay	T	1959-60
Bruce, Betty	T	1964-68
Bruce, Caroline		1933
Bruce, Dana	T	1979
Bruce, Patti	A	1964-67
Brulay, Lucy		1928
Bruner, Alison	A	1946-47,49
Bruner, Julie	T	1966-70
Bruner, Mary	C	1975-82
Bruni, Allison	C	1993-96
Brunner, Claire	A	1995 -96
Brunner, Whitney	T	1995-96
Bruno, Brittany	A	1995-96
Brunson, Iris Ann	A	1945-48
Brunson, Susannah	C	1948-49, 1953-54
Brusenhan, Laura	C	1972-73
Brusenhan, Nancy	T	1971-72
Brusenhan, Susan	T	1971-73
Bruss, Betty	C	1963-66
Bruton, Mary Jane	T	1934
Bruyere, Ann	T	1958-62
Bryan, Alicia	C	1974-81
Bryan, Barbara	C	1947-49
Bryan, Beverly	C	1936-37
Bryan, Carolyn	T	1940-41
Bryan, Elizabeth		1929
Bryan, Jo Ann	T	1950-51
Bryan, Joan	C	1942
Bryan, Marion	C	1955-57
Bryan, Patsy	C	1944-45
Bryan, Virginia	T	1942,44-45
Bryant, Barbara Joyce	T	1943,48
Bryant, Barbara Ann	T	1941,45-47
Bryant, Chaytor	T	1940
Bryson, Kathryn	C	1941-43
Buatt, Aimee	C	1981-87
Buchanan, Betsy	C	1950
Buchanan, Daphne	T	1939
Buchanan, Jane Ellen	C	1942
Buchek, Laura	T	1983-88
Buck, Betty Jo	C	1938
Buck, Elaine	C	1931-33
Buck, Sarah	A	1989
Buckler, Ann	T	1936,38
Buckley, Brenda	A	1966-68
Buckly, Margaret	A	1944
Bucy, Martha	A	1943
Buddendorf, Patricia	C	1974
Buell, Lynn	C	1956-59
Buell, Susan	C	1959-62
Buescher, Betty Jo	T	1941-46
Buescher, Genelle	C	1934-35
Buffington, Diane	A	1943-45
Buffington, Mary	C	1975
Buford, Allison	C	1979-81
Buford, Christy	A	1987
Buhler, Mary Margaret		1929
Buie, Harriet	T	1952
Bulbrook, Kay Anna	C	1954-55
Bullion, Ann	A	1958-62
Bulloch, MLise	A	1979
Bullock, Jane	C	1942
Bumpas, Susan	A	1975-77
Bumpus, Barbara Sue	T	1942-43,45
Bumpus, Karen	C	1971-75
Bundy, Jenness	A	1978-83
Bunger, June	C	1955
Bunkley, Angela	T	1978-83
Bunkley, Mary Lou	A	1945-46
Bunte, Nannette	C	1936
Bunting, Floy Gary	T	1958-63
Bunting, Nancy Ann	A	1960-61
Bunyard, Joann	C	1930-31
Burbridge, Ann	A	1967-72
Burbridge, Karen	C	1970-75
Burbridge, Phyllis	C	1965-67
Burch, Catherine	A	1946-52
Burden, Eileen	T	1963-65
Burden, Julie	C	1963-65
Burdette, Ann	T	1942
Burford, Ashley	A	1977-84
Burford, Blaire	A	1980-88
Burford, Carolyn	C	1940
Burford, Melissa	T	1976-81
Burford, Sherrie	A	1965-72
Burg, Jean	T	1938
Burg, Nan	T	1938
Burge, Corida	T	1940-41
Burger, Kitty	T	1933-35
Burger, Mary Frances	C	1942
Burgher, Diane	C	1940
Burk, Jennifer	C	1983-86
Burk, Lee Ann	T	1965-71
Burke, Barbara	A	1947
Burke, Barbara	C	1973-74
Burke, Bridget	A	1990-96
Burke, Cathy	T	1968-74
Burke, Elizabeth	T	1973-76
Burke, Jennifer	A	1990-94
Burke, Kathleen	T	1956
Burke, Maria	C	1951-57
Burkett, Blake	C	1976-78
Burkhalter, Jane	C	1951-52
Burkhalter, Jean	C	1951-52
Burkhalter, Joanne	A	1944-47
Burkhalter, Mary Dudley	T	1951-52
Burks, Bettina	C	1954-55
Burleson, Bridget	T	1982-88
Burleson, Megan	A	1980-83
Burlingame, Joan	A	1946-49
Burnett, Jeanne	C	1939-40
Burnett, Martha	C	1935-37
Burney, Barbara	C	1930
Burney, Karita	A	1962-67
Burns, Elizabeth	C	1989-91
Burns, Nancy	T	1944-45
Burns, Rebecca	A	1994
Burns, Shannon	T	1991-92
Burris, Martha Glynn	T	1942-43

Name		Years
Burroughs, Billie Jean	C	1935-36
Burrow, Lacee	T	1992-96
Burrow, Lauren	T	1990-96
Burrow, Leah	T	1994-96
Burrus, Cynthia	C	1967
Burrus, Ellie	C	1991-94,96
Burrus, Mandy	A	1970-74
Burrus, Mary Ellis	T	1972-75
Burrus, Vivian	A	1964-69
Burt, Emily	A	1943-44
Burt, Jane	C	1958-62
Burt, Juanita	C	1936
Burton, Chloe	A	1950
Burton, Jackie	A	1950
Burton, Jean	T	1934-35
Burton, Margaret	C	1938-40
Buser, Betty	T	1951
Bush, Joan	T	1941-42, 1944-45
Bush, Madelaine	T	1970-72
Bush, Marianne	T	1935
Bush, Rebekah Jane	C	1933,36
Bush, Sarah Virginia	C	1935-36
Buss, Elizabeth	T	1978-79
Bussey, Casey	C	1982-85
Bustamante, Celina	C	1991-92
Butcher, Margaret Helen	C	1939
Butcher, Mary Ann	C	1952-53
Butler, Ann	A	1946
Butler, Anne	C	1949-52
Butler, Becky	A	1962-69
Butler, Bridget	T	1978-84
Butler, Cathy	C	1957-60
Butler, Francis		1929
Butler, Gretchen	C	1971-77
Butler, Heidi	T	1976-82
Butler, Helen		1929
Butler, Hilairy	A	1974-76
Butler, Ida Jo	A	1943-44,46
Butler, Janice	T	1942
Butler, Jo Anna	A	1980-85
Butler, Kay	A	1965-70
Butler, Kristen Kissy	A	1974-80
Butler, Laura		1929
Butler, Lauren	C	1996
Butler, Libby	C	1975-79
Butler, Lillian		1929
Butler, Maria	A	1974-80
Butler, Mary Jo		1928
Butler, Mary K.	T	1996
Butler, Matilda	C	1952
Butman, Alice Ann	C	1940
Butman, Statira	C	1939-40
Butt, Dana	T	1984-85
Butt, Karen	C	1984-85
Butte, Beth	T	1940-41
Butte, Sarah Catherine	T	1941
Butter, Alexis	T	1978
Butter, Bette	A	1954-57
Butter, Susan	C	1955
Butterworth, Eve	T	1942
Button, Marion		1929
Buxton, Natasha	A	1994-96

Name		Years
Buzzard, Beth	A	1991-96
Buzzini, Barbara	C	1945
Buzzini, Carol Lee	C	1951-52
Byars, Betty	C	1952-55
Byars, Jo Ann	T	1939-41
Byars, Mary Alice	T	1939-40
Bybee, Beth	A	1962-68
Bynum, Patsy	T	1962-63
Bynum, Richie	A	1963
Byram, Brooke	T	1982-85
Byram, Carrielu	A	1945
Byrd, Carol	C	1986
Byrd, Flora Leta	A	1950-55
Byrd, Jane		1928
Byron, Patsy Ruth	T	1937
Bywaters, Phyllis	A	1949-50

C

Name		Years
Cabell, Christine	C	1956-57
Cabell, Sara Lee	C	1936
Cabell, Therese	T	1961-66
Cable, Carol	C	1936-37
Cable, Elizabeth	C	1967-74
Cade, Billie	T	1936
Cade, Eleanor	T	1936
Cade, Martha	T	1975-79
Cadwallader, Leah	C	1975-78
Caffery, Marion	T	1943
Cafiers, Becky	T	1960-61
Cage, Ali	C	1981-86
Cage, Barbara Carol	T	1948-49
Cage, Beverly	C	1954-56
Cage, Chaille	C	1946-48
Cage, Kathryn	T	1946-49
Cage, Lillian		1928
Cage, Sharon	T	1945-49
Cahoon, Corrinne	T	1968-74
Cahoon, Lula Jane	T	1940-41
Cain, Allison	C	1967-68
Cain, Carol	A	1974-76
Cain, June		1929
Cain, Mary Lee	T	1971
Cain, Stephanie	C	1953
Caldarelli, Karen	C	1981-86
Caldwell, Ann	A	1943-44
Caldwell, Erma	C	1932
Caldwell, Frances	A	1976-77
Caldwell, Linda	A	1950-53,55
Caldwell, Lisa	T	1964
Caldwell, Marilyn	C	1980-85
Caldwell, Martha	C	1958-60
Calhoun, Betsy	T	1941-47
Calhoun, Elizabeth	C	1933,35-37
Calhoun, Jill	C	1980-82
Calk, Marilyn	T	1960-61
Calkins, Carol	A	1954
Calkins, Carolyn	A	1960-62
Callaway, Julia	A	1968-72
Calloway, Carrie	A	1992-93
Calloway, Katie	T	1993
Calvert, Catherine	T	1995-96
Calvert, Chris	T	1956-60
Calvert, Libby	C	1956-62

Name		Years
Calvert, Toni	C	1955-58
Calvin, Carolyn	T	1953-54
Cameron, Amanda Toppy	A	1951-56
Cameron, Colleen	A	1976
Cameron, Cyrena	C	1982-85
Cameron, Emily Ann	T	1943-45, 1947-48,50
Cameron, Frances	C	1940
Cameron, Kalen	A	1979-82
Cameron, Libby	A	1954-59
Cameron, Margaret	A	1963-67
Cameron, Mary Jane	T	1940-44
Cammack, Charlotte		1928
Cammack, Jessica	A	1995-96
Cammack, Susan	A	1971
Camp, Katherine	C	1948
Camp, Mary Ann	T	1935-36
Campbell, Amy	C	1975
Campbell, Ann	C	1939-40
Campbell, Anne	A	1978-80
Campbell, Bess	A	1995-96
Campbell, Betty Gene	C	1941
Campbell, Carole	C	1975-78
Campbell, Catherine	C	1968-69
Campbell, Catherine	T	1992-96
Campbell, Cathy	C	1968-73
Campbell, Dianne	C	1944-47
Campbell, Dianne	T	1974-77
Campbell, Dorothy	C	1931
Campbell, Dorothy	C	1934
Campbell, Dorothy		1929
Campbell, Elizabeth	A	1974-77
Campbell, Gael Ann	A	1949-52
Campbell, Gail	A	1950
Campbell, Jere	A	1946-49
Campbell, Karen	C	1967-68
Campbell, Kathryn	T	1980-81
Campbell, Louise	A	1961-66
Campbell, Mandy	C	1972-74
Campbell, Margaret	T	1945
Campbell, Martha	C	1960-62
Campbell, Mary		1929
Campbell, Mary	C	1956-57
Campbell, Maud Evelyn	A	1945
Campbell, Nancy Claire	C	1943-47
Campbell, Nancy Ann	C	1947
Campbell, Patricia	T	1939
Campbell, Rebecca	T	1949-50
Campbell, Sue Ann	T	1966-67
Campbell, Susan	A	1996
Campbell, Toni	T	1974-77
Campbell, Winifred	C	1951
Campdera, Delores	T	1943-44
Canfield, Roberta DAnne	A	1946-50
Cann, Arabella	T	1969-73
Cann, Vada	T	1967-71
Cannan, Beth	T	1946-51
Cannan, Doris Ann	C	1939-40
Cannon, Jan	T	1942-43
Cannon, Lou Rena	T	1944-45
Cannon, Sarah	C	1981-85
Cannon, Thera Dell	T	1935
Canon, Carolyn	C	1935-38

Canon, Elizabeth Ann	T	1992-96
Canon, Kit	T	1975-81
Canon, LoRean	C	1965-68
Canon, Myrtle	C	1935-39
Cantey, Ambler	T	1957-59
Cantey, Samantha	A	1985-91
Cantey, Sandra	C	1950-54
Cantey, Thayer	C	1950-51,54
Capetillo, Juliana	A	1994-96
Cappel, Eloise	A	1943-47
Capps, Whitney	A	1996
Capron, Frances	T	1934
Caravageli, Athene	C	1969-72
Caravageli, Margo	T	1961-64
Caraway, Barbara	C	1935
Carb, Helen Ann		1929
Carey, Brooke	C	1981-88
Carey, Cathy	T	1975-77
Carey, Kathleen	C	1979-81
Cargile, Carolyn	C	1941-42,44
Carlisle, Bitsy	T	1937-41
Carlisle, Margaret	T	1933-35
Carlock, Caroline	C	1937-42
Carlton, Christi	T	1983-90
Carlton, Harriett	A	1945-46
Carmena, Amy	T	1980-81,
		1984-87
Carmena, Janie	T	1974-80
Carmena, Julie	T	1978-81
Carmena, Leslie	C	1981,84-88
Carmichael, Jody Lee	C	1954-59
Carmichael, Mamieola	T	1929-30
Carmichael, Meredith	A	1993-96
Carmichael, Micky Marie	C	1935-37
Carmichael, Taylor	C	1991-96
Carmody, Josephine	T	1942-44
Carnahan, Vicki	T	1960-61
Carothers, Charlotte	A	1985-89
Carothers, Drusilla	C	1944-47
Carpenter, Clare	A	1979-80
Carpenter, Peggy	C	1934,37
Carpenter, Shirley	T	1948-51
Carr, Barbara Ann	A	1943-44
Carr, Catherine	A	1967-72
Carr, Lydia	T	1939,41-42
Carr, Megan	A	1995-96
Carr, Nona Gay	A	1950-52
Carraci, Jean	C	1941
Carrell, DAun	A	1952-56
Carrell, Helen		1948
Carrigan, Laura Lou	T	1940-43
Carrington, Frances	T	1936
Carroll, Alexis	T	1960-65
Carroll, Carolyn	A	1950-53
Carroll, Cathy	A	1951-53
Carroll, Corinne	C	1945
Carroll, Cynthia	A	1949-50
Carroll, Frances	T	1930
Carroll, Janet	C	1939-41
Carroll, Joan	T	1941,43-45
Carroll, Marilyn	C	1936-37
Carroll, Mary Edna		1929
Carroll, Nora Ann	T	1940
Carroll, Polly Lynette	C	1940-41
Carroll, Sally Ann	A	1945-46
Carroll, Virginia	A	1946-48
Carroway, Betty Jean	C	1939
Carruth, Lane	T	1992-96
Carruthers, Carolyn	C	1944-45
Carson, Connie	T	1950
Carson, Kay	C	1944
Carswell, Peggy Ann	C	1935,37
Carter, Allison	A	1977
Carter, Ann	T	1944-46
Carter, Ann	C	1935-36
Carter, Betty Jean	C	1942-44
Carter, Bodessa		1928
Carter, Caroline	T	1992-96
Carter, Celeste	T	1988-94
Carter, Christie	T	1978
Carter, Cornelia Connie	A	1948
Carter, Delia Beth	T	1938
Carter, Eloise	T	1936-37,39
Carter, Erline		1929
Carter, Helen Jane	T	1948
Carter, Jane	C	1934-35
Carter, Janet	A	1949,51-52
Carter, Jennifer	C	1984-89
Carter, Joy	T	1933-34
Carter, June	T	1944-49
Carter, Kathy	T	1970-71
Carter, Kathy	T	1965-67
Carter, Kay	T	1962-65
Carter, Kay	T	1945-47
Carter, Keely	C	1992
Carter, Laura	T	1957-63
Carter, Lydia	T	1939-40
Carter, Marjorie	T	1936-37
Carter, Natalie	C	1989-93
Carter, Nenetta	A	1965-69
Carter, Pamela	A	1955
Carter, Patsy Ruth	T	1939
Carter, Phebe	T	1946-52
Carter, Phyllis		1944-45
Carter, Rondelle	T	1952-53
Carter, Sara	A	1947-48
Carter, Susan	C	1974-77
Carter, Susan	T	1994-96
Carter, Suzy	T	1975-78
Carter, Talmadge	T	1934-36
Carter, Terrell	C	1992-96
Carter, Velma	C	1936
Cartwright, Cathy	C	1962-64
Cartwright, Claire	T	1966-70
Cartwright, Dorsey	T	1955-56
Cartwright, Gayle	A	1964-67
Cary, Alatia	C	1981-85
Cary, Anne	T	1982-85
Cary, Katherine	C	1934-35
Caserta, Helen Jane	T	1941
Casey, Jane	A	1958-60
Casey, Joyce	C	1936
Cashion, Brownie Sue	C	1956-59
Cashion, Martha	T	1951-56
Cashion, Mary Jane	C	1957
Cason, Martha Lee	T	1938
Cason, Mary Helen	C	1942
Casselman, Betsy	C	1960-67
Casselman, Nonie	A	1964-72
Casselman, Prudie	T	1963-70
Caster, Jane	C	1944
Castle, Mary Katherine	T	1937-40
Castleberry, Ann	C	1956-57
Castleberry, Becky	A	1957
Castleberry, Diana Lee	C	1957
Castleberry, Jane	C	1937-40
Castleberry, Mimi	A	1953-56
Castleman, Elizabeth	A	1943
Castleman, Pryor	A	1973-76
Cates, Helen		1929
Cathriner, Cheri	T	1970-75
Cato, Ann	T	1987
Cato, Leigh	T	1987
Cato, Maggie	C	1996
Catterton, Julie	A	1951-53
Caughron, Patricia	A	1943
Cauthorn, Candy	T	1957-60
Cavazos, Cathleen	C	1976-81
Cave, Mary	A	1943-47
Caviness, Nancy Jane	T	1941
Caylor, Diane	A	1954-55
Cazort, Carolyn	A	1961-62
Cazort, Celia	C	1958-59,
		1961-62
Cella, Joan	A	1957
Cepeda, Emilia Mimi	C	1948-53
Cezeaux, Beulah	C	1934
Chabot, Mary		1926
Chaffe, Martha	T	1942
Chalk, Allison	A	1984-86
Chalk, Ann	C	1969
Chamberlain, Meg	T	1992-96
Chamberlin, Carrie	T	1984-86
Chamberlin, Susan	A	1989-95
Chambers, Cathy	T	1959-62
Chambers, Celeste	T	1947-51
Chambers, Claire	A	1993-96
Chambers, Dina	T	1985-88
Chambers, Dorothy D.	T	1941
Chambers, Erminie	C	1942-43
Chambers, Judith Lee	T	1948-50
Chambers, Kay	C	1974-80
Chambers, Molly	A	1979-86
Chambers, Myrna Loy	T	1949-50
Chambers, Neva		1950-52
Chambers, Ruth Patricia	C	1941-44
Chambers, Susie	C	1975-81
Champion, Carole	A	1951-54
Champion, Dana	T	1947
Champlin, Rosemary	T	1941
Chan, Edythe	C	1937-38,
		1940,43
Chan, Florence	C	1936-38
Chance, Patsy	C	1930
Chancellor, Phyllis	C	1942
Chandler, Alice Ann	T	1944
Chandler, Caroline	A	1994-96
Chandler, Joan	A	1946-50
Chandler, Martha Ann	C	1949-55

Name	Camp	Years
Chandler, Mimi	T	1992-96
Chapa, Adriana	A	1986-90
Chapa, Yolanda	A	1952
Chapell, Carol	T	1951
Chapman, Cindy	C	1945-50
Chapman, Cynthia	A	1958-59
Chapman, Finita		1929
Chapman, Helen	C	1957-59
Chapman, Karen	A	1960-63
Chapple, Toya	C	1943-47
Charbonnet, Jan	T	1945-48
Charles, Linda	A	1974-78
Charles, Lisa	A	1974-76
Chase, Susan	A	1978-80
Chastain, Grayson	T	1982-85
Chastain, Mary Alyce	C	1947
Chauveaux, Connor	T	1989-96
Chauveaux, Kelsey	T	1991-96
Chavez, Jennifer	A	1988-92,94
Cheairs, Susan	C	1960-62
Cheaney, Alberta	T	1934
Cheney, Cornelia	C	1942
Cheney, Courtney	C	1957-58
Cheney, Vallye Lou	T	1934
Cherbonnier, Christine	T	1991-96
Chernosky, Christine	T	1943
Chernosky, Ellen	A	1975-79
Cherry, Jane	A	1992-94
Cherry, Jo Ann	C	1938
Cherry, Jo	C	1940-42
Cherry, Mary Carolyn	T	1939
Chesnutt, Helen Marie	C	1937
Chesnutt, Mary Julia	T	1930
Chessher, Sue	T	1954-55
Chew, Dorothy		1929
Chewning, Bess	C	1930
Chiasson, Wanda	C	1936
Chick, Liz	T	1962-69
Chilcote, Edith Lynn	A	1954-58
Childers, Cherie	C	1942
Childers, Lenita	A	1950-51
Childers, Marganna	C	1950-51
Childers, Meredith	T	1982-88
Childers, Terri	C	1968-69
Childre, Frances Anne	C	1948
Childress, Carol	T	1955-56
Childress, Genelle	C	1951-52
Childress, La Vonne	C	1936
Childs, Charlsie	T	1956-60
Childs, Claire	A	1953
Childs, Jan	C	1964-66
Childs, Linda	T	1952-53
Childs, Phyllis	C	1957-60
Childs, Phyllis	C	1931-35
Childs, Roxy Anne	C	1953-58
Chiles, Martha Alice	T	1939-40
Chilton, Mable Lee	T	1940
Chipman, Cindy	C	1969-73
Chittim, Claudia	T	1986-88
Choate, Catherine	C	1968-72
Choate, Cynthia	A	1967-69
Choate, Elizabeth	T	1973
Chowning, Martha	A	1974-78
Christainsen, Avalon	T	1940
Christian, Ann	T	1957-60
Christian, Kathleen	A	1982-88
Christian, Mary	C	1959-60, 1962-65
Christiansen, Pat	C	1940
Christopher, Ginger	T	1986
Chunn, Ann	C	1949-50, 1952-54
Chunn, Patricia	C	1952-53
Church, Barbara		1929
Churchill, Corrie	T	1987-89
Cissel, Georgeann	T	1969-75
Cissel, Jena	T	1975-79
Ciuba, Ellen	C	1996
Clanton, Elaine	T	1955-60
Clanton, Sara	T	1957-62,65
Clark, Amy	C	1984-87
Clark, Ashley	A	1984-87
Clark, Barbara	C	1936
Clark, Becky	T	1964-68
Clark, Betty Jean	C	1942
Clark, Cadien	A	1987-91
Clark, Carol	T	1946-47
Clark, Caroline	A	1979-85
Clark, Carrie	T	1987-88
Clark, Catherine Leigh	T	1977-82
Clark, Catherine	T	1977-80
Clark, Catherine Ann	A	1965
Clark, Catherine	T	1985-92
Clark, Cathy	A	1965-67,70
Clark, Cathy	T	1966-70
Clark, Cathy	A	1984-88
Clark, Christin	T	1937-39
Clark, Connie	C	1980-85,87
Clark, Courtney	T	1931-32
Clark, Edith	T	1975-80
Clark, Elizabeth	T	1957-61
Clark, Gail	C	1931
Clark, Gleith	C	1931
Clark, Iva Louise		1929
Clark, Jane	T	1933-34
Clark, Jean	T	1972-75
Clark, Jenny	A	1965,67-70
Clark, Kathy	T	1962-65
Clark, Kay	C	1949-58
Clark, Lee	C	1989-95
Clark, Martha	C	1934
Clark, Mary	C	1934
Clark, Mary Lena	C	1941
Clark, Meredith	C	1996
Clark, Myrtle Jeanne	T	1933
Clark, Nancy	T	1961-66
Clark, Sara Ann	A	1958-66
Clark, Sarah	C	1967-71
Clark, Sarah		1929
Clark, Susan	A	1989-92
Clark, Vicki	C	1954-56
Clark, Virginia	T	1940-41
Clarke, Elaine		1928
Clarke, La Royce	A	1943-44
Clarke, Mary Catherine	C	1942
Clarkson, Carolyn	C	1950
Clary, Joyce	A	1951
Clawater, Grace	A	1996
Clawater, Jean Rose	A	1996
Clawater, Lynn	A	1961-62
Claxton, Nancy	C	1950
Claxton, Nancy Lee	C	1950
Clay, Marty	A	1963
Clay, Pamela	C	1961-64
Clay, Peggy	T	1968
Clayton, Bertha	A	1943
Clayton, Carmen	C	1941
Clayton, Catherine	C	1981-84
Clayton, Helen	C	1930
Clayton, Jane	C	1930
Clayton, Jane	A	1943
Clayton, Martha	C	1936
Cleary, Marcia	A	1953-58
Cleary, Sandra	C	1955-63
Clemens, Eleanor	T	1931
Clemens, Louise	T	1935
Clement, Frances	T	1931
Clement, Gloria	T	1940
Clement, Suzanne	T	1948
Clements, Adelaide	C	1942,44
Clements, Cathy	T	1974-81
Clements, Mary Leslie	A	1973
Clements, Nancy	A	1952-59
Clements, Pat	C	1942-43
Clements, Peg	A	1979-82, 1984-85
Clemmons, Nancy	C	1955-56
Clemmons, Sara	T	1958
Clemons, Elizabeth	A	1991-96
Clemons, Mary C.	A	1992-96
Clemons, Susannah	T	1987-94
Clendening, Barbara	T	1941
Cleveland, Ann	C	1941
Cleveland, Susan	C	1968
Clevenger, Susan	C	1967-69
Clifford, Betsy	A	1943-45
Clifford, Martha	T	1946-47, 1949-50
Clift, Jeanette	C	1939-41
Clift, Patsy	T	1950-51
Clift, Sondra	C	1950-51
Clifton, Mary Lacy	T	1962-64
Cline, Cathie	A	1957-60
Cline, Charlene	C	1954-58
Cline, Courtney	T	1987-89
Clinton, Lyn	C	1982-84
Cloniger, Diana	T	1969-75
Clough, Sara	C	1940-41
Clower, Allene	T	1937-38
Clower, Cara Jeanne	T	1936-37
Clowers, Betty Jean	C	1940-41
Cloyd, Carey	A	1987-92
Cloyd, Trudi	A	1994-96
Clubb, Mary Elizabeth	T	1932
Clyde, Anna	T	1987-93
Clyde, Eloise	C	1966-71
Clyde, Kitty	A	1959-64
Clymer, Garnett	C	1986-89
Coates, Beth	A	1968-72

Coates, Doris Jean	T	1931
Coates, Jane	T	1933
Coats, Karen	A	1952-53
Cobb, Amanda	C	1958-59
Cobb, Ann	T	1936-38,41
Cobb, Ashley	A	1989-92
Cobb, Betty Lou	T	1937-40
Cobb, Bettye	C	1951-54
Cobb, Bibb	T	1966-68
Cobb, Caroline	A	1968
Cobb, Carolyn	T	1940,46-47
Cobb, Carolynn	A	1973-78
Cobb, Cornelia	A	1961-67
Cobb, Darla	C	1963-69
Cobb, Haley	A	1983-89
Cobb, Janie	C	1966-68
Cobb, Jennifer	T	1986-89
Cobb, Katie	C	1995
Cobb, Kristi	T	1978-81
Cobb, Lallie	T	1976-80
Cobb, Liz	C	1974-77
Cobb, M.M.	A	1978-82
Cobb, Martha	C	1975-80
Cobb, Patricia	C	1941
Cobb, Priscilla	T	1958-66
Cobb, Roberta	C	1963
Cobb, Suzanne	T	1957-62
Cobb, Wendy	T	1978-81
Cochran, Carol	A	1977-80, 1982-83
Cochran, Carolyn	T	1942
Cochran, Helen	T	1934
Cochran, Kimberly	C	1981-87
Cochran, Sara	T	1980-81
Cock, Mary Helen	C	1942
Cocke, Carla Jo	C	1942,44
Cockrill, Emma Jane	T	1945-47
Coe, Brenda	C	1960-65
Coe, Carol	A	1955-56
Coffee, Gayle	A	1975-76
Coffee, Rex Ann	T	1940
Coffeen, Molly	T	1944
Coffelt, Kay	A	1943-49
Coffey, Anna Marie	C	1940-41
Coffey, Gayle	A	1971-76
Coffey, Nancy Jo	A	1949-54
Coffey, Trish	A	1975-78
Coffield, Mary Martha	C	1937-38
Coffin, Kimberly		1974
Coffman, Kitty Lu	C	1948
Coffman, Shirley	A	1948
Cogdell, Carol	T	1965-72
Cogdell, Connie	A	1963,66-68
Cohen, Betty Mae	C	1936
Cohenour, Joyce	A	1964
Cohle, Amy	A	1984-85
Coin, Cindy	T	1960-61
Coiner, Emily	T	1985-89
Coiner, Josie	A	1986-93
Cointment, Carolyn	C	1972-76
Cointment, Chinkie	C	1956-64
Cointment, Janie	A	1948-57
Cointment, Kitty	T	1969-76

Colchensky, Rae Ann	C	1937-38
Colchensky, Sara	C	1936-37
Cole, Carroll	A	1972-73
Cole, Eddye Gene	C	1936-37
Cole, Frances	T	1930
Cole, Georgine	C	1930
Cole, Minnie	T	1930
Cole, Vera	C	1971
Coleman, Caroline	C	1991-94
Coleman, Emma Jean	T	1933
Coleman, Julia Ann	T	1942
Coleman, Julie	A	1977-80,82
Coleman, June	T	1945-46
Coleman, Lilyan Ruth	C	1938-42
Coleman, Macari	A	1987-93
Coleman, Mary LaRue	C	1933
Coleman, Mary Maud	T	1961-64
Coleman, Priscilla	C	1965-67
Coleman, Sue Ellen	T	1953-54
Colgan, Lindsey	C	1990-96
Colgin, Ann	C	1969-74
Colgin, Elizabeth		1928-29
Collens, Mary Ann	T	1942
Collett, Ashley	C	1973-79
Collette, Ann	A	1943
Colley, Bevan	T	1992
Colley, Ellen	A	1943-46
Colley, Lane	A	1987-91
Collie, Carol	A	1965-68
Collie, Gwynne	T	1958-61
Collier, Eleanor Cappie	T	1933-39
Collier, Marguerite	A	1949
Collier, Suzanne	C	1950
Collins, Ann	C	1948-50
Collins, Ann	T	1969-74
Collins, Beverly	A	1944
Collins, Caroline	T	1994-96
Collins, Carolyn	A	1956-60
Collins, Charlotte	T	1937
Collins, Charlotte E.H.	T	1989
Collins, Courtney	C	1992-96
Collins, Delores	C	1939
Collins, Elizabeth	T	1937
Collins, Jane Catherine	T	1991-96
Collins, Jennifer	T	1989-95
Collins, Kelly	T	1974-77
Collins, Kendall	A	1981-86
Collins, Louella	A	1944-46
Collins, Madeline	C	1970-77
Collins, Nanci	A	1963-70
Collins, Nancy	C	1961-66
Collins, Pat	A	1944-46
Collins, Rana	T	1975-79
Collins, Ruth	C	1934-35
Collins, Shannon	T	1987-90
Collins, Shirley	T	1940
Collins, Susan	A	1964-72
Collins, Suzanne	T	1955
Collins, Yuppy	C	1936
Collord, Sharon	A	1950-56
Colly, Bobby	C	1935,38
Colly, Sue	T	1939
Colomb, Beth	C	1972-73

Colquitt, Kit	A	1948
Columbus, Mackenzie	A	1994-95
Colvert, Catherine	A	1944
Colvert, Mary	T	1936
Colvert, Sarah Ellen	T	1935
Colvin, Alice	A	1988-94
Colvin, Brooke	T	1986
Combs, Helen	T	1944
Combs, Julia	T	1996
Compere, Susan	A	1963-66
Compere, Tid	C	1934-37
Compton, Bertita	C	1940-42
Compton, Clarine	C	1933
Compton, Joan	T	1956-58
Compton, Judy	A	1944-44
Compton, Mary Deen	C	1946-47
Compton, Mary	T	1955-59
Compton, Patricia	A	1953-58
Condra, Whitney	C	1986-89
Congdon, Susan	A	1961-62
Conger, Betty	A	1957-61
Conine, Karrah	T	1989
Conkling, Barbara	T	1965-69
Conkling, Kathy	A	1961-64
Conkling, Susan	T	1963-66
Conley, Eloise	A	1947
Conley, Mayriann	T	1940-41
Conley, Thayer	C	1951
Conn, Cornelia	C	1933-34
Conn, Elizabeth	T	1979-84
Connally, Frances	C	1933-35
Connally, Gretta	T	1931-35
Connally, Martha Ann	T	1936
Connell, Brett	C	1958
Connell, Gretchen	C	1955-59
Connellee, Jane		1928-29
Connelly, Beth	C	1945-47,49
Connelly, Eileen	T	1974-81
Connelly, Jennifer	A	1970-74
Connelly, Lisa	T	1990-93
Connelly, Tessa	T	1988-90
Conner, Barbara Jean	T	1938
Conner, Caroline	C	1993-96
Conner, Delrena	T	1952-55
Conner, Erin	A	1975-79
Conner, Mary	C	1986-87
Conner, Mary Peirce	A	1953-57
Conner, Sarah Claire	T	1994-96
Conner, Stacy	C	1989
Connor, Virgie	T	1931
Conover, Connie	T	1941
Conrad, Lori	T	1985-88
Conway, Allison	A	1989-93
Conway, Christie	C	1996
Cook, Aimee	T	1982-89
Cook, Alice Anne	C	1981-84
Cook, Audrey	A	1979-86
Cook, Betty Ann	C	1944
Cook, Eleanor	T	1952-57
Cook, Julia	A	1992-95
Cook, Marie	C	1974-79
Cook, Maybian	T	1944
Cook, Miriam	A	1948

Name		Years
Cook, Nancy	C	1957-58
Cook, Nellie Anne	C	1983-87
Cook, Patricia	A	1944-47
Cook, Patricia Anne	T	1977-84
Cook, Rita	A	1950-51
Cook, Sharon Lynn	T	1950-53
Cook, Sue Cookie	A	1960-61
Cook, Vera	T	1937
Cooke, Margene	C	1948-51
Cooke, Maybian	T	1944-45
Cooksey, Carol	A	1984
Cooksey, Catherine	A	1995-96
Cooksey, Catherine	C	1983
Cooksey, Karen	T	1980-81
Cookston, Ann	C	1967-71
Cookston, Jane	C	1967
Coon, Betty Earl	T	1939
Coon, Margaret	C	1956-60
Coonley, Jean	A	1950
Cooper, Amelietta	T	1941-42
Cooper, Carol	A	1951-54
Cooper, Charlotte	T	1943
Cooper, Erin	T	1986-89
Cooper, Florine		1934
Cooper, Karleen	C	1936
Cooper, Laura	A	1971-74
Cooper, Mary	A	1973-79
Cope, Joan	T	1952
Copeland, Elise	T	1983-88
Copeland, Elizabeth	A	1978-83
Corbett, Isabelle	C	1995-96
Corbett, Karen	C	1975-76
Corbett, Peggy	A	1948
Corbett, Whitney	T	1993,95-96
Corcorran, Bettie Jo	C	1944-45
Corcorran, Johnnie Sue	A	1944-45
Cordell, Carolyn	T	1956
Cordell, Emily	T	1937
Corder, Billie	C	1940
Corder, Mary		1940
Corder, Mickie	C	1940
Corder, Wilma Josephine		1940
Cordts, Anna	C	1982-86
Cordts, Colleen	C	1980-86
Cordts, Connie	C	1956,58-61
Corgey, Elizabeth	C	1934
Corinhas, Clementina	T	1943
Corinhas, Joyce	T	1943
Cornelius, Cecily	C	1985
Cornell, Julie	C	1967-71
Corrigan, Pat	T	1939
Corzelius, Diana	T	1938-39, 1941,44
Corzelius, Frances	T	1944-48
Corzelius, Martha	T	1939,41,44
Cosby, Laura	C	1974-78
Coskey, Julia	T	1996
Cotham, Cathy	C	1974
Cotham, Christy	C	1978-84
Cotham, Elizabeth	C	1980-86
Cotham, Margaret		1926,28
Cotham, Nancy	C	1982-88
Cotham, Virginia		1926,28
Cothran, Adair	A	1975-79
Cothran, Leah	C	1977-81
Cottel, Louise	C	1991
Cotten, Martha	A	1948
Cottingham, Beth	C	1983-88
Cottingham, Carol	C	1948-51
Cottingham, Margot	C	1975-78
Cottingham, Mary Lee	T	1944,46-49
Cotton, Cathy	A	1969-70
Cotton, Michaela	A	1995-96
Cotton, Natalie	A	1995-96
Cottrell, Savery	C	1993-96
Couch, Betsy	C	1972-74
Couch, Carol	T	1955-56
Couch, Catherine Anne	A	1976-79
Couch, Christi	T	1965-69
Couch, Elizabeth Ann	C	1955-60
Couch, Jessie	A	1968-73
Couch, Mary	T	1964-68
Couch, Mary Bea	T	1951-55
Couch, Mimi	A	1953-58
Couch, Nancy	C	1957-61
Couch, Polly	T	1938-39, 1942-43
Courtney, Caren	C	1963-66
Courtney, Catherine	C	1975-78
Courtney, Cynthia	T	1963-69
Cousins, Dorothy	C	1933-34
Covert, Anne	T	1983-86
Covert, Carol	C	1970-77
Covert, Gary Beth	T	1965-72
Covert, Jennie	T	1981-87
Covington, Ann	C	1944-45
Covington, Carol	T	1952-56
Covington, Jane	C	1944-46
Covper, Carol	A	1952
Cowan, Camilla	A	1962-66
Cowan, Jessica	C	1993
Cowan, Ruth		1928
Cowan, Sandra	T	1958-65
Cowan, Susan	C	1970-74
Coward, Anna	A	1991-95
Cowden, Ada Mat	T	1937-38
Cowden, Alma Faye	C	1939-40, 1943-44
Cowden, Barbara	C	1937,39
Cowden, Caran	C	1973-80
Cowden, Carolyn	T	1951-56
Cowden, Christi	T	1986-90
Cowden, Christy	A	1976-79
Cowden, Cynthia	A	1962-68
Cowden, Elizabeth Ann	C	1939-40, 1943-44
Cowden, Julianan	C	1936-37
Cowden, Laura	T	1991-92
Cowden, Linda	C	1956-61
Cowden, Mary Sue	C	1937
Cowden, Sarah	C	1989-95
Cowden, Sharon	T	1977-83
Cowden, Susan	A	1972-78
Cowen, April	A	1983-88
Cowen, Joanne	C	1947-54
Cowen, Katherine	A	1946-51
Cowen, Kathleen Marie	A	1946
Cowen, Mary Alice	A	1948-55
Cowen, Reve	T	1954-56
Cowen, Suzie	C	1954-62
Cowley, Colleen	A	1980
Cox, Ara B	T	1946-47
Cox, Callan	C	1959-63
Cox, Carolyn	C	1945-46
Cox, Daisy	C	1988-91,93
Cox, Elizabeth	C	1935-38
Cox, Jacqueline	T	1939-40
Cox, Jane	C	1930
Cox, Jo Ann	T	1940
Cox, Joyce	C	1940-43
Cox, Lorinda	C	1931
Cox, Margaret	C	1937
Cox, Margarey Ann	C	1932
Cox, Maria	A	1982-85
Cox, Martha Ann	C	1937
Cox, Mary Lucylle	C	1934-35
Cox, Mary Louise		1929
Cox, Melissa	A	1976-82
Cox, Olive Ruth		1928
Cox, Ora Louise	C	1934
Cox, Patsy	C	1942-43,45
Cozad, Sarah	A	1994
Cozean, Tiffanie	T	1985
Crabb, Mary Mack	T	1947-49
Crabtree, Mary Tom	T	1955
Craddock, De Lois	T	1939
Craddock, Emmie J.C.	T	1934
Craddock, Tanya	A	1943-45
Craig, Ann	T	1935-36
Craig, Carter	C	1988-91
Craig, Connie	T	1945-47
Crain, Ann Lacy	A	1956,58-59
Crain, Ann	T	1958-60
Crain, Cara	A	1987
Crain, Eileen		1928-29
Crain, Emily	T	1933-35
Crain, Frances	C	1929-30
Crain, Jane Lynch	A	1990-96
Crain, Julie	C	1975-81
Crain, Katharine	C	1971-73
Crain, Lois	T	1945-51
Crain, Margaret Virginia		1928-29
Crain, Penny	T	1966-67
Cram, Carol	C	1973-76
Cram, Marianne	T	1975-82
Cramer, Alice Lee	T	1942-46
Cramer, Marjorie	C	1941,43-45
Crank, Medley	C	1995-96
Cranston, Carolyn	C	1956
Craven, Elizabeth	C	1991-92
Craven, Emily Ann	T	1953-55,57
Cravens, Mary Ellen	T	1992-96
Crawford, Alicia	T	1971-78
Crawford, Cori	T	1990-96
Crawford, Jill	T	1992
Crawford, Joan	A	1945
Crawford, Kate	A	1990-96
Crawford, Katie	A	1964-68
Crawford, Louise	A	1978-81

Name		Year
Crawford, Mary Jean	A	1943
Crawford, Peyton	A	1952-57
Crawford, Talicia	T	1938-39
Crawley, Georgia Lee	C	1952-55
Creager, Beth		1926,28
Creager, Frances		1926,28
Creamer, Betty	C	1937
Creighton, Luan	A	1944
Crenshaw, Heather	A	1981-86
Cress, Carolyn	A	1977
Creveling, Jodie	T	1982-86
Crews, Angelynn	T	1967-68
Crews, Carolyn	C	1936-37
Crichton, Kate	C	1961
Crim, Camie Dell	C	1934-36,38
Crist, Linda	C	1950
Crites, Katie	C	1990-92
Crittenden, Carol	T	1973-77
Critz, Helen	C	1936-37
Critz, Pottee	T	1953
Crockett, Kathy	C	1960-64
Crockett, Totsy	A	1944-47, 1950-53
Cromwell, Gertrude	C	1948-52
Cromwell, Mildred	C	1951-54
Cromwell, Patricia	A	1957-61
Crook, Catherine	C	1937
Crooker, Carolyn	A	1952-59
Croom, Barbara	C	1945-52
Croom, Carolyn	A	1971-77
Croom, Mary Ann	C	1945-46
Crosbie, Elaine	C	1940
Crosby, Chris	T	1960-61
Cross, Shirley	A	1944
Crossland, Mary Beth	T	1962-63
Crosslin, Hiawatha		1928
Crosswhite, Peggy	T	1941
Crosthwait, Nancylu	T	1942-44
Crouch, Carolyn	T	1945-46
Crow, Carole	T	1951-57
Crow, Kara	C	1992
Crow, Katy	A	1996
Crow, Linda	C	1958
Crow, Lucy	C	1963-69
Crow, Maisie	A	1991-92
Crow, Margaret	C	1994-95
Crow, Nancy	T	1956
Crowder, Emily	A	1983-89
Crowe, Marjorie	T	1934-36
Crowell, Cynthia		1957
Crowley, Leslie	C	1986-90
Croy, Amanda	T	1973-76
Crozier, Anne	T	1945-48
Crozier, Terry	C	1945-49
Crumpler, Karin	A	1952-58
Cruse, Mary	A	1987
Crusemann, Sally	A	1968-71
Crutcher, Allison	T	1963-65
Crutchfield, Cathy	C	1958-62
Crutchfield, Kendall	T	1987-90,93
Crysup, Katie	T	1984-85
Culbertson, Diane	C	1950
Culbertson, Shirley	C	1937,39-40

Name		Year
Cullinan, Barbara	C	1935
Cullum, Carol	T	1943
Cullum, Chloe	T	1941,43, 1945-48
Cullum, Selbia	C	1944-48
Culp, Carrie	T	1981
Culp, Joan	C	1959-63
Culp, Josephine	C	1931
Culp, Tricia Ann	C	1948-49
Culpepper, Dot	T	1950
Culpepper, Mary Mallory Mimi	C	1946-48
Culton, Dorothy Lou	C	1933
Culver, Cathy	T	1980-84
Culver, Cynthia	C	1981-85
Cummings, Katherine	A	1943-45
Cummings, Lynn	C	1946-47
Cummings, Marilyn	T	1948-50
Cummings, Sally	A	1946-50
Cummins, Nelda Ann	A	1949
Cummins, Susan	C	1971-76
Cunningham, Agnes	T	1940
Cunningham, Ann	C	1944-47
Cunningham, Bob Burke	C	1930,33
Cunningham, Carrie	T	1996
Cunningham, Joyce	C	1930,33
Cunningham, Katie	T	1991
Cunningham, Lee	A	1961-68
Cunningham, Leslie	A	1967-68
Cunningham, Marie	C	1968-70
Cunningham, Mary	C	1965-67
Cunningham, Nancy Lynn	T	1948-49
Cunningham, Paige	A	1993
Cunningham, Shirley	T	1936-37
Cunningham, Sue		1926
Cupp, Lauren	C	1992-94
Curelton, Constance	T	1942-43
Curran, Kelly	T	1994
Currey, Dimi	A	1979-82
Currie, Ann	A	1944-47
Currin, Ruth	A	1944
Curry, Virginia	C	1947
Curtis, Anne	C	1944-47
Curtis, Chancy	T	1975-79
Curtis, Eloise	T	1938-39
Curtis, Jane Ann	C	1949
Curtis, Libby	A	1949-53
Curtis, Margaret	C	1942-43
Curtis, Margaret	C	1974-79
Curtis, Sara	C	1978-83
Curtis, Shannan	C	1977-81
Custard, Laura	A	1980-85
Custard, Marla	A	1979-81
Custer, Stacey	A	1994
Cutbirth, Caroline	C	1993-96
Cutbirth, Catherine	A	1990-95
Cutbirth, Sandra	C	1943-46
Cutler, Diana	A	1951,53
Cutler, India King	T	1974
Cutler, Sue	A	1975-76
Cutrer, Mallory	T	1945-52
Cutting, Jane	T	1935

D

Name		Year
Dacy, Catherine	A	1996
Daily, Barbara	A	1953-56
Daily, Lorraine	C	1935-36
Daily, Missie	C	1959-64
Daimwood, Mary	T	1935-37
Dale, Elizabeth	T	1993-96
Dale, Peggy	T	1935
Dalehite, Ellen	C	1972-75
Dallas, Ann	C	1976-82
Dallas, Debbie	A	1968-73
Dallas, Jennifer	A	1974-77
Dallas, Teddy	A	1970-75
Dalrymple, Libby	A	1945
Dalton, Cheryl	T	1988-91, 1993-95
Dalton, Elizabeth	C	1993-95
Dangelmayr, Lauren	T	1993-96
Daniel, Anne	C	1985-87
Daniel, Bailey	C	1995-96
Daniel, Dana	A	1961-68
Daniel, Kay	C	1959-61
Daniel, Marjorie	A	1946
Daniel, Mary Alvis	A	1948
Daniel, Myrtis Beall	C	1947-50
Daniel, Terry	C	1953-56
Daniels, Amy	T	1984-87
Danson, Suzette	C	1942
Darbrandt, Helen Ann	T	1948
Darby, Beth	C	1980-83,85
Darden, Cathy	T	1963-68
Darden, Lucretia	T	1971-76
Darlington, Dorothy		1929
Darnall, Barbara	C	1946
Darragh, Lily	C	1994-96
Darrenburg, Janet E.	A	1943
Dascomb, Kristin	A	1982-85
Dashiell, Em	T	1939
Daughtry, Tiffany	A	1982-87
Dauphin, Alexandra	T	1996
Davenport, Amy	A	1971-78
Davenport, Casey	C	1977-80
Davenport, Gerry	T	1937-38
Davenport, Heather	C	1975-77
Davenport, Leila	C	1984-90
Davey, Marie	T	1934-37
Davidge, Nell	T	1948-52
Davidson, June Ann	C	1953-57
Davidson, Lee	A	1963-64
Davidson, Marsha	T	1961
Davidson, Muggins	A	1943
Davidson, Susan	C	1957-60
Davidson, Van	C	1960-63
Davis, Alann	C	1972-74
Davis, Amanda	T	1982-87
Davis, Angilee	T	1937-40
Davis, Ann Camille	A	1946-47
Davis, Ann	T	1964
Davis, Ann	A	1968-71
Davis, Anne	T	1990-96
Davis, Barbara	A	1953
Davis, Betsy	A	1959-65
Davis, Betty	C	1942-50
Davis, Candy	A	1960-62

Name		Years
Davis, Carol	A	1964-70
Davis, Carol	T	1937
Davis, Cynthia	A	1975-80
Davis, Debbie	T	1981-85
Davis, Diane	A	1950-51
Davis, Dianne	C	1955
Davis, Dora Jean	C	1931
Davis, Eleanor	C	1938
Davis, Elizabeth	C	1930-31
Davis, Elizabeth	C	1961-67
Davis, Elizabeth	T	1967-70
Davis, Fanny	T	1937
Davis, Frances	T	1937
Davis, Georgi	C	1948
Davis, Hallie	C	1973-78
Davis, Heather	T	1992-95
Davis, Jane	T	1993-96
Davis, Jenny Alice	C	1957-65
Davis, Joan	C	1943
Davis, Katherine	C	1995-96
Davis, Kay	C	1966
Davis, Kay	C	1942
Davis, Kristin	A	1977-82
Davis, Lenita Tita	C	1952-57
Davis, Lisa	C	1985-89
Davis, Lucy	A	1952-55
Davis, Margaret	A	1992-96
Davis, Martha Elaine	T	1947-50
Davis, Martha	T	1947-53
Davis, Mary Anne	C	1946
Davis, Mary Margaret	C	1929-30
Davis, Mary Louise	C	1934
Davis, Mary Ann	A	1943-44
Davis, Mary Elizabeth	T	1950
Davis, Mary	T	1973-78
Davis, Marynelle	T	1948-49
Davis, Melissa	C	1979-81
Davis, Pauline	C	1935
Davis, Priscilla	A	1948
Davis, Sara	T	1953-55
Davis, Sara Deane	C	1941
Davis, Sarah	A	1985-91
Davis, Sharon	T	1948-55
Davis, Susan	C	1966
Davis, Sylvia	A	1953
Davis, Veta	C	1965-67
Davis, Virginia	A	1944
Davis, Wesley	A	1994-95
Davison, Alene	A	1959-60
Dawkins, Lela	A	1972-77
Dawkins, Nancy	T	1979-81
Dawson, Becky	T	1954,56,58
Dawson, Carol	T	1964-67
Dawson, Deborah	T	1969-70
Dawson, Dee	A	1975-80
Dawson, Donna	C	1951-52
Dawson, Donna Booch	C	1934
Dawson, Mariella	T	1965-67
Dawson, Mary Louise	C	1964-68
Dawson, Roxanne	A	1967-71
Dawson, Sally Jo	C	1944
Day, Ann	A	1946-49
Day, Becky	C	1982-86
Day, Billie	C	1933
Day, Carolyn	T	1958-66
Day, Dorothy		1934
Day, Ernestine	C	1931
Day, Helen	C	1930-31, 1933-35
Day, Jane	T	1948-51
Day, Jenny	C	1992-96
Day, Marion	T	1945
Day, Mary Catherine	A	1989-92
Day, Sue	T	1957-60
Dayson, Suzette	C	1942,44-45
de Brueys, Johnelle	T	1941
de la Houssaye, Caroline	A	1996
De Arman, Alice Joyce	T	1935
De Arman, Dorothy	T	1934
De Bois, Dianne	T	1958
De Cordova, Anne	C	1948-49
De George, Carmalee	T	1939
De Graffenreid, Nancy	A	1943-44
De Grasse, Leonora	A	1943
De Jean, Kay	A	1961
De la Houssaye, Lyn	T	1957-59
De Larot, Katie	C	1948
De Llano, Cordelia	T	1940
De Long, Josephine	C	1944-45
De Lony, Marie	C	1971-74
De Mana, Joyce	T	1942
De Montrond, Dottie Lou	T	1939-42
De Moss, DAnne	A	1963-65
De Sanders, Diane	C	1950-52
De Shona, Paige	A	1975
De Shong, Betty	A	1943-47
De Shong, Diane	C	1972-75
De Shong, Hallie	C	1938-40
Deakins, Paula	A	1968-73
Deal, Darvaney	A	1976-77
Dean, Bette Jo	A	1950-51
Dean, Carol Joan	C	1953-55
Dean, Diana	C	1956
Dean, Dorothy	C	1936-37
Dean, Nancy Ann	A	1947
Dean, Susan	A	1953-57
Deane, Claire	T	1993-94,96
Dearborn, Susan	C	1944
Dearie, Suelen	C	1958-60
Dearie, Tori	A	1958-59
Deas, Barbara	C	1930-31
Deaton, Abbie	C	1940
Deaton, Deanna	C	1950
Decamps, Jordana	A	1994
Decker, Elizabeth	C	1938-39
Decker, Esther	C	1940-41
Deering, Evelyn	T	1935
Deering, Gladys Marie	C	1930-31
Delamater, Grace	T	1938-41
Delaney, Phyllis	C	1934
Delaune, Valerie	C	1995-96
Delhomme, Doris	C	1940
Delisi, Annie	T	1980-85
Deming, Ann	A	1943
Deming, Bebe	T	1959-62
Deming, Catherine	T	1959-65
Deming, Kate	C	1996
Denby, Mary	C	1930
Denis, Joan	T	1954
Denison, Courtney	C	1978-85
Denison, Darby	T	1974-81
Denison, Dawn	A	1974-81
Denius, Charmaine	T	1965-70
Denman, Amy	T	1977-82
Denman, Berta		1929
Denman, Beth	T	1974-78
Denman, Betsy	C	1956-57
Denman, Destine	T	1973-79
Denman, Frances	T	1934
Denman, Jo Ann	A	1943-46
Denman, Laura	A	1956-57
Denman, Majorie	C	1929-30,33
Denman, Mary Claire	C	1933-34,36
Denney, Lida Lee	A	1943
Denney, Robbie Dell	A	1943-44
Dennis, Jennifer	A	1974
Denson, Deirdre	C	1944-49
Denson, Elizabeth	C	1993-94
Denson, Laura	C	1992-94
Dent, Susan	C	1952-57
Dentler, Barbara	C	1940,43
Dentler, Marilyn	C	1943-47
Denton, Liza	T	1985-92
Denton, Nancy Jane	C	1947-48, 1950-51
Depp, Diane	A	1960
Derby, Mary Louise	T	1930
Derning, Bebe	T	1959
Derrick, Jennifer	A	1989-92
Derrick, Julie	C	1986-90
Derrick, Linda	T	1966-69
Detering, Deborah	A	1950-57
Deu Pree, Del	T	1958-59
Devanney, Anna Noel	T	1942,46-50
Devanney, Dianne	A	1969-73
Devanney, Emily	A	1976-78
Devanney, Gail	A	1948-49
Devereaux, Grace		1929
Deviney, Charla	T	1986
Dewees, Corabel	C	1928,30
Dexter, Dorothy	C	1941
Dexter, Grace	C	1934-36
Dexter, Lindsey	C	1993
Dibble, Harriet	T	1936
Dibrell, Frances Tancy	A	1954-57
Dibrell, Jane	T	1948,50-53
Dibrell, Virginia	C	1953-59
Dickey, Lynn	T	1951-53
Dickie, Mary Martha	T	1946-47
Dickins, Josephine	T	1986-87
Dickinson, Eleanor	C	1984-87
Dickinson, Nan Ellen	T	1958-59
Dickmann, Marilyn	A	1950
Dickson, Angela	T	1973-78
Dickson, Claudia Ross	C	1933-34
Dickson, Laura	T	1977-80
Dickson, Virginia	C	1932-33
Diem, Dorothea	T	1938
Diem, Edith Louise	T	1954-55

Dunlap, Anne	A	1977-81
Dunlap, Kay	C	1953-56
Dunlap, Mary Jo	T	1931
Dunlap, Susan	A	1953,55-57
Dunn, Carmen	C	1942
Dunn, Kathleen	C	1938
Dunn, Patsy	C	1939
Dunnam, Diana	A	1953
Dunnam, Sabra	T	1987-88
Dunnam, Sandra	T	1945-46
Dunnett, Clarene	T	1938-40
Dunning, Katherine	C	1948-49
Dupree, Laura Jean	C	1940
Dupree, Mary		1928
DuPuy, Jeanne	C	1935
DuPuy, Mary Lorraine	C	1935
Durham, Abbie Ruth	C	1937-38
Durham, Barbara	C	1934
Durham, Cliona	T	1973-74
Durham, Janet	A	1965-71
Durham, Kathryn	C	1970-76
Durham, Lara	C	1931,34-35
Durkin, Betty	C	1936-37
Durkin, Kathleen	C	1960-61
Durkin, Terry	A	1961-66
Durland, Diane	A	1959
Durr, Benca	A	1976-79
Durr, Beth	A	1982-85
Duson, Betty	C	1961-62
Duson, Kerr	A	1985-90
Duson, Molly	T	1965-66
Duvic, Joel	T	1942
Dwight, Alyson	A	1986
Dwyer, Emily	C	1990-93
Dybolski, Mildred	T	1937
Dye, Gloria	C	1951-52
Dyer, Cherry	A	1943-45
Dyer, Dorthell	C	1940-43
Dyer, Gerry	T	1947
Dyke, Allison	C	1979-80
Dyke, Debbie	T	1967-69
Dyke, Patricia	C	1974
Dyke, Renee	T	1972-74
Dykes, Deborah	A	1975-79
Dykes, Mary Frances	A	1962-63
DAntoni, Maura Ann	T	1946-49,52

E

Eagle, Suzanne	T	1957-59
Eagleston, Pollyanna	T	1930
Eakin, Betty Claire	C	1947
Eakin, Gretta	A	1970-71
Eakin, Kate	C	1993-95
Eakin, Kelly	T	1995-96
Eargle, Cleo	T	1932
Earl, Carolyn	T	1941-42
Earle, Nancy	T	1958-60
Early, Helen	C	1951-56
Early, Jackie	A	1976-79
Early, Ruth	T	1931
Earnest, Elizabeth		1929
Earp, Mary	C	1941
Earthman, Emily	A	1994-96

Earwood, Elsie	A	1959-61
Earwood, Melinda	A	1966-69
Easley, Jan	A	1969-70
Easley, Megan	A	1989-91
East, Adele	C	1965-68
Easterling, Anne	C	1951-53
Easterling, Ashley	C	1966-69
Easterling, Cindy	A	1963-67
Easterling, Ginger	C	1948-49
Eastham, Elana	A	1943
Eastham, Margaret	T	1953
Eastham, Sally	A	1951-60
Eastman, Terrell	T	1975-78
Eaton, Sally	C	1950-51
Ebaugh, Bettie	C	1940-41
Ebeling, Betty Jane	C	1936-37
Eberle, Phyllis	T	1936
Echols, Cynthia	T	1954
Echols, Fannie Lou	T	1937
Echols, Mary	T	1939-44
Echols, Pat	T	1935
Eckel, Mary Jan	A	1954
Eckert, Nancy	T	1968-74
Eckhardt, Joan	A	1943-45
Eckhardt, Lynn	A	1960
Eckhardt, Marcia	T	1951-55
Eckhardt, Sue	C	1945
Eckhart, Jane	T	1939-40
Eckles, Laine	C	1995-96
Eckles, Nancy	C	1996
Eckman, Virginia	C	1944
Eddleman, Anne	A	1985-86
Edel, Lois	T	1934
Edens, Terri	A	1968-69, 1971-72
Edgar, Dianne	T	1950-55
Edgar, Patricia	C	1942-43
Edge, Altha		1928
Edington, Ashley	T	1976-77
Edmundson, Joanne	A	1952-56
Edmundson, Lacy	A	1949-53
Edmundson, Mary Lou	T	1944-47
Edson, Ashley	C	1987-91
Edson, Betty Ann	C	1938-39,41
Edwards, Amy	C	1977-80
Edwards, Ashley	C	1989
Edwards, Eve	A	1962-67
Edwards, Frances	T	1945-46
Edwards, Janet Patricia	C	1946-47
Edwards, Jaynan	T	1947-54
Edwards, Katherine	C	1961-62
Edwards, Laura	T	1988-92
Edwards, Margaret	T	1934
Edwards, Mary Ann	T	1937
Edwards, Paige	T	1993-96
Edwards, Sadie		1929
Edwards, Sarah	T	1996
Edwards, Seawillow	A	1983-89
Egan, Chesley	A	1977-82
Egbert, Rosa Mae	T	1931
Eggers, Joan	T	1946-47
Eichelberger, Phyllis	C	1941
Eidman, Courtney	C	1991

Eidman, Megan	C	1993
Eisele, Dorothy	T	1934
Eisenberg, Jean	A	1943
Ekholm, Gwen	C	1956-57
Ekholm, Rilla	A	1955-57
Elbert, Janice	T	1947
Elder, Carey	T	1974-80
Elder, Diane	C	1965-68,70
Elder, Joanne	C	1965
Elder, Meriam	C	1945-46
Elder, Minette	C	1946,50
Elkins, Ann	A	1948-49
Elkins, Auab		1928
Elkins, Tiffany	C	1985-90
Ellerbe, Mollie	C	1930
Ellett, Edna	C	1936
Ellett, Mildred	A	1943
Ellington, Cally	C	1975-81
Ellington, Kay	T	1953-56
Elliot, Beryle Jeane	C	1941
Elliott, Edwina	C	1949
Elliott, Elaine	C	1965-72
Elliott, Erin	A	1989-95
Elliott, Janice	C	1956-57
Elliott, Katherine	C	1994-96
Elliott, Lisa	C	1969-71
Elliott, Louise	T	1931
Elliott, Madeline	C	1994-96
Elliott, Mary Ann	A	1946-48
Elliott, Mary Katherine Winkie	T	1936-38
Elliott, Patricia Ann	A	1948
Elliott, Patricia Anne	T	1954
Ellis, Amy	T	1988-92
Ellis, Ethel Lee	C	1938
Ellis, Jeri	A	1975-78,80
Ellis, Kate	A	1994-96
Ellis, Lilian	T	1948
Ellis, Lucy	C	1970-74
Ellis, Margaret	C	1930
Ellis, Margery	T	1932
Ellis, Olive Ann	A	1956
Ellis, Susan	C	1961-64
Ellison, Carol	A	1945-50
Ellison, Jane	T	1948-49
Ellison, Martha Ann	A	1944
Elliston, Dorothy Marie	C	1943
Ellsworth, Ruth	T	1936-37
Elmore, Irene	A	1943-45
Elmore, Meg	A	1974-80
Elmore, Trudie	A	1943-45
Emanuel, Marjorie	A	1943-44
Embleton, Sue	C	1938
Emch, Jeanne	C	1939-41
Emerson, Carol	T	1944-47
Emerson, Lee	A	1995
Emerson, Lindsay	C	1985-88
Emery, Marynell	T	1960-67
Emmons, Mary	T	1942-44
Emmons, Sophia	C	1942-44
Emrick, Sarah	T	1995-96
Engel, Anne Marie	T	1932
England, Milly Ann	T	1935

Englander, Catherine	C	1991-95	Evans, Tanis	C	1955-56	Farrell, Katherine	C	1986-90
Engler, Patsy	C	1942	Everest, Marilyn	A	1959	Farrell, Kay	T	1949
English, Betty Louise	A	1944-45	Everett, Candy	A	1960-63	Farrell, Linda	A	1949
English, Carolyn	C	1941	Everett, Caroline	A	1994-96	Farrell, Sara Helen	C	1961
English, Emily	T	1945	Everett, Elizabeth Libby	C	1929-31	Farrell, Virginia	T	1940-41
English, Kate	C	1994-96	Everett, Emilie	C	1930	Farris, Leigh	C	1986
English, Linda	T	1952	Everett, Eugenia	C	1942-44	Farris, Lindsay	T	1988-92
English, Marsha	T	1950-54	Everett, Jane	C	1935,37	Farris, Martha	A	1956-61
English, Martha Jane	A	1950	Everett, Katharine	C	1992-96	Fasken, Susan	A	1954-60
English, Nancy	C	1943	Everett, Laura	C	1976-79	Faubion, Annette	A	1974-80
English, Sally	T	1946	Everett, Meta	C	1930	Faubion, Tori	C	1981-84
English, Sarah	C	1943	Everett, Sarah	A	1989-96	Faulconer, Sara	T	1976-80
Enle, Eleanor	T	1941	Eversberg, Constance	C	1937	Favrot, Margaret	T	1980
Enochs, Martha	C	1942-44	Eversole, Lona	C	1981-85	Fawcett, Sara Lee	C	1957-58
Enrch, Jeanne	C	1940-41	Eversole, Nancy	A	1982-89	Fawks, Bobbie	T	1941
Epps, Amy	A	1975	Ewing, Betsy	C	1944	Fears, Ann	T	1944-46
Erickson, Dorothea	C	1934	Ewing, Esther	T	1940-41,44	Featherston, Fae Marie	A	1947
Erickson, Suzanne	T	1936	Ezelle, Nell		1926	Fedoroff, Gladys	T	1945
Erigan, Armeen	C	1940-41				Fee, Jane Day	T	1951-53
Erisman, Emily	T	1953-58	**F**			Fee, Kathy	C	1977-81
Ermis, Amy	A	1986-90	Fabacher, Carole	T	1941	Fee, Linda	C	1942-43
Ermis, Vanessa	A	1989-93	Fabacher, Elaine	T	1941	Feiber, Ann	T	1949
Eschenberg, Doris	C	1937	Faber, Betty Jane	T	1933	Feild, Ann	T	1938
Eshleman, Amy	C	1968-69	Faber, Julia		1933	Feitel, Betty	A	1948
Eshleman, Lica	A	1964-66	Fadell, Mary Charles	C	1947	Feland, Evelyn	C	1939
Espy, Mary John	A	1956-61	Fagadau, Junie	T	1938-39	Feland, Lois	C	1938-39
Espy, Tommy	C	1953-56	Fagan, Joan	C	1940-41, 1943-46	Feldar, Frances		1928
Estes, Adrienne	A	1973-79				Feldhaus, Rennie	C	1982-87
Estes, Barbara	A	1948	Fagg, Juanita		1928	Feldman, Mia	T	1991
Estes, Blaine	T	1989-91	Fain, Dianne	T	1948-51	Fell, Frances	T	1939
Estes, Brette	A	1986	Fain, Elizabeth	C	1929-30	Felsenthal, Kathryn	T	1984-91
Estes, Carol Lynn	T	1950-54	Fain, Holley	T	1993-96	Felt, Melinda	A	1951
Estes, Jane	A	1957-61	Fain, Martha	T	1956-57	Felton, Kamme	C	1983-90
Estes, Kris	T	1974-75	Fain, Snow	T	1994-95	Felton, Kelle	A	1977-84
Estes, Mary Jane	T	1937	Fair, Martha	C	1938,40-41, 1943-47	Felton, Suzanne	T	1947-52
Estes, Meg	T	1974-78				Fender, Diane	C	1948
Estill, Emily	T	1985-90	Fairchild, Mamie	C	1930	Fendley, Cynthia	A	1974-79
Estill, Jessica	T	1990	Faircloth, Evalene	C	1938-39	Fendley, Laura Lee	C	1942-44
Estill, Julie	T	1985-90	Fairman, Margaret Ann	C	1929-30	Fendley, Rose Mary	T	1936-37
Estill, Louise	C	1945-48	Falb, Mimi	A	1994-96	Fenley, Carol Elizabeth		1929
Etchison, Barbara	C	1944-47	Falchi, Juliet	T	1995-96	Fenley, Carol	C	1973-74
Etchison, Margaret	C	1934	Falchi, Kate	C	1993-96	Fenley, Leslie	A	1973
Etheridge, Semmes	A	1994-95	Falls, Dorothy Jean	T	1941	Fenley, Margaret	C	1942-45
Ethridge, Charlotte	A	1965-67	Faltin, Helen		1928	Fenn, Nina	C	1941
Etnyre, Yvonne	T	1936	Falvey, Frances	C	1930	Fennekohl, Diane	C	1968-72
Eubanks, Alice	T	1956	Falvey, Linda	C	1950-51	Fennekohl, Rosslyn	C	1946-47
Eubanks, Helen	T	1959	Falvey, Linda	C	1944-45	Fenstermaker, Dotsie	T	1947
Eudy, Cameron	C	1992-96	Falvey, Olive	C	1938-44	Fentem, Janis	A	1963-66
Eudy, Lindsay	A	1991-96	Fambrough, Jean	A	1949-53	Fentem, Lezlie	A	1961-64
Evans, Edith Lee	A	1952-55	Fancher, Ann	A	1977-83	Ferguson, Amy	A	1968-72
Evans, Janet	A	1970-72	Fancher, Lisa	T	1971-77	Ferguson, Ann	C	1945
Evans, Janis	C	1957	Farabee, Valerie	C	1992-93	Ferguson, Barbara	A	1952-55
Evans, Jean	A	1965-67	Faris, Sara Jane	C	1951-52	Ferguson, Billie Jean	C	1936-38
Evans, Jettie	T	1950-52	Farish, Joan	T	1939-41	Ferguson, Carolyn	T	1955-57
Evans, Kim	A	1974-79	Farmer, Alice	T	1936,40-42	Ferguson, Claire	C	1981-87
Evans, Lee-Taylor	A	1991-96	Farmer, Ann	C	1958-66	Ferguson, Gretchen	A	1987
Evans, Lucy		1929	Farmer, Joan	T	1935-36	Ferguson, Jean	A	1943
Evans, Mary M.	T	1953-54	Farmer, Sammie Ann	C	1942-43, 1945-48	Ferguson, Jimmie Ruth	C	1937
Evans, Pamela	A	1996				Ferguson, Jolyn	C	1942-45
Evans, Paula	A	1951-55	Farnsworth, Jane	T	1940-41	Ferguson, Sawnie	C	1980-85
Evans, Priscilla	C	1946-48	Farnsworth, Jennifer	A	1982-87	Ferguson, Sharon	T	1970-76
Evans, Sandra	C	1948-49	Farrell, Elizabeth Ann	C	1988-92	Ferguson, Susan	C	1981-86
Evans, Sue	T	1943	Farrell, Elizabeth	A	1983	Ferguson, Susan B.	T	1953-57

Ferguson, Susan	C	1969-72	Fitzhugh, Peden	A	1987-94	Forbes, Betty	C	1941-43
Ferguson, Virginia	T	1951-52, 1954-56	Fitzhugh, Tissa	T	1965-66	Forbes, Sarah	C	1943
Fernandez, Mignon	T	1930	Fitzpatrick, Kay	C	1956-57	Force, Kristen Ann	T	1994-96
Ferrell, Caroline	A	1985-90	Fitzsimmons, Sea Willow		1929	Ford, Amy	A	1986-87
Ferrin, Mary	T	1929-30	Flack, Alice	C	1945-46	Ford, Diana	A	1956-57
Fertitta, Nicole	T	1992-96	Flack, Jerre Jo	T	1940	Ford, Evangeline	A	1948-53
Feuillan, Diane	T	1945	Flaig, Frances	C	1942-44	Ford, Faith	C	1949-57
Few, Delfred	C	1937	Flaitz, Jane	A	1951-54	Ford, Karen	A	1955-56
Field, Lucy		1928	Flaitz, Marilyn Minnette	A	1949-51	Ford, Laura	T	1954-62
Fielden, Melinda	C	1965-66	Flanagan, Margaret	A	1976-83	Ford, Maegan	C	1989-96
Fields, Christi	T	1976-82	Flanagan, Mary Eileen	A	1974-81	Ford, Martha	A	1950-51
Fields, Fara	A	1985-88	Flanders, Sally	T	1976-80	Ford, Mary Jane	C	1967-68
Fields, Jeanne	C	1936	Flannery, Ann	A	1980-87	Ford, Patricia	T	1956-57
Fields, Melissa	A	1969	Flannery, Gayle	T	1958-63	Ford, Sally	A	1963-64
Fietz, Jane	T	1950	Flannery, Sylvia	A	1978-84	Ford, Stacey	T	1983-86
Fifield, Katie	C	1988-89	Flato, Carolyn	A	1955-61	Ford, Virginia	A	1986-92
Files, Ann	T	1948-50	Flato, Hattie	T	1938	Ford, Virginia	C	1940
Filson, Charlotte	T	1937	Flato, Mary Louise	C	1961-67	Ford, Virgnia Kate	C	1934
Finch, Emily Ann	A	1944-45	Flato, Monica	A	1974-80	Fordyce, Cindy	C	1980
Finch, Eva Jean	C	1940-43	Flato, Shelley	C	1950-56	Fordyce, Lillian	C	1941
Finch, Katherine	C	1926,29-30	Flato, Susan	C	1959-61,64	Foree, Katherine	A	1965
Finch, Mary Alice	T	1936-37	Flato, Winifred	C	1956-60	Foreman, Josephine		1929
Findley, Jane	C	1935	Flatten, Cynthia	T	1990-92	Forester, Julie	A	1987-90
Findley, Sally	C	1972-73	Fleeger, Mary Jean	T	1942-43, 1945-46	Forester, Whitney	T	1990
Finkbeiner, Christa	T	1973-78				Forman, Maxine	T	1935-37
Finks, Anne	A	1945-46	Fleming, Kim	C	1976-77	Fornot, Jane	T	1944
Finks, Julia	A	1944-50	Fleming, Marilyn Mikey	C	1939-40	Forrest, Carolyn	C	1949-50
Finks, Mary Carolyn	A	1949	Fleming, Phoebe	T	1984-89	Forrest, Mary	C	1930-31,33
Finley, Anna	A	1982-88	Fleshman, Martha	T	1931	Forrester, Heather	C	1983-87
Finley, Jennifer	C	1980-85	Fletcher, Bunky	C	1981-82	Forrester, Margaret	C	1988-94
Finn, Catherine	A	1987	Fletcher, Courtney	C	1986-92	Forster, Elaine	A	1955-57
Finn, Patricia	A	1987	Fletcher, June	T	1941,45	Forster, Febe	C	1946
Finney, Cindy	A	1961-64	Fletcher, Louise	C	1940	Forster, Jane	C	1946
Finney, Gale	T	1969-74	Fletcher, Mary Frances	T	1935	Forster, Laura	A	1986-88
Finney, Maurice	C	1929-31	Fletcher, Missie	C	1967-68	Forsythe, Julie	A	1984-87
Fisch, Natalie	C	1935-36	Flippen, Kay	A	1943-45	Fort, Ellie Miles	C	1942
Fischer, Margaret	C	1935,37-38	Floca, Doris	C	1943-44	Fortson, Karen	C	1970-71
Fischer, Meg	T	1995-96	Florence, Florence	C	1930	Fortson, Kim	C	1969-71
Fischer, Samantha	T	1980-86	Florsheim, Susan	A	1984-87	Fortson, Lisa	T	1972-77
Fish, Ann	T	1951-55	Flory, Sarah	A	1995	Forwood, Barbara	C	1935
Fish, Francine	A	1949-55	Flour, Lacey	T	1995-96	Fosdick, Louise	A	1945-47
Fish, Suzanne	C	1952-55	Floyd, Christina	A	1989-95	Foster, Angelique	A	1977-80
Fishburn, Wanda	T	1937	Floyd, Sarah	A	1996	Foster, Eva	T	1936-40
Fisher, Alice Ann	T	1941,43-44	Flucht, Gwyne	T	1963-66	Foster, Fairfax	C	1935
Fisher, Ann	A	1949	Flucht, Sarah	A	1967-70	Foster, Farren	T	1995-96
Fisher, Blossey		1929	Flury, Dorothy		1928	Foster, Glenna	T	1964-71
Fisher, Doris	C	1937-38	Flynn, Marietta	T	1946	Foster, Jan	C	1948
Fisher, Grace	T	1938-39	Flynn, Patricia	T	1942-43	Foster, Joan	T	1939
Fisher, Jean	T	1937-39	Flynn, Susan	C	1957	Foster, Karen	T	1977-80
Fisher, Leila Beth	C	1942-43	Folley, Frances	A	1945	Foster, Katie	T	1989-95
Fisher, Mary Lucille	C	1933	Folse, Laurie	T	1966-71	Foster, Liz	C	1972-76
Fitch, Barbara	T	1947	Folse, Lisa	C	1966-69	Foster, Martha Ann		1927
Fitch, Frances		1926	Foltz, Christine	C	1959-61	Foster, Meghan	C	1996
Fitch, Laura	T	1990-91	Foltz, Eleanor	C	1974-77	Foster, Susan	T	1975-79
Fitch, Melinda	A	1952	Foltz, Sarah	C	1996	Foulkrod, Catherine	A	1992-95
Fite, Ann	T	1938	Fontaine, Eugenia		1926	Foulkrod, Olivia	C	1988-92
Fite, Annita	T	1947-52	Fontaine, Lorraine		1926	Fountain, Rosemary	T	1937
Fite, Claudia	T	1953	Fontaine, Marie		1926	Fouts, Dorothy		1929
Fitzgerald, Bunny	T	1979	Fonville, Clarita Peter	T	1939-41	Fowler, Mary Stahl	A	1968-69
Fitzgerald, Cindy	C	1978-79	Fooks, Frances	C	1946-47	Fowler, Mary Jo	T	1936
Fitzgerald, Kelly	C	1972-73	Fooshee, Margaret Ann	T	1937-38	Fox, Julie	C	1990-92
Fitzhugh, Kathy	A	1962-69	Foote, Marlene	C	1944-46	Fox, Margretta	T	1937-38
			Foote, Sydneye	C	1950-51	Foxworth, Julie	T	1975-80

Foxworth, Susan	C	1974-78	Frels, Marjorie	T	1943-45,49	Furse, Mary	A	1974-81
Fraley, Betty Jo	C	1939-40	French, Alecia	C	1987-93	Fuselier, Carolyn	A	1952-54
Frame, Gloria	C	1936	French, Andrea	C	1977-81	Fussell, Jane	C	1951-53
Frances, Aileen	T	1931,33	French, Drue	A	1960-65			
Francis, Alatia	A	1956	French, Kathleen	C	1988-89	**G**		
Francis, Ann	T	1940-41	French, Lilian	A	1943-44	Gable, Ann	C	1949
Francis, Becky	C	1966-72	Frensley, Joan	A	1957-63	Gable, Jean	C	1949
Francis, Brenda	C	1970-77	Frere, Eleanor	T	1941,43	Gabriel, Carter	T	1987-94
Francis, Jane	A	1956-59	Freret, Elizabeth	T	1941-42	Gaddis, Jean	C	1941-42
Francis, Julia	A	1948-52	Fretwell, Mary Jane	T	1944	Gafford, Arden	C	1979-80,
Francis, Lillian	C	1940	Fretz, Joanne	T	1945-48			1982-84
Francis, Marjorie	T	1992	Frey, Lindsey	C	1994-96	Gage, Ann Elizabeth		1929
Francis, Martha	C	1932,34,36	Fricke, Pat	A	1953-58	Gage, Daria	A	1990-91
Francis, Martha Anne	C	1940-42	Friedrichs, Paige	A	1977-81	Gaido, Kimberly	C	1976-77,
Francis, Martha Muffin	A	1968-69	Friedson, Hortense	C	1936			1980-83
Francis, Martha E.	A	1962-66,	Friend, Ione	C	1961-65	Gaines, Beverly		1949
		1968-69	Friend, Rosalie	T	1945	Gaines, Joan	C	1942
Francis, Martha C.	A	1962-63	Friend, Vicky	A	1949-50	Gaines, Pat	A	1949
Francis, Stacey	A	1966	Frissell, Lou	A	1943-45	Gaither, Billie		1928-29
Francks, Patricia	C	1964-66	Frizzell, Virginia Ann	T	1935	Galbraith, Betty		1929
Francois, Beth	C	1961-68	Frost, Ann	T	1955-59	Galbraith, Frances		1929
Frank, Floy Edna		1929	Frost, Betty	C	1957-62	Gale, Martha	A	1961-62
Frank, Louise	T	1992-96	Frost, Sparky	C	1994-96	Gallagher, Jane	T	1965-71
Frank, Marie Louise	C	1939-40	Fruit, Barbara	A	1945	Gallagher, Karen	C	1965-71
Frank, Mary John	A	1990-96	Fruit, Elizabeth	C	1940-41	Gallagher, Kristen	A	1971-78
Franke, Barbara	C	1959	Fruit, Nance	T	1944-47	Gallagher, Marcia	C	1932-33
Franke, Carol	T	1955-57	Fry, Cynthia	C	1962-63	Gallaher, Martha	C	1952-53
Franke, Christen	T	1990-96	Fry, Karen	C	1965-67	Gallaher, Nancy	A	1954
Frankfurt, Dawn	A	1977-80,82	Fry, Katy	C	1988-94	Gallaher, Virginia	C	1958-61
Frankfurt, Michelle	C	1978-84	Fry, Susan	C	1955-58	Gallaway, Tara	A	1996
Franklin, Ann	C	1977	Frye, Gail	C	1966-70	Gallie, Rosalind	C	1942-43
Franklin, Ellen	T	1975-77	Fullen, Katherine	T	1930	Galloway, Belinda	A	1994-96
Franklin, Jean	A	1947-48	Fuller, Amy	T	1988	Galloway, Jacque	T	1944
Franklin, Lois	T	1950-53	Fuller, Betty Jo	A	1943-46	Galloway, Kay	A	1962-64
Franks, Lynn	T	1952	Fuller, Elizabeth	C	1982-85	Galloway, Nancy	T	1952
Franks, Victoria	T	1980-82	Fuller, Fa Lu	T	1951-54	Galo, Katharine	A	1979-82
Fraser, Babette	T	1956-60	Fuller, Kay	C	1958-61	Galo, Kristen	T	1981-83
Fraser, Donnie	T	1930	Fuller, Lady Myra	C	1937-39	Galo, Lisa	A	1987-88
Fraser, Jerry	C	1930	Fuller, Marjorie	C	1946	Galt, Allison	T	1948-49
Frasher, Ann	A	1948	Fuller, Mary Margaret	T	1935	Galt, Barbara	T	1955
Frates, Keith	A	1973	Fuller, Mimi	C	1968-72	Galt, Diane	A	1977-81
Frates, Robin	C	1973	Fuller, Patricia Ann	T	1953-56,58	Gammage, Amanda	A	1958-64
Frazer, Aubra	T	1972-75	Fuller, Terri	C	1970-76	Gammage, Gail	T	1950
Frazer, Jean Elstner	T	1949-50	Fullerton, Elizabeth	T	1968-69	Gammill, Arlene	A	1944
Frazer, Jeannie		1965	Fullerton, Roberta	T	1952-57	Gammon, Alice	A	1967-72
Frazer, Jennifer	C	1962-63	Fullick, Carol	A	1956-58	Gammon, Eleanor	C	1959-62
Frederick, Alice	A	1946,48	Fullilove, Barbara Ann	C	1948	Gammon, Hallie	A	1964-69
Frederick, Courtney	T	1974-80	Fullilove, Caroline	C	1939-40	Gammon, Lara	T	1986-91
Frederick, Farrell	C	1966-72	Fullilove, Priscilla	T	1957-60	Gandy, Jennifer	T	1971-72
Frederickson, Amanda	A	1992-93	Fullinwider, Kate	T	1985-90	Gandy, Sissy	C	1960-65
Frederickson, Ashley	C	1992-93	Fullinwider, Virginia	T	1935	Gannon, Charlotte	C	1975-77
Freel, Cindy	T	1971-77	Fulton, Geraldine	C	1956-64	Gannon, June	C	1932-38
Freels, Alice	C	1936-37,39	Fulton, Thara	T	1933	Gannon, Repple	C	1931
Freeman, Candy	T	1961-63	Funchess, Betty	A	1944-46	Garbade, Anne	A	1953
Freeman, Larryce	T	1947-48	Funk, Carol	T	1986-88	Garcia, Ale	C	1988
Freeman, Nettye	C	1936	Funk, Catherine	T	1986,88	Garcia, Betty	A	1988
Freeman, Tina	A	1960-65	Funk, Jean	C	1941-45	Garcia, Jacquelyn	A	1994-95
Freeze, Ann	C	1959-64	Fuqua, Stacy	C	1977-80	Garcia, Nikki	A	1994-94
Freeze, Sandra	T	1947-49	Furlow, Beverly	T	1947	Gardes, Betty	A	1964
Freitas, Bitsy	A	1949-57	Furman, Clare	C	1942	Gardner, Alyssa	T	1991-95
Freitas, Patricia	C	1957-65	Furneaux, Katherine	T	1934	Gardner, Frances		1935
Freitas, Shannon	T	1979	Furrh, Mary	C	1939	Gardner, Gina Gay	C	1970-71
Frels, Jo Anne	T	1942-46	Furse, Janie	A	1967-70	Gardner, Linda	C	1993-96

Name		Years
Gardner, Mary Elizabeth		1955
Gardner, Mary	C	1942-43
Gardner, Mary Ann	T	1942-43
Gardner, Mary		1935
Gardner, Melanie	A	1981-85
Gardner, Rebecca	A	1990-96
Gardner, Sharon	C	1972-76
Garett, Sally	C	1941
Garfield, Amanda	C	1991-92
Garison, Carol Ann	C	1960
Garitty, Sara Lee	C	1931-32,36
Garland, Leanne	T	1978-82
Garland, Nancy	T	1949-52
Garmon, Bashie	T	1964-68
Garner, Becky	A	1960
Garner, Betty	C	1960
Garner, Janie	C	1959-60
Garner, Jennifer	A	1979-86
Garnett, Carol	A	1961-66
Garnett, Linda	T	1955-57
Garrett, Betty Jane	T	1931,34
Garrett, Brandie	C	1980,82-83
Garrett, Dianne	A	1967-71
Garrett, Geneva	C	1994
Garrett, Jane Joyslin		1944-47
Garrett, Jane	T	1943
Garrett, Jennifer	T	1978-83
Garrett, Kate	C	1993-94
Garrett, Kim	C	1977-80
Garrett, Laura	T	1981-87
Garrett, Lucinda	A	1976-80
Garrett, Margaret	A	1949
Garrett, Mary Pearl		1928-29
Garrett, Nancy	C	1963-66
Garrett, Penny	T	1953-59
Garrett, Sally	C	1940-46
Garrett, Sarah	T	1992-94
Garrett, Susan	A	1969-70
Garrison, Anna Louise	T	1931
Garrison, Mary	T	1948-52
Garrison, Tiffany	T	1979
Garth, Gayle	C	1968-69
Garth, Leta	C	1969-74
Garth, Lucy	A	1971-78
Gartner, Suzanne	T	1941-42
Garton, Frances		1930
Garwood, Billie	T	1937
Garwood, Yvonne	T	1937
Gasow, Lenore	T	1952-56
Gaston, Alice	T	1996
Gaston, Caroline	C	1995
Gaston, Elizabeth	A	1987-93
Gaston, Frances	T	1930
Gaston, Garvin	T	1990-91
Gaston, Katherine	A	1989-95
Gaston, Katherine C.C.	A	1944
Gaston, Patricia	A	1953
Gaston, Suzanne	A	1950-53
Gates, Carol	T	1941
Gates, Elizabeth	C	1939-41
Gates, Elizabeth Ann	T	1955-59
Gates, Mary Jane	C	1949-55
Gates, Sarah Katherine	T	1949-56
Gates, Valerie	A	1967-68
Gathright, Grayson	T	1973-77
Gau, Benning	A	1987-88
Gaughan, Caroline	C	1951
Gaumer, Forrest Jones	T	1939
Gauntt, Shelley	A	1971-73
Gauthier, Kathy Jo	C	1961
Gavit, Lindsay	A	1993-96
Gaylord, Elinor	C	1942-45
Gaylord, Louise	A	1973-74
Gear, Adrianne	T	1959-62
Gear, Marsha	A	1956-60
Gearhart, Jessica	A	1964-66
Gearhart, Martha	A	1958-60
Gee, Jenifer	C	1963
Gehrkin, Marjorie	T	1945
Geiler, Joan	T	1936-37
Geiselman, Dorothy	T	1934-35
Gentry, Anne	C	1939-40
Gentry, Lisa	T	1991,93-94
Geoghegan, Jan	T	1951-52, 1954-55
Geoghegan, Patty	T	1947-51
George, Dolores Sissy	C	1944-52
George, Kathleen		1928
George, Mary Edith	C	1949
George, Meredith	T	1964-69
George, Ray	C	1945-46
George, Sylvia Anne	A	1947
Gerald, Ashley	A	1994-96
		1929
Gerard, Mary		
Gerdes, Lisa	C	1972-74
Gerdes, Nancy	T	1973-76
Germer, Allison	T	1982-84
Gernert, Joan	C	1936-39
Gessner, Natalie	C	1941
Gettys, Nancy	A	1945-46
Gholson, Martha Marie	C	1930
Gibbons, Mary	A	1972
Gibbons, Molly	A	1980-81
Gibbons, Pat	T	1942-43
Gibbs, Margaret	T	1946-47
Giblin, Sharon	A	1961-67
Gibson, Amy	C	1977-81
Gibson, Annette	C	1941
Gibson, Betty	T	1940
Gibson, Gertrude		
Gibson, Gigi	A	1976-77
Gibson, Gloria	C	1937-41
Gibson, Hagen	C	1979-81
Gibson, Jodie Ann	C	1944
Gibson, Mary C.	A	1994-96
Gibson, Melinda	T	1954
Gibson, Sarah	T	1976-77
Gibson, Sharon	A	1947-49
Giesey, Martha	T	1937
Giffin, Mandy	T	1964-69
Gifford, Barrett	T	1987-88
Gifford, Carrah	T	1984-87
Gifford, Lavon	T	1930
Gilbert, Mary Lee	C	1980-81
Gildersleeve, Caroline	T	1936-37
Giles, Ann	T	1968-73
Giles, Jacklyn	T	1948
Giles, Mary	T	1933
Gill, Ann	T	1949-50
Gill, Gloria	C	1935-36
Gill, Martha	C	1936-37
Gill, Mary	T	1952-53
Gilleland, Dell	T	1956-63
Gillespie, Cathy	T	1963-64
Gillett, Jennifer	C	1985-89
Gilliam, Jeanie	C	1973-79
Gilliam, Marjorie	C	1939-40,43
Gilliam, Patricia	C	1958-59
Gilliam, Sue	T	1958-66
Gilliland, Ann	C	1942
Gilliland, Sara	T	1942
Gillis, Dorothy	C	1938
Gilmer, Day	A	1953-57
Gilmer, Elizabeth	T	1959-64
Gilmer, Laurie	A	1961-67
Gilmer, Margaret	A	1962
Gilmer, Margaret	A	1960-66
Gilmore, Edna		1928
Gilmore, Karen	A	1970-77
Gilmore, Kathy	C	1968-74
Girard, Betty	C	1938-39
Girault, Bunny	T	1956
Giroir, Jan	T	1977-78
Giss, Karen	C	1955-57
Giss, Pam	T	1980
Gissell, Julia	C	1940
Givens, Judith	C	1957-60
Glaber, Joyce	A	1957
Gladney, Ann	C	1938
Gladney, Mary Jane	C	1937
Glasco, Marion	C	1936
Glasgow, Mary Lynn	T	1950
Glasgow, Sylvia	C	1955
Glass, Jane Ann	C	1955-63
Glass, Mary Ell	C	1954-60
Glass, Monta Jo	C	1939-40, 1943-46
Glass, Sharon	C	1974
Glasscock, Camile	C	1972-78
Glasscock, Julianna	A	1980-85
Glasscock, Kathy	T	1958-64
Glasscock, Sharon	C	1951-52
Glassell, Ashton	T	1942-43
Glassell, Emily Ann	C	1939-41
Glassell, Lillian	C	1939
Glauner, Janice	T	1937,40
Glauner, Jeanne	T	1937,39
Glaze, Laura	C	1969-73
Glaze, Lynn	T	1976-77
Glen, Patricia	C	1931
Glenn, Dunlop Scott		1928-29
Glenn, Jill	C	1961-62
Glenn, Maria	C	1975-78,80
Glidden, GiGi	C	1972-77
Glober, Jane	T	1956-59
Glober, Joyce	A	1956-60
Glover, Gay	T	1941-43
Glover, Lindsay	T	1990-96
Glover, Twasy	C	1957-60

Greenwood, Jacquelyn	T	1995-96
Greenwood, Lee	T	1979-85
Greenwood, Mimi	T	1962-65
Greenwood, Nancy	T	1948-49
Greenwood, Nancy	C	1957
Greenwood, Nita	C	1938
Greenwood, Pam	A	1959-63
Greer, Allison	C	1989-92
Greer, Ann	A	1943-46
Greer, Eleanor	A	1945-48
Greer, Linda Lou	A	1952
Greer, Mary	A	1943
Greeves, Kilby	A	1974-80
Gregg, Marthanne	T	1961-65
Gregg, Megan	T	1990-96
Gregg, Pat	C	1940
Gregg, Susie	T	1962-67
Gregory, Carole	T	1966-69
Gregory, Margaret	C	1958
Gregory, Rose	T	1941
Gregory, Shirley	T	1930
Grelling, Ann	T	1989-93
Grelling, Mary John	C	1933-35
Gresham, Marco	C	1932
Gresham, Susan	A	1950-52
Greusel, Charlotte Lynn	T	1931
Greusel, Charlotte	T	1931
Greve, Bernie		1931
Greve, Louise		1929
Grey, Tara	A	1988-91
Gribble, Louise Dugie	C	1938-39
Gridley, Gayle	T	1943,45-46
Griesedieck, Kathleen	C	1957-58
Griesedieck, Lorene	T	1959-62
Griesedieck, Mary	C	1959-62
Griesedieck, Nancy	A	1962
Griffen, Lauren	C	1991
Griffin, Elaine	A	1965-70
Griffin, Elise	C	1982-84
Griffin, Gale	C	1953-58
Griffin, June	A	1943
Griffin, Lea	A	1948-52
Griffin, Mary Ellen	A	1943
Griffin, Mary Alice	T	1938-41
Griffis, Janet	C	1986-92
Griffis, Jennifer	A	1983-89
Griffis, Laura	T	1984-87
Griffith, Ann	T	1930
Griffith, Barbara	A	1943
Griffith, Carolyn	A	1994-96
Griffith, Carolyn	C	1943
Griffith, Gail	C	1968-73
Griffith, Gwen	A	1968-73
Griffith, Kelli	A	1976-77
Griffith, Kendall	A	1979-84
Griffith, Laura	T	1983-86
Griffith, Lena	A	1943
Griffiths, Gail	A	1957-58
Griggs, Mary Lucille	C	1941
Griggy, Jennifer	C	1983-89
Grigsby, Flora Nell	C	1964
Grigsby, Gretchen	T	1956-57
Grigsby, Kathy	T	1958-64

Grimes, Amy	A	1969-75
Grimes, Ann	T	1974-80
Grimes, Mardi	T	1968-73
Grimes, Meredith	C	1970-75
Grimland, Diane	T	1961-65
Grimland, Donna	A	1962-69
Grimland, Gayle	A	1966-73
Grimshaw, Bonnie	T	1989-96
Grimshaw, Robin	C	1992-93
Gripon, Allison	C	1981-87
Grisham, Mary Ellen	C	1930,33
Grisso, Ann	A	1947
Grisso, Kelly	C	1946
Grissom, Charlotte	C	1937-38, 1940,42
Griswold, Martha	T	1941,44
Groce, Sara Lee Sally	C	1948
Groff, Sallie Eleanor	A	1948-49
Groff, Susan Elizabeth	T	1948-49
Grogan, Eden	T	1991-96
Grogan, Jacqeline	T	1935,37
Grogan, Laura Lee	T	1940
Groos, Kristin	A	1984-91
Groseclose, Frances		1929
Gross, Carolyn		1928
Gross, Kristine	A	1987
Gross, Missy	A	1967-70
Grosshart, Rita	T	1945-48
Grossman, Marion	C	1937
Groth, Alison	T	1972-74
Groth, Diane	T	1949-50
Ground, Amanda	T	1990-91
Groves, Betty	A	1943-46
Grozinger, Liza Beth	C	1992-96
Grubb, Hannah	A	1991-96
Grubb, Jackie	C	1936-37
Grubb, Julia	A	1953
Grubb, Lili	A	1953-55
Grubbs, Sherri	T	1972-73
Gruy, Carolyn	C	1968-73
Gruy, Clayton	A	1964-69
Gruy, Dagmar	C	1930,35
Gruy, Hannah	A	1994,96
Gruy, Lisa	A	1970-76
Gruy, Lucy	T	1958-62
Gudger, Betty Jo	T	1939-40
Guerin, Laura	A	1987-94
Guerrero, Patricia Ann	A	1943
Guggolz, Eloise	T	1993-95
Guinn, Jennie	C	1996
Guinn, Jimmie Jean	T	1939
Guitar, Catherine	T	1993-94
Gullatt, Debbie	T	1974-78
Gump, Marilyn	C	1951-52
Gunn, Jill	A	1955-56
Gunn, Julie	C	1987-89
Gunn, Marguerite	T	1955-58
Gunn, Missy	C	1965-68
Gunn, Nell	C	1940,43-44
Gunn, Shannon	A	1980-85
Gunn, Virginia	C	1963,65-69
Gunnell, Lillian	T	1931,33
Gunter, Elizabeth	T	1970-71

Gunter, Mary	T	1951-53
Gurley, Louise		1928
Gurley, Mary Earl		1928
Gurley, Nell		1928
Guseman, Cecilia	C	1941-44
Guseman, Michelene	T	1939-40
Gusmann, Ursula	T	1939
Gust, Jean	A	1970-71
Gustine, Libby	T	1954,58-59
Gustine, Lynn	A	1958-59
Gustine, Pat	T	1948-51, 1953-54
Gustine, Peggy	C	1958-59
Guthrie, Kate	T	1972-73
Guthrie, Kim	A	1961-68
Guthrie, Virginia	T	1938
Guttry, Melinda	A	1969-72
Gutzman, Jane	T	1953
Guy, Christina	C	1985-89
Guy, Janie	C	1953-57,59
Guy, Judy	T	1953-56
Gwens, Judith Ann	C	1957
Gwin, Hannah	A	1965-67

H

Haag, Barbara	C	1953-59
Haag, Heather	T	1986
Haag, Janice	T	1957-65
Haas, Kristy	C	1985-88
Haase, Lindzey	T	1994-96
Haberle, Jean	C	1935-36
Hable, Katharine	A	1979-84
Hable, Susan	C	1981-87
Hackett, Frances		1929
Hadden, Martha	C	1971-77
Haden, Barbara	C	1940-44
Haden, Frances	T	1972-74
Haden, Holly	C	1987-91
Haden, Jean	T	1930-33
Hadley, Elizabeth	C	1937
Haesly, Gretchen	T	1931
Hafner, Nancy	C	1937-39,43
Hagan, Lyle	T	1976-83
Hagelstein, Anne	A	1973-76
Hagelstein, Janie	A	1970-73
Hagelstein, Mary Olive	C	1968-71
Hagens, Alice	C	1989-96
Hagens, Edie	A	1976-79
Hagens, Peggy	T	1935-36
Hager, Courtney	C	1983-87
Hailey, Kelly	T	1976-77
Hails, Jean	T	1936
Haines, Lela	C	1935
Hair, Bonnie	C	1972
Hair, Cecelia	C	1972
Hairston, Barbara	A	1981-84
Hairston, Dee Dee	T	1978-81
Hairston, Jane	A	1945
Hairston, Katie	C	1983-90
Halbert, Bobbie Mae	C	1930
Hale, Betty	A	1943
Hale, Joyce Janice	T	1939
Hale, Lisa	C	1977-82

Name	Code	Years
Harris, Emiy	C	1973-79
Harris, Frances	C	1948-52
Harris, Gina	C	1966-67
Harris, Holly	A	1965-70
Harris, Jane	A	1947
Harris, Kay	A	1952-55
Harris, Krista	T	1978-84
Harris, Lindsey	T	1984-90
Harris, Lynn	T	1946
Harris, Margaret A.	C	1934-37
Harris, Margaret T.	T	1934
Harris, Martha		1934
Harris, Mary Lou	C	1938
Harris, Mary Elizabeth	T	1939-40,44
Harris, Mary Lou	C	1960-62
Harris, Maurice		1928
Harris, Peggy	T	1961-62
Harris, Reagan	A	1986-92
Harrison, Amy	C	1966-68
Harrison, Barbara	C	1932
Harrison, Callan	T	1996
Harrison, Dixie	T	1951
Harrison, Elizabeth	T	1932-33
Harrison, Ellen	A	1962-66
Harrison, Gloria	C	1941
Harrison, Heather	A	1986-92
Harrison, Hester	C	1930
Harrison, Julie	C	1969-72
Harrison, Katherine	C	1938-40
Harrison, Kathy	T	1960-64
Harrison, Lauren	T	1991-94
Harrison, Leslie	C	1968-71
Harrison, Mabel	C	1945
Harrison, Margaret		1928
Harrison, Martha	A	1988-90, 1992-95
Harrison, Melissa	T	1969-72
Harrison, Nancy	T	1962-65
Harrison, Priscilla	T	1942
Harrison, Sadie	A	1987-88
Harrison, Tiffany	C	1973-80
Harrison, Tina	T	1961-64
Harrison, Virginia	T	1934
Harriss, Valerie	C	1958-61
Harsh, Molly	A	1961-63
Harsh, Roxie	A	1965-67
Harston, Marian	A	1946
Harston, Martha	C	1948-49, 1951-52
Hart, Carolyn	T	1942-45
Hart, Dorothy	T	1936
Hart, Gayle	A	1948-49
Hart, Susan	C	1973-77
Hartgrove, Lucia	A	1947-48
Hartley, Jane	C	1975-80
Hartman, Elsa Claire	C	1930
Harvey, Betty Jane	T	1978-80
Harvey, Frances	T	1967-69
Harvey, Inez	T	1936
Harvey, Jane	A	1958-62
Harvey, Kathryn	A	1978,80
Harvey, Laura	T	1982-86
Harvey, Muriel	C	1935

Name	Code	Years
Harvey, Tave	T	1972-78
Harvey, Tootie	T	1961-63
Harvick, Anne	T	1945-46
Harvick, Mary Louise	T	1937-38
Harvin, Chanda	A	1977-83
Harwell, Marilynn	T	1935-38
Harwell, Sara	T	1965-70
Harwood, Anna Lu	C	1961-62
Haslam, Julie	T	1975-77
Hassebroek, Kacey	T	1987
Hasty, Reba Berle	T	1931
Hatch, Roberta	T	1944
Hatchell, Beverly	T	1946
Hatcher, Frances	A	1943-44
Hatcher, Johnny Mae	C	1931,33
Hatchett, Elizabeth	A	1956
Hatchett, Rosemary	C	1935
Hatchett, Susan	A	1954-56
Haus, Ashley	A	1980
Hause, Daryl Anne	C	1960-61
Haves, Ann		1929
Hawk, Jane	T	1936
Hawkins, Anna	T	1984-89
Hawkins, Betsy	T	1944
Hawkins, Sara	T	1996
Hawley, Mary Jane	T	1940
Hawn, Christina	T	1961-64
Hawn, Hailey	T	1996
Hawn, Joy	T	1987-88
Hawn, Katy	C	1980-81
Haws, Holly	T	1983-86
Hawthorne, Hagan	T	1974-77
Hawthorne, Hayley	A	1976-79
Hawthorne, Heather	T	1972-75
Hay, Martie	C	1940
Hay, Mary	C	1940
Hayden, Ann	T	1964-68
Hayden, Martha	C	1974-79
Hayden, Nancy	T	1964-67
Hayes, Cora Ann	A	1947-49
Hayes, Heather	A	1978-83
Hayes, Holly	T	1974-78
Hayes, Janet	C	1948
Hayes, Kandy	T	1967-70
Hayes, Kelli	T	1975-80
Hayes, Lyda	T	1939-44
Hayes, Sammie Jo		1928-29
Hayes, Sarah Jane	A	1950-54
Hayes, Sheryl	A	1969-72
Hayes, Yvonne	T	1939-41
Haynes, Betty	C	1940
Haynes, Kathy	A	1974-75
Haynes, Renee	C	1971-72
Haynes, Vicki	T	1959-62, 1964-65
Haynie, Garland	T	1930-31
Hays, Anne		1926
Hays, Connie Sue	T	1944
Hays, Janet	C	1948
Hays, Sammy Jo		1928
Hayter, Martha Buford	C	1931
Hayter, Mary Elizabeth	C	1933-34,36
Hayter, Penelope	C	1931-32

Name	Code	Years
Hazlip, June	C	1945-46
Head, Eugenia	T	1947
Head, Gwen	T	1949-55
Head, Julie	T	1956-61
Head, Lannie	C	1954-58
Head, Lisa	T	1963-68
Head, Marcy	C	1963-66
Heaner, Anne	C	1951-56
Heaney, Katherine		1929
Heaney, Lizzie	A	1995
Heaney, Pat	C	1938
Heard, Alice	T	1942-44
Heard, Bessie	T	1930
Heard, Eleanor	A	1986-92
Heard, Fannie Lee	C	1938-42,44
Heard, Mary	T	1984-90
Heard, Mildred	T	1931
Heard, Priscilla	C	1949-52
Heard, Susan	C	1988-95
Heard, Susan	A	1958-59
Heare, Helen	T	1938
Hearn, Ruthy	T	1966-69
Hearne, Angela	A	1985-91
Heartfield, Heather	C	1979-82
Heartfield, Lorraine	C	1956-58
Heartfield, Shari	T	1984-86
Heath, Cynthia	A	1945-47
Heath, Heather	A	1976-83
Heath, Hilary	A	1987-93
Heath, Nancy	T	1948-51
Heberling, Natalie	A	1990-96
Hebert, Guy	T	1946-47
Hebert, Jo Ann	T	1942-43, 1945-56
Hecht, Valerie	T	1942-43
Heckmann, Kate	T	1992-96
Hedgcoxe, Clair	C	1996
Hedge, Carolyn	T	1967-71
Hedge, Hollee	A	1968-71
Hedgecock, Mimi	T	1988-89
Hedgecoke, Sallye	A	1982-88
Hedley, Mary Lou	T	1940
Hedrick, Jean	C	1939-40
Hedrick, Mildred	C	1939-40
Heep, Dorothy	C	1939
Heep, Kathryn	C	1937
Heerwagen, Dean	T	1966
Heflin, Charlotte	C	1936-37
Heflin, Delores	T	1936-37
Hefner, Catherine	C	1965-66, 1968-71
Hefner, Virginia	A	1996
Heidenheimer, Jill	A	1973-76
Heidrick, Ellen	T	1969-74
Heidrick, Penny	C	1955-57
Heiligbrodt, Heather	A	1983-86
Heiman, Gigi	A	1971-73,75
Heinisch, Carolyn	C	1954-55
Heinisch, Marie	A	1954
Heinz, Hannah	C	1990
Heinz, Morgane	A	1987-89
Heinzelman, Dru	T	1970-76
Heinzerling, Ann	A	1955-59

Heinzerling, Mary	C	1962-65
Heldenfels, Alice	C	1948,50-51
Heller, Mary	C	1958-66
Heller, Sally	A	1950-53
Heller, Susan	C	1951-56
Helmbold, Roxanna	T	1941
Helmcamp, Jan	T	1956-58
Hemphill, Patricia	C	1941
Hemry, Mary Ann	A	1945
Henderson, Doris		1926
Henderson, Dorothy	C	1930
Henderson, Emily	A	1993-96
Henderson, Frances	A	1966-67
Henderson, Helen	T	1930
Henderson, Hilda	C	1963-66
Henderson, Holly	T	1988-96
Henderson, Honey	C	1985-92
Henderson, Irma Veree Bing	C	1942,44-45
Henderson, Jean B.		1929
Henderson, Jennifer	T	1983-88
Henderson, Jennifer P.	A	1978-82
Henderson, Jenny	C	1967-68
Henderson, Julie	T	1964-68
Henderson, Katie	T	1994-96
Henderson, Laura Sue	C	1946-49
Henderson, Libby Lou	C	1942,44-46
Henderson, Mildred	C	1946
Henderson, Norma		1928
Henderson, Sally	A	1957-58
Henderson, Sistie	C	1941-43, 1945-46
Henderson, Susan	C	1957-61
Henderson, Virginia	C	1942-46
Henderson, Virginia Sister	T	1986-93
Henderson, Virginia	C	1940-41
Henderson, Zuma Legay	C	1941
Hendon, Ernestine	T	1941
Hendon, Martha Ann	T	1941-43
Hendrick, Florence	C	1934
Hendricks, Candy	C	1960-62
Hendricks, Kay	C	1946-52
Hendricks, Lisa	A	1967-69
Hendricks, Patsy	A	1952-53
Hendrickson, Kay	A	1968-75
Hendrickson, Nancy	C	1967-74
Hendryx, Ann	A	1948-55
Hendryx, Caroline	A	1994-96
Hendryx, Deborah Ann	T	1991-96
Henley, Betty	C	1963-66
Henley, Claire	T	1937
Henley, Jenny	T	1965-70
Henley, Lee	C	1959-62
Henninger, Glenn Adelle	C	1936-37
Henry, Allyson	A	1979-84
Henry, Barbara	T	1956-64
Henry, Betty	C	1938
Henry, Carolyn	C	1951
Henry, Christine	A	1957-59
Henry, Ginny	T	1970-76
Henry, Helen	A	1990-91
Henry, Jacqueline	T	1974-78
Henry, Jane Ann	A	1951-52
Henry, Karen	A	1975-79
Henry, Kathryn	C	1983-90
Henry, Margaret	A	1987-90
Henry, Mary Louise	C	1959-61
Henry, Mary Lou	C	1939-40
Henry, Paige	A	1985-86
Henry, Pam	A	1975-78
Henry, Rosmary	T	1967-72
Henslee, Carol	A	1955
Henson, Amanda	C	1987
Henson, Amelia	T	1932
Hentrich, Jennifer	C	1982-84
Herbert, Bessie		1930
Herbert, Joyce	T	1941
Herd, Claire	T	1955-61
Herd, Holly	C	1979-84
Herd, Valerie	T	1992-95
Herder, Mary Elizabeth	C	1929,34
Herder, Sally	A	1958
Herman, Adeline	T	1930
Herman, Louise	T	1930
Herndon, Bennett	T	1983-84
Herndon, Jill	C	1970
Herod, Betty	C	1939
Herold, Ellen	T	1945
Herold, Judy	A	1949
Herr, Sally	C	1974-77
Herrick, Gail	C	1962-67
Herrick, Leslie	C	1972-76
Herrin, Betty	C	1951-54
Herrin, Joan	C	1941
Herring, Ann	A	1948
Herring, Luella	T	1957-60
Herrington, Canice	T	1964
Herrington, Melissa	T	1973-75
Hervey, Kathy	C	1959-60
Hervey, Nancy	C	1959-60
Herzfeld, Elizabeth	T	1937
Herzfeld, Ruth	T	1934
Herzfield, Helene	T	1935
Hess, Dorothea	T	1941
Hess, Karen	T	1958-62
Hess, Penny	C	1949-55
Hess, Priscilla	A	1955-61
Hess, Susan	T	1955-59
Hestwood, Adele	C	1945-49
Hestwood, Jacqueline	C	1955-60
Hewitt, Janith	T	1939
Hewlett, Sherry	A	1964-66
Heyne, Marcia	A	1952-55
Hibbert, Holly	C	1966-72
Hickey, Jill	A	1962
Hickman, Brenda	A	1970-76
Hickman, Emily	A	1989-90
Hickman, Margaret	A	1992-96
Hickman, Mary	A	1964-67
Hickman, Paula	A	1952-55
Hickman, Sally	A	1964-67
Hicks, Gina	A	1967-71
Hicks, Janelle	A	1943-48
Hicks, Janis	A	1943-44
Hicks, Leslie	A	1962-68
Hicks, Marilyn	T	1945-46
Hicks, Sarah	A	1950-54
Hiett, Anna Mitchell	T	1949-55
Hiett, Josephine	A	1943-44
Hiett, Karen	A	1949-50
Higginbotham, Lynn	T	1971
Higginbotham, Norma	C	1941
Higginbothom, Joyce	T	1947-48
Higgins, Amy	T	1988
Higgins, Heidi	C	1973-79
Higgins, Virginia	T	1938
High, Jane	T	1941
Hightower, Camilla	T	1971-75
Hightower, Elizabeth	C	1974-78
Hightower, Jenifer	T	1977-78
Hightower, Lutetia	A	1947-50
Hightower, Martha	T	1965-68
Higigns, Lysle	A	1978
Hildebrand, Nancy	T	1940
Hilker, Dorothy	C	1936-37, 1939-40
Hill, Alexis	T	1981-84
Hill, Alinda Honeybear	T	1958-59
Hill, Amy	A	1974-77
Hill, Angie	A	1982-84
Hill, Carlie	A	1992-95
Hill, Catherine	C	1942-43
Hill, Charlotte	A	1943
Hill, Courtney	A	1981-86
Hill, Debbi	C	1982-85
Hill, Elyse	C	1991-92
Hill, Ernestine	T	1931-32
Hill, Georgette	T	1935
Hill, Gigi	C	1982-87
Hill, Glenn	T	1936-38,40
Hill, Helen Sissy	C	1950-54
Hill, Johannah	T	1969-72
Hill, Kasey	C	1984-86
Hill, Landon	C	1988-92
Hill, Lyda	A	1954-59
Hill, Marilyn	A	1960-64
Hill, Martha	C	1963-68
Hill, Mary Ann	C	1936-37
Hill, Mary Frances	C	1931
Hill, Marynada	T	1940-45,47
Hill, Minta	T	1943
Hill, Nancy	T	1943
Hill, Robin	A	1976-78
Hill, Sarah Jane	C	1937
Hill, Winifred	T	1934-38
Hillard, Lauris	C	1972-78
Hillegeist, Stephanie	C	1933-34
Hillegeist, Virginia	T	1933-34
Hillhouse, Laura	T	1945
Hilliard, Rosemary	T	1931
Hillman, Holly	C	1991-95
Hillman, Lauren	A	1992
Hills, Margery	C	1936
Hills, Mildred	C	1935-36,39
Hime, Hailey	T	1993-96
Hindermann, Lane	A	1961
Hindermann, Mary	A	1961
Hindes, Betty Lou	T	1937-38
Hines, Carol Lee	A	1946-48

Hines, Corley	C	1990-94
Hines, Marie	C	1946-47
Hines, Neely	C	1990-92
Hines, Peaches	C	1956-58
Hinkle, Ferol	T	1972-76
Hinman, Amy	C	1930
Hinman, Genevieve	C	1930
Hinn, Karen	T	1953-58
Hinton, Margaret Ann	T	1981-82
Hinton, Mary Elizabeth	C	1977-80
Hinton, Virginia	T	1935-39,42
Hirschi, Jean Ann	A	1943-44
Hissen, Susanne Skeets	C	1933-35
Hissom, Tamra	T	1970-71
Hivick, Catherine		1928
Hixson, Sue	C	1935
Hobart, Marilyn	C	1941-42
Hobbie, Ethel	T	1935
Hodell, Jane	A	1949-52
Hodge, Anne	A	1954-56
Hodge, Carolyn	A	1944
Hodge, Jane	A	1943-44
Hodge, Lark	A	1985-86
Hodge, Mary	A	1943
Hodges, Acker	C	1987-90
Hodges, Ann	A	1965-72
Hodges, Anne	A	1981-86
Hodges, Cathy	C	1980-84
Hodges, Donna	C	1971-78
Hodges, Hilary	T	1980-83
Hodges, Margaret	A	1957-60
Hodges, Virginia	T	1930
Hoebeke, Shelby	A	1989-94,96
Hoebeke, Whitney	C	1991-96
Hoehn, Louise	C	1950
Hoehn, Mary	T	1941-44
Hoenig, Marsha	C	1953-55
Hoepfner, Frances	C	1937
Hoffman, Caroline	C	1993-96
Hoffman, Ginger	A	1970-76
Hoffman, Kay	C	1962-63, 1965-68
Hoffman, Mary Katherine	T	1941-42
Hogan, Jackie	C	1946-47
Hogan, Janet	C	1951-52
Hogan, Lisa	A	1982-84
Hogan, Maggie	A	1973-78
Hogan, Peggy	A	1951-52
Hogsett, Marguerite	C	1940
Hohorst, Meagan	T	1987
Hoke, Wilma	C	1944
Holbrook, Betty	T	1931
Holcomb, Laura	A	1995-96
Holcomb, Norma Jean	C	1954
Holcomb, Virginia	A	1943-44
Holden, Mary Alice	C	1937
Holder, Lisa	T	1961-66
Holecamp, Cecelia		1928
Holeman, Annette		
Holitik, Kaye	C	1973-74
Holke, Judith Ann	T	1952-57
Holland, Allison	C	1991-94
Holland, Harriett	A	1943-45

Holland, Jean		1929
Holland, Joanna	T	1980-84
Holland, Marie	C	1934
Holland, Nancy Jane	A	1945-46,48
Holland, Sandra Anne	A	1946-49
Holland, Virginia	C	1936
Hollander, Elizabeth		1929
Hollander, Miriam Lee	C	1931
Holleron, Barbara	T	1931
Holliday, Emily	C	1989-95
Hollingsworth, Dawn	C	1963-70
Hollingsworth, Julieann	A	1961-67
Hollingsworth, Martha	T	1954-60
Hollingsworth, Susan	A	1959-62
Hollins, Virginia	C	1969-75
Hollis, Kathryn	T	1994-95
Hollis, Laurie	C	1967-71
Hollis, Rebecca	T	1994-96
Holloway, Anne	T	1934-35
Holloway, Cynthia	T	1932
Hollrah, Rebecca	C	1982-85
Holmes, Allison	T	1990
Holmes, Barbara	T	1955-60
Holmes, Berkeley	C	1982-86
Holmes, Betty	T	1961-68
Holmes, Carol	T	1957-64
Holmes, Caroline	T	1944-45
Holmes, Charlotte	T	1953-56
Holmes, Elizabeth	A	1957-65
Holmes, Elsie	C	1936-37
Holmes, Erin	A	1990
Holmes, Helen	T	1961-67
Holmes, Jane	T	1951-53
Holmes, Jennifer	A	1985
Holmes, Judy	T	1957-59, 1961-63
Holmes, Laura	C	1962-69
Holmes, Lucy	A	1956-62
Holmes, Lyle	C	1996
Holmes, Mary	A	1961-65
Holmes, Milly	T	1956-64
Holmes, Pat	T	1944-47
Holmes, Patty	T	1946
Holmes, Paula	T	1966-69
Holmes, Phyllis	A	1952-55
Holmes, Tavener	T	1966-67
Holmes, Wendy	A	1968-73
Holmgreen, Barbara		1926
Holt, Billie Sue	T	1939-40
Holt, Dorothy Faye	C	1939-40, 1943-44
Holt, Mavour	A	1947-48
Holt, Nettie June	C	1936-38
Holtzman, Sandra		1939
Honaker, Mavis John	T	1931
Honea, Patricia	T	1940-44
Honeycutt, Marie	C	1937
Honnold, Carol	C	1954-57
Honnold, Laine	A	1983
Hood, Bobbie Sue	T	1949-55
Hood, Christie	C	1988,90-92
Hood, Dorothy Rose	T	1934-35
Hood, Evelyn	C	1933-35

Hood, Jo Ann	A	1949-51,54
Hood, Kelly	A	1966-68
Hood, Mindy	C	1967-68
Hood, Sophie	T	1991-95
Hood, Susan	C	1960-63
Hooks, Elise	C	1934
Hooks, Ema	C	1934
Hooper, Ann	A	1988-95
Hooper, Mary	C	1968-72
Hooper, Ruby Laura	C	1934-35
Hoover, Christina	C	1994-96
Hoover, Josie	T	1986-90
Hoover, Marylee	T	1957-58
Hopkins, Aubrey	A	1992-93,95
Hopkins, Beth	A	1993-96
Hopkins, Harriet	T	1942-43
Hopkins, Juanita	C	1930
Hopkins, Pamela	C	1965-68
Hoppe, Ann	T	1970-75
Hoppe, Anne	A	1966
Hoppe, Emily	C	1996
Hoppe, Nellie	C	1996
Hopper, Farrell	C	1990-92
Hopper, Frances	T	1965-72
Hopper, Tany	C	1971-78
Hopps, Dorothy Jeanne	T	1936
Hopson, Anita	T	1935-36
Hopson, Annelle	C	1935-36
Hopson, Nancy	A	1960-65
Horan, Elizabeth	C	1930
Horka, Dee Dee	C	1977-78
Horkan, Patricia	T	1946-47
Horn, Johanna	C	1948
Horn, Patricia	A	1943
Hornberger, Diana	T	1949-56
Hornberger, Dorothy	A	1953
Hornberger, Joan	A	1953
Horne, Joyce	C	1939
Horne, Rose Marie	C	1939
Horner, Evalie	A	1986-92
Horner, Rose	C	1936-37
Horrigan, Nancy	C	1946
Hortenstine, Ann	T	1948-49,51
Horton, Elizabeth	A	1961-65
Horton, Judy	T	1953-55
Horton, Mary Louise	C	1930
Horton, Susanne	A	1954-59
Hoskins, Jo Louise	C	1931
Hospers, Julie	A	1970-76
Hott, Jackie	C	1940
Hotz, Carlene	C	1949-50
Hotz, Gretchen	T	1949-50
Hotz, Nancy	A	1949-50
Houck, Doris	C	1941
Houck, Garland	T	1945
Hough, Beth Anne	A	1972-73
Houghton, Judy	C	1954-57
Houghton, Nancy	T	1959-62
Houghton, Stephanie	A	1988-90
House, Elissa Anne	T	1994
Houser, Melissa Kay	C	1972
Houser, Yvonne	T	1940
Houston, Elizabeth	C	1982-87

Houston, Jane	C	1930-31
Houston, Josephine	T	1931
Houston, Leslie	C	1985-86
Houston, Louise	A	1954-58
Houston, Nancy	C	1947-48
Hovorka, Mary	C	1938-40
Hovorka, Sally Lee	C	1940
Howard, Annlee	C	1931
Howard, Claire	T	1994-95
Howard, Diane	A	1956
Howard, Ellie	C	1993-96
Howard, Haley	T	1994-96
Howard, Kathleen	T	1929-30
Howard, Katie	T	1985-87
Howard, Kay	T	1953-54
Howard, Kristi	A	1966-69
Howard, Sarah	T	1992-95
Howard, Sherry	T	1955
Howe, Carol	T	1981-84
Howe, Diane	A	1947-48
Howe, Jean	C	1931
Howe, Lacy	A	1985-91
Howe, Nancy	C	1947-48
Howell, Alice	T	1959-62
Howell, Ann	A	1943
Howell, Barbara	T	1937
Howell, Betsy	A	1972-73
Howell, Carolyn	T	1945
Howell, Catherine	C	1955-56
Howell, Cornelia	A	1943-45
Howell, Eva Mae	T	1940
Howell, Evelyn		1928
Howell, Jennre June		1933
Howell, Katie	T	1973-75
Howell, Leigh	C	1986
Howell, Marie	A	1943-45,47
Howell, Mary Esther	T	1940-41
Howell, Mitten	T	1937,40
Howell, Nancy	C	1974
Howell, Perry	C	1990-91
Howell, Robertha	T	1940-41, 1945-47
Howell, Rosemary	C	1937
Howsley, Marilynne	C	1938-40
Hoyt, Marcia	C	1940
Hubbard, Kristie	C	1970-71
Hubbard, Lisa	T	1963-64
Hubbard, Missie	C	1964
Hubbard, Norma Jean	C	1944
Huck, Laurie	A	1970-74
Huck, Lew	A	1980-86
Huck, Mary	T	1974-80
Huckins, Barbara		1929
Huckins, Mary Lee	A	1947
Huddleston, Caroline	A	1992-94,96
Huddleston, Erika	A	1989-91, 1993-94
Huddleston, Pauline	T	1938-39
Hudgins, Carol Ann	A	1953-59
Hudgins, Mary Claire	C	1929-30
Hudgins, Nan	A	1967-70
Hudnall, Alicia	A	1972-73
Hudson, Amy	T	1992-96

Hudson, Emily	T	1975-76
Hudson, Frasher	T C	1972-77
Hudson, Ione	T	1931
Hudson, Janis	T C	1949
Hudson, Nancy	T	1960
Hudspeth, Claire	A	1948-49
Huff, Ann	A	1962-63
Huff, Jennifer	T	1963
Huff, Katherine	C	1950
Huffman, Laura	A	1976
Huffman, Patricia Tish	T	1950-53
Huge, Charner	T	1973-80
Huge, Vaughan	T	1970-75
Huggins, Jennifer	T	1974-77
Huggins, Judith	A	1953
Huggins, Marilyn	A	1973-76
Huggins, Suzanne	C	1948-49
Hughes, Alice Ann	T	1947
Hughes, Cody	C	1954-55
Hughes, Gwen	A	1955
Hughes, Jennifer	T	1982-84
Hughes, Leslie	T	1969-72
Hughes, Louise		1928
Hughes, Marion	T	1937-38
Hughes, Mary Leslie	A	1951-55
Hughey, Heather	C	1985-91
Hughey, Hillary	T	1988-94
Hughey, Holland	A	1993-96
Hulcy, Mary	C	1936-37
Hull, Betty Jo	C	1945-51
Hull, Carla	C	1957-60
Hull, Joanna	C	1936
Hull, Margaret	C	1931,33-34
Hull, Sondra	A	1945
Hull, Susan	C	1971-76
Hulme, Michelle	T	1994
Hulsey, Mary Elizabeth	A	1983-85
Hulsey, Natalie	C	1991-96
Hulsey, Sarah	T	1988-95
Humble, Elizabeth	T	1941
Humble, Frances	T	1943
Hume, Lynne	T	1971-78
Humphrey, Jane	A	1955
Humphreys, Celia	C	1941
Humphreys, Patricia	T	1941
Humphries, Ann	T	1941-42
Hundling, Carolyn	C	1951-52
Hundling, Suzanne	A	1946-48
Hunke, Merritt	C	1991-94
Hunsicker, Mary Frances	C	1933
Hunsucker, Elizabeth	C	1945
Hunt, Barbara	C	1963-70
Hunt, Betsy	C	1965
Hunt, Caroline	T	1933-37
Hunt, Ellen	A	1963-68
Hunt, Gene Spencer	C	1934-35, 1937-38
Hunt, Geraldine	C	1945
Hunt, Gladys		1928
Hunt, Helen	C	1931
Hunt, Helen	A	1990-96
Hunt, Hillary	T	1971-78
Hunt, Jennifer	C	1982-83

Hunt, Kathryn	C	1982-85
Hunt, Laura	T	1984-91
Hunt, Laura	T	1937-39
Hunt, Leane	T	1934
Hunt, Libby	C	1964-71
Hunt, Lisa	C	1990-96
Hunt, Mary Anna		1926
Hunt, Mary	T	1963-69
Hunt, Meredith	T	1977-83
Hunt, Myra Lou	T	1934
Hunt, Nancy	A	1950-55
Hunt, Natalie	A	1985-91
Hunter, Elizabeth	A	1949-53
Hunter, Floylee	T	1937-38
Hunter, Fredericka	C	1959-62
Hunter, Ida Mae	T	1940-41, 1943-46
Hunter, Mary Beth	T	1937
Hunter, Sue	T	1946-48
Huntsman, Heather	T	1984-85
Huntsman, Lacey	C	1984-85
Hunzicker, Elizabeth	C	1971-73
Hurd, Karen	T	1959
Hurd, Patricia	A	1956-64
Hurd, Sally	T	1954-63
Hurd, Victoria	T	1961-65
Hurley, Lou Anne	C	1944
Hurlock, Kathryn		1928-29
Hurn, Emily	C	1996
Hurn, Helen	A	1993-96
Hurn, Jennifer	C	1990-96
Hurn, Margaret	C	1989-95
Hurst, Grace Anne	C	1960-64
Hurst, Jacqueline	T	1938
Hurst, Marie	A	1962-64
Hurst, Regina	T	1937-40
Husted, Carroll	A	1961-63
Husted, Holly	T	1987
Husted, Lindsey	A	1988-89
Hutchens, Mary Helen	A	1971-74
Hutcherson, Abbi	A	1995-96
Hutchings, Beryl	A	1948-56
Hutchings, Julie Ann	T	1944-50
Hutchings, Sally	T	1955-61
Hutchings, Trudy	T	1955-59
Hutchinson, Ann	A	1944-47
Hutchinson, Julia	T	1931
Hutchison, Catherine	C	1942
Hutchison, Courtney	C	1983-86
Hutchison, Paige	T	1986-89
Huth, Thelma		1926
Hutton, Heather	A	1983-85
Hutton, Lillian	T	1933
Hutton, Lottie	T	1933
Hyde, Brooke	C	1974-81
Hyde, Chepelle	C	1980-84
Hyde, Corey	A	1983-86
Hyde, Jennifer	T	1984-88
Hyde, Lilla	T	1955-56
Hyde, Molly	T	1985
Hyde, Ninya	C	1955
Hyde, Shanda	T	1981-84
Hyden, Pam	T	1960-62

Hyden, Susan	T	1964	Jackson, Vicky	T	1966-67,	Jay, Janice	T	1956-60
Hyer, Eloise	C	1938			1969-72	Jayred, Peggy Sue	C	1945-46
I			Jackson, Willo	C	1929-30	Jeannette, Harriett	T	1966-67
Ickard, Paula Jane	T	1938	Jacobs, Betty Claire	T	1938	Jefferies, Carol Annette	C	1948-54
Iegenfritz, Martha	C	1964	Jacobs, Elizabeth		1929	Jefferies, Carolyn	C	1947-48,50
Igo, Janet	C	1953-55	Jacobs, Florence	C	1933-34	Jeffers, Ann	A	1954-59
Iiams, Mary Elizabeth	A	1950-56	Jacobs, Grace Babs	T	1933-34	Jefferson, Lucy	A	1996
Ikard, Paula Jane	T	1938	Jacobs, Judy	A	1963	Jeffery, Mary Jo	C	1948-49
Ilgenfritz, Martha	C	1960-66	Jacobs, Lynne	C	1959-60	Jeffrey, Jan	A	1973-76
Illig, Elaine	A	1950	Jacobs, Nell		1929	Jeffrey, Kate	A	1980-82,84
Imler, Ruthann	A	1943-44	Jacobson, Elena	C	1987-91	Jeffrey, Meg	C	1981-82
Ingram, Cherie	T	1988	Jacobson, Maurine	T	1940-42	Jehle, Patricia	T	1933-34,38
Ingram, Katie Rob	T	1990	Jacobson, Phyllis	T	1941-43	Jenkins, Betty	T	1935-38
Ingrum, Estelle	C	1930	Jacomini, Joannie	A	1975-79	Jenkins, Janice	T	1937
Irby, Mary Evelyn	T	1937	Jacomini, Kathy	T	1977-80,	Jenkins, Kelly	T	1989-91
Irona, Karen	T	1965-68			1982-84	Jenkins, Sue Ann	T	1952
Irvin, Amanda	T	1988-93	Jafarzzdeh, Surie	T	1991-92	Jenkins, Virginia	C	1937
Irvin, Jennifer	A	1982-88	Jagoe, Anna Catherine	T	1934	Jennette, Harriett	T	1962-65,68
Irvin, Marilyn	C	1949	Jamerson, Dorothy	C	1930	Jennings, Ann	A	1969-74
Irwin, Kathy	T	1954,56-61	James, Dannie Bea	T	1939	Jennings, Barbara	A	1943-44
Isaacks, Lynn	T	1936,43-44	James, Doris	C	1945-46	Jennings, Jacklyn	T	1973
Isaacks, Margo Lee	T	1951	James, Elizabeth Anne	T	1987-94	Jennings, Jane	C	1937
Isbell, Allison	A	1983-84	James, Frances	C	1931	Jennings, Jean	T	1984-87
Ishmael, Carol Jean	C	1947	James, Jackie	T	1941-43	Jennings, Mary Peyton	C	1935-37
Ishmael, Polly Dee	C	1951-55	James, Jeanette	T	1990	Jennings, Meador	C	1935-37
Itz, Elsa	T	1984-91	James, Kathryn	C	1950-51,53	Jennings, Olivia	T	1995-96
Itz, Mary	A	1992-96	James, Laura M.	A	1943-44	Jennison, Catherine	A	1993-96
Itz, Sarah	T	1987-94	James, Lisa	C	1971-73	Jennison, Lindy	T	1990-95
Ivory, Mary	A	1974-77	James, Mary	T	1931	Jensen, Elizabeth	C	1963
Ivory, Sally	T	1976-77	James, Molly	C	1979-82	Jenswold, Carrie	T	1979-82
Ivy, Caro	C	1940	James, Nancy	C	1969-71	Jernigan, Betty Ann	C	1946-47
			James, Renna	A	1943-44	Jernigan, Jan	A	1956-59
J			James, Susan	C	1949-50	Jernigan, Jane	T	1951-53
Jackson, Alexandra	A	1994-96	Jamison, Emily	A	1993-94	Jersig, Shelby	C	1945-46
Jackson, Ann	T	1980-83	Janes, Judy	A	1960	Jeter, Emily Catherine	A	1995-96
Jackson, Ann	T	1942	Janes, Judy	A	1960	Jewell, Brenda	C	1980-83
Jackson, Arden	A	1984-90	Janse, Susan	C	1940-41	Jewell, Diana	T	1982-83
Jackson, Ashley	C	1978-79	Janssen, Betty Jean	T	1942-44	Jinkins, Ann	T	1958-60
Jackson, Betty Jean	T	1940	Janus, Julianne	A	1995-96	Jirou, Kay	C	1936
Jackson, Debbie	A	1967-74	Japhet, Ann	C	1939-41	Jobe, Marguerite		1928
Jackson, Diane	A	1949-51	Japhet, Gretchen	A	1970-73	Jochem, Eva Lee	C	1942-43
Jackson, Diane	A	1944-45	Japhet, Jane	C	1933-34	Jockusch, Mary	T	1965-66
Jackson, Diane	T	1959-62	Japhet, Larkin	C	1972-75	Johndroe, Pam	A	1977-80
Jackson, Eloise	A	1964	Japhet, Martha Ann	C	1939-40	Johns, Anna	C	1965-68
Jackson, Florine Mary	C	1929-30	Japhet, Susan	A	1973-80	Johns, Lori	T	1982-85
Jackson, Geraldine	A	1945-49	Jardine, Whitney	A	1993-96	Johns, Susan	C	1958-60
Jackson, Hilary	C	1979	Jarrell, Ann	A	1977	Johnson, Allison	T	1991-96
Jackson, Janet	A	1964-67	Jarrell, Ann	T	1951-52	Johnson, Amanda		1929
Jackson, Janis	T	1950	Jarrell, Carolyn	C	1970-72	Johnson, Andee	A	1978-81
Jackson, Jo Anne	T	1944	Jarrell, Edith	T	1940	Johnson, Andrea	C	1995-96
Jackson, Judy	T	1952-57	Jarrell, Kathryn	C	1981-82	Johnson, Ann	A	1971-78
Jackson, Julie	A	1977-81	Jarrett, Cora Jane	A	1946	Johnson, Ann	C	1967-71
Jackson, Kate	A	1987-92	Jarrett, Lourene	C	1954-57	Johnson, Beth	C	1959
Jackson, Kathryn	T	1934,39-40	Jarvis, Ann	T	1945-48	Johnson, Betsy	A	1952-57
Jackson, Linda	T	1961-63	Jarvis, Sarah	C	1939-40	Johnson, Betty	A	1962-63
Jackson, Lindsey	T	1979	Jarvis, Sue	A	1947-52	Johnson, Brittany	C	1989-94
Jackson, Lucy	A	1949	Jaseffy, Ann	C	1957	Johnson, Burdine	C	1950,53
Jackson, Marjem	C	1951-54	Jasper, Winnie	C	1931	Johnson, Carrie	A	1995-96
Jackson, Mary Jane	T	1937-39	Jastram, Cynthia Ann	A	1951	Johnson, Cindy	T	1964-69
Jackson, Sallie Bell	T	1953-54	Jastram, Sylvia	C	1954	Johnson, Courtney	C	1977
Jackson, Sara Lou	C	1944-45	Jaworski, Claire	T	1945	Johnson, Cynthia	A	1952-53
Jackson, Suzy	A	1983-87	Jaworski, Joanie	T	1945,47	Johnson, Cynthia E.	T	1962-68
Jackson, Tomme Nell	C	1934-35	Jay, Gena	A	1956-59	Johnson, Cynthia W.	A	1965-72

Johnson, Debbie	A	1960-67	Johnson, Susan	A	1989	Jones, Jean	C	1940-44
Johnson, DeMar	A	1965-72	Johnson, Vivienne	T	1935-36	Jones, Jeanne	T	1940
Johnson, Diane	A	1962-63	Johnston, Barbara	C	1957-62	Jones, Jennifer	C	1979-84
Johnson, Doris		1928	Johnston, Beth	T	1963-69	Jones, Jerry	T	1953
Johnson, Dorothy Jean	T	1933	Johnston, Carol	A	1954-56	Jones, Joanne	C	1942,45-46
Johnson, Elaine	T	1940-41	Johnston, Claudine	T	1929-30	Jones, Joyce	T	1942-46
Johnson, Elizabeth Ann	T	1936	Johnston, Decie	C	1964-69	Jones, Judy	C	1961-65
Johnson, Elizabeth	C	1981-88	Johnston, Diane	C	1949	Jones, Katherine	A	1959-60
Johnson, Erin	C	1990-93	Johnston, Doll	C	1976-77,79	Jones, Katie	T	1994-96
Johnson, Ernestine		1928	Johnston, Dorothy	T	1933	Jones, Kim	A	1970-75
Johnson, Gail	A	1965-69	Johnston, Elaine	C	1962-67	Jones, Laura	T	1989-93,96
Johnson, Genie	A	1955	Johnston, Frances	T	1930	Jones, Leslie	T	1996
Johnson, Geraldine	A	1949-58	Johnston, Helen	C	1937	Jones, Louella		1928-29
Johnson, Irma	T	1930	Johnston, Jackie	C	1933	Jones, Lucile	A	1954-55
Johnson, Jane	C	1944-46	Johnston, Jan	C	1951	Jones, Marilu Frances	C	1935
Johnson, Janet	T	1941	Johnston, Janet	A	1962-67	Jones, Mary Landon	C	1996
Johnson, Janet	T	1959,61	Johnston, Jeanette	T	1941	Jones, Mary Owen	T	1944-48
Johnson, Jean	T	1948-49	Johnston, Jenny	A	1970-71	Jones, Mary Helen	C	1933-35
Johnson, Jean Louise	C	1959	Johnston, Jerry	T	1948	Jones, Mary Louise	C	1937-38
Johnson, Jean	T	1945	Johnston, Jo Libby	C	1951	Jones, McKinley	A	1987-94
Johnson, Jeanette	C	1931,33-35	Johnston, Jodi	A	1985,87	Jones, Nancy	A	1945
Johnson, Jeanne	C	1934-35	Johnston, Kathy	C	1978-81	Jones, Pamela	C	1956
Johnson, Jeanne	C	1957	Johnston, Kathy	C	1958-63	Jones, Rubye Fay		1929
Johnson, Jessie Lem	T	1957-61	Johnston, Lois	C	1964-70	Jones, Ruth	C	1933 -35
Johnson, Jill	T	1945,47-53	Johnston, Lucretia	C	1937	Jones, Shelley	C	1952-55
Johnson, Jo Addah	C	1957-59	Johnston, Marian Lea	T	1941	Jones, Terry	T	1930
Johnson, Joan	A	1945-47,49	Johnston, Mary Frances	T	1937	Jones, Tracey	T	1980-86
Johnson, Judy	T	1956-60	Johnston, Mary Martha	C	1975,77-80	Jones, Virginia Gigee	A	1943-44
Johnson, Julianne	C	1938-39	Johnston, Mimi	C	1949	Jordan, Barbara Jean	C	1947
Johnson, Julie	A	1961-65	Johnston, Ruth	C	1931-34	Jordan, Beverly	C	1945
Johnson, Julie	C	1990-93	Johnston, Susan	T	1955-58	Jordan, Beverly Mae	C	1934-35
Johnson, Karen Sue	T	1961-68	Johnstone, Jennifer	A	1990-93	Jordan, Hallye	A	1970-75
Johnson, Katherine	A	1988	Jolley, Sandra	C	1950,52-54	Jordan, Jeanne	A	1959-61
Johnson, Katherine	C	1930	Jolley, Toinette	A	1976-80	Jordan, Jennifer	C	1986-93
Johnson, Katie	C	1995-96	Jones, Alice	T	1929,31,33	Jordan, Joyce	T	1930
Johnson, Kylie	C	1994-95	Jones, Alice Jeanne	T	1933,37	Jordan, Julie	C	1946-47,
Johnson, Lacy	C	1992-93	Jones, Ashley	A	1987-94			1949-50
Johnson, Laura Jean	C	1926,31	Jones, Barbara	T	1992-94	Jordan, June	C	1935-36
Johnson, Louise	T	1931	Jones, Betty Sue	T	1940-42	Jordan, Laura	A	1974-75
Johnson, Lucy	A	1950-52	Jones, Betty Jean	A	1944-46	Jordan, Marion Jo	T	1937-39
Johnson, Margaret	C	1931,34	Jones, Candy	T	1956-60	Jordan, Nancy Belle	T	1948
Johnson, Margaret	C	1950-54	Jones, Carla	A	1966-67	Jordon, Marian	T	1939
Johnson, Margie	T	1944-45	Jones, Casteel	C	1994-96	Joseffy, Ann Copeland	C	1957
Johnson, Marjorie Ruth	T	1944	Jones, Christina	T	1991-94	Joseph, Diana	C	1942
Johnson, Martha	C	1956	Jones, Clair	C	1986-92	Joseph, Irene	T	1932-34
Johnson, Mary	T	1931-34	Jones, Dean	C	1950-52	Josey, June	T	1943
Johnson, Mary	A	1969	Jones, Edith	C	1937-38,40	Journeay, Anne	T	1937
Johnson, Maydee	C	1945-47	Jones, Edna Marie	T	1939-41,43	Jowell, Jerelyn	C	1945-47
Johnson, Meredith	C	1994-95	Jones, Elizabeth Ann	T	1940-41,	Joyce, June	C	1936
Johnson, Meredith	T	1964-71			1943-44	Joyce, Michelle	T	1979-83
Johnson, Mollye Catherine	C	1931-35	Jones, Ethel	C	1938	Joyner, Elizabeth	A	1962-65
Johnson, Mollye Bea	A	1951-53	Jones, Florence	T	1960	Joyner, Evelyn	C	1930
Johnson, Myra	C	1946-47	Jones, Frances Gale	C	1935	Joyner, Heidi	A	1982-87
Johnson, Nancy	C	1966	Jones, Frances		1929	Judice, Angelle	A	1991-96
Johnson, Nancy Beth	A	1949-53	Jones, Frances	A	1966	Judice, Natalie	C	1995-96
Johnson, Nita	A	1946-49	Jones, Georgie Lee	C	1936-38,40	Judice, Nicole	T	1995-96
Johnson, Patricia	C	1945-46	Jones, Gladys		1929	Judkins, Jean	A	1944
Johnson, Rainey	C	1990-95	Jones, Gusta Mae	A	1951	Judkins, Joyce	A	1944
Johnson, Rosemary	C	1944-45	Jones, Ilene	C	1979	Judkins, Reba	C	1930
Johnson, Sarah	A	1985-91	Jones, Ivanette	C	1950-54	Juett, Katherine	T	1993-94
Johnson, Shannon	T	1985-92	Jones, Jacklyn Marie	C	1948-49	Jung, Carroll	T	1961-64
Johnson, Staci	T	1985-87,	Jones, Janet	T	1954-56	Junod, Betty	T	1963-66
		1989-90,92	Jones, Janet	T	1946-48	Junod, Rena	C	1961-65

Name	Code	Years
Justice, Ann		1941-42
Justice, Jean	T	1938,40
Justice, Norma Lu	C	1940
Juul, Nancy	C	1943-45

K

Name	Code	Years
Kadish, Laura	C	1992
Kaffie, Lauren	T	1990-94
Kahl, Gay	A	1960-63
Kahl, Jan	C	1960-61
Kahn, Adah Charline	T	1933
Kahn, Barbara Ellen	T	1939-41
Kahn, Betty	T	1937-38
Kahn, Eddy	A	1950
Kahn, Hailey	C	1988-94
Kahn, Marion	T	1963-67
Kahn, Susan Jane	A	1954
Kaiser, Brooke	A	1981-88
Kaiser, Shannon	C	1983-90
Kalhurst, Helen	C	1929-30
Kalmbach, Mary Ellen	T	1978-82
Kameron, Erin	C	1936
Kampman, Carolyn		1928
Kangas, Kristi	T	1991-92
Karcher, Ann	C	1954-56
Karger, Kara Sue	C	1966-69
Karger, Kathy	A	1960-66
Karger, Sherry	C	1961-67
Karlsson, Makenzie	C	1996
Kassahn, Mary	A	1991-92
Katz, Norma	T	1934
Kaufman, Gerry	T	1938
Kay, Allison	A	1972-75
Kay, Betsy	T	1951-53
Kay, Sally Ann	C	1948-51
Kaylor, Connie	A	1968
Kayton, Carol	T	1945,48
Keahey, Hilary	T	1979-85
Keahey, Holly	T	1974-80
Keating, Jane Ann	A	1958-59
Keating, Patsy	A	1943-45
Kee, Dorry	A	1963-68
Keehn, Virginia Ann	T	1952-57
Keene, Mandy	T	1996
Keeney, Elise	T	1959-64
Keeney, Leigh	T	1963-65
Keeney, Mary	T	1962-67
Keepers, Josephine	T	1930
Keepers, Mary Margeret	T	1930,34
Keesee, Martha	C	1930
Keith, Betty	C	1965-69
Keith, Frana	T	1981-88
Keith, Katherine	C	1995-96
Keith, Kimberly	T	1994-96
Keith, Liza	C	1968-74
Keith, Lorena	T	1944
Keith, Marilyn	T	1945-46
Keith, Martha Jane	T	1934
Keith, Megan	A	1996
Keith, Stephanie	T	1995-96
Keitt, Beth	T	1966-71
Keitt, Melanie	T	1979-83
Keitt, Susan	C	1974-78
Keller, Courtney	C	1992-93
Keller, Cynthia	A	1959-61
Keller, Elisabeth	C	1967-70
Keller, Katherine	C	1939
Keller, Katherine Anne	A	1984
Keller, Linda	T	1957-58
Keller, Mary Tom	C	1961-62
Keller, Patty	T	1962-67
Keller, Ramona	T	1934
Keller, Wynona	C	1933-37
Kelley, Colleen	C	1980
Kelley, Fifi	T	1932,34
Kelley, Frank A.	T	1937-38
Kelley, Lucille	C	1940
Kelley, Missie J.C.		1937
Kelley, Nancy	C	1941-43
Kellog, Sara Katherine	T	1938
Kellogg, Abbie	T	1977-84
Kellogg, Ann	C	1991-94
Kellogg, Anne	C	1967-74
Kellogg, Judy	A	1950-53
Kellogg, Lea	A	1966-73
Kellogg, Prudy	A	1953-54
Kellogg, Rhoda	T	1941
Kellogg, Sara Katherine	T	1938
Kelly, Allyne	T	1940-42
Kelly, Ann	T	1974-76
Kelly, Anne	T	1931
Kelly, Colleen	C	1976-79
Kelly, Dorothy	C	1938
Kelly, Elizabeth	T	1931
Kelly, Frances	C	1938
Kelly, Frank	T	1937-38
	T	1950
Kelly, Janice Jo	T	1973
Kelly, Joan	A	1950
Kelly, Judith Ann	T	1930
Kelly, Julia Ann	T	1976-80
Kelly, Kendall	C	1975-80
Kelly, Kirby		1929
Kelly, Mary Anne	T	1957
Kelly, Nancy Brook	A	1954-55
Kelly, Nancy	T	1956
Kelly, Pamela	C	1935-38
Kelso, Jane	C	1935,37-38
Kelso, Jerry	C	1937
Keltner, Sara Lee	T	1951-55
Kelton, Betsy Jane	C	1949-51
Kemble, Carolyn	A	1968-72
Kemp, Camille	C	1970-73
Kemp, Carla	C	1967-70
Kemp, Diane	A	1958-59
Kendall, Frances	C	1960-63
Kenderdine, Claire	A	1950
Kendrich, Edith Kay	C	1985-91
Kendrick, Shannon	A	1993-95
Kendrigan, Annemarie	T	1930
Kenedy, Louise		1929
Kenley, Carol Elizabeth	C	1935,38
Kenley, Marie	A	1950-51
Kennard, Karol	A	1945-48
Kennard, Kay	C	1955
Kennedy, Betty Ann	T	1942-45
Kennedy, Donna		
Kennedy, Elizabeth Ann	C	1942-43
Kennedy, Erin	T	1985
Kennedy, India	T	1983-90
Kennedy, Leigh	C	1990-94
Kennedy, Lin	C	1942
Kennedy, Locke	C	1942
Kennedy, Martha		1942
Kennedy, Neima	C	1971-75
Kennedy, Priscilla	C	1993-95
Kennedy, Sally	T	1942
Kennemer, Nan Ann	C	1933-34
Kennerly, Ann	A	1943-45
Kennerly, Mary Marcia	T	1943-45,47
Kenney, Elise	T	1961
Kenney, Valerie	T	1988-94
Kent, Jane	T	1943
Kent Virginia	T	1933-35
Kepler, Taylor	T	1985-92
Kerby, Patricia	A	1949-52
Kerr, Allison	T	1967-71
Kerr, Alysia	C	1983-87
Kerr, Carolyn	T	1950-55
Kerr, Daphne	A	1949
Kerr, Kallie	T	1987-94
Kerr, Krista	A	1991-96
Kerr, Kyra	A	1949-50
Kerr, Lizabeth	T	1956-61
Kerr, Marie	C	1957
Kerr, Mary Ann	A	1953-56
Kerr, Norie	C	1957
Kerr-Perkinson, Eden	A	1990-96
Kerr-Perkinson, India	T	1985-91
Kerr, Randa	C	1941-42, 1948-49
Kerr, Shirley	T	1940-43
Kertzer, Adriana	C	1988-95
Kertzer, Victoria	T	1994-96
Kessler, Virginia	C	1930
Ketchum, Harriet Ruth	C	1947-51
Ketchum, Kate	T	1982-83
Key, Caroline	A	1991-96
Key, Jane	A	1947
Keyes, Mary	A	1984-87
Kidd, Catherine	A	1988-91
Kidd, Donna	T	1971-76
Kidd, Kelly	T	1967-73
Kidd, Margaret	A	1965-70
Kiehne, Brooke	C	1989-96
Kiehne, Holly	T	1991-96
Kiehne, Klaire	T	1991-96
Kiehne, Mendy	C	1989-96
Kiel, Martha Gene	T	1941-44
Kies, Carol Anne	C	1940-43
Kight, Jan	T	1947
Kihle, Kathryn	T	1983-89
Kihle, Kirsten	T	1981-87
Kiker, Helen	T	1934
Kiker, Sue	A	1975-78
Kilburn, Carolyn	T	1943,45-49
Kilburn, Mynan	T	1940-41,43
Kiley, Jane		1926
Killen, Kandee	T	1959
Killgore, Carole	C	1953-59

Kilpatrick, Elise	C	1965-66
Kilpatrick, Jane	T	1941
Kilpatrick, Kerry	C	1975
Kilpatrick, Laura	A	1977-82
Kilpatrick, Robin	C	1975-82
Kimbro, Penny	A	1954-57
Kimbrough, Peggy	C	1937-40
Kimsey, Kristen	C	1986-91,93
Kincade, Imogene	C	1934
Kincade, Kimberly	A	1991
Kincaid, Bennie Lee	A	1947
Kincaid, Jewel Frances	C	1943-44
King, Carol	T	1957
King, Caroline	A	1968-71
King, Caroline	C	1986-89
King, Carolyn	C	1947
King, Cheryl	C	1952-56
King, Christine	C	1958-64
King, Dorothy Jean	C	1941,43-46
King, Dorothy Faye	C	1934-35
King, Floy		1933
King, Frances	C	1949-52
King, Frank		1929
King, Jean	T	1939-40
King, Jill	T	1945-47
King, Katherine	T	1934,37-38
King, Kay	T	1950-51
King, Margaret	A	1984-91
King, Mary	C	1941-43
King, Natalie	C	1937
King, Patsy		1938
King, Ruth	T	1939-41
King, Thelma	C	1942
King, Virginia Ann	T	1940-41
Kingsberry, Marian	T	1937
Kinnan, Gretchen	A	1960-62
Kinsel, Cathy	A	1959-65
Kinsel, Maxine	C	1935
Kinzbach, Teddy	T	1930
Kinzie, Lauren	T	1970-73
Kirby, Carolyn	C	1949
Kirby, Dorothy	C	1936
Kirby, Nelwyn	C	1938-39
Kirby, Ruth Thompson	C	1930
Kirk, Diana	C	1942
Kirk, Gray	T	1930
Kirk, Mildred	T	1931
Kirkham, Doris		1929
Kirkley, Ella V.		1926
Kirkpatrick, Joan	A	1943
Kirkpatrick, Margaret A.	C	1935
Kirksey, Barbara	A	1943
Kirksey, Carolyn	A	1944-46
Kirksey, Kathryn	A	1949-53
Kirvin, Mary Ellen	T	1930-34
Kitchell, Frances	C	1931
Kite, Shirley	T	1942-43, 1946-51
Kittrell, Betty	C	1939-4143
Kittrell, Patsy	C	1938-39
Kizer, Becky	C	1981-84
Kizer, Marion	C	1948-49
Klein, Kim	C	1974-77

Klein, Marguerite		1929
Klein, Wilma		1929
Kliewer, Nancy	A	1958
Klugh, Nancy	C	1942,45-46
Klugh, Susan	T	1946-47
Knapp, Lynda	T	1951-54
Knapp, Margaret Jean	C	1949
Knapp, Marsletta	C	1979
Knickerbocker, Jean	T	1936
Knickerbocker, Nancy	A	1945
Knight, Ann	A	1947
Knight, Bonnie Marie	C	1934-35
Knight, Dorothy Jean	T	1940-41
Knight, Emilie		1952
Knight, Fayrene	T	1932
Knight, Francille	C	1944-45
Knight, Helene	C	1930-32
Knight, Jean	T	1944-46
Knight, Joan	T	1947-50
Knight, Laurie	C	1973-77
Knight, Lynda	T	1952
Knight, Martha Lake	T	1939
Knight, Nadyne	T	1931-33,35
Knight, Taylor	T	1995
Knighton, Ruth	C	1941
Knolle, Karin	C	1974-80
Knolle, Katherine	C	1978-84
Knolle, Marjorie	C	1935
Knolle, Martha	A	1981-88
Knouse, Susanna	T	1995-96
Knowlton, Angela	C	1980-83
Knox, Camilla	A	1952-55
Knox, Kaye	C	1978-84
Knox, Lyndee	T	1972-75
Koch, Betty	T	1953-58
Koch, Gloria	A	1967-71
Koch, Virginia	T	1953-56
Koehler, Frances		1929
Koehler, Helen	A	1943-48
Koehler, Lauren	C	1996
Koehring, Norma	A	1944
Koelsch, Frances	A	1981
Koen, Betty	T	1937-41
Koen, Carolyn	C	1942
Koerner, Francesca	A	1966-67
Koger, Nelda	T	1935
Kokernot, Gay	C	1954-55
Kokernot, Joy	C	1954-55
Kokernot, Mary Ann	C	1935
Kokernot, Sarah	A	1992-94
Kollhoff, Becky	C	1988-95
Kollhoff, Jennifer	T	1986-92
Kolstad, Evelyn		1926
Kolter, Karol	T	1950-54
Kooken, Julia	T	1950
Koonce, Caroline	C	1928,30
Kopp, Devin	A	1996
Kothmann, Kayla	T	1967-68
Kouns, Lauren	T	1971-75
Kouns, Leigh	T	1967-71
Kouns, Merrill	T	1979-82
Kralj, Nicole	T	1988-89
Kramer, Adriane	T	1981-84

Kramer, Becky	A	1968-69
Kramer, Sally	T	1946
Kramer, Theo A. Teetie	T	1941-42
Kraus, Ann	C	1985-88
Kraus, Leah	C	1986-88
Krause, Della Bel	T	1941
Krause, Susan	T	1962
Krausse, Carolyn	A	1963-67
Krausse, Susan	T	1961-64,66
Kreager, Elizabeth	C	1993-96
Kreager, Gretchen	T	1972-77
Kreager, Heather	C	1968-74
Kreager, Lilly	A	1993-96
Kreager, Paige	A	1975-81
Krenz, Jamie	A	1993-95
Krister, Gail	T	1958-60
Krister, Moylan	C	1959-60
Kritser, Ann	A	1964-69
Kritser, Gentry	C	1982-86
Kroeger, Beret	T	1992
Kroeger, Beryl		1928
Kroeger, Jane	C	1950-53
Krohn, Ann	A	1948-50
Krohn, Carolin	A	1949-51
Krook, Betsy	T	1947-49
Kropp, Marion		1926
Krouse, Alicia	C	1977
Krueger, Carol Ann	C	1937-42
Krueger, Carolyn	C	1959-63
Krueger, Eleanor		1928
Krupp, Carlyn	T	1932
Krupp, Elinor	T	1932
Kruse, Elaine	T	1940-41
Kubecka, Kay	A	1958-59
Kubecka, Martha Ann	C	1960-61
Kucera, Kathy	A	1952-54
Kuhlman, Amanda	A	1986-93
Kuhn, Nell	T	1930
Kumpuris, Kate	A	1986-90
Kumpuris, Katherine	C	1964-67
Kumpuris, Victoria	T	1986-90
Kunc, Bobbie	T	1945
Kuntz, Betty	T	1934
Kuntz, Dolly	T	1934
Kuper, Karen	A	1957-60
Kuper, Kitty	A	1959-62
Kurth, Emily	C	1945-46
Kurth, Florrie	C	1931
Kurth, Judy	T	1960-64
Kuykendall, Holly	T	1966-69
Kuykendall, Jo Ann	A	1943
Kuykendall, Martha	C	1939
Kyle, Emilie	T	1944
Kyle, Lucia	A	1949
Kyle, Margaret	T	1944

L

La Cour, Henrietta	T	1936
La Due, Suzy	A	1967-69
La Font, Gail	A	1955
La Force, Nancy	C	1939-40
La Force, Suzanne	C	1939-40
La Force, Laurie	T	1968-74

La Force, Cliffy	A	1970-76
La Fortune, Kay	A	1963-65
La Fortune, Linda	A	1963
La Fortune, Jeanne	T	1936-37
La Fortune, Mary Ann	T	1936-37
La Fortune, Suzanne	C	1962-66
La Fortune, Shelly	T	1963
La Roe, Joie	A	1961
La Roe, Mary Lois	A	1958-60
La Rue, Martha	C	1952-58
La Rue, Nancy	C	1954-59
La Rue, Ruthie	C	1933-34,36
La Rue, Betty	C	1934
La Rue, Terry	T	1952-55
La Vigne, Mary	C	1970-76
La Vigne, Lila	A	1974-81
Labbe, Marie Elise	T	1948
Label, Sara Betty	C	1930
Lacey, Margaret	C	1937
Lacy, Ann		1933-34
Lacy, Ann	A	1963,65
Lacy, Elizabeth	C	1959-62
Lacy, Florence	C	1956-58,60
Lacy, Golda	A	1969-72
Lacy, Kathryn	C	1934
Lacy, Kristin	T	1982-85
Lacy, Martha	T	1956-59
Lacy, Patsy	C	1934
Ladner, Loreliu Larry	C	1940-44
Lafland, Macbeth	C	1942
Lair, Gaylen	A	1948
Lair, Jacque Elaine	C	1948
Laira, Lois	C	1937
Laird, Evelyn	T	1937
Laird, Kathleen	C	1938-40
Laird, Lois	C	1935,39-40
Lalla, Leslie	C	1958,60-66
Lamb, Cornelia	C	1941-44
Lamb, Dolly	T	1951-53
Lamb, Elizabeth	C	1939
Lamb, Jessie Lee	T	1959-60
Lamb, Nancy	A	1952-55
Lambert, Elizabeth	A	1985-87, 1991-96
Lambert, Jean	T	1965-71
Lambert, Sarah	T	1991-94
Lambert, Susan	C	1986,88-90
Lambert, Susan	C	1961-65
Lamberth, Lauren	A	1988-90
Lamkin, Marguerite	T	1940-41,44
Lamm, Sacha	C	1987-90
Lammers, June	C	1946-47
Lampkin, Julee	C	1961-64
Land, Gracie	C	1969-70
Lander, Clare	T	1953-57
Lander, Joan	A	1944-49
Landers, Hilda	T	1942
Landers, Libby	T	1980-81
Landers, Susan	T	1975
Landess, Amy	C	1976-80
Landford, Carlee	A	1953
Landon, Mary Jean	T	1944
Landon, Sandra	T	1947,49-50

Landram, Elsie	T	1942
Landreaux, Christie	C	1986-87
Landreth, Anjie	A	1986-90
Landreth, Jane	T	1954-56
Landreth, Lynda	C	1951-54
Landreth, Sandra	T	1962-71
Landreth, Sherry	C	1964-68
Landreth, Susan	T	1962-66
Landry, Claire	A	1953-59
Lane, Charline	C	1928-31
Lane, Charlotte	C	1928-31
Lane, Dianne	A	1969-70
Lane, Ginger	T	1948
Lane, Katherine	A	1996
Lane, Kelley	T	1973-78
Lane, Marian	T	1955
Lane, Megan	A	1986-90
Lane, Peggy	T	1966-70
Lane, Stacey	C	1975-79
Lane, Tenney	C	1991-92
Lanford, Mary Alden	C	1995-96
Lang, Jean	C	1936
Langdon, Jane	C	1953-58
Lange, Katherine	C	1935
Lange, Mary Ann	T	1944
Langen, Jane	C	1957
Langford, Carlee	A	1954
Langford, Leah	C	1941-42
Langford, Lou Anne	C	1947-51
Langford, Sue	T	1943-48
Langford, Sylvia Ann	C	1949-53
Langlas, Catherine	C	1995-96
Langley, Evan	T	1987-90
Langley, Lindsey	C	1984-88
Lanier, Rachel	C	1983-88
Lansdale, Sally	C	1934
Lansden, Mary	A	1968,70-71
Lanyon, Lisa	A	1960-61, 1963-67
Lanyon, Sally	C	1956,58-60
Lapeyre, Cici	A	1974
Larcade, Gloria	T	1936
Larimore, Susan	C	1977-83
Larson, Sumarie	T	1942
Lary, Mary		1929
Lasater, Ann	T	1958-60
Lasater, Carolyn	C	1977-83
Lasater, Lauren	T	1973-79
Lasater, Lera	T	1975-81
Lasater, Lynne	A	1955-58
Laskey, Ann Marie	T	1942-44
Laster, Carolyn	C	1935-38,41
Latham, Anna	C	1975
Latham, Kathy	A	1958-59
Latham, Laura	T	1971-75
Lathram, Mary Pharr	T	1941-42
Lathrop, Sharon	T	1960-63
Latimer, Christine	C	1930
Latimer, Price	A	1987-92
Latimer, Sarah	A	1995-96
Latta, Laura	T	1979-85
Lattimore, Meghan	A	1988-91
Lattimore, Seaneen	T	1988-89

Laufman, Kathryn	T	1937
Laughbaum, Patricia	A	1944-45
Laughlin, Cary	T	1967
Laughlin, Helen Jane	T	1938-39
Laughlin, Lisa	T	1962-65
Laughlin, Nancy	C	1964-66
Laughlin, Phyllis	T	1945
Laughlin, Robin	A	1965-67
Laughlin, Susy	A	1963-66
Laughlin, Suzanne	A	1947,49
Laughlin, Yvonne		1929
Lautenschlaeger, Addie	C	1972-80
Lavender, Cynthia	T	1946-50
Lavender, Margaret Anne	A	1949,52-53
Lavin, Sally	A	1962
Lavin, Vicki	A	1962
Law, K. C.	T	1964
Law, Kathryn	T	1963
Law, Virginia Gray	C	1935
Lawhon, Anne	A	1947
Lawhon, Christine	T	1986-90
Lawhon, Jane	C	1944-45
Lawhon, Laura	T	1987-93
Lawhon, Leslie	C	1982-88
Lawhon, Mary	A	1949
Lawhon, Virginia	C	1948-49
Lawliss, Carrie Frances	A	1945-48
Lawrence, Amy	C	1969-74
Lawrence, Ann	T	1969-75
Lawrence, Anne	A	1991-92
Lawrence, Anne	A	1985-90
Lawrence, Dana	C	1981-88
Lawrence, Elizabeth	C	1975
Lawrence, Elizabeth	A	1993-96
Lawrence, Frances	C	1967-71
Lawrence, Helene	A	1957-59
Lawrence, Kay	C	1950
Lawrence, Libby	C	1976-81
Lawrence, Linda	A	1953
Lawrence, Nikki	C	1994-96
Lawrence, Patricia	A	1982-83
Lawrence, Patsy	A	1948-49, 1951-52
Lawrence, Stephanie	T	1995-96
Lawson, Caroline	C	1994-96
Lawson, Jane	A	1943
Lawyer, Brooke	A	1988-92
Lawyer, Marjorie	T	1941-43
Laycock, Barbara Nell	T	1939-40,43
Layden, Mary Ann	T	1967-72
Lazarz, Ginger	C	1979-84
Le Barre, Jessica	C	1996
Le Bees, Mary Nell	C	1940
Le Blanc, Jane	A	1979-85
Le Bus, Jacquelyn	C	1945-46
Le Bus, Jo Ann	C	1940,43
Le Flore, Mary	A	1943
Le Mond, Evelyn		1928
Le Sage, Susie	A	1964-66
Le Sage, Sherry	A	1963-65
Lea, Kathryn	T	1993-96
Lea, Kristen	T	1968-74
Lea, Mary Ida Sherrill	C	1940-42,45

Name		Years
Lea, Melissa	C	1989-94
Leach, Jane	T	1942-43
Leach, Mary Laura	A	1944-47
Leach, Patsy	A	1945
Leachman, Elizabeth	T	1936,38
Leak, Virginia Ann	C	1940-41
Lear, Ann	A	1945
Learning, Marilyn	T	1959
Leath, Francis		1929
Leavith, Anne Christine	A	1964
Leavitt, Chris	A	1965-66
Lebow, Melissa	A	1989
Ledbetter, Barbara Ann	C	1937-38
Ledbetter, Joyce	C	1940
Ledbetter, Mary Ann	C	1941
Ledford, Angela	T	1946-47
Ledford, Phyllis	C	1938
Ledoux, Karen	T	1971-74
Ledoux, Kathy	C	1971-72
Lee, Amy	A	1994-96
Lee, Anita	C	1940
Lee, Carolyn	A	1948
Lee, Carrie	C	1986
Lee, Casey	C	1983-84
Lee, Courtney	T	1988
Lee, Donna	C	1947-48
Lee, Elizabeth	C	1930-31
Lee, Janet	T	1969-72
Lee, Jerilyn	T	1962-64
Lee, Kathryn		1928
Lee, Mary Lucy	C	1936-39
Lee, Mary Nell	T	1945
Lee, Mary	T	1989
Lee, Sally	T	1950-51
Lee, Terry	C	1963-67
Leedy, Clara	T	1939,41
Leftwich, Maryann	A	1976-82
Leftwich, Maurine	C	1941
Leftwich, Rose Marion	C	1947-51
Legarde, Anita	T	1930
Lege, Shirley	T	1929, 31
Leggett, Nancy	A	1948-49
Leggia, Joy Ellen	C	1947
Lehman, Mary Ann	A	1950-51
Lehmann, Melissa	T	1985-88, 1990-91
Lehmberg, Michelle	T	1990-91
Lehrack, Norma Jean	C	1934
Lehrer, Dorothy Jane	T	1930-33
Leibowitz, Jessica	A	1995
Lemak, Lacey	A	1992
Lemert, Tiffany	C	1979-84
Lennon, Mary Anita	T	1941
Lents, Ann	A	1958-64
Lents, Caroline	T	1992-96
Lents, Sarah	C	1990-96
Lentz, Lois	T	1931
Lentz, Margaret	T	1931
Leon, Madge	C	1935-36
Leonard, Elizabeth	T	1970,72-73
Leonard, Elizabeth	C	1966-69
Leonard, Ellen	T	1964-65
Leonard, Emily	C	1965-69
Leonard, Laura	T	1975-76
Leonard, Liz	T	1971,74-75
Leonard, Lou	T	1944-46
Leonard, Louise	A	1965-67, 1969-70
Leonard, Madelon	A	1956
Leonard, Mary Dean	C	1967-71
Leonard, Tubby	C	1936
Leopold, Jean	T	1937-38
Lesh, Jane	T	1935
Lesh, Phyllis	C	1935
Leshin, Leigh	A	1991-95
Lesikar, Leslie	A	1992-96
Lesley, Norma	T	1944
Lester, Gloria	T	1933-37
Lester, Margaret	C	1969-70, 1972-73
Lett, Donna	C	1951-57
Lett, Sandra Winkie	T	1950-52, 1954-55
Leuthold, Linda	T	1977-78
Leutwyler, Cara Lee	A	1943-45
Levering, Janice	T	1980-85
Levering, LeAnn	T	1982-89
Levert, Lee	A	1974
Leverton, Jane	C	1935
Levi, Judith	T	1944
Levine, Doris	C	1938-39
Levine, Rose Marion	T	1938-39
Levy, Mathilde	C	1937
Lewis, Ann	T	1949
Lewis, Bessie	T	1930
Lewis, Cannon	C	1992-96
Lewis, Caroline	T	1995-96
Lewis, Catherine	T	1960-61
Lewis, Elizabeth	C	1958-60
Lewis, Ellen	A	1980-84,86
Lewis, Flora Louise		1929
Lewis, Hannah	T	1995-96
Lewis, Harriet	T	1955-62
Lewis, Jane	T	1953-54
Lewis, Jane		1929
Lewis, Janie	A	1975-78
Lewis, Jennifer	T	1975-80
Lewis, Jenny	T	1953-60
Lewis, June	T	1941
Lewis, Laura	C	1977-80
Lewis, Linda Ann	T	1950
Lewis, Margaret	T	1940-44
Lewis, Margaret	A	1966
Lewis, Martha	T	1952-54
Lewis, Mary-Ayres	C	1986-87
Lewis, Mary	C	1984
Lewis, Mary Ann	C	1937-39
Lewis, Mary Jon	C	1951-54
Lewis, Nancy	A	1944-46
Lewis, Patricia Lee	C	1950-53
Lewis, Rebecca	T	1937
Lewis, Terese	T	1935
Lewis, Thelma	T	1936
Ley, Diane	A	1952-59
Ley, Judy Ann	T	1949-55
Ley, Katherine	A	1977-83
Ley, Linda	T	1953-57
Ley, Nancy	C	1952-56
Liakos, Kee	C	1973-77
Lide, Mary	A	1960-62
Lide, Nita	A	1962
Lieb, Emily	C	1984-89
Liebman, Carol	C	1937-38,40
Liebmann, Laura	A	1969-74
Liedecker, Juliet		1928
Liggett, Carol	T	1934-35
Light, Kay	C	1949-57
Ligon, Gretchen Dutch	T	1951-54
Ligon, Kendall	A	1978-83
Ligon, Lacey	A	1979-89
Lilly, Elizabeth	T	1994-96
Lilly, Elyse	A	1987-89,91
Lilly, Laura	C	1991-93
Limerick, Arden	C	1958-59
Limerick, Patricia	T	1944-47
Linbeck, Betsy	T	1972-79
Linbeck, Mary Clark	A	1977-84
Linbeck, Suzanne	C	1950
Linbeck, Tammy	A	1969-75
Lincoln, Viola	A	1944,46
Linden, Dorothy	T	1936
Linden, Patsy	T	1936
Linderman, Helen		1928
Lindsay, Marilyn	T	1944,46
Lindsay, Rosemary	C	1941,44
Lindsey, Betty	T	1940-41
Lindsey, Claire	C	1968-71
Lindsey, Laurie	C	1969-73
Lindsey, Mary	C	1962-66
Lindsey, Mary Nell	T	1939-40
Lindsey, Myra	A	1967-70
Lindsey, Robin	T	1961-65
Lindsey, Rosamay	C	1940-41,44
Lindsley, Cathy	C	1961-66
Lindsley, Katherine	C	1936-39
Lingenfelter, Margaret	A	1943
Lingo, Ann	T	1948-51
Lingo, Mary Sissy	T	1948-51, 1953-54
Link, Adrienne	T	1946-48
Link, Lyndall	C	1975-82
Link, Margaret	C	1981-87
Link, Patsy	C	1939-41
Link, Rita	A	1953
Linn, Erin	C	1954-59
Linn, Mary	T	1935
Linnartz, Shirley		1929
Lintz, Mary Jane	C	1938-40
Lippman, Ruth Ellen	T	1934-37
Lipscomb, Diane	T	1947-48, 1950-51
Lipscomb, Lottie Lou	C	1945-48,50
Lipscomb, Lucille		1928-29
Lipscomb, Weston	C	1993-96
Liston, Bonne Rhea	C	1951
Litle, Mary Frances	C	1941-43
Little, Ann	A	1951-55
Little, Cynthia	T	1937-38,40
Little, Dana	A	1980-86

Little, Gail	A	1949-55		Lomax, Barbara	C	1942-43		Lovett, Eliza	C	1943
Little, Janna C.	C	1978-83,85		Lomax, Louise	C	1943		Lovett, Hilary	C	1989
Little, Janna Lou	T	1954-59		Lomax, Mary Helen	A	1944		Lovett, Jane	A	1959-66
Little, Julie	C	1977-84		London, Mary Lee	T	1936		Lovett, Mary	C	1971-78
Little, Karen	A	1972-73		London, Mary Jean	T	1942-43		Lovin, Sally	A	1959-63
Little, Kathleen	A	1943-44		Long, Betty Anne	C	1941		Lovin, Sandra	C	1954-59
Little, Kathy	T	1972-74		Long, Cleo	C	1932		Lovin, Vicki	A	1957-62
Little, Linda	C	1971-76		Long, Frances	C	1932		Loving, Joyce	C	1936-37
Little, Lloydelle	C	1942		Long, Jane	C	1932-33		Low, Courtney	T	1981-87
Little, Lutie	T	1966-68		Long, Lyda	A	1943-44		Low, Rachael	C	1975-81
Little, Mary Elizabeth	C	1940-43,		Long, Margaret Ann	T	1942-45		Lowden, Betty		1928
		1945-46		Long, Mary Ellen		1928		Lowe, Beryle		1928
Little, Molly	T	1984-91		Long, Sarah	A	1995		Lowe, Martha	C	1937
Little, Penny	A	1956-64		Longford, Sue	T	1942		Lowe, Susan	C	1937-38
Little, Yvette	T	1970-77		Longoria, Adrienne	A	1993-96		Lowe, Suzette	C	1975-82
Littleton, Mary	C	1983-87		Longoria, Bettina	T	1975-82		Lowell, Betty Rae	C	1947-49
Littleton, Nancey	C	1978-84		Longoria, Cassandra	A	1991-94		Lowenstein, Elaine	T	1937
Lively, Mary Katherine	C	1936		Longoria, Sarah	A	1995-96		Lowery, Eileen	C	1951-54
Liverman, Camille	A	1984-90		Looke, Elizabeth	C	1993-96		Lowery, Kathryn	A	1949-53
Livermore, Christy	C	1982-84		Loomis, Lynn	A	1955-63		Lowery, Margaret	A	1945-51
Livezey, Anne	A	1974-79		Loomis, Mary	A	1954-61		Lowery, Virginia	A	1958-62
Livingston, Linda	T	1952		Loomis, Mary Kathryn	T	1994-96		Lowrey, Mary Elaine	T	1939,41
Llewellyn, Julia	T	1979		Looney, Courtney	T	1987-94		Lowry, Jean	C	1935
Lloyd, Anne	C	1955		Looney, Harriett	A	1946-48		Lowry, Lee Ann	C	1975-76
Lloyd, Anne	C	1933-34		Looney, Lorin	A	1983-89		Lowry, Mary Elaine	T	1939
Lloyd, Kathleen	C	1942		Looney, Martha		1929		Lowry, Suzanne	C	1954
Lloyd, Lauren	A	1996		Looney, Thyrza Lee	A	1948-49,		Lubin, Kathleen Anne	T	1988
Lloyd, Marian	T	1935				1951-52		Lucas, Candy	A	1968-73
Lloyd, Rachel	T	1936		Loose, Nancy	T	1955		Lucas, Caroline	T	1972-76
Lochhead, Cameron	C	1996		Lopes, Carla	A	1944		Lucas, Susan	T	1981-82
Lockart, Olive	T	1931,36-37		Lord, Ashley	A	1993-96		Lucke, Allison	C	1990-94
Locke, Aimee	T	1955-63		Lord, Conley	A	1982-88		Luckett, Lucille	T	1939-40
Locke, Geralynn	T	1941,44-45		Lord, Katherine	A	1990-96		Lucky, Barbara	T	1946
Locke, Jennifer	T	1965-66		Lord, Robyn	C	1987-93		Ludwig, Karen	T	1954-55
Locke, Lynnan	T	1964-66		Lorentzen, Carrie	A	1987-90		Lummis, Allene	C	1938
Locke, Mary	C	1961-62		Lorentzen, Katie	A	1986-87		Lummis, Ann	C	1939
Locke, Mary	T	1931		Lorenz, Janis	T	1931		Lumpkin, Katherine	T	1978-81
Locke, Nancy	A	1943		Lorio, Jerry	T	1942		Lumpkin, Libby	A	1978-81
Lockett, Hester	C	1945-47		Lorton, Tracy	T	1976		Lunn, Myrle	A	1967
Lockewitz, Daisy	T	1936-37		Lott, Pamela	C	1964-67		Lupe, Elizabeth		1928
Lockhart, Ann	T	1936-37		Lottinger, Amy	C	1985		Luppen, Jeanne	A	1957
Lockhart, Kathleen	C	1940-43		Lottman, Jennifer	A	1978-85		Lupton, Gloria	T	1934,38
Lockwood, Ann	T	1939-40		Lottman, Linda	T	1971-77		Lupton, Shirley	T	1938-41
Loeb, Emily	C	1991-96		Lottman, Louise		1928		Lusk, Annette	T	1970-71
Loeb, Rebecca	C	1989		Lottman, Susan	T	1973-79		Lusk, Charlene	C	1960-63
Loffland, Barbara	C	1949-57		Loughbaum, Patricia	A	1943		Lusk, Lauren	A	1993-96
Loffland, Joan	C	1950-54		Loughridge, Laurie	C	1976		Lusk, Mary Catherine	C	1946-51
Loftis, Cathey	C	1961-64		Loughridge, Lisa	A	1979		Lusk, Miki	A	1958-61
Loftis, Lynn	C	1960-64		Love, Barbara	T	1949		Luten, Dora	T	1944-45
Loftis, Nancy	A	1959-63		Love, Dawn	C	1985-88		Luther, Nan	T	1958-62
Loftis, Sallee	T	1968-72		Love, Jan	T	1965-68		Luther, Sherrill	T	1969-75
Lofton, Anne	T	1953-59		Love, Julie	A	1966-69		Lutken, Kate	C	1966-69
Logan, Betty	T	1937		Love, Paula	C	1987-92		Luttrell, Meg	C	1981
Logan, Chris	T	1936-37,41		Love, Robyn	C	1990		Lydick, Anne	C	1937-40
Logan, Frances	C	1938		Love, Sandra	A	1946-47		Lydick, Patsy	T	1941
Logan, Jerry	T	1936-37,41		Love, Shellie	T	1989-95		Lyle, Beverly	T	1943
Logan, Kitty Anne	A	1948-50		Lovejoy, Jean	C	1972-73		Lyle, Yvonne	T	1943
Logan, Mary	C	1938		Lovejoy, Marianne	C	1971-72		Lyles, Martha Elizabeth	T	1930
Logue, Fanelle	C	1945-47		Loveless, Dilyn	T	1991-92		Lynch, Alice Ann	T	1951-56
Lohman, Susan	T	1974-75		Lovell, Marilyn	T	1934-36		Lynch, Mary Kathryn	C	1952-55
Lokey, Jacque	C	1986-89		Lovell, Patty	T	1941-42		Lynn, Jean	T	1939-44
Lokey, Mary Alice	T	1951-53		Lovell, Teri	C	1957		Lynn, Mary Virginia	A	1996
Lolland, Barbara	C	1951		Lovett, Ann	C	1965-71		Lynn, Peggy	T	1939-42

Name		Years
Lyons, Leslie	A	1993-96
Lyons, Linda	T	1974-78
Lytle, Betty Jean	C	1930
M		
Maberry, Jacquelyn	C	1961-67
Mabray, Shirley	A	1943-44
Mabry, Winnie Lee	C	1933
MacArthur, Kathryn	T	1969-72
Macaulay, Joan	T	1945-46
Macdonald, Martha	T	1941
Machac, Melissa	T	1989-93
Machac, Stephanie	T	1990-95
Machen, Carolyn	C	1958-61
MacIntyre, Henley	T	1991-96
MacIntyre, Katie	T	1995-96
MacKellar, Jennie	C	1984-89
Mackin, Beverly	T	1945-48
MacPherson, Caroll	C	1931-34
MacPherson, Charlotte	C	1945-46
Macy, Thelma		1928
Madden, Leslie	A	1979-85
Madden, Tawney	A	1969-74
Maddox, Carolyn	T	1955-59
Maddox, Cynthia	A	1958-61
Maddox, Lou	C	1931,34-36
Maddox, Lula Belle	C	1955-59
Maddox, Marjorie	T	1930-31
Maddox, Marlene	T	1950
Maddox, Patricia Anne	C	1959
Madeley, Catherine	T	1987-94
Madeley, Jennifer	T	1983-90
Madeley, Mary Ann	T	1959-65
Madeley, Mary Clare	C	1988
Madison, Mary Moss	T	1940-41
Madison, Sue	A	1943-44
Maedgen, Mary Ellis	C	1939-40
Maer, Kelly	C	1981-82
Magaw, Lynnie	T	1970-71
Maggart, Jeanne	T	1937
Maginnis, Mary Lei	C	1951-54
Magruder, Elaine	A	1962-66,70
Magruder, Frances	A	1961-68
Magruder, Kay	T	1965-69
Magruder, Mary Jean`	T	1942-45
Mahaffey, Doris	C	1940-42
Maida, Marty	C	1990-94
Mailandt, Anya	A	1989-95
Mailandt, Tonia	C	1986-89,91
Mainer, Jackie	C	1946
Mains, Lindsay	A	1985-88
Major, Diane	A	1954-56
Majors, Genevieve	T	1931
Malcom, Lissa	T	1994
Maledon, Molly		1959
Maley, Mary Ann	C	1945-47
Mallick, Morgan	C	1996
Mallinson, Barbara	T	1936,37
Mallory, Grace	A	1989-92
Mallory, Laura	C	1963-67
Mallory, Trudy	T	1967-70
Malloy, Connor	A	1982-88
Malloy, Peg	A	1958-62
Malone, Ella Mae	C	1930
Malone, Jennifer	A	1985-89
Malone, Katie	C	1988-92
Malone, Martha	C	1958-64
Malone, Meg	C	1987-88
Malone, Nancy	C	1946-48
Maloney, Ashley	C	1995-96
Maltz, Annette	T	1936
Maltz, Janice	T	1936
Man, Jennifer	T	1974-77
Manahan, Leah	C	1937
Manahan, Loretta	C	1935,37
Mancuso, Jean	C	1942
Maness, Gillian	T	1988-93
Mangin, Elizabeth	C	1980-83
Mangum, Jimmie Jean	T	1930
Mangum, Margaret	C	1948-50
Manhart, Martha	C	1957-60
Manion, Beth	T	1956
Manking, Lynn	C	1962
Mann, Elizabeth	C	1994-96
Mann, Helen	C	1980-86
Mann, Jayne	T	1951
Mann, Liz	A	1983-89
Mann, Lois Ann	T	1943
Mann, Merideth	T	1930
Mann, Terry	T	1951
Manning, Ann	T	1951-55
Manning, Julie	C	1984-87
Manor, Margaret	T	1931-34
Manske, Donna	A	1952
Manske, Julie	A	1973-74
Manske, Melissa	A	1990-95
Manske, Rosemary	A	1943
Marburger, Billie Mae		1932
Marbury, Martha	C	1936-37
Marchant, Nancy	A	1946
Marchbanks, Claudia	C	1968-72
Marchbanks, Gwen	C	1964-71
Marchbanks, Karen	C	1967-74
Marchbanks, Linda	A	1963-68
Marchen, Carolyn	C	1960
Marchman, Madalyn	C	1957-62
Marchman, Marylyn	T	1956-57
Marcom, Mary	T	1969-76
Marcus, Arlene	C	1935-36
Marcus, Becca	T	1988-91
Mardis, Mary	C	1934
Mares, Charlotte	T	1947-51
Maresca, Melissa	A	1990-92
Marian, Isabel	A	1970
Maris, Pat	C	1937-39
Markham, Elaine	C	1931-35
Markham, Princess Louise	T	1931-34
Marks, Ellen	A	1981
Marks, Mary Theresa	C	1941-42,45
Marks, Sherrill	A	1960-65
Markus, Mildred	T	1936
Marmaduke, Jane		1929
Marrero, Dolores	A	1951
Marrero, Lydia		1951
Marse, Susan	T	1977-84
Marsh, Audrey	T	1981-87
Marsh, Betsy	A	1956-58
Marsh, C.C.	C	1991-94
Marsh, Estee	A	1979-84
Marsh, Holly	A	1974-75
Marsh, Lucy	T	1990-96
Marsh, Mary Sue	C	1937
Marshall, Geraldine	T	1941
Marshall, Katherine	C	1933
Marshall, Kathryn	C	1970-77
Marshall, Laura	C	1973-80
Marshall, Margaret	A	1976-83
Marshall, Mary Jon	C	1978-85
Marshall, Melinda	A	1975-81
Marshall, Rebecca	A	1960-63
Marshall, Rosemary	T	1959-63
Marthinson, Jan	T	1944-45
Martin, Ann	C	1964-67
Martin, Betty	T	1943-44
Martin, Cali	C	1982-88
Martin, Carol	T	1954-55
Martin, Carolyn	A	1990-96
Martin, Colby	T	1983-90
Martin, Elizabeth	T	1934-35
Martin, Geraldine	T	1930
Martin, Jaclyn	C	1987-88
Martin, Jane	A	1962-63
Martin, Johnni Ruth	T	1935-36
Martin, Judy	C	1948,53-54
Martin, Kim	T	1986-90
Martin, Margaret	C	1931
Martin, Margaret	T	1930-31
Martin, Marilyn	C	1939-40,43
Martin, Marion	T	1946-48,50
Martin, Marja	C	1976-77
Martin, Mary Carolyn	A	1943-45
Martin, Mary	C	1961-65
Martin, Mary M.	T	1987-93
Martin, Mary Vance	T	1942
Martin, Melissa	C	1975-80
Martin, Michelle	A	1973-78
Martin, Mimi	C	1968-75
Martin, Molly	C	1977-81
Martin, Patricia	T	1934,37
Martin, Pattie	A	1944
Martin, Patty Lou	C	1940,43
Martin, Ruth	C	1931
Martin, Sally	A	1959-60
Martin, Shirley	C	1939
Martin, Suzanne	A	1952-58
Martindale, Katherine	T	1938-41
Martindale, Sally	T	1939-43
Martinez, Margot	C	1975-76
Marvin, Mary	T	1984-86
Mary, Betty	T	1938
Mason, Jane	A	1956-59
Mason, Jennifer	C	1985-91
Mason, Jo Ellen	T	1978-83
Mason, Molly	C	1940
Mason, Shirley	T	1935-36
Massengill, Sandra	A	1953-56
Massengill, Sharon	C	1953-57
Massengill, Suzy	T	1954-60,62
Massey, Dorothy	T	1934-35,37

Massey, Marilyn	T	1937	
Massey, Marion	C	1930	
Massey, Sherry	C	1961-64	
Massie, Helen	C	1941-42	
Massingill, Nancy	C	1936-39, 1941-42	
Massingill, Suzy	T	1959	
Masters, Estelle (Sissy)	A	1954-60	
Masterson, CiCi	T	1982-86	
Masterson, Clare	T	1945-47	
Masterson, Martha Ann	C	1940	
Mastin, Tallie	T	1991-95	
Matchett, Dorothy	C	1941	
Matheney, Diana	A	1969-71	
Mathews, Alexandra	T	1992-93	
Mathews, Betty Jane	C	1939-42	
Mathews, Norma	C	1941-42	
Mathews, Wilma	C	1941-42	
Matlock, Candy	A	1955-63	
Matlock, Martha Jane	C	1942	
Matlock, Norma	C	1948-52	
Matteson, Sarah Belle	T	1932-33	
Matthew, Kathleen	T	1985-91	
Matthew, Marjorie Ann	T	1994-96	
Matthews, Bonnie	C	1961-67	
Matthews, Catherine	C	1956-61	
Matthews, Helen	C	1931	
Matthews, Judy	C	1961-64	
Matthews, Leslie	T	1981-86	
Matthews, Lila	A	1946-49,51	
Matthews, Lisa	A	1965,67	
Matthews, Meredith	A	1977-82	
Matthews, Sammy Louise	C	1932	
Matthews, Somers	A	1946-48	
Matthews, Stephanie	T	1988	
Matthews, Susie	A	1964-70	
Matthews, Virginia	T	1936	
Mattison, Blanche	C	1971-74	
Mattison, Meredith	T	1969-72	
Mauboles, Etta Wanda Petite	T	1936	
Mauritz, Carrin	C	1942	
Maxey, Elaine	T	1931	
Maxey, Katharyn	T	1941	
Maxey, Marcia Ann	T	1950-53	
Maxson, Amanda	A	1996	
Maxson, Barbara		1928-29	
Maxson, Katie	A	1993-96	
Maxson, Peggy		1928-29	
Maxwell, Sally Kay	T	1950-53	
May, Caroline	C	1947	
May, Doris	T	1939	
May, Karla	T	1972-77	
May, Margaret	T	1938	
May, Marilyn	A	1948-49	
May, Marjorie	C	1934,39	
May, Myra	T	1945	
May, Phoebe	A	1947	
Mayer, Bonnie Lou	T	1973-80	
Mayer, Diana	T	1971,74	
Mayer, Diane	T	1967	
Mayer, Dina	T	1984-88	
Mayer, Doris	T	1940-42,45	
Mayer, Jean	A	1944	
Mayer, Marjorie	T	1938	
Mayfield, Ann	A	1944,46-47	
Mayfield, Jeannie	C	1952	
Mayfield, Natalie	C	1949-51	
Mayfield, Sandra	A	1946-47	
Mayhew, Anna Lea	T	1938	
Mayhew, Mandy	T	1963-64	
Maynard, Kim	T	1970-71	
Maynard, Mary	C	1945-50	
Mayor, Diana	T	1968-74	
Mays, Christy	A	1979-85	
Mays, Stephanie	A	1982-88	
Maze, Molly	C	1952-53	
Mazoch, Kortney	T	1991-96	
Mazoch, Kristin	A	1988-91	
Mazur, Dorothy	A	1949-55	
Mazzola, Cecile	A	1986-92	
McAbee, Betty	C	1953-59	
McAdams, Minnetta	T	1944	
McAden, Ann	C	1962-65	
McAden, Lyn	T	1960-63	
McAden, Nancy	A	1964-68	
McAfee, Betty	C	1947-49	
McAfee, Sara Jane	T	1955-58	
McAlister, Ann	A	1952-54	
McAllen, Elizabeth	A	1980-84	
McAllen, Mary Margaret	A	1977-79	
McAllen, Melissa	A	1978-81	
McAllen, Stephanie	T	1987-93	
McAllister, Lida	C	1979-80	
McAnally, Alice	T	1930	
McAndrews, Carey	C	1992-94	
McAndrews, Kristine	C	1992-93	
McAnelly, Nancy	C	1945	
McBrian, Hazel Dell	T	1937-38	
McBride, Eugenia	A	1943	
McBride, Eula Lee	C	1950	
McBrine, Betty Ann	A	1957	
McBurnett, Virginia	C	1936	
McCabe, Claire Ann	T	1987-93	
McCain, Callie	A	1986-93	
McCain, Frances	C	1963-67	
McCall, Carolyn	C	1947-49	
McCall, Laura	T	1972-73	
McCall, Leslie	C	1972-76	
McCall, Lorraine	T	1936	
McCall, Lyndsey	C	1989-91	
McCall, Margaret	C	1953-56	
McCall, Rosemary	T	1943	
McCall, Sharon	T	1951-54	
McCamey, Sara Elizabeth	T	1930	
McCann, Mary Alma	T	1940,42	
McCanne, Marian	T	1940	
McCants, Leslie	A	1973-75	
McCard, Margaret	C	1965	
McCarter, Bettie	C	1966-71	
McCarthy, Ellen	C	1962-67	
McCarthy, Eugenie	C	1990	
McCarthy, Mary Anne	T	1954-58	
McCarthy, Megan	C	1956-60	
McCarthy, Sheila	T	1952-55	
McCarthy, Shelley	A	1958-65	
McCartt, Kathy	C	1975-76	
McCarty, Anne	C	1988-91	
McCarty, Betty	T	1947-50	
McCarty, Elizabeth	T	1983-88	
McCarty, Luanne	C	1938	
McCarty, Mary Kay	A	1983-87	
McCaskill, Leslie	A	1965-70	
McCaslin, Ann	T	1966-67	
McCauley, Anne	A	1972-77	
McClancy, Gail	A	1947-48	
McClenaghan, Judy	A	1953-56	
McClenahan, Cristin	A	1980-86	
McClendon, Betsy	C	1944,46	
McClendon, Linley	C	1985-91	
McClendon, Marian	C	1946-49	
McClerkin, Katherine	C	1976-78	
McClerkin, Lauren	T	1979-80,83	
McClerkin, Martha	A	1976-77	
McCloy, Ruth		1928	
McClung, Trixie	C	1941-43	
McClure, Betty	C	1951-53	
McClure, Cathie	C	1964-71	
McClure, Janena	A	1961-62	
McClure, Kathy	C	1964	
McClure, Marjorie	T	1944	
McClure, Mary	C	1940	
McClure, Ruth		1926	
McClymonds, Katherine	T	1989-96	
McCollum, Myrtle	T	1932,34	
McComiskey, Allison	T	1979-86	
McComiskey, Jamie	T	1972-79	
McConnell, Karen Kam	C	1970-75	
McConnell, Kathleen Kem	C	1970-75	
McCook, Norma Ann	T	1942-44	
McCord, Margaret	C	1961-67	
McCord, Nanette Netta	T	1955-60	
McCorkle, Mary Jo	T	1940	
McCormick, Carolyn	A	1954-55	
McCormick, Lorna	A	1943	
McCormick, Marietta	C	1939	
McCormick, Martha	A	1943	
McCormick, Nancy	C	1949-50	
McCormick, Olive		1928	
McCoy, Helen	T	1935	
McCoy, Jane	A	1945-47	
McCrary, Kelly	C	1976-79	
McCrary, Sandra	A	1951-53	
McCrea, Beth	A	1968-73,75	
McCrea, Melissa	C	1969-73	
McCreary, Raye Virginia	C	1941-45	
McCreery, Meredith	A	1984-91	
McCrummen, Claire	T	1971-74	
McCue, Kay	C	1952-53	
McCullars, Ann	C	1948	
McCulloch, Ann	C	1948,50	
McCulloch, Norma Sue	T	1940	
McCulloh, Jane	C	1943	
McCullough, Judy	C	1953	
McCullough, Linda	A	1950-51	
McCullough, Margaret	A	1968-70	
McCullough, Marilyn	T	1951-53	
McCullough, Nelda	C	1950-53	
McCurdy, Betty		1938	

McCure, Gwenliana	A	1955	McFaddin, Jerry	T	1953-56	McHenry, Laura	C	1979-85
McCurry, Marsha	T	1962-65	McFaddin, Lalah	C	1966-67	McHenry, Marion	C	1968-71
McCutchen, Carla	A	1960-63	McFaddin, Mamie	T	1934	McIlhenny, Elizabeth	C	1930
McCutchen, Linda	T	1955,58	McFaddin, Nan Rebecca	T	1948-50	McIlyar, Kathy	A	1968-73
McCutchern, Jean	C	1937	McFaddin, Susan	A	1986-92	McIlyar, Kelly	T	1975-82
McCutchin, Morgan	C	1994-96	McFadin, Lola Ann	C	1938-39	McIlyar, Kirby	C	1980-86
McDade, Betty	T	1951	McFadin, Nancy	T	1930	McInnis, Brandon	T	1982-85
McDade, Diana	T	1965-69	McFarland, Barbara	T	1935	McInnis, Frances	T	1941,43
McDade, Evelyn	T	1957	McFarland, Beth	T	1943	McInnis, Katherine	A	1984-87
McDaniel, Ann	T	1939-40	McFarland, Emily	T	1948-53	McIntosh, Jane	T	1936
McDaniel, Carol	T	1939-40	McFarland, Hattie Veigh	T	1931,33-36	McIntosh, Sara Elizabeth		1928
McDaniel, Erin	C	1987-91	McFarland, Isabel	T	1931	McIntyre, Danya	C	1976-83
McDaniel, Kathryn	C	1938-39	McFarland, Isobel	T	1964-70	McIntyre, Jeanette	C	1937-38
McDaniel, Lisa	T	1995-96	McFarland, Louise	C	1963-68	McIntyre, Mary Virginia	C	1936
McDaniel Lisa	T	1996	McFarland, Louise	T	1931	McIntyre, Ruth	C	1941-42
McDaniel, Marilyn Beth	C	1949-53	McFarland, Lucy	T	1958-62	McIntyre, Sandra	T	1950-54
McDaniel, Martha Ann	T	1937	McFarland, Lynn	A	1961-65	McJimsey, Barbara	T	1971-75
McDaniel, Mary Ellen	T	1933	McFarland, Mary	C	1966-70	McKallip, Susan	A	1966-69
McDavitt, Gail		1926	McFarland, Paula	C	1945-47	McKay, Elaine	C	1958-60
McDermott, Holly	A	1972-78	McFarland, Virginia	A	1968-73	McKay, Kay	C	1961-64
McDermott, Katherine	A	1977-84	McFarlane, Eulalie Lee	C	1933	McKay, Lauri Ann	C	1973-75
McDermott, Lisa	T	1970-72	McFarlane, Thelma	T	1942	McKay, Nellie May		1928
McDermott, Margaret	T	1980-85	McGaha, Sara	C	1944-47,49	McKean, Dorothy	C	1937,40
McDermott, Mary Dees	C	1935-36	McGaha, Sue	C	1945-47,49	McKellar, Kathryn	T	1936
McDermott, Patricia Ann	A	1944-46	McGahhey, Flo	T	1950-51	McKelvy, Marcelle	C	1958-60
McDonald, Ainslee	T	1970-77	McGar, Katherine	C	1944	McKendry, Betty	T	1936
McDonald, Ann	C	1936-38	McGaughey, Motsie	T	1934	McKenna, Mary Lil	T	1941
McDonald, Blair	C	1989	McGaughy, Caroline	T	1989	McKenzie, Alison	A	1985-92
McDonald, Dee	A	1966-74	McGee, Betsy	A	1989-91	McKenzie, Brooke	A	1995-96
McDonald, Emily	T	1965-69	McGee, Louan	T	1950-55	McKenzie, Cara	A	1982-84
McDonald, Eve	C	1983-87	McGee, Mary	T	1953-54	McKenzie, Caroline	T	1996
McDonald, Janie	A	1956-59	McGehee, Cleo	T	1943-44	McKenzie, Leanne	A	1957-58
McDonald, Kay	A	1945-46,48	McGehee, Jamie	C	1935	McKenzie, Margaret	C	1955-58
McDonald, Margaret	T	1972	McGehee, Lacy	T	1956-62	McKenzie, Martha	C	1970-74
McDonald, Martha	T	1942	McGill, Ada Reed		1928	McKigney, Shannon	C	1982-83
McDonald, Molly	C	1965-72	McGill, Julie	T	1970-73	McKim, Caroline	T	1994
McDonald, Susan	C	1972	McGill, Shelley	T	1973-79	McKinley, Georgea	A	1958-61
McDonnell, Cherry	C	1935	McGinley, Lou Ellen	C	1949-53	McKinley, Judy	C	1961
McDonough, Ann	T	1974-80	McGinn, Rosemary	C	1948	McKinley, Mary	A	1956-59
McDonough, Lauren	C	1978-84	McGinnes, Jewel	T	1934	McKinney, Arden	T	1985-87
McDonough, Nancy	A	1944-48	McGivney, Elizabeth	A	1960	McKinney, Brooke	A	1991
McDonough, Rita	A	1944-47	McGoldrick, Mary Jane	C	1941,43	McKinney, Florine		1929
McDougal, Anita	T	1944	McGowan, Anne	A	1963-69	McKinney, Georgia	T	1949-50
McDougal, Bennet	A	1991-95	McGowan, Callie	T	1991-96	McKinney, Jane	T	1945-46
McDougal, Margo	A	1989-95	McGowan, Dorothy Anne	C	1996	McKinney, Janet	C	1956-59
McDowell, Carol Ann	A	1943	McGowan, Elizabeth	A	1971,73-75	McKinney, Joan	A	1947-48
McDowell, Mary Ann	A	1943-44	McGowan, Jane	A	1974-78	McKinney, Lauren	T	1988-95
McEachern, Dorothy	C	1931	McGown, Kathleen	C	1961-66	McKinney, Marian	A	1946
McEldowney, Amy	A	1979-81	McGown, Mary Beth	A	1962-65	McKinney, Mary	C	1960-61
McEldowney, Ann	C	1958-60	McGraw, Brooke	T	1983-85	McKinney, Mary Elizabeth	C	1940-41
McEldowney, Lucy	C	1992-96	McGreevy, Elizabeth	A	1975-81	McKinney, Mary	T	1960-65
McEldowney, Mia	C	1962-64	McGreevy, Martha	A	1976-82	McKinney, Meredith	A	1980-83
McElhenney, Amy	T	1966-72	McGregor, Megan	T	1993-96	McKinney, Susan	C	1957-59
McElhenny, Sidney	C	1962-67	McGregor, Patsy	C	1931	McKinnon, Margaret	C	1939
McElhinney, Daphene	C	1935	McGregor, Rosetta	T	1947	McKinsey, Mazie	A	1944
McEniry, Jean	T	1934	McGuehee, Lucy	T	1960	McKnight, Betsy	C	1991-96
McEnnis, Margie	T	1937	McGuffey, Emily	C	1987-94	McKnight, Jane	C	1963
McEvoy, Marianne Boo	A	1990-94	McGuffin, Meredith	A	1979-84	McKnight, Jerry Anne	A	1954-55
McEwen, Barbara	A	1943	McGuire, Demar	C	1990-96	McKnight, Joan	A	1949
McEwen, Joanne	T	1936	McGuire, Monica	T	1985-90	McKnight, Martha	A	1987-90
McEwen, Lauren	A	1995-96	McHaney, Elizabeth	C	1937-38	McKnight, Molly	T	1988-94
McFaddin, Ida	C	1946	McHaney, May Evelyn	C	1945	McKnight, Stella		1928-29
McFaddin, Janet	C	1947-48	McHenry, Cornelia	T	1940-42	McKnight, Vivian	T	1940

McKown, Emily	T	1973-78	McNab, Scottie	C	1986-91	Meek, Virginia	T	1937-38
McLain, Mary	T	1938	McNabb, Allison	A	1994-96	Meekins, Connell	A	1992-95
McLaughlin, Ann	T	1946-47	McNabb, Margaret	C	1988-95	Meekins, Maury	A	1992-96
McLaughlin, Anna	A	1993	McNabb, Wynne	T	1990-96	Megarity, Mary D.	C	1945-47
McLaughlin, Jennifer	T	1992-93	McNamara, Betty	T	1962-63	Mehlburger, Katie	A	1985-91
McLaughlin, Kae	T	1966-70	McNatt, Markeeta	C	1963-70	Mehr, Carolyn	C	1955-58
McLaughlin, Marianne	A	1968-71	McNeal, Carolyn	T	1940	Mehr, Ida		1929-30
McLaughlin, Sheryl Sue	C	1960-62	McNeal, Mary Ann	C	1983-88	Mehrens, Judy	T	1955-57
McLaurin, Farrior	C	1930	McNearney, Anne	C	1966-71	Mehrens, Marilyn	C	1956-59
McLaurin, Margaret	C	1935-36	McNearney, Claire	T	1966-71	Mehring, Molly	T	1978-81
McLaurin, Mary	C	1930-31	McNearney, Eileen	C	1965-70	Meier, Anne	C	1971-73
McLean, Alice Lee	C	1978	McNeil, Ann	T	1944-47	Meier, Stacey Anne	A	1994
McLean, Dorothy	C	1934	McNeill, Aleene	C	1937	Meili, Marilyn	C	1951-56
McLean, Ellen	C	1972-73	McNeill, Dawn	A	1974-79	Meili, Mildred	C	1950-54
McLean, Harriett	T	1941	McNeny, Mary Agnes	T	1941-42	Meindl, Mary	A	1969-72
McLean, Lisa	C	1941	McNicholas, Graham	T	1963-66	Meiring, Marcia	T	1970-73
McLean, Mary Elizabeth	C	1978	McNutt, Dawn	T	1967-70	Melch, Maxine	A	1944-46
McLean, Peggy	C	1953,55	McPike, Linda	A	1951-52	Melton, Linda	A	1958-60
McLemore, Anne	A	1945	McRae, Colin	A	1987-90	Melton, Rosemary	A	1947
McLemore, Beverly	A	1949-52	McReynolds, Doris	T	1928-30	Melton, Ruth		1929
McLendon, Anna	A	1962-66	McReynolds, Karen	A	1974-78	Melton, Sue	A	1956-58
McLendon, Jan	A	1955-60	McRoberts, Virginia Ruth	T	1935-36	Menefee, Ann	T	1946
McLendon, Kristen	C	1961-66	McShane, Frances	C	1952-53	Menefee, Joan	A	1947
McLeod, Ann	A	1947-52	McShane, Mary	A	1958	Menges, Suzanne	A	1987-92
McLeod, Dorothy	A	1953-59	McShane, Susan	A	1969-73	Menke, Connie Jo	C	1940
McLeod, Gail	A	1957-62	McShane, Susan	C	1954-56	Menking, Lynn	C	1961-67
McLeod, Joanie		1993	McWilliams, Barbara	A	1946-49	Merchant, Catherine	T	1934-35
McLeod, Judy	C	1949-50	McWilliams, Diane	A	1946-49	Meredith, Barbara	T	1941,43-45
McLeod, La Juanda	C	1942	McWilliams, Ruth	C	1931	Meredith, Mary Mimi	C	1935-38
McLeod, Merle	T	1937	Mead, Lanier	C	1988	Meredith, Nancy	T	1935-37
McLeod, Opal	C	1936-37	Meador, Betty	C	1942	Meric, Jean	T	1941-44
McMackin, Trish	C	1975	Meador, Emily	C	1993-95	Meriwether, Rachel	C	1991-95
McMahan, Beth	A	1947,49-50	Meador, Megan	C	1996	Merrem, Mary Elizabeth	A	1943-44
McMahan, Susannah	A	1983-89	Meador, Mildred	C	1935	Merrick, Valda	A	1961-63
McMahon, Cristi	A	1986-88	Meador, Nancy	C	1995-96	Merrill, Sarah	C	1983-87
McMahon, Gretchen	A	1962,64-68	Meador, Rosalie Anne	C	1932-33	Merrill, Suzanne	T	1982-85
McMahon, Mary	C	1968-74	Meadors, Reinette	C	1937-38	Merriman, Beatrice	C	1935
McMahon, Pat	T	1957-59	Meadows, Beth	T	1970-71	Merriman, Cornelia	C	1935
McMakin, Maconda	T	1969-73	Meadows, Brooke	A	1984-91	Mertz, Minnie	T	1930-31
McMeans, Mary Beth	C	1939-40	Meadows, Kristin	A	1994-96	Mertz, Susan		1970
McMillan, Brittany	C	1987-89	Meadows, Lisa	C	1948	Merveldt, Betty	C	1942
McMillan, Grace	T	1931	Meadows, Mary Anne	A	1967-70	Metcalf, Curtis Jean	C	1941
McMillan, Marcy	C	1986-89	Meadows, Susanna	A	1989-94	Metcalf, Emily	A	1983-90
McMillan, Martha	C	1939	Mean, Jane	A	1959-61	Metcalf, Megan	A	1987-92
McMillan, Mary	C	1939	Means, Martha	A	1979-84	Metcalf, Rachel	C	1987-94
McMillen, Betty Jean	C	1936	Means, Suzanne	T	1958-60	Metcalfe, June	T	1932
McMillen, Carol Jean	A	1943-44	Meazel, Mary	C	1946	Methvin, Betty Jo	T	1943
McMillian, Evelyn	T	1942-45	Meck, Laura	A	1995-96	Metni, Maya	T	1986-87
McMullan, Dixie	A	1944	Medders, Marilyn	A	1969-75	Metteauer, Julie	T	1969-72
McMullan, Margaret Tibba	A	1943-44	Medders, Martha Ann	T	1935-36	Meyer, Andrea	C	1972-77
			Mee, Abby	A	1944	Meyer, Donna	A	1970-72
McMurray, Eugenia	T	1934	Mee, Deva	A	1974-75	Meyer, Molly	A	1991-96
McMurray, Lula Belle	T	1934,36	Mee, Kathryn	T	1981-84	Meyers, Frances	C	1935-37
McMurrey, Ann	T	1939-40	Mee, Marilyn	A	1951	Meyers, Ruth	C	1931
McMurrey, Betty	C	1966	Meek, Blanche	T	1936	Mickel, Mary Alice	T	1941,43
McMurrey, Julia	A	1958-59	Meek, Carol	C	1972-77	Mickey, Dawn	A	1972-74
McMurrey, Laura	C	1976-83	Meek, Janet	T	1961-66	Middlebrook, Claire	T	1950
McMurrey, Odette	A	1968-74	Meek, Kathy	A	1968-73	Middlebrook, Eddie	T	1930-31,33
McMurry, Mary	T	1931-32	Meek, Linda	T	1975-79	Middlebrook, Joel Ann	A	1949,51
McMurtray, Lorena		1926	Meek, Marian	T	1936	Middleton, Anne	T	1993-96
McMurtry, Sharon	A	1948-51	Meek, Mary	C	1979-85	Middleton, Carol Anne	T	1954
McNab, Adeline		1928	Meek, Paula	C	1967-71	Middleton, Dorothy	T	1956-58
McNab, Esther	T	1986-90	Meek, Suzanne	A	1993-96	Middleton, Elizabeth	C	1976-83

Name	Code	Years
Moore, Ann	A	1973-76
Moore, Anne	C	1969
Moore, Cara Lou	T	1960-63
Moore, Clair	T	1994-96
Moore, Cynthia	C	1975-76
Moore, Delight	C	1942,44
Moore, Diane	A	1958-59
Moore, Elizabeth	C	1991-94
Moore, Elizabeth	A	1980-83
Moore, Emily	C	1994-96
Moore, Evalene	C	1940
Moore, Georgia	A	1993-96
Moore, Gina	T	1962-66
Moore, Jane	C	1940
Moore, Jennifer	A	1973-80
Moore, Joanie	A	1977-78
Moore, Karen	A	1961-64
Moore, Katherine	T	1948-54
Moore, Kathleen	C	1980-87
Moore, Lila Susie	A	1947-52
Moore, Madison	C	1989
Moore, Maggie	C	1984
Moore, Marissa	A	1989-94
Moore, Marsha	C	1956-60
Moore, Martha	C	1945
Moore, Mary Elizabeth	T	1992-96
Moore, Mary	A	1968-72
Moore, Melissa	A	1971-77
Moore, Meredith	T	1988-95
Moore, Nancy Lee	A	1974-77
Moore, Nancy	T	1946
Moore, Patricia	T	1942-47
Moore, Ruth	C	1969-73
Moore, Susie	A	1949,52
Moorehead, Katy	A	1980
Moorehead, Lucinda	A	1953
Moorer, Gatna	T	1942
Moorer, Patricia	T	1942
Moores, Frances	T	1937
Mooring, Jo Ellen	A	1946-47
Moran, Caitlin	A	1988-94
Moran, Heather	C	1980-86
Moran, Linda	A	1955
Moran, Linda	A	1951-57
Moreau, Noel	T	1990-93
Moreau, Suzanne	A	1992-93
Morehead, Barbara Ann	T	1946-47,50
Morehead, Katy	A	1978-84
Morehead, Lucinda	A	1953-55
Morel, Patty	T	1938-41
Moreman, Alice	C	1980-85
Moreman, Florence	T	1976-82
Moreton, Dana	A	1967-73
Moreton, Laura	A	1966-72
Morgan, Amanda	T	1930
Morgan, Annie Blake		1929
Morgan, Betty	C	1963-66
Morgan, Billie Lee	A	1944
Morgan, Claire	C	1989-95
Morgan, Doris	T	1929-30
Morgan, Dorothy		1929
Morgan, Elaine	C	1939-40
Morgan, Elizabeth	A	1967-68
Morgan, Elizabeth	T	1939-40
Morgan, Elizabeth	T	1939
Morgan, Gene	T	1943
Morgan, Helen	T	1930
Morgan, Holly	T	1984-86
Morgan, Katherine	T	1929-31
Morgan, Kelly	T	1968
Morgan, Layne	C	1973-74
Morgan, Lee Ann	C	1972
Morgan, Leigh	A	1960
Morgan, Lou	T	1960-63
Morgan, Lynn	T	1968-69
Morgan, Marlowe	A	1981
Morgan, Meg	A	1957-60
Morgan, Nancy	T	1946
Morgan, Patty	C	1966
Morgan, Velma		1929
Morian, Bel	A	1970-71
Morlang, Betty	T	1939-40
Morledge, Susan	C	1972-75
Morris, Ann	T	1945
Morris, Ann	C	1958-60
Morris, Becky	C	1983-84
Morris, Belle	C	1976-80
Morris, Betsy	C	1965-68,72
Morris, Bette	A	1968-72
Morris, Betty	A	1951-54
Morris, Camille	C	1987
Morris, Charlotte Kay	C	1950-51
Morris, Christina	C	1990-92
Morris, Cindy	T	1980-81
Morris, Cissy	T	1996
Morris, Gail	T	1949-52
Morris, Helen	C	1934-37
Morris, Jean	T	1960
Morris, Kathryn	C	1987-89
Morris, Louise	T	1932
Morris, Marilyn	T	1945-48
Morris, Mary Elizabeth	C	1943-45
Morris, Mary Ernestine	A	1944
Morris, Melissa	T	1952-57
Morris, Nancy	T	1954-57
Morris, Sharon Kay	A	1952
Morris, Virginia	C	1936-37
Morrison, Catherine	C	1930
Morrison, Elizabeth	C	1980-85
Morrison, Frances	C	1944
Morrison, Herrise	T	1949
Morrison, Joan	A	1950
Morrison, Kay	C	1945-50
Morrison, Maria Mary	C	1938
Morrison, Sara Cole	T	1934
Morrison, Sara L.	T	1940
Morrison, Tinker	A	1961-62
Morriss, Annelle	T	1948-49,52
Morriss, Fran	A	1956-60
Morriss, Helen B.	C	1934
Morriss, Nancy	C	1932-33
Morriss, Penny	A	1968-72
Morrow, Emily	T	1984-87
Morrow, Ethel June	C	1945-46
Morrow, Harriet	C	1967-70
Morrow, Jan	T	1961-68
Morrow, Julia	T	1941
Morrow, Laura	T	1991-95
Morrow, Martha Mopsi	C	1961-63
Morrow, Nancy	C	1941
Morrow, Pamela	C	1952
Morrow, Patsy	A	1951-53
Morse, Marilyn	T	1942,45
Morse, Norma Lou	T	1942,45
Morton, Betty	A	1947
Morton, Blair	C	1939-40
Morton, Martha	C	1947
Morton, Mary Delilah	C	1935-37
Moseley, Betty	A	1943-44
Moseley, Marian	T	1941
Moser, Meme	T	1935
Moser, Suzanne	C	1939
Moses, Billie June	T	1938-41
Moses, Jan	T	1940-41
Moses, Marejane	A	1970-73
Moses, Maxine	C	1930
Mosher, Jean	C	1944-49
Mosier, Juli	A	1980-82
Mosier, Susan	A	1977-80
Moss, Camille	T	1940-41
Moss, Cindy	T	1980-84
Moss, Louise		1929
Moss, Moatka	T	1944
Moss, Vivian	C	1942
Mosser, Suzanne	C	1938-42
Mossler, Bonnie	C	1945-47
Mossler, Evelyn	T	1946-47
Mossler, Marilyn	C	1946
Mott, Becky	T	1967-69
Mott, Debbie	T	1969-70
Mott, Jacqueline	T	1946
Mott, Rebecca	T	1967,69
Moulder, Ann	A	1943,45
Mouledous, Gayle	T	1949
Mounger, Katherine		1926
Moursund, Mildred	C	1937
Moutray, Jeanne	A	1943
Moxley, Kay	A	1953
Moxley, Suzette	T	1948-53
Mroz, Juanita	T	1952
Muckleroy, La Merle	C	1935-36
Mueller, Barbara	C	1940-41,43
Mueller, Francis Louise		1929
Mueller, Louise	C	1966-67
Mueller, Louise	T	1941
Mulford, Elizabeth	A	1951-53, 1955-58
Mulkey, Mary Lynn	T	1944
Mulky, Sue	C	1966-67
Mullally, Madge	C	1936-37
Mullen, Talmadge	C	1957
Mullins, Jean	T	1936-38
Mullins, Lisa	C	1969-70
Mullins, Neely	T	1989
Mullins, Peggy	T	1940-41
Mumford, Sondra	C	1953-56
Muncy, Jo	C	1945-46
Munden, Marcia	C	1966-70
Munden, Vanessa	C	1991-95

Munger, Anna	T	1935-37
Munger, Doris	T	1940-41
Munger, Virginia	T	1940-41
Munro, Diane	T	1944
Munro, Mary	A	1945-49
Munsey, Audrey	T	1933
Munsey, Rosemary	C	1933
Munson, Betty	C	1932-33,35
Munson, Dee Dee	A	1978-85
Munson, Diana	A	1979
Munson, Kathryn	T	1986-91
Munson, Mary Martha	T	1960-64
Munson, Meg	C	1988-91
Munson, Merry	A	1985-91
Munson, Nancy	C	1982-84
Munson, Peggy	C	1940-42
Munson, Regina	C	1991-96
Munson, Regina	A	1964-69
Murchison, Ashley	A	1981-83
Murchison, Jennifer	C	1986-93
Murchison, Pat	T	1940-43
Murdock, Linda Dale	C	1958
Murdock, Sarah Jane	A	1949
Murell, Cindy	T	1974
Murfee, Jeanne	C	1931
Murfee, Roberta	C	1939-44
Murphey, Bertie	C	1933,37, 1939,41
Murphey, Dorothy	T	1935-36, 1939-40
Murphey, Malinda	C	1981-87
Murphey, Melrose	C	1940
Murphree, Catherine	C	1941
Murphree, Mary Charlie	C	1955-56
Murphree, Sarah	C	1947
Murphy, Agnes		1928
Murphy, Amy	C	1990,92
Murphy, Camille	T	1954,57
Murphy, Harriet	A	1943
Murphy, Karen	T	1965-70
Murphy, Kathleen	C	1956
Murphy, Kathleen	T	1961-65
Murphy, Martha	T	1963
Murphy, Meg	C	1992
Murphy, Nancy	A	1964-68
Murphy, Patricia	T	1950-53
Murphy, Polly	C	1933,36-37
Murphy, Theodosia	C	1933
Murrah, Ann	C	1946
Murray, Cameron	T	1986-91
Murray, Carla	T	1956-65
Murray, Catherine	T	1940
Murray, Deidra	A	1973-78
Murray, Dorothy	C	1938-40
Murray, Janie	A	1965
Murray, Katie	A	1970-72
Murray, Marilyn	T	1945
Murray, Marilyn	T	1941-45
Murray, Mavis	C	1934,36
Murray, Melissa	T	1970,72
Murrell, Barbara	C	1946-48
Murrell, Cindy	T	1969-76
Murrell, Jill	C	1976-83

Murrell, Julie	T	1976-83
Murrell, Melinda	T	1974-78
Murrell, Nora	C	1994-96
Murrin, Lou Gayle	A	1976-83
Murtaugh, Mary	T	1965-68
Muse, Christi	C	1976
Musselman, Mary Anna	T	1989-92
Musslewhite, Lysbet	T	1987-88
Myatt, Mary Lucille	T	1960-62
Myers, Ann	A	1943
Myers, Betty Sue	C	1944,47
Myers, Caroline	C	1930
Myers, Dorothy	C	1931
Myers, Frances		1938
Myers, Joanne	T	1985-92
Myers, Ruth	C	1931
Myers, Virginia	T	1933-34
Myers, Winifred	C	1932
Mytinger, Micki	A	1960

N

Naber, Nancy	C	1957-60
Nachlas, Emma		1928
Nadler, Carla	A	1949-55
Nadler, Juliane	T	1951-55
Naiden, Charlotte	T	1944
Nail, Jessica	A	1995-96
Nance, Gail	C	1949,51
Nash, Carol	A	1943-44,46
Nash, Catherine	C	1930
Nash, Eleanor	C	1936
Nash, Paige	A	1972-75
Nau, Evangeline	T	1941
Naylor, Noel	T	1947-48
Neal, Melissa	A	1988
Neal, Nancy	C	1932
Neale, Mary Ellen	A	1943-46
Neale, Sallie	C	1946-47
Nealy, Shelly	A	1986-90
Neary, Heather	T	1984
Neathery, Nancy	A	1951-54
Needham, Gayle	T	1956-60
Neel, Betty	C	1936-37, 1940-41
Neeley, Bonnie Mary	C	1935,37
Neeley, Kathleen	A	1944-47
Neeley, Marian	A	1943-45
Neeley, Shirley	A	1944-46
Neely, Jane	A	1947-48
Neely, Susan	A	1962-67
Neely, Susan	A	1976-79
Neff, Lucille	T	1934
Neil, Ina Claire	C	1938-39
Neill, Kathryn	A	1983-85
Neill, Sherry	A	1951
Neimeyer, Agnes	T	1945-46
Nelms, Nancy	C	1962-66
Nelson, Ashley	C	1991-96
Nelson, Becky	A	1968-72
Nelson, Cathy	A	1964-68
Nelson, Dale	C	1964-71
Nelson, Elizabeth	T	1985-88,91
Nelson, Evelyn	T	1979-86

Nelson, Gerry	C	1937-38
Nelson, Harlan	C	1990-96
Nelson, Janie	C	1947-48
Nelson, Katherine	A	1983-88
Nelson, Laura	C	1971-74
Nelson, Leigh	C	1995-96
Nelson, Margaret	C	1935-38
Nelson, Mary	C	1983-84
Nelson, Nancy	C	1954-55
Nelson, Terry	T	1954-57
Nelson, Virginia	A	1954-57
Nelson, Yvonne	A	1946
Nesbitt, Wilmuth		1928
Nesby, Susan	A	1962
Nettles, Mary	A	1962-67
Neudoerfer, Betty Jean	C	1938
Neuenschwander, Christy	A	1983-89
Neuhaus, Grace	C	1941-47
Neuhaus, Peggy	T	1938
Neuhoff, Carolyn	T	1970-77
Neuhoff, Catherine	T	1945-49
Neuhoff, Donna	C	1977-80, 1982-84
Neuhoff, Ellen	A	1967-74
Neuhoff, Emily	T	1978-85
Neuhoff, Ginger	T	1982-89
Neuhoff, Helen	A	1971-77
Neuhoff, Jennifer	A	1981-83
Neuhoff, Laurel	T	1976-80
Neuhoff, Linda	C	1972,74-77
Neuhoff, Mary Ann	T	1941-48
Neuhoff, Mary Jane	T	1972-79
Neuhoff, Michelle	C	1974-81
Neuhoff, Nancy	T	1941-50
Neuhoff, Patty	T	1986-91
Neuhoff, Sarah	C	1995-96
Neuman, Lee	C	1945-49
Neusel, Emily	C	1991-96
Neusel, Gretchen	C	1986-92
Neusel, Heidi	T	1989-96
Nevill, Heather	T	1982
Neville, Carolyn	A	1944
Nevins, Merry Helen	A	1947-49
Newberry, Beth	A	1970
Newberry, Josephine	T	1932
Newbury, Margaret	T	1930
Newby, Bernadine		1933
Newby, Dorothy	C	1938-39
Newby, Elsie	T	1935,37-38
Newcomb, Nancy	C	1951-53
Newell, Ada	C	1931
Newell, Ashley	C	1986
Newell, Valerie	A	1986
Newhill, Barbara		1928
Newhouse, Lynn	C	1949
Newhouse, Nancy	A	1949
Newkirk, Lynn	C	1967-70
Newman, Ernestine	T	1962-63
Newman, Jo	C	1936
Newman, Lee	C	1949
Newman, Margaret	C	1936-37
Newman, Robbie	C	1962-64
Newquist, Lauren	A	1994

Newsom, Janice	C	1949-50		Noble, Lois	T	1937-39		Novy, Melissa	A	1983-84
Newsom, Mary Lewis	C	1950		Noble, Mary Anne	C	1939-42		Nowell, Jo Jo	C	1944-46
Newton, Ailsa Craig Scottie	A	1950-51		Noble, Pat	T	1949-54		Nowery, Ellie	A	1985
				Nobles, Jane	C	1958-60		Nowlin, Alice	A	1981-85
Newton, Ansley	A	1995-96		Noe, Claire	C	1978-84		Nunn, Martha	C	1940
Newton, Clary	A	1987-93		Noe, Erin	A	1970-72		Nussbaum, Barbara	A	1974-75
Newton, Dominique	C	1988-89		Noe, Gay	T	1937-40		Nussbaum, Beverly	T	1934
Newton, Doris	C	1942		Noe, Linda	T	1946-50		Nutto, Janey	T	1942
Newton, Ethel		1929		Noe, Lisa	T	1966-69				
Newton, Evelyn	A	1954		Noel, Catherine	A	1947-48		**O**		
Newton, Iva		1929		Noel, Diana	T	1947-48		Oakes, Mary Agnes	T	1941-43
Newton, Janice		1926		Nofal, Zizi	T	1988		Oakes, Nancy	T	1942
Newton, Julia		1926		Nolan, Caroline	A	1979-84		Oakley, Ada Marie	A	1945-47,49
Newton, Kathy	A	1962-67		Nolan, Diny	C	1969-74		Oakley, Day	T	1959-67
Newton, Lindsay	C	1993-95		Nolan, Mary	A	1975,77		Oakley, Francesca	A	1967-74
Newton, Martha	C	1989-95		Nolan, Tia	C	1958-59		Oatley, Virginia	C	1989
Newton, Opal	T	1933-34		Noland, Judy	T	1952		Oatman, Mary	A	1972-79
Newton, Pam	A	1953-57		Nolen, Lois	T	1930		Obenhaus, Casey	A	1993-96
Newton, Roxana	T	1992-96		Noles, Julie	T	1989-94		Oberman, Lauren	C	1993-94
Newton, Shelby	T	1985-89		Nolte, Ann	A	1947-49		Oberwetter, Valerie	C	1934
Newton, Whitney	T	1994-95		Nolte, Janie	A	1952-54		Ochsner, Skye	A	1985
Niblo, Elizabeth Betty	T	1936-37		Norfleet, Nellie	T	1990-96		Oden, Anna	T	1982-87
Niblo, Virginia	T	1936-37		Norfolk, Claire	C	1968-70,72		Oden, Barbara	T	1965,67-69
Nichols, Annella	C	1939		Norfolk, Lynn	T	1965-69		Oden, Caroline	T	1978-85
Nichols, Betty Ann	C	1956-58, 1960-61		Norfolk, Nancy	A	1975-77		Oden, Frances	C	1934
				Norman, Brenda	T	1954-57		Oden, Lynn	A	1978-84
Nichols, Diane	T	1958-61		Norman, Mary	T	1983-85		Oden, Marilyn	C	1940-41
Nichols, Judy Lea	C	1948-51		Norman, Morgan-Leigh	T	1992-93		Oden, Nell	C	1953-56
Nichols, Nancy	A	1960-61		Norman, Nanette	T	1941		Oden, Sarah	A	1974-80
Nichols, Nancy	A	1945-46		Norman, Nina Wade	A	1943		Odom, Donna	T	1946-54
Nichols, Nancy	C	1940		Norman, Sarah Lee	C	1944-45		Offutt, Betty	C	1935,37-40
Nichols, Penny	A	1956		Norris, Anne	C	1967-70		Offutt, Virginia	C	1935,37-40
Nichols, Priscilla	A	1953-54		Norris, Carol	A	1974-77		Ogden, Catherine	C	1988-91
Nichols, Sally	T	1985-87		Norris, Hillary	T	1988-89, 1991-92		Ogilvie, Margaret	C	1955-57
Nichols, Sally	A	1946-51						Ohlin, Lucy G.	T	1930-31
Nichols, Sandy	T	1957-60		North, Eleanor	C	1937		Old, Andrea	A	1976-81,83
Nicholson, Ann	A	1949		North, Lucy	C	1935-36		Oles, Kaki	C	1965
Nicholson, Carmelle	T	1940		North, Margery	T	1934,36-37		Oles, Mary Michael	A	1955-58
Nicholson, Danya	A	1952-53		Northcutt, Aurelia	T	1981-82		Oliphant, Allene	T	1937-38
Nicholson, Helen	T	1936-37		Northcutt, Cissy	C	1975-81		Oliphant, Nancy	T	1962-63
Nicholson, Jane Ellen	A	1950-51		Northington, Mona	A	1982-87		Oliphint, Mary Brooke	A	1965-71
Nicholson, Mary Ellen	T	1939		Northrup, Dena Beth	C	1981		Olivard, Joanne	A	1943-44
Nickel, Jarrott	T	1964-70		Northrup, Julie	T	1940,44		Olivard, Lois	A	1943-44
Nickel, Lisa	C	1969-73		Norton, Christy	C	1978-79		Oliver, Betty	T	1937
Nicol, Dorothy	T	1942-44		Norton, Marie Louise	T	1940-42		Oliver, Christina	C	1986-93
Nicol, Margery	T	1941-42		Norton, Maud Lynette	C	1937		Oliver, Eleanor	A	1949
Nicol, Martha	T	1943-44		Norton, Melanie	C	1980-81		Oliver, Eloise	T	1931
Niedermann, Phyllis	T	1939,42		Norton, Nancy	T	1941-43		Oliver, Jessie Fay	C	1948-53
Niedermeyer, Emily	C	1994-95		Norton, Robin	T	1942		Oliver, Joan	A	1947-50
Niedermeyer, Susan	A	1994-96		Norton, Sarah Jane	T	1942		Oliver, Kate Ann	C	1954
Ninde, Norma	C	1941		Norvell, Mary	T	1931		Oliver, Laura	T	1979-83
Nini, Taryn	A	1970-75		Norvell, Nicole	T	1977-83		Oliver, Louise	C	1981-86
Nislar, Joan	C	1941-44		Norvell, Noell	T	1980-86		Oliver, Marianne	A	1943
Nislar, Virginia	T	1938		Norvich, Ruth	C	1930		Oliver, Marion	C	1979-85
Nix, Betty	T	1948-52		Norville, Nancy	A	1951		Oliver, Mary Lynn	T	1963-67
Nix, Helen		1928		Norwood, Carol	A	1955-57		Oliver, Mary Vaughn	T	1936-37
Nix, Josephine		1928		Norwood, Mickey	T	1938		Oliver, Mary Lou	T	1946-47
Nix, Marjorie	T	1948-49		Norwood, Paula	T	1969		Oliver, Patsy	T	1946-47
Nixon, Cindy	T	1962-63		Norwood, Ruby	T	1938		Oliver, Sallie	A	1950,52
Nixon, Jane	T	1938		Norwood, Sally	T	1983-86		Oliver, Stacey	C	1985-90
Nixon, Ro	T	1937-40		Notestine, Alice	A	1968-73		Oliver, Susan	A	1982-85
Noble, Ann	T	1941,43		Notestine, Martha	A	1977-84		Olmstead, Kay	A	1972-75
Noble, Leslie	T	1980-81		Novakov, Isabell	C	1990-91		Olsen, Karolyn	C	1942-43

Parrott, Mary Charlotte	C	1950-58	Pearson, Ellen	T	1953-58	Perry, Kathryn	T	1966-71		
Parry, Gaye	C	1962-69	Pearson, Kay	T	1946-47	Perry, Kathy	A	1968-73		
Parsons, Marilyn	T	1948-50	Pearson, Maurnie	T	1940	Perry, Martha	T	1966-71		
Partain, Laura	C	1984-91	Pearson, Rosemary	C	1935-36	Perry, Patricia	C	1953-59		
Partain, Mary Emma	C	1987-94	Pease, Helen Marie	T	1928-30	Perry, Quin	C	1947,49-53		
Partee, Cecille	C	1996	Peay, Charlotte	C	1951-53	Perry, Rachel	T	1987-94		
Partee, Clarice	A	1996	Pech, Lyndall	T	1952-57	Persia, Gloria	A	1960-63		
Partridge, Elizabeth	T	1940	Peck, Alison	T	1967-69	Persia, Sherrie	A	1960-65		
Paschal, Kathleen	T	1937	Peck, Ashley	A	1971-74	Person, Amy	A	1973		
Paschal, Parris	T	1996	Peck, Capi	A	1966-67	Person, Currie	T	1988-91		
Paschall, Elizabeth	A	1992-94	Peck, Diane	A	1961-63	Person, Karen	A	1971-73		
Paschall, Stephanie	T	1992-93	Peck, Frances	A	1943	Peterkin, Pat	T	1939		
Pass, Alex	T	1988-90	Peck, Patti Jo	C	1955-58	Peterman, Frances	A	1947		
Pate, Betty Sue	C	1952-53	Peckham, Grace		1929	Peterman, Julia	T	1941		
Patee, Jean Marie	T	1942	Peckham, June	A	1948-51	Peters, Audrey	T	1945-51		
Paternostro, Anne	T	1986-89	Peckham, Mary		1928-29	Peters, Charlotte	C	1956-60		
Paternostro, Christina	A	1988	Peddie, Bettie	T	1938	Peters, Jennifer	A	1984-87		
Paterson, Blair	A	1995-96	Peddie, Julie	C	1944-45	Peters, Katherine		1934		
Patman, Kay	C	1985	Peden, Martha	A	1949-50	Peters, Margaret	C	1977-82		
Patrick, Erin	T	1931	Peden, Nancy	C	1990-96	Peters, Margaret Ann	A	1943		
Patten, Ann	C	1970-76	Pedrolie, Nancy	C	1952-53	Peterson, Amanda	C	1990		
Patterson, Dorothy		1929	Peebles, Henrietta	C	1941	Peterson, Ellen	A	1972-77		
Patterson, Emily Ann	T	1953-56	Peel, Dorothy	T	1940	Peterson, Kathleen	T	1931		
Patterson, Frances	C	1940	Peery, Sally	C	1940-41	Peterson, Kristin	A	1978-83		
Patterson, Grace	C	1965-71	Pegues, Garland	C	1934	Peterson, Laura	A	1970-75		
Patterson, Iris	C	1931	Peirce, Corinne	T	1932,34	Peterson, Laura	C	1967-69		
Patterson, Jean	C	1947-48,51	Pendergrass, Jinny	C	1950,52	Peterson, Marilyn	C	1934-35		
Patterson, Julianne	C	1967-71	Penders, Sunny	A	1992-95	Peterson, Mary Clare	C	1967-70		
Patterson, Laynie	A	1985	Pendley, Ann Elizabeth	A	1947-51	Peterson, Nora Jo	T	1936,38		
Patterson, Marilyn	C	1929-31,	Penick, Barbara	C	1965-69	Peterson, Norma	C	1942		
		1933-35	Penick, Mary	C	1962	Peterson, Sally	C	1967-70		
Patterson, Patricia Maris	T	1949	Penick, Mary	C	1963-66	Peterson, Waldine	T	1946-50		
Patterson, Priscilla	T	1957-61	Penick, Nancy	C	1940-41	Petitjean, Loretta	T	1936		
Patterson, Susan	A	1958-62	Penn, Patricia	A	1943	Petitjean, Melba	T	1936		
Patterson, Suzanne	C	1940	Pennington, Suzanne	T	1972-73	Petrie, Diana	C	1947		
Pattillo, Pat	C	1945-48	Penny, Mary Sam	C	1941-44	Petrus, Amy	A	1979-84		
Patton, Annette	C	1939	Perez, Jean Beverly	C	1966	Petrus, Leslie	A	1979-82		
Patton, Connie	C	1952-54	Perkins, Ann	A	1955-57	Petry, Dianne	C	1959-65		
Patton, Kay	C	1953-56	Perkins, Cherrie	C	1940-44	Pettit, Carol	A	1978-82		
Patton, Mary Lynn	T	1959-63	Perkins, Diane	A	1948-52	Pettit, Pene	A	1953-57		
Patton, Patricia	C	1941	Perkins, Dorothy	T	1935	Pettit, Sally	T	1965-69		
Patton, Patti Jo	A	1947	Perkins, Elizabeth	C	1933-34	Pettit, Susan	C	1976-80		
Patton, Paula	T	1961-66	Perkins, Laura	C	1958-61	Pettus, Ada Virginia		1928		
Patton, Polly	A	1980-86	Perkins, Lucille		1927	Pettway, Patricia Ann	T	1950		
Patton, Shirley	C	1947	Perkins, Martha	C	1942-44	Petty, Cherry	T	1985-89		
Paulus, Elsie	A	1946,48-51	Perkins, Mauryne	C	1937-38	Petty, Elizabeth	T	1986-89		
Paulus, Rose	T	1930	Perkins, Nancy	C	1944	Petty, Judy	C	1954		
Paup, Jessica	A	1994-96	Perkins, Pat	C	1955-56	Petty, Mary Buford	T	1931		
Paup, Mary Catherine	T	1990-94	Perkins, Patsy	C	1942-47	Peveto, Ann	C	1954-61		
Paup, Patty	A	1958-61	Perkins, Patty		1927	Peyton, Mary Clare	C	1946		
Pawkett, Patricia	T	1943	Perkinson, Martha Gene	T	1928-31	Peyton, Meredith	A	1996		
Payne, Donna	A	1954	Perlitz, Arvilla	C	1975-80	Peyton, Ruth	T	1937		
Payne, Melanie	T	1975-76	Perlitz, Caliste	T	1980-87	Pfeffer, Peggy	C	1936-38		
Payne, Melissa	A	1963	Perlitz, Stacy	T	1967-71	Pflaffenberger, Janelle	A	1979		
Payne, Peggy	C	1941-42	Perner, Mary	T	1942	Pfluger, Amy	A	1978-85		
Payne, Susan	A	1950-53	Perot, Carolyn	A	1980-84	Pfluger, Audrey	T	1968-71		
Payne, Suzanne	A	1954-61	Perot, Katherine	A	1981-84	Pfluger, Bette	A	1981-87		
Peace, Hazel	T	1937-38	Perot, Nancy	T	1973-76	Phares, Edith	T	1967-70,		
Peacock, Martha	A	1943-44	Perot, Suzanne	C	1974-80			1972-73		
Peacock, Robbie	A	1960-66	Perrin, Elizabeth	T	1982-84	Phares, Lenore	C	1976-80		
Peak, Dorothea	T	1942	Perry, George Ann	C	1944	Phares, Melinda	A	1973-76		
Pearce, Anne	T	1965	Perry, Jamie	A	1995-96	Phelan, Colleen	A	1947-48		
Pearce, Margaret	T	1946-49	Perry, Jessica	C	1941-45	Phelan, Johannah	A	1947-48		

Phelan, Katherine	C	1947-48	Pinkston, Hazel	T	1934	Potter, Polly Lou	T	1946,49
Phelan, Lillian	C	1948	Pipkin, Catherine	A	1980-86	Potts, Carol	C	1952-55
Phelan, Margaret	T	1947-48	Pipkin, June	T	1954	Potts, Evantha	A	1943-45
Phelan, Mary Ellen	C	1947-48	Pipkin, Laura	A	1981-84	Potts, Marie	C	1929-30
Phelan, Mary Ann	A	1953-61	Pipkin, Patricia Ann	C	1933-34	Potts, Ruth	C	1932
Phelan, Patsy	T	1946-47	Pitman, Bonnie	T	1945	Powell, Barbara	T	1961-63
Phelps, Kathy	C	1959-60	Pitman, Helen Ann	C	1941-44	Powell, Beverly	T	1951
Phelps, Laura Louise		1928	Pitman, Peggy		1945	Powell, Chrissy	T	1976-83
Phelps, Nancy	C	1942-43	Pittman, Jeannette	C	1941-43	Powell, Crystal	T	1974
Phelps, Vicki	A	1959-60	Pittman, Virginia	C	1939-40	Powell, Elizabeth		1929
Philbin, Jennifer	A	1983-88	Pitts, Linda	C	1969-70	Powell, Hallie	A	1967-71
Philen, Edna Sophia	A	1949-50	Pitts, Sally	C	1961-68	Powell, Holly	C	1964-69
Philip, Margaret	C	1992	Pitts, Sally	C	1950-54	Powell, Janis	C	1959-64
Philips, Susan	A	1961	Pitzer, Barbara	A	1961-68	Powell, Judy Ann	A	1949
Phillips, Abby	T	1984-90	Pitzer, Pamela	C	1958-66	Powell, Kathryn	T	1966-70
Phillips, Anette	A	1967-71	Pitzer, Susan	T	1953-59	Powell, Kimberly	C	1979-85
Phillips, Anne	A	1985-88	Pivoto, Bessie Margaret		1929	Powell, Lorrie	C	1972-78
Phillips, Ashley	T	1989-95	Pivoto, Mary Lula		1929	Powell, Marie	C	1936
Phillips, Bennie Gail	T	1942-43	Plankey, Ann	C	1949-52	Powell, Nancy	T	1961-66
Phillips, Corinne	T	1942	Platt, Jessica	T	1990-96	Powell, Nicole	C	1993-96
Phillips, Dana	A	1964-67	Platt, Julia	T	1993-96	Powell, Nixon	T	1992-96
Phillips, Evelyn	C	1934	Platt, Mary Jane	T	1995-96	Powell, Paige	A	1980-83
Phillips, Gail	A	1959-64	Plowman, Jane	C	1929-30	Powell, Varina	A	1943
Phillips, Jane	C	1963-66	Plumb, Mariquita	A	1947-50	Powell, Victoria	A	1975-79
Phillips, Kay	T	1964-65	Plumb, Susan	T	1956-57	Powers, Elizabeth	T	1968-71
Phillips, Lavon	C	1937-40	Plunkett, Linda	A	1956	Powers, Nancy	A	1943-44
Phillips, Lisa	C	1980-83,85	Poage, April	C	1945	Powers, Patricia	A	1944
Phillips, Marilyn	A	1944	Poe, Jenny	T	1986-91,93	Powers, Patty	A	1951-55
Phillips, Mary Frances	C	1935-36,	Pohl, Jennifer	A	1994-96	Powers, Shannon	T	1989
		1938,43	Pohl, Mindy	A	1989-94	Poyner, Ann	C	1940-43,45
Phillips, Mary Ashton	T	1994-96	Pohli, Anne	T	1965-70	Prather, Johnetta	C	1982-85
Phillips, Missy	C	1991-96	Poland, Jennifer	T	1989-91	Pratt, June Lucille	T	1933
Phillips, Nancy	T	1961-68	Poleski, Kristen	A	1992-96	Pratt, Kelley	C	1986-91
Phillips, Patti	A	1971-75	Poleski, Lauren	C	1995-96	Pratt, Lauren	C	1985-90
Phillips, Phyllis Ann	A	1945-52	Pollard, Dorothy	T	1938	Pratt, Marian	T	1988-94
Phillips, Ruth Dee	C	1937	Pollard, Patti	T	1947-54	Pratt, Shawn	A	1988-90
Phillips, Windi	A	1975-76	Pollard, Tany	T	1942-48	Preble, Marlene	C	1943
Phinizy, Kate	T	1981-85	Pollard, Virginia	T	1946	Prehn, Mary Virginia	C	1936
Phy, Elizabeth	A	1985-88	Pollock, Sylvia	C	1937	Preis, Katie	T	1996
Pichinson, Lisa	A	1974-79	Ponder, Virginia		1928-29	Prejean, Thelma	T	1936
Pickens, Jean	C	1937-38	Ponderon, Ruth	T	1930	Prendergast, Martha Marty	T	1937-38,40
Pickens, Patricia	A	1982-88	Pool, Iris Ruth	C	1951-52	Prentice, Catherine	C	1929-30
Picton, Jan	T	1962-67	Pool, Nancy	C	1937	Prentice, Linda	A	1956-59
Pierce, Diane	T	1955-61	Pope, Geralyn	C	1959-60	Prescott, Paula	A	1954-55
Pierce, Krista	C	1995-96	Pope, Katherine	T	1951-55	Presley, Jacquelyn	C	1987-93
Pierce, Martha	C	1942	Pope, Mary	T	1968-74	Presley, Joan	T	1944
Pierce, Mary Jane	C	1931	Pope, Ruthie	C	1931, 33-34	Presley, Kathleen	C	1996
Pierce, Patricia	C	1956-57	Pope, Sandra	C	1951	Pressler, Margaret		1929
Pierce, Susan	T	1958-59	Porch, Judy	T	1942	Pressly, Catherine	C	1995-96
Pierce, Vicky	C	1930-31	Porter, Becky	T	1939	Pressly, Laura	C	1972-74
Pierre, Patricia	C	1957	Porter, Betty	T	1935-36,38	Pressly, Lisa	C	1967-68
Pierson, Anne	C	1960	Porter, Gerry	A	1954-56	Preston, Eleanor	C	1947-50
Pierson, Judith	A	1946	Porter, Jane	T	1940-41	Preston, Eugenia	T	1931
Pierson, Martha	T	1941	Porter, Louise	C	1947-49	Preston, Frances	T	1951-59
Pierson, Patsy	A	1943	Porter, Mary Alva	T	1940	Preston, Laura	A	1950-53
Pierson, Pattie	C	1959-60	Porter, Phyllis	C	1944	Preston, Ruth	T	1930
Pierson, Roma	T	1946	Posey, Sandra	A	1948	Pribyl, Sally	C	1966-68
Pierson, Sybil	A	1943	Postlethwaite, Stratton	T	1948-49	Price, Alice	A	1985-91
Pierson, Windley	A	1970-73	Pote, Nola Clay	C	1931	Price, Ann	T	1950-54
Pincoffe, Louise	T	1933,35	Poth, Elizabeth Anne	T	1929-30	Price, Anne Bratton	C	1989-91
Pincoffe, Rosalind		1933	Potishman, Boots	T	1934-35	Price, Becca	A	1980-85
Pincus, Louise	C	1931,34	Potter, Joan	T	1938	Price, Dorothy	C	1955-57
Piner, Robbie	T	1938,40	Potter, Mary Lee	C	1958	Price, Dorothy Ruth	C	1941

Price, Dorsey	C	1942
Price, Elaine	C	1930-31
Price, Elizabeth	C	1955-59
Price, Jana	T	1972-73
Price, Jeanne	C	1944-51
Price, Kelsey Virginia	T	1954-55
Price, Lelah	C	1946-50
Price, Linda	C	1959-64
Price, Pat	C	1944-47
Price, Paula	T	1960-63
Price, Penny	T	1962-63
Price, Rosalie	C	1936-37
Price, Sally Sue	C	1952-54
Price, Sara Jo	C	1956-59
Price, Sarah	A	1988-92
Price, Virginia Dinny	T	1953-54, 1956-59
Price, Zoe	C	1930
Priddy, Ann	T	1941-42
Priddy, Barbara	A	1966-69
Pride, Virginia	T	1935
Prideaux, Doris	T	1937
Prideaux, Francis	C	1938
Priest, Dannie Jane	C	1937
Priestly, Abbe	T	1981-86
Prigmore, Phyllis	T	1941
Primm, Lucy	C	1948-49
Primos, Amanda	T	1988-91
Primos, Jessica	A	1991-92
Princes, Louise	C	1931
Pring, Patricia	T	1930
Pringos, Angela	C	1958-59
Probst, Marilyn	T	1940-41
Procter, Bettye	C	1956-57
Procter, Debbye	T	1956-57
Procter, Pennye	A	1954-57
Proctor, Evelyn	C	1935
Proctor, Jeannine	C	1941
Proctor, Jolene	C	1940-41
Proctor, Mary Lou	A	1950-51
Pross, Molly	T	1994-96
Prothro, Holly	A	1981-88
Prothro, Kathy	T	1970-72
Prothro, Kay	T	1950-54
Prothro, Mary Margaret	C	1942-47
Prothro, Mary	A	1973-77
Prouty, Alice Lynn	C	1947-49
Prouty, Joan	C	1941-44
Provosty, Miriam	A	1945
Prowell, Marianne	C	1939
Pruet, Paula	A	1962-63
Pruitt, Mindy	A	1960-61
Pryor, Cornelia	C	1946
Pryor, Elizabeth	C	1966-71
Pryor, Laura	A	1964-69
Pryor, Molly	A	1978-79
Pryor, Susan	A	1963-68
Puckett, Frances Jane	T	1935-38
Puckett, Mary Ann	T	1935,37-38
Puckett, Prissy	A	1948-51
Puckett, Terry Gay	T	1951-53
Pullen, Elizabeth	C	1977-81
Pullin, Janet		1940

Pullin, Jean		1940
Purcell, Diane	C	1972-73
Purcell, Laura	C	1978-83
Purdie, Patricia	A	1943
Purnell, Marjorie	A	1948-51
Purvines, Norma	T	1936-40
Pustka, Audrey	C	1996
Putman, Jean	C	1942
Putman, Lucy	C	1981-83
Putman, Mandy	C	1987-92
Putnam, Sa San	T	1938-42
Putney, Elizabeth Bibba	A	1946-50
Putty, Mary Kell	A	1952-55
Pyle, Gene Ann	C	1974-81
Pyle, Mary	T	1970-75

Q

Quantz, Anne	T	1953
Querans, Bettie	T	1950
Querbes, Carolyn	T	1990-93
Querbes, Elizabeth	A	1978-81
Querbes, Jennifer	T	1987-90
Querbes, Marjorie	C	1977-81
Querbes, Mary Jane	C	1934
Querens, Agnes		1950
Quinn, Cathy	A	1965
Quinn, Frances	T	1944-49
Quinn, Kathy	A	1965-67
Quinn, Kendal	T	1978-80
Quinn, Kim	A	1973
Quinn, Patton	T	1990-95
Quinn, Susan	A	1982-88
Quirk, Barbara	T	1977-78
Quisenberry, Laura	C	1995-96

R

Rabon, Diane	C	1949-53
Race, Chandler	C	1991-94
Rader, India Ann	A	1949-50
Ragan, Amy	T	1974-79
Ragan, Sarah	C	1975-81
Ragland, Sarah Lou	C	1937
Ragsdale, Amele	T	1931
Ragsdale, Jamie		1928
Ragsdale, Silky	C	1934-37
Rahmberg, Lauren	A	1996
Rainey, Becca	A	1987-90
Rainey, Mary Katherine	A	1990-96
Rains, Misti	A	1972-79
Rains, Sherri	C	1968-75
Rakestraw, Cathy	A	1954-55
Rall, Linda	A	1989-93
Rall, Olive	T	1937
Rall, Stephanie	T	1989-96
Ralston, Jo B.	C	1940-41
Ramirez, Jane	A	1960-63
Ramirez, Nan	A	1961-67
Rampy, Donna	C	1942-43
Ramsay, Jan	T	1972-74
Ramsay, Laura Marie	A	1943-44
Ramsay, Mackie	C	1947-50
Ramsey, Allison	C	1995-96
Ramsey, Doris	T	1939

Ramsey, Jan	T	1972
Ramsey, Mackie	C	1949
Ramsey, Mary Ann	C	1952-56
Ramsey, Mildred	T	1934
Ramsey, Mysti	C	1992-93
Ramsey, Rachel	C	1974-75
Ramsey, Randa	C	1971-74
Ramsey, Reade	C	1968-69
Ramsey, Rosemary	T	1984-91
Ramsey, Sally Lou	A	1945
Randall, Anne	A	1972-75
Randall, Betsy	C	1966-70
Randall, Leigh	C	1971-74
Randall, Lynne	C	1969-72
Randall, Rose	C	1939
Randolph, Judy	C	1952-53
Randolph, Margaret Ann	C	1931
Randt, Ashley	C	1994
Raney, Amanda	T	1971
Raney, Mary	C	1970-71
Raney, Myra	A	1990
Raney, Sharon	T	1952-55
Ranfrang, Sibyl	T	1943
Ranfranz, Mary Alice	T	1942-43,45
Rankin, Sylvia	C	1946-47
Ransom, Helen	C	1935
Ransom, Majorie	C	1931
Rao, Shannon	A	1980-83
Raper, Lori	A	1980-81
Rapier, Helen	T	1942
Rappeport, Jennifer	A	1982-89
Rasbach, Jane	C	1962-64
Rascoe, Mary	T	1952-53
Rasdire, Carol Jeane	A	1943
Rase, Victoria	A	1973
Ratcliff, Grace	A	1943-44
Ratcliff, Isolina	C	1932
Ratcliff, Ruby Moss		1933
Ratcliff, Virginia	T	1946
Ratcliffe, Evangeline	T	1942-43
Ratcliffe, Ruth Ann	T	1942
Rathbone, Eleanor	T	1941-43
Rathbun, Kelly	A	1978-83
Rathbun, Stacy	A	1983-90
Rathburn, Kelly	A	1982
Rather, Carol	A	1955-59
Rather, Francis		1929
Ratliff, Claire	C	1981-88
Ratliff, Lillie	A	1978-82
Ratliff, Louise	A	1966-67
Ratliff, Rosemary	A	1981-83
Ratz, Leslie	A	1984-87
Rau, Sally	A	1948
Rauch, Ann	T	1934
Rauch, Veda Mae	C	1934
Rauth, Kit	T	1964
Rawland, Bettye Lu	T	1945-49
Rawland, Carol Jeanne	C	1957-61
Rawland, Marianne	T	1946-53
Rawlins, Jane	C	1946
Rawlins, Josephine	T	1941
Ray, Alicia	T	1968-74
Ray, Bobby Jean	T	1945-47

Ray, Coletta	C	1942
Ray, Julie	T	1972-74
Ray, Martha	C	1941
Ray, Melodie	A	1972-73
Ray, Patricia	C	1944
Rayce, Elaine	A	1964
Rayes, Rebecca	T	1963-67
Rayford, Bess	T	1932-35
Raynor, Betty Lee	C	1938-39
Rayzor, Jackie	A	1943
Rayzor, Sallie	T	1984-90
Rayzor, Wispy	C	1982-87
Rea, Gracie Catherine	C	1931
Read, Kay	T	1949
Read, Penny	A	1983-84, 1986-89
Read, Susan	A	1985-90
Reagan, Mary Bell	A	1952-54
Reardon, Becca	C	1995-96
Reasoner, Caroline	C	1975-77
Reble, Marleen	C	1943
Rebsamen, Mary Lee	T	1949-50
Rector, Nancy	C	1968-73
Red, Alice	C	1953-54
Redburn, Betty Jo	T	1934-35,39
Redding, Dana Kay	T	1958-62
Redding, Marsha	T	1960-65
Redford, Davalyn	T	1975-81
Redford, Meredith	A	1975-81
Redington, Katherine	C	1992
Redman, Sarah		1928
Redmont, Pamela	A	1957-61
Redmont, Sondra	T	1982-85
Redwine, Elizabeth	C	1990-94
Reed, Alyce Jean	T	1933
Reed, Annette	T	1947
Reed, Betsy	A	1978-82
Reed, Billie	T	1928-31
Reed, Carolyn	T	1976-80
Reed, Christie	T	1955-56, 1958-59
Reed, Ida	A	1945-46,48
Reed, Jennifer	T	1963-64
Reed, Jenny Lou	T	1979-80
Reed, Lucy	C	1952,54
Reed, Meredith	A	1967
Reed, Nancy	T	1933
Reed, Nancy Sue	C	1948
Reed, Peggy	T	1939
Reed, Ruth Nell		1928-29
Reed, Vicky	T	1949-51
Reeder, Ann	A	1945-47
Reeder, Caroline	T	1994
Reeds, Helen	C	1940-41, 1943-44
Reese, Ann	A	1946-49
Reese, Billie Ruth	T	1939,42
Reese, Rachel	C	1981-87
Reese, Sharon	A	1985-88
Reese, Stacey	C	1977-83
Reeves, Dolores	A	1943
Reeves, Jan	A	1954-56
Reeves, Julie	C	1956-64

Reeves, Patsy	C	1940
Reggan, Kathryn		1929
Rehbeger, Barbara	A	1950
Rehm, Dorothy	T	1978-83
Reib, Jane	C	1936
Reichert, Barbara	C	1958-62
Reichert, Heidi	A	1959-62
Reid, Leslie	T	1975
Reids, Helen	C	1943
Reiger, Jennifer	C	1982
Reilly, Kathryn	C	1944
Reilly, Lillian		1928-29
Reilly, Mary Elizabeth	T	1939-40
Reilly, Nancy	A	1943-45
Reinhardt, Mary Kathryn		1928
Reinhardt, Stephanie	T	1991
Reitmeyer, Jillian	T	1995
Rektorik, Becky	C	1988-89
Remes, Alice	T	1940
Remmel, Becky	T	1961,63-64
Remmel, Carrie	C	1932
Remmel, Cathie	T	1952-57
Renaudin, Elise	C	1971-72,74
Rendleman, Ann	A	1951-56
Rendleman, Janet	A	1947-48
Renfro, Laura	C	1930
Renfro, Nancy	T	1930-31
Renger, Rosalie	C	1935
Rennie, Allis Ann	T	1957-62
Renshaw, La Vega	C	1947
Replogle, Majorie		1929
Repschleger, Lillian	T	1932
Ressman, Ashley	C	1986-90
Ressmann, Courtney	A	1987-93
Ressmann, Lindsey	T	1991-94
Rettger, Priscilla	C	1946
Reynolds, Andrea	C	1980-83
Reynolds, Dina	C	1958-59
Reynolds, Jean	T	1941
Reynolds, Jean	C	1965-68
Reynolds, Margaret	A	1960-62
Reynolds, Martha	T	1961-62
Reynolds, Muffet	T	1978-84
Reynolds, Virginia	A	1987-93
Rhea, Mary Ida		1929
Rhine, Kelly	T	1949
Rhoades, Marci	A	1968-74
Rhodes, Amy	C	1971-75, 1977-78
Rhodes, Jane	C	1935-37
Rhodes, Ranelle	T	1948-49, 1951-52
Rhymes, Jane	T	1939-40
Ribelin, Lucia	C	1946-47
Ricci, Laura	A	1981-84
Rice, Amy	T	1990
Rice, Ashley	A	1986-88
Rice, Doll	T	1985-88
Rice, Dolores	T	1945-48
Rice, Finley	C	1963-65
Rice, Jackie	A	1951
Rice, Jane	T	1936
Rice, Jerilyn	A	1950-52

Rice, Joanne		1951
Rice, Martha	C	1993
Rich, Connie Sue	C	1958-60
Richard, Anna	A	1946
Richard, Kate	A	1994
Richard, Kim	C	1972-73
Richard, Nancy	A	1961-63
Richards, Amy	A	1977-79
Richards, Ann	C	1942-50
Richards, Beverly	A	1954-55
Richards, Carrie	T	1987-88
Richards, Edith	A	1960
Richards, Jane	A	1958-61
Richards, Jean	T	1941,45-46
Richards, Julie	A	1946
Richards, Morgan	A	1992-96
Richards, Norma Joyce	T	1939-40
Richards, Pam	T	1975-81
Richards, Patricia Ann	C	1934
Richards, Peggy	C	1936
Richards, Susan	T	1960-64
Richards, Trudy	A	1972
Richardson, Alexis	A	1995-96
Richardson, Ann	T	1964-66
Richardson, Ann	A	1944-45
Richardson, Barbara	C	1939-40
Richardson, Caroline	T	1986-89
Richardson, Connie	T	1994-96
Richardson, Elizabeth	C	1969-73
Richardson, Francie		1970
Richardson, Janis	T	1942,44
Richardson, Lucy		1928
Richardson, Martha Ann	A	1949
Richardson, Patty	C	1944
Richardson, Robin	A	1964-66
Richardson, Robin	C	1963-68
Richter, Amy	A	1982-85
Richter, Elizabeth	T	1960
Richter, Patricia	A	1959-60
Rick, Connie	C	1958-60
Rickard, Claire	C	1967-71
Ricker, Maribel	T	1938
Rickland, Claire	C	1968
Riddle, Jane	T	1951,54-55
Riddle, Rose Marie	C	1931
Ridgeway, Allison	A	1975-80
Ridley, Jill	A	1959-65
Ridley, Lauren	C	1992
Ridley, Rachel	T	1992-95
Riedel, Nancy	T	1951-54
Rieger, Jeanie	C	1982-83
Rieke, Courtney	C	1987-90
Riff, Selma	C	1937
Riggs, Marci	A	1976-77
Riggs, Susan	C	1948
Rihelin, Ree		1947
Riley, Maggie	C	1982-87
Riley, Mary Elizabeth	T	1939
Riley, Nan	T	1964-67
Riley, Polly	T	1947-48
Riley, Tex Ann	C	1940
Rinaman, Peggie	C	1934-35
Rindy, Beverly	T	1940

Rindy, Rowena	C	1940
Riner, Ronnie	C	1958-62
Ring, Rosalie		1934
Ringer, Margaret	T	1942
Ripley, Elsie Rose	T	1937
Rippel, Ann	T	1942-43
Rippel, Jane	T	1940-42
Riser, Deanna	A	1974
Riser, Melissa	A	1975
Risinger, Jane	T	1968-69
Risser, Sally	C	1953-55
Ritchie, Sally	T	1947-48
Riter, Melinda	A	1963-67
Rivenbark, Betty Mac	A	1952
Rivers, Dawn	T	1970-74
Rivers, Lucy	A	1972-75
Rivers, Robin	T	1974
Rives, Jen	C	1941-43
Riviere, Alice	A	1945-51
Riviere, Carolyn	C	1938,40
Riviere, Dorothy Belle	T	1937-38
Rixon, Patricia	A	1951-53
Rizos, Joanne	C	1996
Roach, Ann	C	1960-67
Roach, Katie	T	1993
Roach, Martha	T	1937
Roach, Robyn	A	1965-66
Roach, Sheri	C	1969-75
Roach, Shirley	T	1935,37-38
Roach, Susan	T	1966-69
Roach, Whitney	A	1994-96
Roadhouse, Ashley	T	1975,77-78
Roadhouse, Kelley	C	1977-78
Roadhouse, Sarah	C	1986
Roane, Alice	A	1953-54
Roane, Barbara	T	1948-51
Roane, Julia	A	1958-60
Roane, Therese	T	1942
Roark, Courtney	A	1972
Roark, Janie	T	1988-93
Roark, Robin	A	1981-85
Roark, Ryan	C	1993-95
Robb, Janet	T	1938-41,43
Robb, Peggy	C	1961-65
Robb, Shay	A	1959-63
Robberson, Becky	A	1980-81
Robbins, Beverly	A	1950
Robbins, Cynthia	T	1947-50
Robbins, Marion	T	1935
Robbins, Peggy	T	1972
Roberdeau, Ann Elizabeth	T	1934
Roberdeau, Virginia		1929
Roberson, Lois		1953
Robert, Ada	C	1941-42
Roberts, Alice Mae	T	1934-35, 1939-40
Roberts, Barbara	T	1961-66
Roberts, Betty	T	1939-40
Roberts, Catherine	C	1945-46
Roberts, Helen Howie	C	1940
Roberts, Hester	T	1936
Roberts, Jean	T	1940
Roberts, Jennifer	T	1966-73
Roberts, Jessica	C	1983-88
Roberts, Jill	T	1967-72
Roberts, Julie	C	1968-71
Roberts, Kristy	C	1969-73
Roberts, Lee	T	1977-79, 1981-83
Roberts, Margaret	C	1983-90
Roberts, Mary Elizabeth	C	1964-66
Roberts, Mary Alan	T	1964-69
Roberts, Nancy	T	1954-56
Roberts, Nancy	C	1962-66
Roberts, Pamela	A	1982-85
Roberts, Patsy	A	1947-53
Roberts, Peg	C	1936-38
Roberts, Rachel	C	1990
Roberts, Rebecca	C	1986
Roberts, Rebecca	T	1933-36
Roberts, Sara	A	1967-72
Roberts, Wendy	A	1979-83
Robertson, Beth	T	1983-84
Robertson, Christi	C	1970-76
Robertson, Colleen	A	1974-79
Robertson, Jan	C	1957-65
Robertson, Jana	A	1987
Robertson, Kaylea	C	1994-96
Robertson, Lee	T	1957-61
Robertson, Mary	T	1929-30
Robertson, Nan Lee	A	1957-59
Robertson, Natalie	A	1990-94
Robertson, Renie	C	1942,44, 1946-48
Robertson, Susan	C	1957-58
Robertson, Virginia	T	1935-36, 1938-40
Robillard, Jennifer	A	1986
Robinowitz, Beverly		1928
Robinowitz, May Tee		1928
Robins, Margaret	C	1942-44
Robins, Martha	C	1942-47
Robinson, Becky	A	1966-70
Robinson, Beth	C	1978-81
Robinson, Betty Jane	T	1941
Robinson, Beverly	C	1940-41
Robinson, Beverly	T	1945-48
Robinson, Brooks	C	1947-49
Robinson, Carla	T	1954-59
Robinson, Diane	T	1950-52
Robinson, Emily	C	1973-76
Robinson, Flora	A	1960-64
Robinson, Flora Teddy		1928
Robinson, Frances	A	1969-71
Robinson, Gail	C	1963-69
Robinson, Janey	T	1963-68
Robinson, Jill	C	1995-96
Robinson, Kathryn	C	1936
Robinson, Kathy	T	1962-67
Robinson, Laurie	T	1994-96
Robinson, Lois	T	1953
Robinson, Margaret	C	1933-35
Robinson, Maxine	C	1933
Robinson, Nancy	C	1931
Robinson, Rachelle	A	1984-85
Robison, Maxine	C	1933-35
Roby, Kay	C	1959-61
Roche, Rosa Lee	C	1932
Rochelle, Marinelle	T	1930
Rockefeller, Andrea	T	1984
Rockefeller, Katherine	C	1984-85
Rockefeller, Valerie	C	1982-83
Roddie, Diane	T	1949,51-52
Rodgers, Elizabeth	T	1956-57
Rodgers, Renee	T	1964-67
Rodrigues, Alexa	A	1993
Rodriguez, Carolina	C	1984-85, 1987-91
Roe, Haise	T	1982-88
Roe, Hallie	A	1995-96
Roedahl, Sandra	T	1955
Roessler, Judy	C	1957-62
Rogers, Anita	T	1945
Rogers, Betty	A	1981-85
Rogers, Beverly	C	1936
Rogers, Carroll	C	1946-49
Rogers, Charlotte	T	1976-78
Rogers, Cita	A	1954-57
Rogers, Diane	C	1964-68
Rogers, Dolores	A	1945
Rogers, Elizabeth	T	1972-73
Rogers, Elizabeth	C	1958-63
Rogers, Emily	T	1984-90
Rogers, Eryn	A	1983-87
Rogers, Grace		1928
Rogers, Grace	T	1938-39
Rogers, Jane	C	1941
Rogers, Jean	C	1935-36
Rogers, Jillian	C	1988
Rogers, June	A	1976-80
Rogers, Linda	C	1943
Rogers, Lois	T	1936
Rogers, Louise	T	1959-64
Rogers, Lynn	C	1948-49
Rogers, Marcella	T	1939
Rogers, Marcia	C	1942-43
Rogers, Margaret	T	1978-80
Rogers, Mary McGee	C	1935-36
Rogers, Mary	C	1938
Rogers, Rosalin	A	1961-66
Rogers, Wendy	A	1984
Rohan, Nancy	T	1941-46
Rohde, Jamie	A	1991
Rollins, Betty Sue	A	1943
Rollins, Melanie	C	1973-75
Rollins, Rosalind		1929
Rolston, Andra	A	1950-53
Roman, Alice Sue	C	1938
Romano, Carole	C	1957-59
Rome, Jennifer	T	1992-93
Romo, Alexandra	A	1996
Romoser, Marcie	A	1974-78
Rone, Lynn	T	1960-62
Roney, Sharon	T	1954
Roodhouse, Ashley	T	1975-81
Roodhouse, Kelley	C	1976-83
Roodhouse, Sarah	C	1981-85,87
Rooke, Jean	C	1945—49
Rooke, Roberta	C	1941-48

Sargent, Betty	C	1934	Schmidt, Patty Ann	T	1946-48	Schwend, Susan	C	1957
Sartin, Anne Lea	T	1948	Schmidt, Sally Anne	C	1989-90,92	Schwing, Amy	T	1980-83
Sartor, Georgie	C	1996	Schneider, Ellen	T	1941-42	Schwing, Kelly	A	1977-84
Sarvtelle, Caroline	C	1953	Schneider, Kathy	T	1970-75	Schwing, Lilla Anne	T	1956-64
Satel, Tracie	A	1988-89	Schneider, Margaret	T	1941-42	Schworz, Barbara	T	1979
Sauder, Alane	T	1963-67	Schneider, Patsy Gay	T	1942-44	Scisson, Jane	C	1961-64
Sauder, Suzanne	T	1974-77	Schneider, Susan	A	1972-78	Scisson, Judy	A	1962-64
Sauer, Betsy	A	1954-60	Schneider, Susan B.	T	1974-79	Scott, Amanda	C	1985-88
Sauer, Cassie	T	1977-84	Schnitter, Mary Louise	T	1945-48	Scott, Ashley	T	1973-77
Sauer, Ellen	T	1975-81	Schoch, Harriet	C	1951-52	Scott, Betty Jane	C	1929-30
Saunders, Anna Katherine	C	1959	Schoch, Sandra	T	1951	Scott, Betty Jane	C	1940-43
Saunders, Mary Frances	T	1937-40	Schoellkopf, Harriett	A	1956	Scott, Betty	C	1952-54
Saunders, Nancy	C	1945,47-49	Schoenmann, Bernice	T	1934-35	Scott, Betty Ruth	C	1946
Saunders, Suzanne	A	1946-49	Schoenmann, Harriett	C	1931	Scott, Cathy	C	1965
Saunders, Vicki	T	1975-77	Schoenvogel, Emily	C	1991-95	Scott, Claire	A	1944
Savage, Anne	A	1956-60	Schofield, Kinsey	C	1995	Scott, Doris Elaine	T	1952-53
Savage, Betsy	T	1956-57	Schofield, Rebecca	A	1992-95	Scott, Elizabeth	T	1966-69
Savage, Kathleen Ann		1960	Schoonover, Ann	C	1936	Scott, Helen Anne	A	1946-48
Savage, Susan	A	1962-63	Schott, Lois Scottie	C	1934-35	Scott, Jane	C	1939
Savell, Vicki Jo	A	1951-53	Schoverling, Lynn	T	1961-63	Scott, Joan	T	1942-43
Savers, Virginia	C	1950-51	Schreier, Barbara	T	1939,41	Scott, Judy	C	1941-42,44
Saville, Floy	T	1936-37	Schrock, Phyllis Ann	A	1953-57	Scott, Kathy	A	1970-75
Saving, Delores	T	1938	Schroeder, Kristi	A	1988-93	Scott, Lila	C	1945-46
Sawtelle, Caroline	C	1953-54,56	Schroeder, Olga		1928	Scott, Linda	C	1965-68
Sawtelle, Priscilla	C	1954-56	Schubert, Ann		1939	Scott, Martha	C	1939-40
Sawyer, Heather	T	1978-80	Schubert, Edna Marie	T	1955	Scott, Mary Leslie	C	1938
Scales, Jean	C	1931	Schubert, Virginia	A	1943-45	Scott, Mitzie	T	1976-79,
Scales, Mary Ann	T	1934	Schuch, Brenda	A	1960-63			1981-82
Scarborough, Karen	A	1953-54	Schuch, Helene	A	1947	Scott, Nancy	T	1960-65
Scarborough, Margaret	A	1962-63	Schuch, Mary Louise	C	1944	Scott, Pat	C	1948-49,
Scarborough, Margaret Ann	C	1948-50	Schuch, Susan	T	1967-71			1951-52
			Schuelke, Marilyn	C	1946-47	Scott, Patricia	C	1941-42,44
Scarbrough, Courtney	C	1993-96	Schuessler, Bridget	C	1987-90	Scott, Peggy	T	1941
Scarff, Tiffany	T	1987-91	Schuessler, Catherine	C	1985-86	Scott, Shannon	A	1981-83
Schaefer, Frances	C	1937-39	Schuh, Margaret	T	1949-50	Scott, Shirley	T	1936-38
Schaefer, Margaret	T	1933	Schuhmacher, Dineen	C	1945-46	Scott, Shirley	C	1931-32
Schafer, Deborah	C	1978-84	Schuhmacher, Katherine Sandy	C	1946-48	Scott, Sue	T	1946-53
Schafer, Margaret	C	1972-76				Scott, Susan	C	1965-68
Schafer, Shelby	C	1949-54	Schuhmacher, Nancy	C	1945-48	Scott, Susan	C	1958-60
Schaffer, Susan	A	1978-84	Schule, Mary Jean	T	1942	Scott, Tandy	A	1956
Schairbaum, Nicki	T	1996	Schulte, Bridget	T	1978-81	Scott, Terry	C	1930
Schalk, Susan	C	1970-76	Schulte, Paige	A	1991-94	Scott, Tiffani	A	1984-88
Schallhorn, Susan	A	1973-80	Schultz, Robin	C	1968-69	Scott, Virginia	A	1989-92
Schapers, France	C	1991	Schulz, Charlotte	T	1942-46	Scrafford, Suzy	A	1956-59
Scharbauer, Pamela	A	1966-67	Schulz, Sarah	C	1979-83	Scranton, Barbara	T	1938-39
Scharold, Margaret	C	1989-91	Schumacher, Katherine	C	1947	Scroggins, Berkley	C	1995-96
Schaufele, Ann Blair	C	1985-86	Schumacher, Nancy	C	1947	Scroggins, Kelsey	A	1992-96
Schaufele, Janet	T	1981-88	Schumaher, Mary Lou	C	1944	Scruggs, Bettie	T	1938,40
Scheffer, Carole Ann	C	1948	Schuman, Rebecca	C	1932	Scruggs, Jan	A	1961-62
Scheid, Missy	C	1962-64	Schurr, Mary Louise	C	1940	Scull, Beverly	C	1943
Schein, Doris		1926	Schuster, Lyndall	C	1987-93	Scurlock, Amy	T	1967-70
Schein, Frances		1926	Schutts, Emily	T	1965-67	Scurlock, Laura Lee	C	1940-44
Schendle, Maggi	C	1984-88	Schutts, Martha	A	1964-68	Scurlock, Lucia	A	1969-70
Scheyd, Ann	T	1954-55	Schutts, Mary	C	1967-71	Seagler, Dixie	T	1942-43
Schieffer, Susan	T	1978	Schwab, Joan	T	1949-52	Seagler, Sylvia	T	1940,42
Schlachter, Ellen	T	1989-96	Schwartz, Aline	T	1931-32	Seale, Betty Sue	C	1940
Schlachter, Gretchen	T	1979-86	Schwartz, Fanchon	C	1936-37	Seale, Betty Blount	C	1941
Schlacter, Jane	T	1984-88,90	Schwartz, Mary Ellen	T	1937	Seale, Gene	C	1935
Schmidt, Catherine	C	1982-85	Schwartz, Sarah	T	1994-96	Seale, Ilene	A	1947-50
Schmidt, Deidra	T	1954-60	Schwarz, Barbara	T	1975-81	Seale, Ilene	A	1947
Schmidt, Ewing	C	1966-71	Schwarz, Mary Lynn	C	1951-55	Seale, Joanne	A	1948
Schmidt, Kack	T	1938-40	Schwarz, Susan	C	1959-64	Seale, Julia	C	1982-86
Schmidt, Marilyn	A	1944-45	Schweinle, Susan	T	1951-53	Sealy, Deborah	C	1969-70

Sealy, Mallory	A	1995-96	Shamburger, Susan	A	1955-63	Shepherd, Stephanie	A	1982-87
Sealy, Martita	C	1990-96	Shanks, Cynthia	A	1947-49	Shepherd, Sue Ann		1928
Sealy, Nancy	C	1955-58	Shanks, Judy	T	1946	Sheppard, Elizabeth	C	1937
Seaman, Suzanne	T	1946-47	Shanks, Lily	C	1991-96	Sheppard, Jane	A	1960-65
Seanor, Nicole	T	1985-92	Shanks, Slaige	C	1989-92	Sheppard, Lucille	T	1935
Seanor, Noelle	C	1985-92	Shanks, Suzanne	T	1947-49	Sheppard, Shelly	A	1988-89
Searcy, Catherine	A	1976	Shannon, Ashley	T	1995-96	Shepperson, Camille	T	1953-57
Searcy, Cleo		1926	Shannon, Becky	C	1964-66	Shepperson, Sherry	A	1953-58
Searcy, Meredith	T	1984-88	Shannon, Mary Kay	T	1967-69	Sherman, Carroll	C	1954
Searls, Cathey	T	1950-53	Shannon, Patricia	C	1952-58	Sherman, Mary	T	1935
Searls, Susan	C	1949-53	Sharkey, Sara	C	1984-91	Sherpa, Sarah	C	1995-96
Sears, Sally	C	1948-49	Sharman, Jo-Anne	A	1958-60	Sherrill, Adele	C	1950
Seay, Kara	A	1977	Sharman, Martha	T	1960-64	Sherrill, Mary Jane	T	1939-40
Seay, Pauline	T	1979-86	Sharman, Mary	C	1954-58	Sherrill, Patti	C	1963-65
Seay, Soeurette	A	1954-57	Sharman, Teal	T	1992-93	Sherrill, Sara Lynn	T	1957
See, Beverly	A	1956-58	Sharp, Elizabeth	T	1931,33-34	Sherrod, Judy	C	1966-72
Seeley, Maxine	T	1935	Sharp, Frances	A	1947-49	Sherrouse, Ann	A	1959-67
Seelig, Mary Ann	T	1942-44	Sharp, Libby	A	1947-49	Sherrouse, Jane	A	1958-62
Seeligson, Sherri	C	1961-69	Sharp, Mary	T	1936	Sherrouse, June	T	1941
Seeligson, Suzanne	T	1956-62	Sharp, Mary Nell	T	1931,33-34	Sherrouse, Susan	T	1957-62
Seever, Betty	T	1946	Sharp, Susan Louise	C	1949	Sherry, Margie	A	1944,46-48
Seevers, Jean	T	1944-46	Sharpton, Mary Lenore	T	1950-51	Sherry, Mary	A	1944,47
Seewald, Elaine	C	1953-57	Shartle, Sandra	C	1937,39-42	Sherry, Teresa	A	1958
Seewald, Gloria	A	1958-62	Shartle, Sonia	C	1937,39-42	Shield, Dolores	A	1943-45
Seewald, Gretchen	T	1977-83	Shaver, Kathryn	C	1959-64	Shield, Patricia	A	1943
Seewold, Elaine	C	1957	Shaw, Amy	A	1979-82	Shields, Billie	C	1936-38
Seger, Katie	C	1956-57	Shaw, Gloria	T	1935	Shields, Judy	C	1953-54
Seigle, Gwendolyn	T	1934	Shaw, Jean Elizabeth	A	1951-55	Shipley, Martha Doris	T	1934
Selby, Sherrill	T	1960-61	Shaw, Jean	T	1938	Shipman, Katie	A	1995-96
Selby, Susan	T	1957-60	Shaw, Julie	T	1968-71	Shipman, Sarah	T	1982-88
Self, Nancy	T	1964-71	Shaw, Karen	C	1978-79	Shipp, Betty Jane	T	1948
Self, Sandra	T	1960-66	Shaw, Lavan	T	1930	Shivers, Cissie	C	1959
Seliger, Sidney	T	1995-96	Shaw, Reube Gene	T	1932,35	Shivers, Morris	C	1930
Sellers, Sally	C	1990-96	Shaw, Sally	C	1963-65	Shoff, Annie	C	1988-95
Sellers, Tammy	T	1971-75	Shaw, Setta	C	1951-52	Shook, Carol	C	1937
Semaan, Freida		1926	Shaw, Shari Anne	T	1944	Shook, Gail	C	1941-44
Senevey, Suzie	C	1954-60	Shaw, Susan	C	1955-56	Shook, Gwyn	C	1954-55
Sengelmann, Betsy	T	1967-71	Shawell, Sherry	A	1955-58	Short, Ashley	T	1983-88
Sentell, Jean	C	1948	Shayes, Suzanne	T	1936-37	Short, Marilyn	C	1950
Sessions, Betty	T	1936	Shea, Biddley	A	1945	Shotts, Barbara	T	1939
Sessums, Mary Jean	C	1961-63	Sheerin, Kate	T	1983-86	Shotwell, Betty Sue	T	1940-44
Sessums, Patricia	T	1963-69	Shelburne, Joan	A	1944-45	Shotwell, Ernestine		1928
Settegast, Carol	C	1944	Shelby, Dorothy		1926	Shotwell, Mary Elizabeth	T	1964-71
Settle, Ashley	T	1987-90	Sheldon, Helen	T	1939-42	Shotwell, Sally	A	1965-70
Settle, Emy	C	1990-96	Sheldon, Jacqueline	C	1933	Shotwell, Sherry	C	1968-72
Settle, Janice	C	1970-71	Shell, Kelley	A	1986	Shouse, Polly	T	1962-66
Sewell, Jan	C	1941	Shelor, Mary Lynn	A	1953	Shroeder, Olga		1928
Sewell, Susanne	T	1945-46	Shelton, Bippy	A	1979-85	Shryoc, Alice Ann	A	1953-57
Sexton, Patricia Ann	T	1934	Shelton, Cathy	C	1994-96	Shryoc, Cindy	T	1966-67
Seymour, Claire	T	1967-74	Shelton, Claire	A	1950-57	Shryoc, Sharon	A	1971-73
Seymour, Louise	T	1971-74	Shelton, Elise	T	1966-70	Shryoc, Susan	A	1974-75
Seymour, Shelly	A	1969-75	Shelton, Elizabeth	C	1982-88	Shubert, Edna Mae	T	1931
Shaddock, Evelyn	T	1938,40-41	Shelton, Emily	C	1936	Shuffield, Kim	T	1970-73
Shade, Louisa	A	1943-46	Shelton, Jane	C	1955-58,60	Shuford, Adriane	A	1996
Shafer, Ruth	C	1928-30	Shelton, Kelly	C	1992-96	Shuford, Elizabeth	A	1996
Shaffer, Pat	T	1942	Shelton, Kristin	A	1980-83	Shuford, Tommie		1929
Shaffer, Tracy	A	1970-77	Shelton, Maria	A	1977-79,81	Shuler, Sandra	A	1949-52
Shafto, Ann	T	1945-46	Shelton, Marjorie	C	1935	Shuler, Sharon	A	1949-51
Shafto, Neville	C	1976-80	Shelton, Mary Ellen	C	1969-74	Shuler, Sonya	A	1949
Shafto, Sallie	C	1972-74	Shelton, Saphronia	C	1987-91	Shuler, Susan	A	1972-73
Shallcross, Sandra	T	1951	Shepard, Suzanne	T	1960	Shult, Ann	C	1942-46
Shambaugh, Wilma Jean		1928	Shepherd, Francesca	T	1983-90	Shulting, Barbara Ann	T	1940
Shamburger, Lynne	T	1951,53-56	Shepherd, Mary Louise	T	1939-41	Shults, Catherine	C	1978-84

Shultz, Martha Dell	A	1943-44	Singer, Madge		1928	Smith, Alexa	T	1996
Shultz, Oneil	T	1937	Singletary, Jamie	T	1950-53	Smith, Alice	T	1937,40
Shultz, Tomy	T	1937,41	Singletary, Johanna	A	1953-59	Smith, Alycia	A	1974-77
Shurley, Guyon	T	1934	Singleton, Annis	C	1947	Smith, Andrea	C	1975-79
Shurr, Mary Louise	C	1938-40	Sipes, Marietta	T	1944	Smith, Ann	A	1944-45
Shutts, Eleanor	T	1938	Sisk, Allie Joy	T	1937	Smith, Anne	T	1975-77
Sibley, Ginny	C	1975	Sisk, Allison	A	1996	Smith, Ashley	T	1975
Sibley, Pamela	C	1953	Sisk, Jessica	T	1993-96	Smith, Avon	T	1938
Sibley, Serin	T	1951-53	Sivalls, Betty Rae	C	1944-51	Smith, Barbara Mae	C	1931-32
Sickles, Katie	T	1994-96	Sivalls, Mary Martha	C	1938-39,	Smith, Barbara	T	1938
Sides, Sara	A	1943,45	Puddin		1941-46	Smith, Barbara Preston	C	1953
Sieber, Catherine		1929	Sivley, Carolyn	T	1940-41	Smith, Beverly	T	1940
Siegel, Samantha	A	1995-96	Sivley, Edith	T	1940-41	Smith, Blythe	A	1988-95
Sifford, Elizabeth Ann	C	1934	Sivley, Signa June	T	1937-40	Smith, Bobby Sue	T	1951
Sifford, Medora	C	1943	Skaggs, Merrill Ann Bebe	C	1944	Smith, Brenda Elizabeth		1950
Sigler, Beth	C	1981-85	Skeeters, Susan	A	1964	Smith, Carol Lynn	C	1959,60
Sikes, Allyson	T	1987-92	Skelton, Sandra	C	1947	Smith, Carol	T	1961-62
Sikes, Charlotte	C	1989-90	Skelton, Sue	C	1945-47,49	Smith, Carolyn	A	1945
Sikes, Sylvia	C	1947	Skidmore, Jane	T	1948-49	Smith, Carolyn	T	1951-53
Sikes, Tory	T	1990-91	Skidmore, Linda	C	1951-54	Smith, Carrie	C	1976-81
Silk, Linda	T	1967-70	Skillern, Jean	C	1937-43	Smith, Cathy	A	1963-65
Sillers, Mary	T	1942-44	Skillern, Sandra	C	1951-52	Smith, Cinda	C	1960-61
Silverman, Elsie	T	1940-41	Skillman, Frances		1928	Smith, Claire	T	1994-96
Silvers, Jean	C	1932	Skinner, Grace Moon	C	1931-32	Smith, Claire	A	1947-48
Simmon, Jane	T	1934,36-38	Skipper, Caroline	A	1947-51	Smith, Claire Monday	C	1931,33-34
Simmon, Mary Ann	A	1946	Slack, Kara	C	1995	Smith, Clara Mae	C	1937
Simmons, Cindy	A	1988-91	Slack, Paula	T	1963-67	Smith, Clare Wilkerson	C	1940
Simmons, Elizabeth	T	1939	Slagle, Clarice	T	1940-41	Smith, Courtney	A	1983-1992
Simmons, Gay	C	1963-68	Slagle, Lee	T	1940-42	Smith, Crenez		1928
Simmons, Jennie	T	1994-96	Slauford, Adriane	A	1996	Smith, Creo Lynn	C	1949
Simmons, Peggy	C	1955-59	Slaughter, Agnes	T	1945-46	Smith, Devereux	T	1938,40-41
Simmons, Sherye	T	1970-73	Slaughter, Betty Kate	T	1935-36	Smith, Di Ann	C	1948
Simms, Bailey Ann	T	1977-81	Slaughter, Brooke	A	1990-93	Smith, Dorothy Lee	C	1939
Simon, Carol	T	1973-76,	Slaughter, Ginger	A	1945	Smith, Elizabeth	A	1988-1994
		1979-80	Slaughter, Josie	C	1938	Smith, Elizabeth Ann	C	1952-53
Simon, Michele	T	1979-81	Slaughter, Sally	C	1960-63	Smith, Ella Lou	A	1964-1970
Simon, Renee	C	1970-74	Slayton, Lee Ann	T	1964-65	Smith, Ellen	C	1972-1978
Simon, Valerie	A	1971-76,78	Sleeper, Frances	T	1964-70	Smith, Elmera	T	1942-45
Simons, Barbara	C	1945-47,	Sloan, Alice	T	1989-93	Smith, Emmalyn	C	1931
		1950-51	Sloan, Antoinette	C	1944,47-48	Smith, Erica	A	1989-92
Simons, Mollye	C	1935-36	Sloan, Dana	T	1969-72	Smith, Ferrell	C	1980-85
Simonton, Merrie Jo	A	1958-63	Sloan, Grayson	C	1970-72	Smith, Florence	T	1935
Simpkins, Jeannette	T	1940	Sloan, Jule	C	1935	Smith, Frances	T	1937,40
Simpkins, Susan	C	1984-88	Sloan, Martha Ann	C	1950-57	Smith, Gwendolyn	C	1932
Simpson, Barbara	C	1945	Sloan, Martha	T	1975	Smith, Gwyne	T	1957-62
Simpson, Caroline	T	1994-96	Sloan, Mary Katherine	C	1940	Smith, Helen Sue	C	1948
Simpson, Catherine	T	1972-73	Sloan, Mary	A	1968	Smith, Ida Ruth	C	1936
Simpson, Cynthia	C	1965	Sloan, Sally	T	1971-73	Smith, Irene	C	1951-54
Simpson, Elizabeth	T	1989-91	Sloan, Susan	T	1955-56	Smith, Jackie	T	1941
Simpson, Janice	T	1968-72	Slocum, Lena	T	1992-95	Smith, Jamie Anne	T	1975-81
Simpson, Jeanette	C	1936	Small, Cecily	T	1982-86	Smith, Jane	A	1946-47,49
Simpson, Lynda	A	1968-75	Small, Martha	C	1986-93	Smith, Jean	T	1941
Simpson, Lynne	C	1991-96	Smead, Anna	C	1955-56	Smith, Jennifer	A	1993
Simpson, Margaret	C	1940-42	Smead, Catherine	T	1975-79	Smith, Joanne	C	1940,42
Simpson, Martha	T	1975-80	Smead, Frances	C	1934	Smith, Josephine	C	1936-37
Simpson, Rowena	C	1930-31	Smead, Mary	C	1943	Smith, Julia Bess	C	1944-47
Simpson, Sally	T	1964-67	Smead, Susan	C	1970-74,	Smith, Julianna	A	1976-79
Sims, Margaret	T	1945			1976-77	Smith, Karen	T	1960-67
Sinclair, Anne	C	1956-59	Smiley, Elizabeth	T	1986	Smith, Kathryn Ann	C	1945
Sinclair, Mary Lynn	T	1937	Smiser, Lynn	C	1963	Smith, Kay	T	1950
Sinclair, Patsy	A	1947	Smiser, Sharon	C	1952,55-56	Smith, Kristin	C	1985-92
Sinclair, Sally	C	1957-58	Smith, Albertina		1929	Smith, Lacey	C	1990-96
Sindelar, Kim	C	1976-82	Smith, Aldra	T	1938-39	Smith, Laura	T	1966-72

Name	Code	Years
Smith, Lauren	T	1986-91
Smith, Lee	C	1950
Smith, Leslie	T	1957
Smith, Linda Jane	C	1954-57
Smith, Lizbeth	C	1958
Smith, Lori	A	1992-96
Smith, Lottie	C	1938
Smith, Lynne	T	1968-73
Smith, Margaret Clissy	C	1933-34
Smith, Margaret Ann	C	1943
Smith, Margaret T.	T	1933
Smith, Marilyn	C	1937,40-41
Smith, Marlive	A	1962-66
Smith, Martha	A	1950-53
Smith, Marvin Gene	C	1937-39
Smith, Mary Len	C	1945-46
Smith, Mary Pearl	T	1930-31
Smith, Mary Michael	T	1951-52
Smith, Mary Alice	T	1941-45
Smith, Maxine	T	1935
Smith, Maybelle	C	1931,35-36
Smith, Melissa	A	1951-52
Smith, Mimi	A	1951-55
Smith, Missie	A	1976-78
Smith, Mollye	C	1978-82
Smith, Nancy Ann	T	1938
Smith, Nancy Jane	T	1954-59
Smith, Nancy	T	1961-62
Smith, Nancy	A	1967-73
Smith, Olivia Ann	C	1953-54
Smith, Patricia	C	1942-43
Smith, Pearl	T	1942
Smith, Randee	C	1970-74
Smith, Rebecca	C	1960-65
Smith, Ripple	C	1972
Smith, Rondee	C	1973
Smith, Sally	C	1952-55
Smith, Sandra Sue	A	1946-49
Smith, Sandra	C	1944-45, 1947-51
Smith, Sarah	T	1934-35
Smith, Sarah	T	1991
Smith, Sawnie	T	1944-45
Smith, Sharan Lee	A	1951
Smith, Sheila	T	1951-53
Smith, Sherrill	C	1962-65
Smith, Shiela	T	1951
Smith, Shirley	C	1943
Smith, Sidney	T	1980-86
Smith, Sonja	T	1950-51
Smith, Sophie	A	1949
Smith, Stacey	C	1984-91
Smith, Starlett	T	1950
Smith, Susan	C	1959-67
Smith, Susan E.	T	1970-76
Smith, Susan B.	A	1975
Smith, Susan Lee	T	1963-69
Smith, Susan	A	1954
Smith, Suzanne	A	1989-91
Smith, Suzanne	C	1972-75
Smith, Sylvia	C	1957-62
Smith, Thresa Dean	C	1937
Smith, Tracy	T	1976-81
Smith, Tricia	A	1981-84
Smith, Tweed	T	1952
Smith, Virginia	T	1933-34
Smith, Wahleeta	C	1948-50
Smith, Whitney	A	1991-95
Smith, Winzer	C	1993-95
Smither, Mary	T	1984-88
Smither, Sallie	C	1976-82
Smitherman, Geraldine	C	1937-38
Smitherman, Gloria	C	1938
Smotherman, Ann	A	1973-74
Smyth, Beth	A	1943-48
Smyth, Beverly	A	1943-46
Smyth, Sallee	A	1973-77
Smythe, Kathleen	T	1937
Snead, Jenny	A	1981-88
Snead, Katy	A	1981-88
Sneed, Betty Alice	T	1936
Sneed, Lucille	C	1941
Snell, Caroline	C	1992-93
Snell, Stephanie	T	1993-96
Snell, Susan	A	1985-88
Snelling, Lynda	T	1968-71
Snelling, Satchie	T	1978-79
Snetcher, Sue Ann	T	1955-56
Snider, Harriet	A	1960-65
Snodgrass, Brannon	T	1982-89
Snyder, Ann Cecilia	T	1948-53
Snyder, Helen	T	1938
Snyder, Lynn	T	1958-59, 1961-62
Snyder, Mary Emily	T	1939
Sockwell, Patricia	C	1960
Solomon, Alex	C	1988-93
Solomon, Kirksey	C	1991-96
Solomon, Lois	T	1931,34
Solomon, Margaret	C	1931,34-36
Solomon, Merdith	C	1979-86
Solow, Rita	T	1937
Somerville, Shannon	T	1982-89
Sommer, Hilberta	C	1935
Sommer, Mary Ann	T	1935
Sommerville, Sara	C	1947
Sones, Megan	C	1993
Soniat, Nettie		1942
Soper, Mary Helen Dick	T	1930-31
Sorelle, Nita Ray	T	1933-35
Sorley, Summer	A	1988-89
Sorrells, Garland	A	1959-63
Sory, Dorothy	T	1931,35
Soule, Mary Brooks	T	1942
Soules, Laura	A	1985-92
Soulsby, Sloane	T	1992-94
Sour, Nancy	C	1938-39
Souter, Madeline	T	1935-36
South, Diane	C	1952-58
South, Helen Louise	A	1943
Southern, Alison	T	1989-92
Southmayd, Janet	C	1965-69
Sowden, Crozier	A	1976-83
Sowden, Kerry	A	1973-80
Spain, Bettye		1934
Spain, Sharon	A	1958-62
Sparkman, Ann	T	1961
Sparkman, Betty	T	1957-58
Sparks, Cathleen	T	1940,44, 1946-47
Sparks, Janyth	T	1955-56
Sparks, Jo	C	1937-39
Sparks, Lisa	C	1978-82
Sparks, Martha Clayton	T	1945-48
Sparks, Neldalee	C	1940
Sparks, Patti	T	1944-48
Sparks, Susannah	A	1978-83
Sparling, Sarah	A	1996
Spaulding, Ansley	C	1930
Spaulding, Martha	T	1942-47
Spear, Lucy	T	1969-71
Spears, Helen	T	1937
Spears, J.A.S.	C	1993-96
Spears, Susan	C	1961-66
Spence, Judy	A	1963-67
Spence, Louise	C	1961-64
Spencer, Amy	A	1948-50
Spencer, Gail	C	1965-66
Spencer, Louise	A	1943
Spencer, Maidie	C	1947
Spencer, Melissa	T	1991-95
Spencer, Patricia	C	1941-45
Spencer, Priscilla	C	1994-96
Spencer, Shirley	C	1948
Spencer, Susie	A	1947-48
Spice, Susan	A	1950-53
Spickard, Andra	T	1945-47
Spickard, Janice	A	1945-46
Spiers, Merik	C	1984-85,87
Spies, Shelly	A	1975-76
Spillman, Hannah	A	1974-80
Spillman, Janie	T	1977-83
Spinnler, Ann	T	1934-35
Spires, Cindy	A	1963-66
Spires, Cindy	A	1964
Spires, Susan	C	1963-66
Spivy, Pauline	C	1930
Sponberg, Carolyn	A	1995-96
Sponberg, Jennifer	T	1992-96
Sporl, Patricia	C	1948-51
Spratt, Eleanor		1929
Springer, Heather	C	1985-86
Springer, Sue	C	1950-53
Springfield, Cassie	T	1930
Sproull, Flo	C	1955
Spruiell, Carolyn Ann	C	1949
Spruiell, Mary Helen	A	1949
Spurney, Nancy	A	1943
St. Clair, Kay	C	1965-69
St. Clair, Elizabeth	T	1986-93
St. Clair, Shelley	C	1962-65
St. Clair, Cynthia	C	1965,67-71
St. Germaine, Beverly	C	1941
St. John, Sandra	C	1943-44,46
St. Paul, Andrea	C	1970
Stacy, Gay	C	1964-67
Stafford, Beth	T	1976-81
Stafford, Dixie	T	1948-53
Stafford, Frankie	A	1944-46

Name		Year
Stafford, Ginger	T	1984-88
Stafford, Leslie	A	1977-83
Stagg, Bettye Jane	C	1930-31
Stagg, Julie	A	1960-66
Stagg, Margaret	C	1961-67
Stalcup, Dana	C	1980-87
Stalcup, Kara	C	1979-82,84
Staley, Bea	A	1993-96
Staley, Delia	A	1948-56
Staley, Jennifer	A	1989-95
Staley, LuAnne	C	1977-81
Staley, Nancy	C	1945-49
Staley, Stefanie	C	1972-78
Staley, Wynne	T	1980-87
Stambaugh, Jananne	T	1956
Stanbra, Diane	T	1947-48
Stancliff, Jo Ann	C	1939,42
Standefer, Jane	T	1937
Standiforth, Margaret	C	1931
Stanfield, Marie	C	1953
Stanford, Jean	A	1946-49
Stanford, Jerry	T	1946-49
Stanford, Shirley	C	1938
Staniforth, Betty Jane	C	1937
Staniforth, Sarah	A	1985-88
Stanley, Jane	A	1943
Stannus, Claire	A	1946-48
Stansberry, Karen	C	1955
Stanton, Jerry	C	1941-44
Stanton, Jo Nan	A	1949
Stanton, Judy	C	1949
Stanzel, Rachel	A	1988-92
Stanzell, Rose	T	1968-71
Staples, Adele	C	1935-36
Staples, Julia	C	1935-36
Stark, Peggy	T	1937
Starke, Maxine	T	1931
Starkey, Sue	A	1946-48
Starr, Suzy	A	1950-57
Starry, Kathryn	T	1937
Stasney, Elizabeth	C	1982-89
Stasney, Kathryn	A	1980-87
Stasney, Kathryn	A	1980
Stasney, Kathryn	C	1965
Staurt, Laura	C	1965
Staurt, Terry	C	1964
Stayart, Sheila	T	1946
Steadman, Ann	T	1972
Steber, Betty Ann	T	1940-41
Steck, Ellen	C	1930-31
Steck, Ethel	C	1929-31
Steck, Mary Frances	C	1930-31
Stedman, Ann	T	1969-74
Stedman, Jo Anne Jody	T	1941-44
Stedman, Susanne	C	1945-47
Steed, Nita	A	1946-49
Steele, Clarabele	T	1938
Steele, Doris Dolly	T	1930,33
Steele, Kristen	T	1976-82
Steele, Mary Louise	T	1937
Steen, Anna	C	1987-94
Steen, Lee-Wilson	T	1994-96
Steen, Margaret	C	1961-65
Steen, Nancy	T	1958-63

Name		Year
Steen, Susan	C	1958-59
Steger, Mary Stewart	C	1941-42
Stein, Joey	T	1942
Stein, Kristi	C	1988-95
Stein, Laura	T	1995-96
Stein, Sarah	A	1995-96
Steinberger, Joan	C	1941
Steinberger, Mitzi	C	1979-80
Steinhagen, Gretchen	T	1953-54
Steinhauser, Anne	A	1964,66
Steinhauser, Linda	A	1954-59
Steinhauser, Susan	C	1959-62
Steinhoff, Katherine	A	1993-96
Steinhoff, Kelsey	C	1995-96
Stell, Janet	T	1955-59
Stell, Mary Ann	T	1958-61
Stengl, Lorraine	T	1934-36
Stenling, Patsy	T	1945
Stephens, Ann	A	1971-75
Stephens, Barbara Beth	C	1937,40-42
Stephens, Beverly	C	1953,56
Stephens, Caroline	C	1983-84
Stephens, Carolyn	T	1950-52
Stephens, Claire	A	1972-73
Stephens, Elizabeth	A	1971-75
Stephens, Jan	A	1975-80
Stephens, Jennifer	A	1976
Stephens, Julie	T	1951
Stephens, Margaux	A	1994-96
Stephens, Mary	C	1974-77
Stephens, Mary Wells	T	1934-37
Stephens, Pam	A	1972-76
Stephens, Shannon	C	1979-85
Stephens, Susan	C	1961-63
Stephens, Tay	A	1993-96
Stephenson, Beverly Ann	T	1950-56
Stephenson, Cynthia	T	1942
Stephenson, Jancy	C	1966-68
Stephenson, Jane	T	1984-87
Stephenson, Jill	C	1985-91
Stephenson, Kathy	T	1957-60
Stephenson, Marjorie	T	1937
Stephenson, Martha	C	1965-67
Stephenson, Steffani	T	1953-58
Sterling, Elizabeth	C	1937
Sterrett, Suzanne	A	1943,45-46
Stevens, Carrie	C	1976-81
Stevens, Francie	A	1978-82
Stevens, Leila	T	1946-47
Stevens, Mary Katherine	T	1956-61
Stevens, Meg	A	1975
Stevens, Patricia	C	1951-52
Stevens, Sally	T	1962
Stevenson, Dorothea		1929
Stevenson, Sara	T	1969-75
Steves, Gloria	C	1991-95
Steves, Savanna	C	1954-57
Steward, Ann	T	1940
Stewart, Ann	C	1941-43
Stewart, Betty	C	1977
Stewart, Betty Jane	C	1932-35
Stewart, Cathy	A	1963,66-67
Stewart, Doris	T	1937

Name		Year
Stewart, Lucy Guess	C	1948-50
Stewart, Mary Knowles	C	1946-49
Stewart, Mary Lou	T	1941
Stewart, Mary Catherine	T	1958-60
Stewart, Nancy	T	1952-53
Stewart, Roberta	C	1947-49
Stewart, Ryan	A	1988-94
Stewart, Stacy	C	1987-93
Stewart, Stephanie	C	1953
Stewart, Stephanie	C	1949
Stewart, Stephanie	T	1970-73
Stewart, Susan	C	1959-60
Stewart, Susan	C	1949-54
Stewart, Sylvia	T	1942-43, 1945-46
Stillwell, Cathy	C	1970-76
Stillwell, Kay	A	1953-54
Stillwell, Susan	C	1972-76
Stinchcomb, Mary	A	1956-60
Stinnett, Ann	C	1953-56
Stinnett, Cherry	C	1950-53
Stinnett, Jeanne	T	1955-58
Stinnett, Laurel	C	1941
Stinnett, Sidney	A	1945-46
Stinson, Dana	A	1953-54
Stites, Susan	T	1979-80
Stockard, Jan	T	1955-61
Stockard, Sue	T	1954-59
Stockbridge, Zippy	T	1942-44
Stocker, Peggy	C	1969-72
Stokely, Joan	A	1961-64
Stokes, Gale	T	1952-56
Stokes, Kathy	C	1962-65
Stokes, Sue Ann	C	1952
Stokes, Totsie	C	1930
Stollenwerck, Brooke	C	1966-71
Stollenwerck, Elizabeth	T	1974-78
Stollenwerck, Ellison	A	1970-74
Stoltenberg, Lynne	C	1956-57
Stoltenberg, Sue Anne	T	1956-57
Stolz, Dorothy	T	1935
Stone, Barbara	A	1952-61
Stone, Betty	T	1941-42
Stone, Beverly Bunny	A	1964-66
Stone, Cynthia	C	1960-61
Stone, Diane	C	1947-49
Stone, Gloria	A	1947
Stone, Jacqueline	C	1948
Stone, Lois	T	1931
Stone, Margaret	T	1933-34
Stone, Marie	A	1948
Stone, Marilyn	T	1949-53
Stone, Martha	T	1944
Stone, Mary Lou	T	1943-45, 1947-49
Stone, Nancy	T	1940-42
Stone, Rusty	T	1940-48
Stone, Sally	A	1954
Stone, Sarah	T	1945-48
Stone, Tal	T	1941-42
Stone, Wendy	T	1958,60
Storey, Anne	A	1953-58
Storey, Dorothy Nell	T	1951-54

Dottie			Stroud, Sharon	C	1964-68	Sullivan, Toni	A	1967-70

Name	Col	Years	Name	Col	Years	Name	Col	Years
Dottie			Stroud, Sharon	C	1964-68	Sullivan, Toni	A	1967-70
Storey, Jo	T	1946-51	Stroud, Tracy	T	1977-82	Summers, Kathy	A	1985-87
Storey, Susan	T	1957-61	Stuart, Anita	C	1937	Summers, Marianne	C	1963-64
Storm, Anne	C	1954-57	Stuart, Dianne	C	1958	Sumner, Diane	C	1947-49
Storms, Holly	T	1988-95	Stuart, Francita	C	1942	Sumner, Vera Lee	A	1946
Story, Dolly	C	1961-64	Stuart, Jan	A	1959-62	Sundgren, Sherry	C	1965-67
Stouffer, Sherrie	T	1942	Stuart, Kit	A	1954-57	Surratt, Marifrances	A	1943-44
Stouffer, Shirley Lori	T	1942	Stuart, Laura	C	1965-67, 1969-70	Sutherland, Yvonne	T	1935-36
Stough, Beverly	T	1951-52				Sutton, Douglas	A	1959-60
Stout, Flora Beecher		1928	Stuart, Lisa	T	1965-67, 1969-71	Sutton, Ida	T	1943-45,48
Stout, Sally	A	1947-48				Sutton, Jean	T	1941-42
Stovall, Norma Ann	C	1931	Stuart, Liz	A	1969-72	Sutton, Joy	C	1953-54
Stover, Stacy	C	1972-75	Stuart, Mary Louise	C	1931	Sutton, Judy	A	1950-53
Stowers, Nancy	A	1960-67	Stuart, Randi	A	1958-60	Sutton, Linda	C	1954
Stowers, Sally	T	1958-62	Stuart, Sarah	T	1955-57	Sutton, Lucile	C	1940
Stowers, Susan	C	1956-59	Stuart, Stephanie	C	1964-65, 1967-70	Swain, Ann	C	1969-76
Strain, Carol	C	1963-66				Swain, Carol	A	1972-78
Strain, Claire	A	1965-72	Stuart, Susan	A	1968-70	Swain, Cathy	T	1968-74
Strain, Claire	C	1993-96	Stuart, Terry	C	1963-70	Swain, Jeannie	C	1960-64
Strain, Lynn	A	1957-59	Stuart, Tracy	A	1989	Swain, Lou	A	1945-47
Strain, Martha	C	1969-74	Stubbs, Helen Jean	T	1937	Swander, Elizabeth	T	1989-90
Strausner, Ann	C	1986-93	Stubbs, Sue	A	1952-53	Swann, Carolyn	C	1940
Strauss, Sally	A	1950,52	Stuck, Marguerite	A	1962-66	Swann, Helena	T	1963-67
Strauss, Suzanne	C	1936	Stuck, Nancy	T	1964-68	Swann, Hilary	C	1966-70
Streckfus, Barbara	T	1941	Stuck, Susan	A	1958-63	Swanson, Betsy	C	1961-64
Streckfus, Patricia	T	1941	Stuckey, Jane	C	1930	Swarts, Gloria	C	1947
Street, Allison	T	1981-86	Stuckey, Jane	T	1934	Swartz, Lauren	T	1991-93
Street, Allison	T	1988	Stueve, Anne	T	1937	Swearingen, Jonilu	C	1944-45
Street, Amy	T	1982-84	Stulting, Beverly	T	1940-44	Sweeney, Mary Etta	T	1935-36
Street, Anna	C	1986-89	Stumberg, Belle	T	1960-63	Sweeney, Rachel	C	1930-31
Street, Anna	T	1976-82	Stumberg, Lou	A	1962	Sweeney, Sandra	C	1953-56
Street, Betsy	T	1980-81	Stumberg, Sara	A	1993-96	Sweet, Dora		1929
Street, Frances		1929	Sturgeon, Elizabeth	T	1941-42	Swift, Francie	A	1980-82
Street, Melissa	T	1973-80	Sturm, Marti	A	1973-78	Swindell, Suzanne	T	1945-47
Street, Rachel	A	1993-96	Suarez, Rebecca	C	1989-93	Swinford, Jerrie Nan	T	1946-48
Stribling, Ann	Y	1940	Suberbielle, Ann	A	1957-65	Swisher, Ann	A	1972
Stribling, Karen	C	1984	Sudderth, Martha	A	1949-52	Swisher, Kelly	C	1972-74
Stribling, Mary Ellen	T	1944	Sudderth, Mary	A	1943-47	Syfan, Sally	C	1971-74
Stribling, Sara	A	1947-48	Sudik, June	A	1945-49	Sykes, Leigh	C	1984-90
Strickland, Betty	C	1938-40	Sugg, Julia	A	1986-91	Sykes, Sarah	C	1987-89
Strickland, Maidye	T	1954-55	Sugg, Kristin	T	1977-82	Synott, Ann	C	1945
Strickland, Pauline	T	1932-34	Suggs, Dona Gail	T	1950	Syrratt, Marie Frances	A	1943
Strickler, Josephine		1926	Suits, Catherine	T	1937			
Stringer, B. Lee	C	1938-43	Sullenberger, Teel	C	1940-43	**T**		
Stringer, Courtney	T	1986-89	Sullivan, Anne	T	1942-44 ,46	Tabb, Winifred	A	1943-44,46
Stringer, Lucille	C	1930	Sullivan, Charlene	C	1942	Tabor, Elizabeth	C	1985-89
Stringer, Sarah	C	1944-45	Sullivan, Elizabeth	A	1987-89	Taggart, Betty	C	1951-54
Stringer, Stephanie	C	1987-90	Sullivan, Estelle	T	1939	Talbert, Jean	C	1952-57
Stringer, Sue	C	1945	Sullivan, Jane	C	1947-52	Talbot, Anne	A	1963-68
Stringfellow, Jan	A	1959-60	Sullivan, Jean	T	1938	Talbot, Eme	C	1974-80
Stripling, Elizabeth		1929	Sullivan, Jill	C	1985-86	Talbot, Frances		1929
Stripling, Jane	C	1928-29,31	Sullivan, Kathryn	A	1984-87	Talbot, Jennifer	C	1973-76
Strobeck, Suzanne	T	1949-51	Sullivan, Katy	T	1980-87	Talbot, Martha	A	1966-71
Strom, Gloria	T	1938-39	Sullivan, Kelly	C	1978-84	Talbot, Nancy	A	1957-59
Strong, Charlotte	T	1965-68	Sullivan, Kim	T	1964-67	Talbot, Nora Sue	A	1966-69
Strong, Georgeann Gigi	T	1963-68	Sullivan, Lane	T	1968-70	Talbot, Sue	T	1946-47
Strother, Edna Ruth	T	1940	Sullivan, Laura	C	1973-74	Taliaferro, Dorothy	A	1971-73
Strother, Martha	T	1943	Sullivan, Lee	T	1987	Talkington, Lynn	T	1960-64
Stroube, Susan	T	1966-67	Sullivan, Margaret	T	1936	Talley, Martha	T	1976-82
Stroud, Charlene	C	1944-46	Sullivan, Mary	C	1962-67	Talley, Tiffany	T	1979-85
Stroud, Gloria	C	1969-74	Sullivan, Patty	A	1986-87	Tamm, Alice	C	1930
Stroud, Jo Ann	C	1942	Sullivan, Susan Silky	A	1958-62	Tamm, Marion	C	1930
Stroud, Kimball	C	1977-81	Sullivan, Talley	T	1989	Tankersley, Ann	T	1942-44

Name		Year	Name		Year	Name		Year
Tankersley, Karen Kay	T	1954-60	Temple, Kenton	C	1960-65	Thomas, Joy	T	1985-88
Tankersley, Marilyn	T	1940-41	Temple, Samantha	T	1977-80	Thomas, Julie	C	1982-87
Tankersley, Sharon	T	1953-59	Temple, Tress	C	1987-89	Thomas, Kay	A	1950-53
Tannehill, Marietta		1929	Temples, Claire	T	1996	Thomas, Lera	T	1952,54,
Tannehill, Mary	A	1975-82	Temples, Mary	A	1995-96			1956-58
Tannehill, Sudie	C	1972-77	Tenison, Auban Adele	T	1930	Thomas, Marji	C	1960
Tanner, Kathleen	A	1992-96	Tennant, Lisa	C	1977-80	Thomas, Mary Helen	T	1955
Tapp, Carolyn	A	1948-51	Tennis, Margo	T	1971-74	Thomas, Mary Galen	A	1955-57
Tarleton, Rachael	T	1982-84	Tennison, Jil	T	1965-71	Thomas, Meredith	A	1983-90
Tarner, Grace	C	1950	Tennison, Kit	C	1963-66	Thomas, Nancy	T	1940
Tarpley, Vicki	T	1957-59	Tennison, Margo	A	1993	Thomas, Nellie Frances	T	1938
Tartt, Courtnay	A	1975-82	Tennyson, Betty Sue	T	1939	Thomas, Patsy	T	1939
Tarver, Grace	C	1950-54	Terrell, Carolyn	T	1948	Thomas, Read	T	1933
Tatum, Barbara	A	1944	Terrell, Janet	C	1966-70	Thomas, Rebecca	T	1974-77
Tatum, Carter	T	1991-96	Terrell, Kathleen	A	1963-67	Thomas, Sue Ann	C	1938-43
Taub, Cate	A	1994	Terrell, Lara	T	1993-96	Thomas, Suzie	T	1972-77
Taylor, Ann Catherine		1928	Terrell, Lynn	T	1954	Thomas, Taylor	T	1987-88
Taylor, Ann	A	1967-73	Terry, Ann	T	1948-53	Thomas, Tommie	T	1946-49
Taylor, Barbara	A	1971-78	Terry, Elizabeth	T	1936	Thomas, Tracy	T	1973-77
Taylor, Chris	T	1957-58	Terry, Jane	C	1964-68	Thomas, Viola	T	1934-36
Taylor, Christi	C	1994	Terry, Julie	A	1957-58	Thomason, Jan	C	1954-55
Taylor, Cindy	C	1969-72	Terry, Lou	A	1960-61	Thomason, Zaidee	A	1956
Taylor, Claire	C	1978-83	Terry, Patricia	A	1963,65-66	Thompson, Amanda	C	1994-95
Taylor, Diane	T	1970-72	Terzia, Louise	T	1965	Thompson, Angela	C	1967-71
Taylor, Evelyn	T	1939	Terzia, Sara	T	1941	Thompson, Ann	A	1956-58
Taylor, Jamie	T	1960-64	Tesoro, Kim	A	1986-89	Thompson, Anne	A	1957-62
Taylor, Jane	T	1948-50	Tevis, Kelly	C	1974-77	Thompson, Betty Jean	C	1947
Taylor, Janet	T	1958-59	Tevis, Sharon	C	1969-70	Thompson, Charlotte	C	1937
Taylor, Jennifer	T	1974-77	Tevis, Susan	T	1968-69	Thompson, Diane	A	1948
Taylor, Judi	C	1968	Tevis, Terry	A	1967-68	Thompson, Eloise	T	1975-78
Taylor, Julie	A	1980-86	Tewes, Frances	T	1944	Thompson, Erin	T	1980-82,
Taylor, Karen	A	1959-66	Thames, Amanda	C	1986-90			1984-85
Taylor, Kim	C	1978-84	Thames, Caroline	T	1987-93	Thompson, Frances	C	1955
Taylor, Lacy	A	1961-62	Thames, Mary Hershel	T	1989-96	Thompson, Gladys	T	1939-40
Taylor, Lee Ann	A	1943	Thankeiser, Adele	T	1973-78	Thompson, Helen	A	1978-84
Taylor, Libby	C	1988-94	Tharpe, Betty	A	1945	Thompson, Helen	T	1945
Taylor, Lillian	C	1935	Tharpe, Lola May	T	1945	Thompson, Judy	A	1948
Taylor, Lindsay	C	1992-96	Thatcher, Karen	A	1945-46	Thompson, Kate	T	1996
Taylor, Lisle	T	1985-91	Thatcher, Stephanie	T	1981-85	Thompson, Katrina	A	1945
Taylor, Lynn	A	1973-75	Thaxton, Betsy	T	1937	Thompson, Kay	A	1955
Taylor, Mary Lyn	T	1949-51	Thetford, Madeline	C	1934	Thompson, Lauren	A	1996
Taylor, Mary Lynn	C	1944-47	Theus, Helen	T	1952-53	Thompson, Lynn	C	1967-71
Taylor, Meg	T	1979	Theus, Lynn	C	1952-53	Thompson, Maley	C	1993
Taylor, Michelle	C	1985-88	Thibaulet, Caroleu	C	1935	Thompson, Margaret	A	1943
Taylor, Molly	A	1961-66	Thixton, Janie	C	1953	Thompson, Margaret W.	C	1964-68
Taylor, Peggy		1929	Thoman, Laurie	C	1975-78	Thompson, Margaret	T	1937-38
Taylor, Penny	C	1950-53	Thomas, Alexandra	A	1996	Thompson, Margaret E.	T	1967-70
Taylor, Sally	T	1947-49	Thomas, Ann	C	1947-48	Thompson, Margaret Ann	T	1954-55
Taylor, Sammie	T	1953-56	Thomas, Anne	A	1952,54	Thompson, Marie	T	1930
Taylor, Sidney Maxine	C	1944-47	Thomas, Anne	C	1964-66	Thompson, Mary Elizabeth	C	1941
Taylor, Susan	T	1965-69	Thomas, Barbara	T	1934-35,38	Thompson, Mary E.	A	1943-44
Taylor, Susan	A	1980-86	Thomas, Caroline	A	1994-96	Thompson, Mary	C	1950-55
Taylor, Tamara	C	1975-79	Thomas, Dorothy	C	1953-61	Thompson, Megan	T	1985-89
Taylor, Teresa	C	1969-71	Thomas, Elaine	T	1978-81	Thompson, Nancy	A	1968-71
Taylor, Whitney	T	1995-96	Thomas, Eliza	T	1984-87	Thompson, Nancy	C	1936-44
Tayor, Ann	A	1967	Thomas, Elizabeth	T	1931-32,	Thompson, Patricia Oxford	T	1979-85
Teague, Debbie	C	1960-65			1934-35	Thompson, Patricia Marie	C	1954-55
Teas, Sue	T	1937	Thomas, Ellen	A	1973-81	Thompson, Patricia	T	1934-35
Teasley, Brooks	T	1976-82	Thomas, Emma	T	1989-92	Thompson, Peggy Joy	T	1938
Teasley, Holland	C	1973-77	Thomas, Hilda	C	1942-45	Thompson, Peggy	T	1960
Teeling, Nancy	T	1947-50	Thomas, Jill	C	1981-86			
Teis, Susan	C	1963	Thomas, Jo Ann	A	1949-51			
Temple, Amy	T	1979-82	Thomas, Jo Ann	T	1944			

Tullos, Peggy Dean	C	1938	Underwood, Amy	T	1962-69	Vaughan, Erin	A	1990-92
Tullos, Ruth	T	1930-31	Underwood, Dorothy	C	1934,39	Vaughan, Kathy	T	1954-55
Tully, Mary Jane	T	1937-43	Underwood, Gwynne	A	1958-60	Vaughan, Lou	C	1958-60
Tunnell, Eva Ruth	C	1931	Underwood, Helena	T	1961-62	Vaughan, Mary	T	1968-71
Tunstill, Gayle Ann	C	1949	Underwood, Jane	A	1957	Vaughan, Nan	T	1950
Tupper, Betty	A	1943-48	Underwood, Jennifer	A	1983-88	Vaughan, Shannon	A	1979
Turbeville, Elizabeth	T	1951-56	Underwood, Lesley	A	1959-63	Vaughan, Sue	C	1957-60
Turci, Lara	A	1994-96	Underwood, Lynn	C	1951-54	Vaughan, Vanessa	C	1987-94
Turley, Elizabeth	T	1977-79	Underwood, Mary	A	1957-62	Vaughan, Whitney	T	1994
Turnbull, Becky	C	1963-68	Underwood, Mary	T	1966-72	Vaughn, Alice	T	1929-30
Turnbull, Jane	A	1956-57	Underwood, Mary	T	1933-34	Vaughn, Barbara	C	1947-50
Turnbull, Mills	C	1988-93	Katherine			Vaughn, Ella Frances	T	1942-44
Turner, Amanda	T	1979-83	Underwood, Nancy	A	1962	Vaughn, Genevieve	T	1952-53
Turner, Ann	A	1943-44	Underwood, Robin	A	1952-55	Vaughn, June	A	1948-51
Turner, Anne Jo		1933	Underwood, Shelley	A	1959-63	Vaughn, Kathy	T	1955
Turner, Betty	A	1948-49	Underwood, Susan	T	1950-53	Vaughn, Marci	T	1987-88
Turner, Charlotte	C	1976-80	Underwood, Trina	T	1976-83	Vaughn, Sally	A	1943-44
Turner, Clare	T	1937-40	Unger, Charlotte	T	1941,43-44	Vawter, Gretchen	A	1990-94
Turner, Denise	T	1963-64	Ungren, Marcia	C	1941-44,46	Veale, Callie	A	1995
Turner, Diane	A	1957-64	Upchurch, Josephine	C	1934	Veirs, Ann	A	1957-59
Turner, Dorothy	C	1939-44	Upshaw, Ainsley	C	1978-79,82	Veirs, Laura	A	1963-65
Turner, Elaine	T	1989-96	Upshaw, Allison	C	1979	Veirs, Susan	A	1960-63
Turner, Freda Fae	C	1933-34,	Upshaw, Brenda	A	1954-57	Veltman, Krista	C	1981
		1936-37	Upshaw, Rosemary	A	1974-76	Venable, Ann	A	1945-48
Turner, Jan	C	1952-54	Urbanic, Janie	C	1957-62	Venne, Victoria		1926
Turner, Janet	A	1945-47	Urbar, Katherine	C	1934	Verschoyle, Becky	T	1978-84
Turner, June Bug	T	1955-58	Ussery, Elizabeth	A	1987-92	Vick, Mary Elizabeth	C	1938-39
Turner, Karen	T	1965-71	Utzman, Grace	C	1938	Vick, Mary Ann	C	1942
Turner, Laura	A	1990-94				Vick, Taylor	C	1995-96
Turner, Leigh	C	1994-96	**V**			Vickers, Betty	T	1937
Turner, Leslie	C	1968-71	Vaccaro, Suzanne	T	1950	Vickers, Margi	C	1955-57
Turner, Lisa	A	1971-72	Vackar, Kristin	C	1994	Vila, Alexandra	T	1990-91
Turner, Nancy	C	1941-42	Vahlberg, Patricia	C	1940	Villareal, Judy	T	1941,43-46
Turner, Nancy	T	1969-74	Vahlburg, Jeannee	C	1940	Vincent, Olivia	T	1940
Turner, Sharon Lynn	C	1967-71	Valla, Kendra	A	1970-74	Viney, Landon	C	1994-96
Turner, Sterling	T	1995-96	Vallee, Ann	T	1942-43	Viney, Norma	A	1958-64
Turner, Virginia Jinx	T	1931-32,34	Van Cronkhite, Kathryn	A	1981-84	Viney, Reagan	T	1992-96
Turney, Claire	A	1980-86	Van Dornick, Charlotte	A	1945	Viney, Rhonda	A	1964-67,
Turpin, Jessica	C	1939,43	Van Everdingen, Jean	T	1939-41			1969-70
Turpin, Lucy	C	1955	Van Holsbeke, Lynda	A	1953-56	Vineyard, Kelly	C	1978-79
Turpin, Margaret Helen	A	1949-53	Van Hook, Beth	C	1960-63	Vinson, Ann		1951
Turrentine, Noelie	T	1947-48	Van Hoose, Adeline	C	1931	Vinson, Joan	T	1942-45
Tuttle, Frances		1929	Van Hyck, Mimi	T	1987	Vinson, Susie	T	1945
Tuttle, Sharon Duston	T	1948	Van Loan, Martha Jane	C	1934	Vinsonhaler, Jancy	A	1950-54
Tuttle, Winifred		1929	Van Meter, Constance	T	1946-47	Vogel, Nancy	T	1976-80
Twyman, Cecelia	A	1953-54	Van Patten, Phyllis	T	1934	Vogelsang, Katie	A	1985-88
Tygrett, Carroll	T	1979,81	Van Riet, Chantal	T	1984-88	Vogelsang, Merle	C	1940
Tyndall, Ann Barry	T	1959-60	Van Wyck, Mimi	T	1987-88	Vogtel, Connie	A	1945-46
Tynes, Jenny	T	1970-74	Van Zandt, Eugenia	C	1959-62	Vollrath, Linda	T	1942
Tynes, Marion	T	1944-45	Vanberg, Cara	C	1985-88,	Von Gal, Marney	C	1956-59
Tyrrell, Elizabeth	T	1942			1990-91	Von Gal, Suzanne	T	1963-64
Tyrrell, Frances	T	1949-53	Vanberg, Morgan	T	1988-94	Von Zandt, Eugenia	C	1959
Tyson, Dee Dee	A	1984-88	Vanderpool, Janet Ann	C	1959-61	Vornkahl, Jennifer	C	1994-96
Tyson, Janet	A	1948	Vandervoort, Mimi	A	1993-96	Vornkahl, Susan	C	1974-80
			Vandeveer, Cindi	A	1967-68	Vose, Martha	T	1940-43
U			Vandeveer, Vicki	T	1966-67	Vose, Virginia	T	1940
Ullman, Talia	C	1995	Vandever, Bette Lou	T	1934			
Ulmer, Ann	C	1944	Vandevier, Ann	C	1967-69	**W**		
Ulrich, Karen	C	1977	Vaneman, Gloria	C	1937-38	Wachtel, Carolyn	T	1938-39
Ulrich, Mary Liz	T	1975-77	Vardaman, Jan	T	1950	Wade, Nancy	T	1968-71
Umbenhour, Ada	C	1938	Varnell, Valerie	C	1996	Wadsworth, Hope	C	1944
Umphrey, Paige	T	1979-82	Vaughan, Anna	C	1971	Wager, Madeline	C	1995-95
Umpleby, Joanna	T	1954-55	Vaughan, Cathy	A	1972-77	Wagers, Joyce	T	1936,42,44

Waggoner, Amy	C	1978-86	Wallace, Laura	C	1974-79	Warner, Morgan	C	1981-86
Waggoner, Caroline	T	1978-83	Wallace, Martha	T	1942	Warner, Thera	A	1952-53
Waggoner, Jean	T	1938	Waller, Abby	A	1995-96	Warnock, Mary	T	1936-38
Waggoner, Johnnie Marie	T	1936-39,41	Waller, Alison	T	1993-96	Warren, Ann	C	1938-39
Waggoner, Judy	C	1957-61	Waller, Calada	C	1931	Warren, Caroline	T	1970-73
Waggoner, Katie	A	1989-96	Waller, Elaine	A	1962-68	Warren, Dawne	T	1949-51
Waggoner, Lee Ann	C	1985-89	Waller, Elizabeth	C	1975-76	Warren, Margaret	C	1939
Wagner, Betty Ruth	T	1938-39	Waller, Emily	A	1988-92	Warren, Martha	A	1945-46
Wagner, Catherine Ann Kay	T	1949-50	Waller, Heather	C	1983-89	Warren, Mary	A	1972-77
			Waller, Kathy	T	1966-70	Warren, Sue	T	1942
Wagner, Genevieve Sissy	C	1972-77	Waller, Megan	T	1992-96	Washmon, Dorothy	T	1976-79
Wagner, Kelly	C	1987-88	Waller, Rebecca	A	1974-75	Washmon, Wendy	T	1977-81
Wagner, Kim	C	1972-74	Waller, Ruth	C	1975-76	Wasson, Dot	A	1943-47
Wagner, Margaret	C	1937-38	Waller, Sissy	C	1961-66	Wasson, Sue	A	1946,49
Wagner, Peggy	C	1961-62	Waller, Stancy	T	1967-72	Waters, Audrey	C	1990-95
Wagner, Sally	C	1953-55	Walling, Charles Ann	C	1941	Watkins, Geneva	C	1945
Wagner, Sherwood	C	1982-85	Walls, Emily	C	1984-90	Watkins, Liza	C	1989
Wagner, Virginia	T	1939	Walsh, Amy	A	1975-80	Watkins, Mary Lou	T	1945-50
Wahlenmaier, Jane	C	1939-40, 1943-45	Walsh, Ellen	A	1978-85	Watkins, Meghan	C	1984-91
			Walter, Carole	A	1966-70	Watkins, Shana	T	1987-90
Waite, Lucille		1926	Walter, Gladie Jo	T	1936-37	Watkins, Sue	A	1946-49
Waite, Nina		1926	Walters, Caroline	T	1936-37	Watson, Ann	C	1942-48
Wakefield, Sally	A	1958-66	Walters, Karen Ann	A	1948	Watson, Ann Sheridan	C	1947-52
Wakeman, Laura	A	1981-84	Walters, Valerie	A	1949-52	Watson, Becky	A	1968-75
Walcher, Marjorie Sue	T	1954-61	Walton, Alice	T	1940-41	Watson, Bennie	T	1931
Walcher, Prissy	A	1951-58	Walton, Ann	T	1945	Watson, Betsy	T	1963-67
Walden, Ann	A	1945,47	Walton, Anne	A	1990-96	Watson, Carroll	A	1984-89
Waldron, Genie	C	1951-57	Walton, Caroline	A	1945,48	Watson, Daffan	C	1979-85
Waldron, Martha	C	1966-68	Walton, Cynthia	C	1945,48	Watson, Diana	A	1992-96
Waldron, Nancy	C	1966-68	Walton, Emily	A	1996	Watson, Eleanor	T	1937,40-44
Waldrop, Gladys	A	1964-67	Walton, Gage	C	1975-78	Watson, Ellen	T	1930-31
Waldrop, Nancy	A	1966-71	Walton, Sue	T	1943,45-46	Watson, J.C. Ann	C	1930-31
Walker, Ainsley	A	1995-96	Walvoord, Ginger	C	1941	Watson, Jennifer	A	1972
Walker, Alice	C	1941	Wander, Jo	C	1932	Watson, Kendall	T	1994-96
Walker, Alice	T	1944,46	Wander, Ruth	C	1932	Watson, Larkin	C	1968-71
Walker, Ann	T	1974	Ward, Ann	T	1934	Watson, Laura	T	1978-84
Walker, Anne	A	1962-65	Ward, Claudia	A	1981-84	Watson, Lindsey	T	1958
Walker, Annis	T	1950	Ward, Evelyn	T	1930	Watson, Lou	C	1941-44
Walker, Becky	A	1946-51	Ward, Kay	A	1953-56	Watson, Marcia	A	1947-52
Walker, Bernice	T	1942-43	Ward, Laura Frances		1937	Watson, Meredith	A	1987-90
Walker, Betsy	C	1978-84	Ward, Lois Ann	A	1948-49	Watson, Olivia	A	1962-66
Walker, Betty	A	1949-52	Ward, Mary Lois	C	1937	Watson, Patsy	A	1946-48
Walker, Bobbie	A	1944-46	Ward, Maryhill	C	1994-96	Watson, Suzy	C	1975-76
Walker, Carter	T	1990-96	Ward, Rita	C	1966-67	Watson, Vera Jo	C	1945-48
Walker, Cherre	T	1955-63	Wardlaw, Jennifer	C	1987-89	Watt, Elora	T	1935
Walker, Francie	T	1974-76	Wardlaw, Rachel	C	1938	Watts, Ann	T	1945
Walker, Jane	T	1964-68	Wardlow, Cerissa	T	1996	Watts, Dorothy	C	1939-41
Walker, Jean	C	1934-35	Ware, Allison	A	1984-88	Watts, Jane		1936
Walker, Kay	C	1963-67	Ware, Andrea	T	1981-87	Watts, Linda	A	1956-62
Walker, Lana Kay	A	1953-59	Ware, Anne-Clayton	C	1984-91	Watts, Michelle	T	1976-81
Walker, Lucinda	C	1970-71	Ware, Bebe	C	1962-64	Watts, Otis Neal	T	1933,35
Walker, Margaret	T	1933	Ware, Mary Jane	T	1953-58	Watts, Sharon	T	1961-68
Walker, Martha Annis	T	1949-50	Ware, Missy	T	1981-84	Watts, Waynette	T	1950-53
Walker, Mary Helen	T	1941	Wareing, Julie	A	1988-94	Wave, Missy	T	1982
Walker, Rebecca	A	1946	Wareing, Laura	C	1986-92	Wavell, Pamela	T	1957
Walkup, Marian	T	1937	Warner, Allison	A	1985-91	Waycott, Betty Jane	A	1943
Wall, Jennifer	C	1987-91	Warner, Barbara	T	1937-40	Wayland, Anna	T	1986-91
Wall, Kay	C	1945-50	Warner, Beth	T	1978-83	Weaker, Rhoda	A	1974
Wall, Mary	C	1954-56	Warner, Betty Anne	C	1941	Weakley, Nancy	T	1937
Wallace, Anne	C	1968	Warner, Betty Lou	T	1938-39	Wear, Jessica	C	1993-96
Wallace, Carol	A	1969-73	Warner, Elizabeth	T	1937	Wear, Susie	C	1981-82
Wallace, Cathy	A	1968-72	Warner, Janet	T	1937-41,44	Wear, Whitney	C	1996
Wallace, Fay	T	1990	Warner, Lorraine	C	1939	Weatherby, Eleanor Ann	T	1936-37,39

Weatherby, Sarah	C	1952-55	Wells, Nancy	T	1974-75	Wheless, CeCe	C	1960-65
Weatherly, Winifred		1926,28	Wells, Rachel	A	1988-95	Wheless, Lee	C	1957-59
Weaver, Allison	C	1980-87	Wells, Suzanne	T	1966	Wheless, Marti	A	1973-76
Webb, Emily	C	1985	Wells, Whitney	T	1978-83	Wherritt, Vassar	C	1938
Webb, Ethel		1929	Welsh, Anne	A	1943	Whitaker, Ann	A	1951
Webb, Frances	C	1941,44	Welsh, Mary Lou	T	1957	Whitaker, Lori	A	1976-79
Webb, Gladys		1929	Welt, Sabina	T	1982-85	Whitcomb, Dee	T	1956-60
Webb, Margaret	T	1931	Wenmohs, Juanita	C	1940	Whitcomb, Jan	T	1955-59
Webb, Martha	C	1941	Werkenrthin, Louise	C	1939-40	White, Betty Agnes	T	1942
Webb, Mary Claire	A	1945-48	Werlein, Phyllis	C	1960	White, Betty Jane	T	1940-41
Webb, Mary	T	1931	Werlin, Sharon	C	1954-60	White, Carolyn	A	1946-51
Webb, Nancy Lee	T	1946-49	Werner, Jessica	C	1988-91	White, Charlotte	C	1938
Webb, Nelle	T	1929,31	Werst, Sally Ann	T	1947-49	White, Chick	A	1945-48
Webb, Olive	C	1949	Wertz, Charlotte	A	1949-53	White, Cynthia	C	1978-85
Webb, Tori	A	1983-87	Wertz, Ida Mae	T	1929-31	White, Dianne	C	1955-59
Webster, Holli	C	1975-77	Wesson, Ida	C	1939	White, DAnn	C	1981-87
Webster, Sari Jane	A	1950	West, Allison	T	1987-93	White, Elizabeth	C	1930
Wedgeworth, Anne	A	1965-68	West, Angie	C	1986-91,93	White, Elizabeth	A	1985-91
Weed, Elizabeth	A	1970-74	West, Ann	A	1943	White, Evelyn		1928
Weed, Jere	T	1962-67	West, Betty Ann	C	1942	White, Frances	T	1939
Weed, Kathy	T	1957-61	West, Billie Jo	C	1937-38	White, Geraldine G.G.	A	1944-45
Weed, Margaret	C	1972-78	West, Catharin	A	1984-91	White, Heather	A	1994
Weedon, Amy	T	1985-86	West, Cindy	T	1969-71	White, Huetta Gene	C	1936-37
Weedon, Dana	A	1982-85	West, Dolores	C	1942	White, Jean	T	1940
Weedon, Shelly	C	1967-71	West, Elizabeth	C	1937	White, Jennifer	A	1978-85
Weeks, Carrie	C	1968-69	West, Jane	C	1934	White, Jessica	T	1979-86
Weems, Meredith	T	1990-91	West, Janice	A	1957-61	White, Joella		1926
Weems, Whitney	A	1990-91	West, Joyce	T	1942	White, Joy	T	1944,46
Weichsel, Nancy	C	1977-81	West, Kristin	A	1981	White, Marjorie	A	1943-44
Weinert, Clara	C	1941-43	West, Mary Helen	C	1937-38	White, Martha Nell	T	1940-41
Weinert, Jane	T	1930-31	West, Mary Frances	C	1934	White, Mary Kay	C	1971-77
Weinert, Johnnye	C	1940-41,43	West, Mazie	T	1996	White, Mary Ray	T	1938,40
Weinert, Karen Dale	C	1947-53	West, Roxy Anne	T	1952	White, Mary Alice	T	1959-63
Weisberg, Emily	T	1936	West, Saxton	T	1930	White, Mimi	C	1946-47
Weisberg, Marie	C	1936	West, Shirley	C	1942	White, Missy	T	1976-82
Weiss, Marilyn	C	1950	Westbrook, Margaret	C	1954-57	White, Morgan	A	1994-96
Welch, Anna	A	1950-56	Wetzel, Mary Elizabeth	T	1937	White, Sara Frances	C	1929-30
Welch, Francine	C	1941	Weyman, Carol	T	1968-72	White, Sophie Anne	T	1943
Welch, Lynann	C	1955-56	Weymouth, Betsy	C	1931	White, Winifred	T	1939,41
Welch, Marjorie	T	1942	Weymouth, Mary Ann	C	1931	Whited, Carolyn	C	1929-30,32
Welder, Elizabeth	A	1948-51	Weyrich, Mary Frances	T	1950-54	Whitehead, Barbara	T	1930
Welder, Heather	C	1991-92	Wharton, Neene	C	1947-48	Whitehead, Bo Dell	C	1947-48
Welder, Jane	A	1950-53	Wharton, Rita	A	1953-58	Whitehead, Bobbie Lou	A	1943-47
Welder, Mary Heather	C	1989-92	Wheat, Evan	A	1991-95	Whitehead, Cody	T	1992-93
Welder, Pat	T	1939,41	Wheat, Lauren	C	1993-1995	Whitehead, Kelly	A	1981-85
Welge, Kathleen	T	1996	Wheat, Lettie	T	1968-72	Whitehead, Lea	C	1977-83
Welge, Kirsten	C	1991-96	Wheat, Ruby Ruth	T	1935	Whitehead, Leisa	C	1960-68
Welk, Suzanne	T	1936-39	Wheatley, Mollie	T	1965	Whitehead, Lou Emma	T	1941
Welks, Emily	A	1985	Wheeler, Anne	A	1961	Whitehead, Lucie Jean	C	1936-39
Weller, Kate	A	1987-92	Wheeler, Barbara	C	1939-42	Whitehead, Rosemary	T	1938
Weller, Kathryn	A	1987	Wheeler, Barbara	C	1934,36	Whitehill, Ashley	C	1989-93
Wells, Alice	A	1947-52	Wheeler, Connie	T	1955-56	Whitehill, Kristen	C	1985-90
Wells, Breece	A	1973-78	Wheeler, Enid	C	1944	Whitehurst, Charlotte	T	1938-39
Wells, Burkely	C	1975-80	Wheeler, Freddie	A	1946	Whitehurst, Margaret	T	1938-39
Wells, Diane	A	1945-48	Wheeler, Marilyn	C	1947,49	Whitely,Willye		1928
Wells, Elizabeth	C	1981-86	Wheeler, Mollie Jo	C	1947-49	Whiteside, Betty Helen	C	1930
Wells, Elizabeth	C	1967	Wheeler, Sara	T	1961	Whiteside, Billie Jo	T	1946
Wells, Joannna	A	1991-96	Wheelock, Diana	A	1962-65	Whiteside, Carolyn	C	1944
Wells, Katherine	C	1996	Wheelus, Collier	A	1970-76	Whiteside, Lenore	T	1944
Wells, Kelli	A	1989-91	Wheelus, Marilyn	C	1930	Whiteside, Margie	C	1934
Wells, Marjorie	T	1987-93	Whelan, Jeanne	C	1937	Whiteside, Mary Jane	A	1979-86
Wells, Mary	A	1943-44	Whelan, Kay	C	1937	Whitley, Jessie Ruth	C	1941
Wells, Mollie	C	1969-74	Whelees, Barbara	C	1938	Whitley, Joan	C	1943-44

Whitley, Mitchell	A	1985-86	Wilkinson, Amy	A	1995-96	Williams, Liz	C	1993-96
Whitley, Sheree	C	1983-86	Wilkinson, Barbara	T	1936-37	Williams, Lucy Ann	C	1938
Whitmeyer, Edna Marie	A	1945-47	Wilkinson, Ginny	C	1992-96	Williams, Lyn	T	1957-65
Whitmire, Wendy	A	1965-67	Wilkinson, Jane	T	1948	Williams, Lynne	T	1974-80
Whitney, Blythe	C	1979-84	Wilkinson, Kate	T	1991-96	Williams, Margie	C	1935,37
Whitney, Susan	T	1980-84	Wilkinson, Margaret	T	1938	Williams, Marilyn	A	1950-51
Whitson, Mary	T	1995-96	Wilkinson, Susybelle	C	1934-36	Williams, Marnie	A	1979-82
Whitson, Nancy	A	1972-79	Wilkinson, Virginia Lou	C	1946-49,	Williams, Martha Jane	C	1930
Whittaker, Ambra	A	1961			1951-53	Williams, Martha	T	1935,37-38,
Whitten, Becky	T	1962-66	Wilkinson, Virginia	C	1930			1940-42
Whitten, Clair	C	1938	Wilks, Emily	A	1983-86	Williams, Mary	C	1931
Whitten, Laura	T	1977-84	Willard. Mary Lou	T	1934-35	Williams, Mary Elizabeth	T	1934
Whitten, Marian	T	1955-58	Willeford, Emily	T	1986-93	Williams, Melanie	T	1944-46
Whitten, Peggy	C	1961-63	Willeford, Nancy Kate	T	1989-96	Williams, Mimi	A	1946
Whittenburg, C.C.	C	1966-71	Willet, Alissa	T	1981-87	Williams, Nancy	T	1971-76
Whittenburg, Catharine	T	1986-88	Willet, Amber	A	1983-88	Williams, Nell Pope	C	1940,42
Whittenburg, Francie	C	1954-58	Willet, Ashlea	A	1978-84	Williams, Patricia	C	1995-96
Whittenburg, Jeanne	C	1962-69	Willett, Dorothy	T	1931	Williams, Phoebe	A	1957
Whittenburg, Lelah	T	1963	Williamns, Laurie	T	1968	Williams, Rebecca	T	1990-94,96
Whittenburg, Leslie	A	1974	Williams, Adelaide	C	1938	Williams, Sandy	A	1946-50,52
Whittenburg, Liz	T	1963-70	Williams, Agnes		1929	Williams, Sheila Tot		1961
Whittenburg, Wenda	T	1951-52,54	Williams, Alden	A	1965-69	Williams, Suzanne	C	1959-60
Whitworth, Ann	A	1962-67	Williams, Allen	C	1969-74	Williams, Suzanne	C	1955
Whitworth, Anne	C	1986-92	Williams, Angela	C	1990-95	Williams, Wendy	C	1961
Whitworth, Elizabeth	T	1990-96	Williams, Ann	A	1946-49	Williams, Wendy	C	1972-77
Whitworth, Julie	T	1965	Williams, Ann Leland	T	1953-55	Williams, Whitney	C	1978-81
Whorton, Anna	T	1980-86	Williams, Beth Ann	T	1978-84	Williams, Wilma	T	1936-39
Whyte, Imogene	T	1942-43	Williams, Betty	A	1946-47	Williamson, Amy	C	1983
Wick, Pamela	T	1977-80	Williams, Carole	T	1949-52	Williamson, Janie	A	1950-57
Wicker, Helen	C	1958-63	Williams, Caroline	C	1968-74	Williamson, Mary Lyn	T	1957-63
Wickman, Jan	A	1979-81	Williams, Carolyn	T	1950-53	Williamson, Nancy	T	1969-74
Widen, Alma	C	1933,35	Williams, Cayce	C	1980-83	Williford, Ann	T	1942-43
Widen, Charlotte	C	1932-34	Williams, Charlotte	C	1936	Willis, Callen	C	1994-96
Widen, Edna	C	1936-37	Williams, Doris	C	1935-36	Willis, Deborah	T	1982-89
Wiesner, Falon	A	1991-93	Williams, Dorothy	C	1930	Willis, Rebecca	C	1930-31
Wiesner, Lauren	T	1990-93	Williams, Dorothy	T	1939-43	Willoughby, Clara	C	1945
Wiggins, Esther	C	1942-46	Williams, Dotty	A	1955-56	Willoughby, Jan	A	1955-63
Wiggins, Jane	A	1946-48	Williams, Elizabeth	A	1963	Willoughby, Joan	C	1949-56
Wiggins, Margaret	T	1934	Williams, Elizabeth	A	1959-64	Wills, Flo	C	1945
Wight, Jan Helen	T	1949-51	Williams, Ellen	A	1968-72	Wills, Virginia	C	1945
Wightman, Julie	A	1985-86	Williams, Ellie	A	1985-91	Willson, Camille	C	1971-72
Wiginton, Lauren	A	1986	Williams, Evelyn	C	1931	Willson, Louise	C	1939
Wiginton, Nan	A	1947-49	Williams, Gwynn	C	1969-73	Willson, Margaret	T	1970-72
Wiginton, Sue	A	1955-61	Williams, Harriet	A	1952-58	Willson, Oragene	C	1944-45
Wikert, Margretta	A	1996	Williams, Jane	C	1971-74	Willson, Rebecca	C	1931
Wikins, Nicole	T	1982	Williams, Jeannie	C	1993-94	Willy, Rosetta	A	1995-96
Wilbert, Carolyn	T	1941-43	Williams, Jerry	C	1936	Willy, Susan	C	1978-81
Wilbert, Etta Lee	A	1943-45	Williams, Joan	C	1954-55	Wilson, Adrienne	T	1987-93
Wilbur, Christy	A	1981	Williams, Joanne	A	1954-57	Wilson, Barbara	T	1944-45,
Wilcox, Dana	C	1985-90	Williams, Julia		1928			1947-48
Wilcox, Lauren	A	1990-96	Williams, Julie	T	1960-67	Wilson, Carolyn	T	1937
Wilcoxson, Karla	A	1961	Williams, June	T	1937	Wilson, Charlotte	T	1955-59
Wilder, Bettye Hayes	T	1950-53	Williams, Kathryn	C	1962-68	Wilson, Cherie	C	1959-65
Wileman, Anne	C	1951-53	Williams, Kay	C	1952-59	Wilson, Cheryl	T	1972-77
Wiley, Eloise	A	1988-95	Williams, Lane	T	1974-79	Wilson, Christina	C	1989-95
Wilkeret, Margetta	A	1996	Williams, Laura	T	1934	Wilson, Clara E.		1929
Wilkerson, Mary Ruth	T	1949-50	Williams, Laura	C	1978-81	Wilson, Claudia	C	1962-66
Wilkes, Elizabeth Libba	A	1961-62	Williams, Laurie	C	1978-79	Wilson, Courtney	T	1990-94
Wilkes, Jenny	C	1993-96	Williams, Laurie	T	1967-71	Wilson, Darby	T	1973-79
Wilkes, Rachel	C	1994-96	Williams, Laurie Ann	C	1970	Wilson, Edna Marion	T	1933
Wilkie, Mary Lynn	C	1951	Williams, Leigh Alice	C	1964-68	Wilson, Ellen	T	1969-73
Wilkins, Margaret	A	1943	Williams, Leslie Ann	C	1965-70	Wilson, Evalyn	C	1939
Wilkins, Nicole	T	1983-87	Williams, Liz	A	1985-91	Wilson, Evelyn	T	1944

Name	Type	Years
Wilson, Helen	C	1937
Wilson, Hope	T	1970-77
Wilson, Jeanne	A	1963,65
Wilson, Jennifer	T	1989-92
Wilson, Jo Ann	A	1943-44
Wilson, Joan	T	1945-46
Wilson, Joanne	C	1978-80
Wilson, Josephine		1929
Wilson, Kay	T	1976-82
Wilson, Kristilea	A	1988-92
Wilson, Lane	T	1994-96
Wilson, Margaret	T	1971-74
Wilson, Mariann	C	1948-50
Wilson, Marie	T	1953-60
Wilson, Marnerleen	C	1940-41
Wilson, Martha	T	1952
Wilson, Mary	A	1957-61
Wilson, Mary Ann	C	1940
Wilson, Mary Adele	T	1930
Wilson, Mary Jo	C	1933
Wilson, Meador	C	1961-68
Wilson, Michelle	A	1974-75
Wilson, Milly	T	1946
Wilson, Missy	A	1973-79
Wilson, Molly Lou	C	1950
Wilson, Mozelle	T	1941-42
Wilson, Nancy	T	1976-79
Wilson, Nancy Ruth	T	1961-63
Wilson, Nancy Jane		1939
Wilson, Peggie Lou	C	1932
Wilson, Peggy	T	1946
Wilson, Rosine	T	1966-70
Wilson, Sandra	T	1955-57
Wilson, Sharon	A	1974-77
Wilson, Shelley	A	1976-82
Wilson, Virginia	T	1944
Wimberly, Bonner	A	1992-93
Wimberly, Hallie	C	1996
Wimberly, Melissa	A	1988,91-92
Wimbish, Georgann	C	1956-60
Winburn, Mary	A	1970-73
Windham, Allison	A	1976-82
Windham, Ann	T	1934
Windham, Barbara	A	1973-79
Wingate, Agnes	A	1943-45
Wingate, Martha	T	1940
Wingate, Mary	C	1939-40
Wingfield, Carrie Jones	C	1949-52
Winn, Ellen	C	1964-69
Winn, Susie	C	1968-74
Winsett, Mary	A	1945-48
Winship, Diana	C	1948-50
Winship, Kimberly	C	1976-78
Winship, Michelle	C	1978,81-83
Winson, Ann	C	1951
Winston, Anne	C	1990-93
Winston, Dorothy	A	1943
Winston, Janne	T	1959
Winston, Karen	T	1962-66
Winston, Lacey	T	1987-91
Winston, Lauren	T	1962
Winston, Lou Ann	C	1969-72
Winston, Nancy	A	1987-94
Winter, Anna	T	1983-89
Winter, Brittany	C	1995-96
Winter, Kathleen	A	1974-78
Winterirnger, Kay	C	1950-51
Winterringer, Gay	A	1967
Winterringer, Lynn	C	1971-72
Winterringer, Rudi	C	1966-69
Winterringer, Susan	C	1965-68
Winters, Amanda	A	1978-83
Winters, Caroline	T	1978-82
Winters, Catherine	C	1971-74
Winters, Jane	C	1963
Winters, Leila	T	1961-65
Winters, Martha	C	1970-73
Wirth, Beverly	A	1976-78
Wirth, Kelly	T	1975-77
Wise, Ann	C	1944-50
Wise, Betsy	A	1949-55
Wise, Louise	T	1962-67
Wise, Lousanne	C	1956-58
Wise, Margaret	T	1946
Wise, Mary	T	1935
Wise, Wendy	A	1981-84
Wiseman, Eleanor		1929
Wither, Georganna	A	1981-84
Wither, Jennifer	C	1982-85
Withers, Allison	A	1981-86
Withers, Betty Rae	A	1953-55
Witherspoon, Dorothy	C	1938
Witherspoon, Irene	A	1950-54
Witmer, Sally	T	1945
Witt, Susan	C	1995-96
Wittman, Patsy Jo	T	1950
Wittmer, Gay	C	1949
Wittmer, Judy	A	1949
Woeff, Harriet	A	1964
Woldert, Lee	A	1959-62
Woldert, Sarah Lee	C	1934,37
Wolf, Delia	C	1982-87
Wolf, Diane	C	1952-55
Wolf, Edith	T	1937
Wolf, Josephine		1926
Wolf, Martie	A	1986-92
Wolf, Mary J.	T	1930
Wolf, Sonia	C	1945-48
Wolfe, Betty	A	1946-48
Wolfe, Betty	C	1934-37,40
Wolfe, Icia Belle	C	1950
Wolfe, Jane Ellen	C	1934-35
Wolfe, Sara Belle	C	1950
Wolff, Harriet	A	1963-66
Wollery, Vivian	C	1933
Wolslager, Rachelle	A	1989-92
Womack, Betty Ann	C	1940-46
Womack, Jan	T	1947-48, 1950-52
Womack, Louisa	T	1985-89
Womack, Louise		1929
Womack, Mary Eva	A	1954-57
Womack, Nikki	C	1958-63
Womack, Pauline		1929
Womack, Stephanie	A	1978-79
Womack, Virginia Nell	C	1987-89
Womble, Dee	T	1961-64
Womble, Janey	A	1950-54
Womble, Sara	A	1970-71
Wommack, Carroll	T	1969-76
Wood, Charlotte	T	1941
Wood, Edna	T	1934-35
Wood, Ellen	A	1971-76
Wood, Florence	T	1934-35
Wood, Jackie	T	1946-47
Wood, Jane	A	1956-61
Wood, Jean	C	1934-36
Wood, Jean	A	1950
Wood, Kathy	T	1972-78
Wood, Kim	A	1969-76
Wood, Laura Virginia	C	1931
Wood, Laura F.	C	1937
Wood, Martha Kay Marty	A	1949-53
Wood, Mary	T	1936-37
Wood, Mary	C	1949-54
Woodall, Sue	A	1943-46
Woodard, Faye	A	1945-47
Woodforth, Gwendolyn	C	1931
Woodley, Evelyn	C	1935
Woodmansee, Florence	C	1943-44
Woodrome, Jane	C	1940-42
Woodruff, Beverly	T	1956
Woodruff, Joan	T	1939-40
Woodruff, Sharon	A	1955-56
Woods, Chloe	A	1996
Woods, Heather	A	1973-74
Woods, Jane Ann	T	1947
Woods, Larke	C	1967-74
Woods, Marian	T	1936-37
Woods, Martha	C	1936-39, 1941-43
Woods, Roberta	C	1930,33
Woods, Sara	T	1995-96
Woodside, Elizabeth	T	1983-85
Woodson, Ann	T	1947
Woodson, Anne	C	1947-49, 1951-56
Woodson, Ashley	T	1986-89
Woodson, Colleen	C	1950-55
Woodson, Helen		1927
Woodson, Judy	A	1945-51
Woodson, Kata	T	1939-43
Woodson, Kirby	T	1983-89
Woodson, Lucinda	C	1952-56
Woodson, Mary Lynn	T	1933,35
Woodson, Pat	T	1947-51
Woodson, Virginia Anne	C	1948
Woodul, Katherine	A	1995-96
Woodward, Jan	C	1948
Woody, Lyn	A	1963-69
Wooldridge, Betty	A	1956-60
Wooldridge, Linda	T	1959-60
Wooldridge, Sue	A	1956-60
Wooldrige, Mindy	C	1996
Wooley, Grace	A	1945
Wooley, Margaret	C	1936
Woolley, Barbara	T	1970-74
Woolley, Caroline	C	1968-70
Woolley, Cecilia	T	1939,40-41

Name	Code	Years
Woolley, Leslie	C	1967-69
Woolley, Susanne	A	1972-77
Woolley, Vivian	C	1933
Woolridge, Betty	A	1956-59
Woolridge, Linda	T	1959
Woolridge, Sue	A	1956-59
Woolsey, Alice Ann	C	1942
Woolsey, Margie Nell	C	1936,38-40
Wooten, Anne	A	1977-80
Wooters, Virgina	C	1928-31
Wootten, Vendla	A	1944
Word, Joyce	T	1940
Worden, Ann	T	1935-36
Workman, Susan	C	1970-74
Works, Joan	A	1948-49
Works, Mary Sue	A	1949
Works, Smith	C	1986-87
Worley, Betty	A	1948
Worley, Katherine		1926
Worsham, Cynthia	A	1964
Worsham, Gail	A	1963-64
Worsham, Julie	C	1990
Worthing, Ashley	C	1988-91
Worthing, Doris Sue	C	1941,44
Worthy, Ann	A	1970-73
Worthy, Marjorie	T	1933
Worthy, Rose Helen	T	1933-34
Wrage, Kay Lee	C	1941-43
Wray, Betty	C	1958
Wray, Jennifer	C	1989-92
Wray, Lauren	A	1988
Wray, Lois	C	1953-56
Wray, Mary Virginia	C	1961-62
Wren, Josephine	T	1934
Wren, Pamela	T	1949
Wright, Allison	A	1984
Wright, Allyson	C	1985-86, 1988-89
Wright, Amanda	A	1990-94
Wright, Anita	C	1959-60
Wright, Beth	C	1978-81
Wright, Brooke	T	1978-79
Wright, Cathy	C	1962-65
Wright, Clayton	T	1982-88
Wright, Elizabeth	A	1995-96
Wright, Emma Ruth	T	1940
Wright, Erin	T	1971-75
Wright, Heather	T	1969-73
Wright, Irene	C	1936
Wright, Jeannie	A	1961-64
Wright, Jennifer	C	1994
Wright, Jennifer	A	1960
Wright, Katherine	A	1979-86
Wright, Katie	A	1992-96
Wright, Malloy	T	1942-43
Wright, Margaret	C	1945-46
Wright, Mary Ellen	C	1984-91
Wright, Mary Anna	A	1954-58
Wright, Myrlee	C	1938
Wright, Phyllis	A	1946-49
Wright, Rose Marie	T	1938
Wright, Sue		1929
Wroten, Nancy	C	1953-54
Wunsch, Elizabeth	T	1993-96
Wyatt, Lyla Sue	C	1942
Wyche, Wendy	C	1985-88
Wyly, Ann	T	1949
Wynn, Elizabeth	A	1960-62
Wynn, Jennifer	C	1954-57
Wynn, Margaret	A	1943
Wynn, Mary	A	1968-73
Wynne, Chesley	A	1967-71
Wynne, Esther	C	1966
Wynne, Jerry Jane	T	1932,34
Wynne, Jo Alice	C	1937-38, 1941-42
Wynne, Marietta	C	1969-71
Wynne, Sissy	T	1934
Wynne, Staley	A	1971-76
Wynne, Virginia	T	1974-77

Y

Name	Code	Years
Yaeger, Marian	T	1937-38
Yakey, Bess Hal	T	1935,37
Yarberry, Vicky	A	1943-46
Yarborough, Ann	T	1941
Yates, Billie	T	1934-35
Yates, Joyce	A	1943-44, 1946-47
Yeager, Elizabeth	C	1971-78
Yeager, Kathleen	C	1978-85
Yeager, Linda	C	1971-79
Yeary, Alden	T	1986-87
Yelvington, Judy	C	1958-59
Yelvington, Susan	C	1957
Yerger, Rivers Gay	A	1948-49
Yett, Carolyn	T	1935
Yoakam, Anne	C	1981-84
Yoakam, Sarah	C	1984
Yocum, Laura	C	1991
Yoder, Jan	T	1972-73
Yolton, Jesse Marie	T	1937
Yosh, Lynda	C	1948
Yost, Clayton	C	1985-89
Yost, Lynda	C	1949
Yost, Sally	A	1958-64
Yost, Samantha	T	1987-89
Youman, Lucy Lyn	A	1954-55
Young, Ann	A	1946-50
Young, Ann	T	1936
Young, Beth	A	1973
Young, Billie	T	1936
Young, Carolyn	T	1946
Young, Cissy	T	1957-61
Young, Elaine		1939
Young, Ione	T	1934
Young, Jane	A	1946-47
Young, Jean	A	1943
Young, Karita	A	1945
Young, Linda	T	1944,48-49, 1951-52
Young, Mahala	T	1940
Young, Merrie	C	1981-88
Young, Michael	T	1946
Young, Michelle	C	1977-83
Young, Molly	T	1991-93
Young, Patricia	A	1946
Young, Priscilla	T	1957-58
Young, Rebecca Jo	T	1939
Young, Sara Jane	A	1945
Young, Sarah Ann	C	1941
Young, Yvonne	T	1951
Young, Yvonne	A	1960-62
Youngblood, Mary Anne	A	1951-58
Youngblood, Penny Lee	A	1951-52
Youngblood, Sheridan	A	1943
Yuill, Catherine	C	1981-83
Yuill, Margaret	C	1982

Z

Name	Code	Years
Zachry, Emma	T	1942
Zahn, Betsy	A	1964
Zamorano, Courtney	A	1988-92,94
Zamorano, Lauren	T	1994-95
Zanes, Mary		1937
Zappe, Joan Sue	T	1948-49, 1951-52
Zarkle, Renny	T	1949
Zarr, Lucy	T	1948-50,52
Zedler, Gay	C	1940-45
Zehntner, Margaret	T	1941
Zeigen, Mary Frances Bunny	T	1941
Zellers, Ernie Ruth	T	1929-30
Zelsman, Anne	C	1970-74
Zelsman, Martha	C	1972-76
Zelsman, Mary	C	1967-71
Zerboni, Cheryl Anne	T	1962
Ziegler, Mary Kathrine	C	1996
Ziegler, Susan	C	1955-57
Zimmerman, Jeanne	T	1947-51
Zimmerman, Nancy Lee	C	1940
Zimmerman, Nicole	T	1995-96
Zimmerman, Sarah	A	1957
Zimmerman, Ursula	C	1940-41
Zimmerman, Virginia Gypsy	C	1944-46
Zirkle, Margaret	A	1956
Zirkle, Mary	T	1959-60
Zirkle, Renny	T	1948-50
Zivley, Claire	A	1967-73
Zivley, Lisa Jane	A	1969-75
Zoch, Chandler	C	1988
Zoch, Frances	C	1946-48
Zoeller, Frances		1926
Zoeller, Katherine		1926
Zork, Frances	T	1942
Zork, Marian	C	1939-40
Zvolanek, Melissa	T	1980-81
Zweifel, Doris	T	1931
Zwiener, Jane	A	1956-57
Zwiener, Wendy	A	1960-61

CAPTIONS FOR PHOTO SECTION

1 identified
2 identified

3
A—Kampongs & Athletic Field, 1927
B—Office, 1927
C—Original Dining Hall, 1928
D—Rippling Waters, 1930
E—Original Kampong
F—Round-up Lodge, 1931
G—Waldemar Gates, 1929
H—Athletic Field and new Dining Hall
I—In 1938 Catalogue
J—Ideal Waldemar Girl Trophy
K—Crest
L—Bridge over Guadalupe River, 1936
M—Drama presentations, 1932
N—Waldemar Girls, 1936
O—Original Waldemar Gate, 1926

4 — Daily Activities
A—Staff members of 1932
B—Waldemar bugler, Dorothy Milroy, 1929
C—Fencing
D—Horseback riding
E—Schedule
F—Clothing-equipment
G—Swimming
H—Riflery
I—Archery
J—Waldemar girls posing on station wagon
K—Cowgirls
L—War Canoe
M—Tennis
N—Waterfront
O—Golf
P—Ballet
Q—War Whoop

5—Familiar faces of Waldemar
A—Dolly Kelton, Revere, Mac Johnson, Doris Johnson, Squish Willett, Bess Richard
B—Squish Willett, Reba Lucy, Ruth Greene, Bess Rayford
C—Roe Johnson
D—Billie Johnson
E—Sarah Jayne Johnson
F—Connie Reeves
G—Jack Reeves
H—Doris Johnson
I—Dolly Downes Kelton
J—Waterfront staff
K—Ferdinand Rehbeger
L—Squish Wilett

M—Ellen Easley
N—Squish Willett
O—Swimming staff
P—Ruth Tatum
Q—Betty Meyers
R—Carmen Crain Williams
S—Johnny Regan
T—Kay Mitchell Estes
U—Fanny Bollinger
V—Mary Louise Schuch
W—Moey Rutledge
X—Laura Wallace
Y—Mary Kelley

6
A—Riding stables
B—Fencing
C—Picnic
D—Diving
E—Map
F—Mural
G—Girls arriving by train
H—Shannon Harber & Connie Reeves
I—Horse show "Monkey Drill"
J—"Legend of the Guadalupe" Vesper
K—Jan Cannon
L—Katherine Ross, Tejas Cheerleader
M—Tribal officers
N—Dining Hall
O—Johnny Regan
P—Robert and Bessie Munson
Q—Riflery-Floy Hume
R—Waldemar Band
S—War Canoe
T—Jack Reeves

7
A—Doris Johnson Lodge
B—D.J. Lodge window
C—Waterfront
D—Tennis courts
E—D.J. Lodge exterior
F—Rick Robertson, Lodge Architect
G—Swiss Chalet
H—Dining Hall
I—Happy Haven
J—Aerobics class inside DJ Lodge
K—Monterrey Kampong
L—Estrella Kampong
M—Casa interior
N—Casa interior stairs
O—Boots
P—French Chateau
Q—K-10
R—"The Girls" statue and campers
S—Happy Haven
T—Bella Vista porch

U—Junior Dining Hall
V—Gazebo
W—Office
X—Gate
Y—Fence

8
A—Connie Reeves
B—Waldemar staff
C—Josh Elmore, Teak Elmore, Robert Keith
E—Roy Spears
F—Sudie Tannehill Mann
G—Sue Vaughan
H—Shannon Harber
I—Marsha and Dale Elmore
J—Shannon Harber, Carolyn Wheat, Squish Willett
K—Kitchen staff
L—Ruth Smith
M—Anna Spears
N—Splash (Mary Fell)
O—Barbara Tyson
P—Jan Cannon
Q—Julie Menges
R—Dr. English
S—Dr. English and nurses
T—Bebe Bloxsom, Eva Jean Blount, Rita Williamson
U—Allison Ragle
V—B.J. Gray and Jaye Sanford
W—Barb Keller
X—Louise Bivins
Y—Jeannie McKay
Z—Millie von Tungeln
AA—Marguerite Clawson
BB—Laura Jean Johnson
CC—Golden girls
DD—Katherine Greeves
EE—Carolyn Means
FF—Jill Johnson
HH—Liz O'Neill
II—Ethel Roescheise
JJ—Dale Elmore
KK—Vicky Bixler
LL—Suzanne Menges
MM—Mary Vaughan Lester
NN—Rita Granberry
OO—Debbie Norton
PP—Joyce Jordon
RR—Mary Brooke Oliphint Casad
SS—Peg Malloy & Linda Pipkin
TT—Helen Thibodeaux
UU—Waldemar Band
VV—Carolyn Mayo
WW—Chrissy Powell, Anna Whorton, Dorothy Rehm
AAA—Sonya Mikeska
BBB—Waldemar counselors
CCC—Laura Dickens Lee

DDD—Geanne Jeffery
EEE—Lela Eakins
GGG—Amy Stewart
HHH—Amy Brooke
III—Christy Carlton
JJJ—Kate Fullinwider
MMM—Florida
NNN—Ruby Ceasar
OOO—Waldemar Hombres
PPP—Ellen Easley
RRR—Meg, Teak, and Josh Elmore
SSS—Berle Van Zandt
TTT—Clarice Johns
UUU—Sarah Brooke
VVV—Karen Harlan

9
A—Kampong group
B—War Canoe
C—Ideal Waldemar Girl
D—Vespers
E—Cross
F—Tribal leaders and Ideal Girl
G—Dining Hall and all camp
H—Liz Pohl
I—Church service
J—Balance beam, Carolina Rodriguez
K—Campfire and Liz Pohl
L—Waldemar staff
M—Etta Thurmond
N—Legend of Guadalupe
O—Quadrille
P—Weaving and stitchery
Q—Pat Jackson
R—Jewelry
S—*African Queen*
T—Polocrosse
U—Volleyball
V—Pickers
W—Soccer
X—Choir
Y—Golf
Z—Peg Malloy (Third Term)
AA—Riflery
BB—Play "The Wiz"
CC—Tejas War Canoe girls
EE—Happy Jack and Danny Pate
FF—Bush patrol
GG—Kitchen staff
HH—Dining room
II—Diver
JJ—Pep rally
KK—Canoe drill
LL—Counselors
MM—Fencing
NN—Ropes course

10 identified

Index